NATIONAL ——————
AUDUBON
——————— SOCIETY
FIELD GUIDE TO THE
Pacific Northwest

To Benjamin Andersen

From Scout Monte Bill Danner

July 20, 1999

A Chanticleer Press Edition

NATIONAL
AUDUBON
SOCIETY
FIELD GUIDE TO THE
Pacific Northwest

Peter Alden

Amy Gregoret   Richard Keen

Daniel Mathews   Eric A. Oches

Dennis Paulson   Robert Sundstrom

Wendy B. Zomlefer

 Alfred A. Knopf, New York

This is a Borzoi Book.
Published by Alfred A. Knopf, Inc.

Copyright © 1998 by Chanticleer Press, Inc.
All rights reserved under International and Pan-American Copyright Conventions. Published in the United States by Alfred A. Knopf, Inc., New York, and simultaneously in Canada by Random House of Canada Limited, Toronto. Distributed by Random House, Inc., New York.

Prepared and produced by
Chanticleer Press, Inc., New York.

Printed and bound by
Dai Nippon Printing Co., Ltd., Hong Kong.

First Edition
Published May 1998
First Printing

Library of Congress Cataloging-in-Publication Data

National Audubon Society field guide. Pacific Northwest / Peter
  Alden . . . [et al.]. — 1st ed.
      p.   cm.
  Includes index.
  ISBN 0-679-44679-6 (hc)
    1. Natural history—Northwest, Pacific.   I. Alden, Peter.
II. National Audubon Society.
QH104.5.N6N38   1998
508.795—dc21   97-31246

National Audubon Society® is a registered trademark of National Audubon
Society, Inc., all rights reserved.

Front Cover: Wildflowers, Columbia River Gorge National Scenic Area,
  Washington
Spine: Sea stacks, Olympic National Park, Washington
Back Cover: Aurora borealis; Western Pasqueflower; Spotted Owl;
  Sullivan Lake and Selkirk Mountains, Colville National Forest, Washington
Table of Contents: Alpine meadow, Mount Rainier National Park,
  Washington; full moon; Grande Ronde River, Washington
Title Page: Cannon Beach, northern coast of Oregon
Pages 8–9: Twin Sisters Rock, Wallula Gap, Columbia River Gorge,
  Washington
Pages 52–53: Field of Arrowleaf Balsamroot, Okanogan County, Washington
Pages 74–75: Pacific Treefrog on azaleas
Pages 370–371: Moss-covered Bigleaf Maples, Hoh Rain Forest, Olympic
National Park, Washington

National Audubon Society

The mission of NATIONAL AUDUBON SOCIETY, founded in 1905, is to conserve and restore natural ecosystems, focusing on birds, other wildlife, and their habitats for the benefit of humanity and the earth's biological diversity.

One of the largest, most effective environmental organizations, Audubon has more than 550,000 members, numerous state offices and nature centers, and 500 + chapters in the United States and Latin America, plus a professional staff of scientists, lobbyists, lawyers, policy analysts, and educators. Through our nationwide sanctuary system we manage 150,000 acres of critical wildlife habitat and unique natural areas for birds, wild animals, and rare plant life.

Our award-winning *Audubon* magazine, published six times a year and sent to all members, carries outstanding articles and color photography on wildlife and nature, and presents in-depth reports on critical environmental issues, as well as conservation news and commentary. We also publish *Field Notes,* a journal reporting on seasonal bird sightings, and *Audubon Adventures,* a children's newsletter reaching 450,000 students. Through our ecology camps and workshops in Maine, Connecticut, and Wyoming, we offer professional development for educators and activists; through Audubon Expedition Institute in Belfast, Maine, we offer unique, traveling undergraduate and graduate degree programs in Environmental Education.

Our acclaimed *Wild!Life Adventures* television documentaries, airing on TBS Superstation and in syndication, deal with a variety of environmental themes, and our children's series for the Disney Channel, *Audubon's Animal Adventures,* introduces family audiences to endangered and threatened wildlife species. Our weekly birding series, *All Bird TV,* which airs on Discovery's Animal Planet Channel, provides viewers with birding tips and takes them to some of the greatest bird locations in the United States. Other Audubon film and television projects include conservation-oriented movies, electronic field trips, and educational videos. National Audubon Society also sponsors books and interactive programs on nature, plus travel programs to exotic places like Antarctica, Africa, Australia, Baja California, Galápagos Islands, and Patagonia.

For information about how you can become an Audubon member, subscribe to *Audubon Adventures,* or to learn more about our camps and workshops, please write or call:

NATIONAL AUDUBON SOCIETY
Membership Dept.
700 Broadway
New York, New York 10003
212-979-3000
http://www.audubon.org/

Contents

Part One: Overview

Part Two: Flora and Fauna

Part Three: Parks and Preserves

Appendices

Overview

Natural Highlights

The Pacific Northwest states of Washington and Oregon, covering 165,173 square miles, offer a nearly limitless assortment of natural wonders. Within a day's drive of many of the larger cities, the sea crashes on a rugged rocky coastline, flower-filled subalpine meadows bloom against a background of distant mountains, and the searing heat of the sun bounces from canyon walls. Wet coastal forests and dry interior scrub—less than 100 miles apart in much of the region—look like they belong on different planets, and support plants and animals that are likewise amazingly varied. The stormy Pacific Ocean, high glacier-covered mountains, and lush temperate rain forests add grandeur to the variety.

Coastlines

High, rocky headlands and sea stacks alive with noisy seabird colonies alternate with long, low sand beaches whose sculpted dunes are adorned with windblown grasses. Tidepools are everywhere, sheltering a rich array of animal life; beneath the

Cape Kiwanda State Natural Area, Oregon

water live the world's largest species of octopus, sea star, and chiton. Whales and seabirds congregate in nutrient-rich offshore waters.

Ponds, Lakes, and Rivers

Beaver ponds abound in wooded parts of the Northwest, cold alpine lakes are spread like jewels across the high mountains, and fabulously productive marshes in the interior teem with insects and fish that attract great colonies of waterbirds. The mighty Columbia River, which cuts the Cascades in half and forms part of the Oregon–Washington border, furnishes a pathway for salmon and enriches the landscape along its 1,200-mile course.

Lower Klamath Lake, Oregon

Pillars of Rome, interior Oregon

The Dry Interior

Grasses, other herbaceous (nonwoody) plants, and shrubs cover the plateaus and rolling hills of much of eastern Washington and Oregon. These wide-open spaces give this part of the Northwest a totally different character than that of the coast and forested mountains. With no tree cover in much of the area, the geology is vividly apparent. Spectacular canyons and basalt formations furnish habitat for many plants and animals that are unique to the region.

Mount Baker, Washington

Mountains

The Cascades form the spine of this mountainous region. Most Cascade peaks have volcanic origins—some, like Washington's Mount St. Helens, have been active within historic times—and the higher ones, like Mount Baker and Mount Rainier, are frosted with glaciers. Flanking the Cascades are the Olympic, Coast, and Siskiyou ranges to the west, and the Okanogan, Selkirk, Blue, Wallowa, and Steens ranges toward the interior. All of these mountains have large areas of undisturbed wilderness.

Forests

Storm after storm arrives from the open Pacific, drenching Northwest coastal slopes to create the nation's only temperate rain forest. In the magnificent old-growth forests, huge fallen logs serve as shelter for small mammals and salaman-

Moss-covered Bigleaf Maples, Olympia, Washington

ders and as nursery beds for the next generation of trees. The forest floor is home to a glorious assortment of wildflowers.

Topography

Two mountain ranges trend north–south through the western part of the Pacific Northwest: the Coast Ranges rise from southwestern Oregon as the Klamath Mountains and culminate in northwestern Washington as the rugged Olympic Mountains; the Cascade Range runs 600 miles northward from northern California. Between the ranges lies the Puget-Willamette lowland, extending from the Puget Sound, a deep inlet to the Pacific Ocean, to the broad, fertile plains of the Willamette Valley. The northern Rockies reach into northeastern Washington, while the Columbia Plateau—layer upon layer of ancient lava flows—spreads across southeastern Washington and north-central Oregon. Arid south-central Oregon sits upon the vast geological foundation known as the Basin and Range Province. An extensive network of rivers and mountain streams drains the region; the largest is the Columbia River, one of the longest rivers in North America.

Mount Rainier

Washington's Mount Rainier, at 14,410 feet, is the highest of the relatively young chain of volcanic peaks that make up the High Cascades. It is also the most seismically active peak in the Cascades, generating more than 30 earthquakes annually. A huge glacier field, with 27 major glaciers, covers its slopes, making it one of the most po-

Mount Rainier

tentially dangerous volcanoes in the world. During an eruption of a glacier-covered volcano, meltwater combines with hot volcanic debris and slides rapidly down the mountain as a highly destructive mudflow called a lahar.

Olympic Mountains, Washington

Olympic Peninsula

Reaching to nearly 8,000 feet on Mount Olympus, the glacier-carved Olympic Mountains began forming about 50 million years ago when tectonic plates of the Pacific Ocean floor collided with the North American Plate. The mountains were later isolated on a peninsula when glaciers gouged out the Hood Canal and Puget Sound. The Olympics presently receive more precipitation than any other area in the contiguous United States. This water, falling as rain or snow, supports one of the world's largest temperate rain forests in the lowlands of the peninsula.

Columbia River and Gorge

Draining a quarter million square miles of the Pacific Northwest, the Columbia River flows more than 1,200 miles from its headwaters in southeastern British Columbia to the Pacific Ocean and forms nearly 300 miles of the border between Washington and Oregon. The Columbia River Gorge, which stretches nearly 75 miles between The

Dalles and Portland, was formed during the past 2 million years as the river sliced through the rapidly uplifting Cascade Range and hundreds of feet of basalt that had poured out over the region between 17 and 6 million years ago. The gorge was enlarged and reshaped by massive flooding at the end of the last ice age; today it has 71 waterfalls, 11 of which are more than 100 feet high.

Columbia River Gorge, Oregon

Crater Lake

Some 7,700 years ago, Mount Mazama—then a 10,000- to 12,000-foot-high volcano in the High Cascades of southern Oregon—violently exploded, releasing huge amounts of ash and pumice. Following the eruption, the cone collapsed, reducing the elevation of the peak by 2,500 feet and forming a broad basin known as a caldera. It filled with water, forming Crater Lake, the deepest lake in the United States at 1,932 feet deep. Six miles wide, the lake is surrounded by cliffs up to 2,000 feet high. In the center is Wizard Island, the top of a small volcano that rose from the lake floor.

Crater Lake

Basin and Range Province

The expansive Basin and Range Province covers an area of about 300,000 square miles—nearly a tenth of the continental United States. It was formed around 17 million years ago, when tension in the earth's crust caused stretching and faulting that resulted in a pattern of tilted, uplifted blocks separated by wide, steep-walled, down-dropped basins that subsequently filled with hundreds of feet

of sediments from the eroding highlands. In south-central Oregon the Basin and Range Province is mainly desert, with streams that dry up on broad valley floors before reaching an outlet to the sea, and alkaline lakes, such as Lake Abert and Summer Lake, that fill the floors of several valleys.

View of Steens Mountain from Alvord Desert, southeastern Oregon

Ocean and Coastal Topography

Stretches of straight or gently curved sandy beaches alternating with rocky headlands, small coves, bays, and sand dunes characterize the 450-odd miles of Pacific Northwest coastline. Much of the Oregon coast is dominated by rocky headlands, while the southern Washington coast is distinguished by smooth, sandy beaches and occasional wide, shallow tidal flats at estuaries such as Grays Harbor and Willapa Bay. North of Grays Harbor the Washington coast becomes rocky and irregular, with rugged bedrock headlands and high cliffs. Wave energy from the Pacific Ocean is fairly high, causing sea-cliff recession along exposed coasts. A strongly seasonal pattern of wind and waves transports sediments south along the coast in summer and north in winter, resulting in sand spits that grow in both directions across the mouths of river estuaries. The average tidal range (from low to high tide) is 6 to 10 feet.

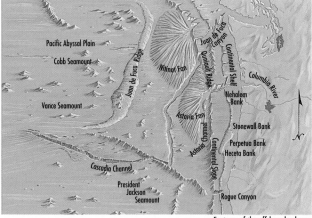

Features of the offshore landscape

Offshore Landscape

The continental shelf off the Pacific Northwest slopes gently seaward for about 40 to 70 miles, with depths to about 600 feet, then plunges to the Pacific abyssal plain, where the seafloor is more than 9,000 feet below the water's surface. At the base of the continental slope is the subduction zone, where the Juan de Fuca tectonic plate is being forced beneath the North American continental plate. Rich populations of marine invertebrates and fish thrive among the rocky banks that rise up from the muddy continental shelf to within 200 feet of the sea's surface. In deeper water, submarine canyons and channels cut across the continental shelf and slope, carrying vast amounts of sediment to the deep ocean floor, creating large submarine sediment fans. Isolated undersea volcanoes that rise from the abyssal plain form submarine mountains called seamounts, while chains of volcanoes form ridges where new ocean crust is created.

Sea Stacks

Peninsulas or headlands that jut out into the ocean are eroded unevenly by waves, and hard basalt or limestone is left behind after softer sandstone has been worn away. These headlands are frequently undermined in places and become bridges;

Sea stacks at Rialto Beach, Washington

further erosion causes the arches to collapse, creating the isolated mounds called sea stacks that dot the Pacific Northwest coast. Sea stacks are especially abundant along Oregon's mountainous coastline between Cape Blanco and Coos Bay, farther north in Oregon between Seal Rock and Tillamook Head, and along Washington's Olympic Peninsula between Hoh Head and Cape Flattery.

Oregon Dunes

Oregon Dunes

A 2- to 3-mile-wide swath of sand dunes rises 10 to 100 feet above sea level and parallels a 55-mile stretch of coast between Coos Bay and Sea Lion Point, Oregon— the largest coastal dune area in the United States. Groundwater-fed lakes fill long, narrow basins between the dunes. Sand began accumulating here several thousand years ago, when the shoreline stood east of its present position. As the coast migrated westward, beach sands were picked up by winds and deposited as the large dune fields present today.

Columbia River Mouth

The lower 20 miles of the Columbia River, where fresh water mixes with ocean water, is a nutrient-rich estuary. Salinity of the estuary, and of the ocean near the river mouth, changes rapidly and frequently as daily tides interact with seasonal variations in river flow. High tides sometimes bring ocean salt

Mouth of the Columbia River, Oregon

as far as 50 miles upriver. The Columbia's outflow of fresh water extends over many square miles of the surface of the coastal Pacific, reaching as far south as the California border in summer and as far north as Vancouver Island in winter.

Tectonic Origins

For hundreds of millions of years the Pacific Northwest has been positioned at the boundary between the North American continental plate and the oceanic Farallon Plate. As the Farallon Plate pushed beneath the continent about 40 million years ago, it spawned the Juan de Fuca Plate, the part of the Pacific Ocean floor that continues to be subducted beneath the Pacific Northwest today. Hundreds of millions of years of plate-tectonic interactions have resulted in the folding, squeezing, stretching, and breaking of the Pacific Northwest crust and the subsequent formation of mountain ranges, volcanoes, and basins.

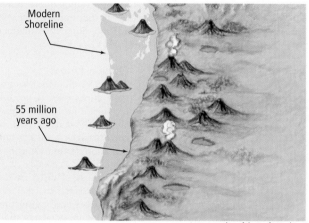

Ancient coastline of the Pacific Northwest

Ancient Coastlines

Rifting of an ancient supercontinent nearly 1 billion years ago tore what is now Siberia and China from North America, forming the western coast of the new North American continent in the area of what is presently central Idaho. For the next several hundred million years, shallow seas rose and covered what has since become the Pacific Northwest, depositing tens of thousands of feet of marine sediments. From about 300 million to 70 million years ago, islands of continental crust began to be carried eastward by the oceanic plate. Too light to sink into the subduction trench between the oceanic plate and the continental plate, these blocks of foreign rocks were welded onto the continent. As convergence of the plates continued, volcanic island arcs that formed above the subduction zone were also thrust onto the continent along with slabs of oceanic crust and marine sediments that had accumulated in the deep offshore trench. The mountains of the Coast Ranges originated as this type of volcanic island chain; they were sutured to the coast beginning about 20 million years ago. The Pacific Northwest shoreline began to take its present shape by about 55 million years ago. Tectonic activity continues to add land to the western shoreline.

Plate Tectonics

According to the theory of plate tectonics, earth's surface is broken into a dozen major plates that constantly move as a result of convection currents generated by the planet's internal heat. Three types of motion occur along the boundaries of these plates.

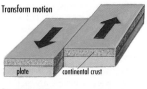

Transform motion

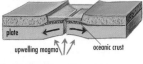

Divergent motion

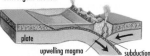

Convergent motion

Transform boundaries, or fault lines, where plates are laterally sliding past each other, are the sites of earthquakes. At **divergent** plate boundaries, the plates move away from one another, or rift apart. Magma (molten rock) rises from within the earth and fills the void that was created, solidifying under the ocean as new seafloor or on land as a rift valley. At **convergent** plate boundaries, two plates collide, causing a buckling of the continental crust and/or forcing one plate beneath the other in a process called subduction, which can result in earthquakes and volcanoes. All the major mountain chains, including the Cascades, and 80 percent of earth's volcanoes are located along convergent plate boundaries.

Blue Mountains

Northeastern Oregon is dominated by the Blue Mountains Province, a cluster of mountain ranges that includes the Wallowa, Elkhorn, Greenhorn, Ochoco, Aldrich, Strawberry, and Sheephead Mountains. This region, which includes the oldest rocks in Oregon, is a patchwork of foreign rocks that were plastered onto the North American shoreline between about 300 million and 55 million years ago. Many of the rocks may have originated in the western Pacific Ocean at about 18 degrees north latitude (the approximate latitude of the Hawaiian Islands today).

Sheephead Mountains

Rocks of the Blue Mountains represent ancient oceanic crust, marine sandstones and limestones, volcanic islands, and intrusions of granite that were solidifed deep within the earth's crust.

Volcanic Features

The Pacific Northwest's volcanoes are commonly associated with subduction zones. As a plate descends (subducts) into the earth beneath another plate it begins to melt, and the molten rock, less dense than the rock around it, begins to rise, forming an underground mass of magma that becomes a volcano if it reaches the surface. The Western and High Cascades run parallel to the offshore subduction trench from northern California to southern British Columbia; in Oregon the Western Cascades lie west of the High Cascades, while in Washington the two ranges are pretty much in line with one another. The Western Cascades were volcanically active about 40 to 20 million years ago and have since been worn down by erosion. The High Cascades volcanoes began erupting only a few million years ago. The youngest and highest ones are dormant, and (except for Mount St. Helens) retain the classic cone shape. Volcanoes dominate the region's landscape because they are relatively young features less worn down by erosive forces than older features, and because they lie above and cover many older formations.

Mount St. Helens before (left) and after (right) 1980 eruption

Mount St. Helens

The most active volcano in the contiguous United States during the past 4,500 years, Washington's Mount St. Helens was a symmetrical cone before its explosive eruption in 1980. After the volcano blew off steam and generated a series of small earthquakes, a bulge began to grow in the mountain's north flank, caused by a rising of viscous magma. As the bulge grew, the slope of the north flank steepened dangerously until it collapsed under its own weight, releasing the confining pressure on the underlying magma. Columns of ash shot 15 miles into the air, ash and rock debris fell to the ground more than 900 miles away, and a torrent of volcanic debris raced northward, flattening trees and killing wildlife in a 230-square-mile zone. Much of the destruction resulted from mudflows of melting snow and glacier ice mixed with thick ash accumulations that sped down the mountainside, clogging river valleys below.

Exposed basalt, Grande Ronde River Canyon, Washington

Columbia Plateau Basalts

The spectacular lava flows that make up the Columbia Plateau of southeastern Washington and north-central Oregon began to pour out of fissures in the ground more than 17 million years ago. This activity continued intermittently for more than 11 million years, covering the region with 42 cubic miles of basalt by the time the eruptions came to an end. Such volcanic events, called fissure eruptions, produce successive flows of highly fluid basaltic lava, termed flood basalts, which spread out as flat layers across the landscape. More than 300 individual flows have been identified, some hundreds of feet thick.

Lava Cast Forest

Volcanic Formations

Newberry National Volcanic Monument, south of Bend, Oregon, comprises a variety of volcanic formations, including craters, lakes, and volcanic cones, as well as large obsidian flows. Obsidian, a dark, translucent glass, forms either when lava is so viscous that it is unable to form crystals or when it cools and solidifies instantly. In the Lava Cast Forest, a lava flow surrounded a forest, leaving basalt casts of standing and fallen trees. All of these features are the result of volcanic activity around Newberry Volcano from about 500,000 to 2,000 years ago.

Glacial Features

Several ice ages have occurred over the past 2 million years, with the most recent one ending about 10,000 years ago. During these glacial expansions, large reaches of North America and Eurasia were covered by thick sheets of ice. The Cordilleran Ice Sheet, which covered about a third of Washington and much of western Canada, was up to 3,000 feet thick over Washington about 15,000 years ago. As the ice advanced and retreated it scoured surfaces, carved the underlying bedrock, and captured eroded debris and deposited it elsewhere. Massive ice sheets and local mountain glaciers sculpted many symmetrical volcanic cones into sharp, jagged peaks.

Deming Glacier, Mount Baker, Cascade Range, Washington

Types of Glaciers

Glaciers are masses of ice that move or spread over land. Ice sheets are continent-size glaciers, often a mile or more thick, that slowly advance outward from the center of ice accumulation; such ice sheets presently cover Greenland and Antarctica. During ice ages, sheets of ice can extend across entire mountain ranges. Even outside of ice ages smaller mountain glaciers or valley glaciers form in cold, high mountains when accumulated snow compresses into ice and begins to move downhill, extending for tens of miles into otherwise unglaciated lowlands. In the Cascades, Washington's Mount Rainier has more than two dozen such glaciers on its slopes and Oregon's Mount Hood has nine. The Olympics of northwestern Washington have too many to count.

Channeled Scablands

The melting of the continental glaciers of the last ice age created large glacial lakes and sometimes caused catastrophic floods. Between 18,000 and 12,000 years ago, Glacial Lake Missoula, which lay to the east, repeatedly broke through an ice dam and flooded westward

Channeled Scablands, Washington

across Washington and into northern Oregon, carrying sediment and icebergs that cut canyons up to 1,300 feet deep in the underlying basalt. The resulting landscape is called the Channeled Scablands.

Glacial Troughs and the San Juan Islands

Puget Sound, Hood Canal, Admiralty Inlet, Possession Sound, Lake Washington, Sammamish Lake, and the Strait of Juan de Fuca are all glacial troughs in northwestern Washington. These deep basins were gouged out of the bedrock by a lobe of the Cordilleran Ice Sheet

Strait of Juan de Fuca

during the last ice age. The San Juan Islands, located at the convergence of Puget Sound and the Strait of Juan de Fuca, were also extensively sculpted by the ice sheet, which cut deep sounds between the islands and left thick deposits of glacial debris over large areas of bedrock.

Loess Deposits

Loess is thick deposits of wind-blown silt or dust that frequently accumulate downwind of glaciers, where winds transport fine particles of sediment that have been flushed from beneath the ice by meltwater. Composed of "rock flour"—fine particles of quartz, feldspar, hornblende, mica, and clay—loess provides a mineral-rich base for the formation of exceedingly deep and fertile soil. Loess deposits are up to 200 feet thick in the Palouse Hills of eastern Washington.

Willamette Valley meteorite, 1904

Willamette Valley

The floods of the end of the last ice age scoured eastern Washington and further eroded the channel of the Columbia River. Water repeatedly backed up into the mouth of the Willamette River, a tributary of the Columbia, creating Glacial Lake Allison and depositing tremendous amounts of sediment, including the deep layer of fine-grained silt that makes the Willamette Valley so fertile. The sediment also includes glacial erratics, or "haystack rocks"—large boulders transported by icebergs or glacial floodwaters. More than 300 erratics, including a meteorite possibly transported from Montana, have been identified in the valley.

Alpine Lakes and Glacial Moraines

Covered by thick ice caps during the last ice age, the Wallowa Mountains of northeastern Oregon still have mountain glaciers on their peaks, as well as nearly 100 alpine lakes whose beds were ground out of the hard granite bedrock by long tongues of ice advancing downslope. These lakes are frequently impounded by glacial moraines, ridges of debris (fine silt to huge boulders) pushed ahead of advancing ice sheets.

Wallowa Lake with granite boulder in foreground

Fossils

A fossil is any indication of past plant or animal life, including petrified wood, dinosaur bones, ancient seashells, footprints, or animal-shaped casts left in rock after the organisms themselves disintegrated. Almost all fossils are discovered in sedimentary rocks, frequently in areas that were once underwater, which explains why

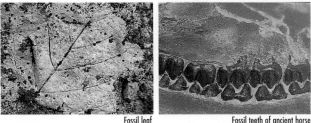

Fossil leaf   Fossil teeth of ancient horse

many fossils are of aquatic species. Fossils of ichthyosaurs (aquatic reptiles) and pteranodons (flying reptiles) can be found in Oregon in rocks from the Cretaceous period, which began about 136 million years ago. Overall, few dinosaur fossils have been found in the Northwest, but the appropriate sediments exist in the region, so it may just be a matter of time. The oldest rocks now found in much of the Pacific Northwest probably originated in the middle of the Pacific Ocean (see Tectonic Origins, page 16) and thus preserve records of life from other parts of the world.

John Day Fossil Beds

The 14,000-acre John Day Fossil Beds National Monument of eastern Oregon preserves a wide range of plant and animal species buried in layers of exposed volcanic deposits. The Clarno Formation was laid down by a series of mudflows some 50 to 35 million years ago, when a hot, wet climate nourished tropical and subtropical forests. Plant fossils found in the Clarno Formation include nuts, fruits, and seeds of hundreds of plant species, among them palms, figs, and avocadoes. The John Day Formation, created about 30 to 20 million years ago when the climate had become a bit cooler and more temperate, was formed when enormous clouds of volcanic ash blew there from the southern

Painted Hills at John Day Fossil Beds National Monument

mountains of the Western Cascades. Some 100 species of animals are preserved in the John Day Formation, including a variety of cats, dogs, pigs, rabbits, opossums, three-toed horses, camels, tapirs, and rhinoceroses.

Pleistocene Mammals

The diverse array of mammals that roamed the Pacific Northwest from around 2 million to 10,000 years ago were members of a robust, highly integrated ecosystem adapted to an extreme climate of cold, harsh glacial periods.

Among the region's Pleistocene inhabitants were mammoths, giant bison, beavers the size of Black Bears, and 7-foot-tall ground sloths. The cause of their demise is hotly debated; some experts speculate that it resulted from climate and vegetation

Giant Ground Sloth

changes associated with the end of the last ice age combined with overhunting by humans, who had only recently arrived in North America. Many fossils of Pleistocene mammals are found in swamp deposits in northern Oregon, and teeth can be found in glacial outwash throughout the region.

Petrified tree from Ginkgo Petrified Forest State Park, Washington

Opalized Wood

Petrified trees may be found in various locations in the Columbia Plateau region of southeastern Washington and north-central Oregon. Forests that grew between periods of basalt flooding were entombed by layers of volcanic ash and basalt. The wood was soaked with and fossilized by silicate minerals and the trees are thus preserved in forms of silica, such as beautiful opal or chalcedony.

Minerals and Natural Resources

Minerals, the building blocks of rocks, are naturally occurring inorganic, crystalline substances with characteristic chemical compositions and structures that determine their appearance. A mineral may be a single native element, such as copper or gold, or a compound of elements. Minerals are recognized by such physical properties as hardness, cleavage (breakage along well-defined planes of weakness), fracture (any type of rough and uneven breakage), luster (the way the surface reflects light), and crystal structure. Color may be an unreliable identifying feature, as minor impurities can cause significant color variations.

CINNABAR
Mercury sulfide, mercury's most common ore, found and mined as cinnabar. Usually brilliant red, with earthy texture, splintery fracture. Cinnabar used as pigment is called vermilion. McDermitt caldera complex in Basin and Range Province of south-central Oregon has produced richest supply of mercury in Western Hemisphere.

GOLD
Forms mainly in hydrothermal veins (lodes); often associated with quartz. Released through rock erosion; becomes concentrated in resulting sands. Butter-yellow color and malleability distinguish gold from copper and silver. Can be scratched by knife; lacks cleavage; jagged fracture. Present along Columbia and Similkameen Rivers.

QUARTZ
Crystals commonly six-sided, with pyramidal ends. Many colors: white, gray, red, purple, pink, yellow, green, brown, black; transparent or milky; glassy luster. One of the most common minerals; abundant in all kinds of rocks, including granite. Frequently found with gold, especially in Western Cascades and Blue Mountains; may also be found wherever ores are mined and on beaches as sand-size particles.

OLIVINE
A heavy silicate mineral containing varying proportions of iron and magnesium; thought to be important constituent of earth's mantle. Varies in color from dull green and yellow to brown. Occurs frequently as granular crystals associated with basalt, and in ophiolites, seafloor basalt and other rocks thrust up on land that comprise parts of Blue and Klamath Mountains. Source of the gemstone peridot.

Geothermal Resources

The tectonic and volcanic activity occurring beneath the crust of the Pacific Northwest—especially in the regions between the High and Western Cascades, and in much of the Basin and Range Province of south-central Oregon—makes the area a prime region for exploration of geothermal resources. Hot springs indicate geothermal heat being produced underground, some of which may be tapped for energy.

Willow Creek Hot Spring, Oregon

THUNDER EGG

Official "rock" of Oregon. Agate-filled geodes (stone nodules containing crystals or minerals) are found in rhyolite, tuff, or perlitic (all volcanic rocks); form when water filled with silica circulates through spaces in rock and precipitates crystals. Dull and bumpy on outside; reveal star-shaped mass of agate or opal when split. Sizes range from less than 1 inch to more than 4 feet in diameter. Best known from John Day Formation (volcanic deposit in eastern Oregon), but may be found in various locales throughout eastern Oregon.

PYROXENES

A group of silicate minerals whose crystal structures vary according to which elements—such as iron, magnesium, calcium, and aluminum—they contain. May be translucent to transparent; color ranges from white to pale green to, more commonly, dark green or black. Cleavage perfect in two directions at nearly right angles. Significant constituent of andesite and basalt, as well as peridotite. Crystals visible in outcrops in Blue and Klamath Mountains.

FELDSPARS

A large group of rock-forming aluminum silicates; earth's most common minerals. Light in color (pink to white and gray); relatively light in weight; glassy luster if fresh, dull if weathered; good to perfect cleavage at right angles. Potassium feldspars common in rhyolite and granite; plagioclase feldspars common in basalt and gabbro. Easily recognized in granite batholiths (large masses of exposed granite) of Western Cascades.

Rocks

A given rock may be composed of only one mineral or it may be an aggregate of different minerals. Rocks provide a tangible record of many geologic processes that are impossible to observe directly—for example, the melting of rocks in the earth's interior. The identification of rocks can be difficult, but clues are provided by their constituent minerals, grain size, and overall texture.

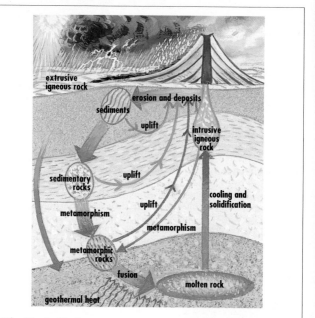

The Rock Cycle

The three basic classes of rocks undergo processes that convert them from one form to another. *Igneous* rocks form through solidification of molten material from earth's interior. Extrusive igneous rock forms on earth's surface through volcanic activity; intrusive igneous rock solidifies below the surface. *Sedimentary* rocks form from consolidation of layers of sediment (fragments of older, weathered rock ranging in size from submicroscopic particles to boulders, and/or organic or chemical matter) deposited at earth's surface. *Metamorphic* rocks form when existing rocks are transformed through heat and/or pressure. Deep within the earth metamorphic rock melts to become magma. As the small arrows on the above drawing indicate, the complete cycle can be interrupted at any point. The Pacific Northwest has an abundance of volcanic rock, but examples of all three types are readily found in the region.

Tuff   Ignimbrite   Pumice   Obsidian

VOLCANIC ROCKS

Lava composed of rhyolite (*constituent minerals:* quartz, feldspar, mica, amphibole); explodes out of volcanoes, unlike basaltic lava; takes various forms. **Tuff:** explosively ejected ash and small volcanic fragments that have settled to earth, eventually cemented into rock by minerals in groundwater. *Appearance:* predominantly light-colored; fine-grained; commonly occurs in layers. **Ignimbrite:** ash and volcanic blocks welded quickly by own heat when hot lava mass near top of erupting volcano collapses, causing incandescent gas and ash to flow at great speed. *Appearance:* hard rock of various-sized fragments with banded structure and visible glass shards. **Pumice:** formed when blocks of rhyolitic lava with high gas content explode from volcanoes. Frothy mass of molten rock and gas cools almost instantly. *Appearance:* Medium to light-colored; very porous, floats on water. **Obsidian:** a volcanic glass usually formed when rhyolitic magma with little or no water vapor cools very quickly. *Appearance:* Reddish brown to black; translucent.

BASALT

Igneous rock formed as thin, flowing lava erupts at or near earth's surface. *Constituent minerals:* feldspar and pyroxene. *Appearance:* dark green to black on fresh surfaces, weathers to reddish brown or gray; very fine-grained; shape depends on where rock came to surface. **Columnar basalt** (pictured) is a formation of geometrically shaped pillars that form as a lava flow cools and shrinks at or near surface. Abundant on Columbia Plateau.

SCHIST

When metamorphosed, shale becomes slate, and at higher grades of metamorphism, schist and eventually gneiss. *Constituent minerals:* vary; mica, quartz, feldspar, chlorite, almandine, many others. *Appearance:* thin, wavy flakes of mica visible; entire rock may look as if it is made of thin stacked plates of minerals. Color varies: usually rather dark at low grades, then separates into dark and light bands as minerals segregate in metamorphic process.

SANDSTONE

Sedimentary rock; may contain fossils. *Constituent minerals:* predominantly quartz, with feldspar, mica, and other minerals. *Appearance:* fine- to medium-grained; tan to dark colored. Silty sandstones of marine origin common in coastal areas, including tectonically uplifted terraces marking former shorelines in Pacific Northwest.

Sandstone coastline, Oregon

Habitats

Habitats are divisions of the natural landscape usually defined by their plant communities. Some of the factors that influence an area's habitat are availability of water, topography, elevation, soil and underlying rock types, and climate (temperature, precipitation, exposure, and wind). Because of the great variation in topography and rainfall in the Pacific Northwest, the habitats of the region are among the most diverse in the country, ranging from temperate rain forest on the coast to desert in parts of the interior. On the slopes of the steepest mountains, a different habitat occurs with each few thousand feet of elevation gain, though the elevations at which particular habitats occur vary with terrain, climate, and, most significantly, latitude. Precipitation plays its part as well, as trees grow higher on drier mountains because there is less winter snowpack.

Forests make up much of the land area of the Pacific Northwest, especially in the west, and are dominated by conifers, which are better adapted than deciduous trees to withstand the region's extremes of heat, cold, and drought. West of the Cascade Range, wet forests cover large areas of mountains and lowlands, while east of the Cascades wet forests blend with dry interior forests, which extend into the sagebrush steppes and deserts of the Columbia Plateau.

During the last century, many forests have been replaced by pastures and settlements, coastal wetlands have been filled, and sagebrush steppe has been replaced by farmland and orchards over large parts of eastern Oregon and Washington. Nevertheless, the Pacific Northwest remains a landscape that is rich in habitat variety and suitable for a lifetime of exploration.

The following pages discuss the habitats pictured below and the natural communities they encompass.

ALPINE AND SUBALPINE   WET FORESTS   DRY FORESTS

STEPPES AND DESERTS   FRESHWATER WETLANDS

COASTAL HABITATS   MARINE HABITATS   DISTURBED HABITATS

Alpine and Subalpine Habitats

The highest peaks in the Cascades and the Olympics—Mount Baker, Glacier Peak, Mount Hood, and Mount Adams in the former and Mount Olympus in the latter, to name a few—are mostly covered with glaciers and snow, with a narrow band of alpine and subalpine meadows between the glaciers and the forests below. Some high peaks in the interior—such as Tiffany Mountain in Washington and Eagle Cap and Steens Mountain in Oregon—are too dry for glaciers, so their meadows are much drier than those in the Cascades. The long winters at high elevations bring cold temperatures and strong winds survived only by low plants and a few uniquely adapted animals. The subalpine forests have scattered, stunted trees that grow larger and denser as the elevation decreases until they blend with the mountain forest below.

Subalpine Firs and Engelmann Spruces, Mount Baker–Snoqualmie National Forest

Subalpine Forests

Typically above 4,300 feet in the north and 5,600 feet in the south are distinctive high-elevation forests with trees considerably less massive than their lowland relatives. Such stands are found widely in the Cascades and Olympics and in higher parts of eastern Washington and northeastern Oregon. Although fewer plant and animal species occur here than in the lower forests, many, such as Showy Jacob's Ladder and the Pine Grosbeak, are uniquely adapted to this habitat. High-elevation conifers such as Mountain Hemlock are densely leafed to protect them from drying winds; most species, including Subalpine Fir and Engelmann Spruce, are narrow and spire-shaped to shed heavy snowfall. Trees at highest elevations are low, stunted, and strongly wind-pruned, forming a characteristic growth called krummholz. Many of the small mammals of subalpine forests stay under the heavy snow in winter, and those that travel on top of it, such as the Snowshoe Hare and Lynx, have large, furry feet. Clark's Nutcrackers and Steller's Jays cache seeds, but most other birds migrate elsewhere during winter.

Subalpine meadow with firs and hemlocks,
Mount Baker Wilderness, Washington

Subalpine Meadows

Also in the subalpine zone are lush, flower-filled meadows alternating with clumps of spire-topped conifers. Subalpine meadows, sheltered by trees and with deeper soil than the rocky alpine meadows, provide a more hospitable environment for both plants and animals. Marmots and pikas graze in the meadows and are in turn hunted by eagles and ravens. This open, park-like habitat is characteristic of the wet mountains of the Pacific Northwest. The wildflower displays of July and August in these meadows are the finest in the region.

Alpine meadow with paintbrush in bloom,
Mount Rainier National Park, Washington

Alpine Meadows

Alpine meadows occupy a very narrow belt just below the glaciers and mostly above 6,000 feet. They are dry, rocky, and treeless, with low cushion plants scattered over the rough terrain and talus slopes of accumulated rock debris. Few animals live in this harsh climate, but some are restricted to it. Mountain Goats, rock specialists with suction-cup-like hooves, survive by migrating downslope in winter. Saxifrage and many other alpine wildflowers are able to grow in the thin veneer of soil; some thrive in only the most protected crevices.

Wet Forests

Covering the landscape from the Pacific Ocean to the tree line in the Cascades and Olympics are wet forests—those that receive more than 60 inches of precipitation annually and have soils that retain water well. Wet forests also clothe the higher mountains east of the Cascade crest: the Selkirks and the Blue–Wallowa complex in northeastern Washington and northeastern Oregon. These forests are dominated by conifers but often also have a rich array of broadleaf trees, which occur in pure stands in areas where the soil stays moist through the summer. Temperate rain forests are found along the very wet seaward slopes of the Olympics and Cascades. The most ancient of these are old-growth forests.

Hoh Rain Forest, Olympic National Forest, Washington

Lowland Old-growth Forests

Wet lowland old-growth forests are the most complex forests of the Pacific Northwest, with a mixture of huge old trees up to 260 feet high and 10 feet in diameter, clearings from fires and landslides, and all stages of growth in between. It takes about two centuries for an old-growth forest to develop; most in this region are from 350 to 750 years old. The varied stature of the trees of a mature forest allows light to reach the forest floor, fostering an abundance and diversity of shrubs and low herbaceous plants. Western Hemlock, Western Red Cedar, and Sitka Spruce dominate lowland old-growth forests. Douglas Firs remain as scattered giants long after their seedlings have been shaded out. Snags (standing dead trees) and downed logs furnish essential hiding places for the many small animals of the forest, such as Southern Red-backed Voles and Northern Flying Squirrels. These mammals in turn are food to Northern Spotted Owls, a threatened species found only in this habitat because it requires heavy forest with substantial nesting platforms.

Lowland Second-growth Forests

Fire, windstorms, and logging have toppled many of the big trees in the wet lowland forests of the Pacific Northwest, and second-growth forests now exceed the acreage of old growth. After clearing, forests begin a cycle of regeneration—from herbaceous plants to shrubs to saplings to mature trees—that may take two or three centuries. Early on, sunlight is abundant, productivity is high, and there is a great diversity of wildflowers, shrubs, insects, birds, and mammals. Within 50 to 75 years, young Douglas Firs fill the space

available, shading the understory and considerably reducing productivity and diversity. The wildlife that inhabits the second growth changes along with the forest structure: within a human generation, Townsend's Voles and Bewick's Wrens of open areas are replaced by smaller, darker Creeping Voles and Winter Wrens of the forest. Needing less to eat, smaller species fare better in a less productive habitat, and darker species are better camouflaged where light levels are low.

Mount Baker–Snoqualmie National Forest, Washington

Coastal Rain Forests

Bathed by moist air from the Pacific, the magnificent forests in parts of western Oregon and in the river valleys of Washington's Olympic Peninsula are called "rain forests" by many, though to others they are simply an extreme manifestation of the region's characteristic wet

lowland forests. Epiphytes (plants that grow on other plants, deriving moisture and nutrients from air and rain, including certain lichens, mosses, and ferns) abound, as do huge old Sitka Spruces and nurse logs (fallen trees that serve as nursery beds for future trees). Bigleaf Maples support epiphytes while taking some nourishment from them by sending aerial roots into the dense masses where nutrients and water collect. Among the animals that frequent these forests is the Roosevelt race of Elk.

Rain forest in Golden and Silver Falls State Park, Oregon

Bigleaf and Vine Maples, Mount Baker–
Snoqualmie National Forest, Washington

Lowland Broadleaf Forests

With leaves too paper-thin to store much moisture, broadleaf trees need more consistent year-round water than conifers, so where the soil stays moist through the summer—as along rivers and in valley floors and bottomlands—extensive groves of Bigleaf and Vine Maples, Red Alders, and other broadleafs occur within and beside stands of conifers. These forests are quite seasonal: in summer they are more productive than conifers, and are full of insects and birds, but in winter many more species reside in the more constant environment amid the conifers.

Firs and hemlocks, Mount Baker–Snoqualmie
National Forest, Washington

Mountain Forests

Conifer forests extend up all Pacific Northwest mountain ranges to the 5,000- to 7,000-foot level. Pacific Silver Fir and Noble Fir dominate forests on the western slopes of the Cascades, while Douglas Fir, Engelmann Spruce, Lodgepole Pine, and Western Larch do so on the eastern slopes and in the interior ranges. These mid-elevation mountain forests foster an often highly diverse mixture of lowland and highland plants and animals. Indeed, the middle elevations of the Washington Cascades have one of the world's most diverse conifer collections, and each of the ten genera of conifers that occurs in the Pacific Northwest has its largest species here. Plants and animals that live in these forests must be adapted to heavy snowpack and cold winter temperatures. Many mammals, such as ground squirrels, hibernate, and many of the birds migrate. Indian Pipes and other saprophytes with no chlorophyll and therefore no need for sunlight live in near darkness on the forest floor and gain nourishment solely from organic matter in the soil.

Dry Forests

Most of the Pacific Northwest's dry forests are in the eastern, interior region. They are typically more open than wet forests, with sunlight reaching the ground everywhere and nurturing a carpet of herbaceous vegetation. The dominant tree species of dry forests have long taproots that can reach the subterranean water table. Ponderosa Pine and Western Juniper are common at the driest extremes of tree growth in the interior, while Lodgepole Pine dominates old burn sites. Pure stands of Oregon White Oaks grow in well-drained dry soils within the Northwest's wet forests. Moister forests spring up in interior areas with water at or near the surface; an integral part of interior landscapes, these broadleaf and riparian forests are discussed here, along with the drier forests.

Ponderosa Pine Forests

Ponderosa Pines dominate lower mountain slopes east of the Cascade crest, growing in open stands interspersed with the herbaceous plants—balsamroot and phlox—of the nearby grasslands. The animals of this forest are mostly arboreal. The Pygmy Nuthatch

Ponderosa Pines, Deschutes National Forest, Oregon

probes with its slender bill for insects in dense needle clumps. The Yellow-pine Chipmunk feeds primarily on seeds on the ground but will climb a 100-foot pine in late summer when the cones are opening.

Lodgepole Pine Forests

Unlike those of most conifers, the cones of Lodgepole Pines stay closed on the branches for years, until the heat from a forest fire opens them. Afterward, the fire-resistant seeds sprout en masse, producing tall, straight Lodgepoles in extensive pure stands that support many of the birds and mammals widely distributed in other coniferous forests.

Lodgepole Pines, Mount Hood National Forest

Juniper Forests

Surviving with as little as 8 inches of precipitation annually, Western Junipers are the only trees in much of their range. They grow on rocky slopes in the high plateaus of eastern Oregon and on sand dunes in south-central Washington. Their long taproots penetrate the water table, and their flat, waxy needles retain water.

Western Junipers at John Day Fossil Beds National Monument, Oregon

One of the few animals specialized for this forest type is Townsend's Solitaire, a thrush that survives the winter on a diet of juniper berries.

Oak Forests

The Oregon White Oak, found in many parts of the Willamette Valley, on drier soils throughout western Washington, and halfway up the eastern side of the Cascades, is slow-growing for a deciduous tree. It thrives where faster-growing conifers are limited by soil moisture—such as areas near Tacoma, where glaciers left behind fast-draining sandy soils. Pacific Madrone, another dry-soil tree, often occurs in large stands in oak forests, and Western Poi-

Oregon White Oaks, eastern Washington

son Oak is common in the understory. Oak forest animals include the acorn-eating Western Scrub Jay and the Western Gray Squirrel.

Quaking Aspens at Okanogan National Forest, Washington

Interior Broadleaf Forests

In the dry interior, broadleaf forests are found in low areas where water is readily available to the roots of fast-growing decidu-ous trees, such as Quaking Aspens. This shade-intolerant tree can-not compete in mixed forests, but flourishes where fires and avalanches clear the landscape of the conifers that would displace it over time. Such groves are full of Gray Catbirds, American Red-starts, and Veeries. If flooded in spring, they host breeding popula-tions of amphibians such as Long-toed Salamanders.

Riparian Forests

Strips of riparian forest occur along rivers and lakeshores (riparian means "along water") throughout the dry interior, forming a transi-tional environment that joins wetlands to their surroundings. In these strips of cottonwoods and willows, wildlife is much more

diverse than in the sur-rounding shrub- and grasslands. Birds are abundant, and some, such as Red-eyed Vireos and Yellow Warblers, are largely restricted to this habitat. Many other animals occupy riparian forests on their way to and from water.

Riparian cottonwoods, Ridgefield National Wildlife Refuge, Washington

Steppes and Deserts

The driest parts of the region, like the coldest, cannot support trees. In the low-lying Columbia Basin and on Oregon's high plateaus there are expanses of true steppe (grassland) and shrub steppe (grassland with scattered sagebrush and other shrubs), and smaller areas of even drier desert shrub. In April and May these areas are productive and green during the short burst of growth of grasses and other plants; they turn brown and lifeless-looking by July. Animal activity also peaks in spring. With such light vegetation cover, the underlying rock is visible; indeed many of the most spectacular rock formations of the Pacific Northwest can be found here.

Steppe habitat, Columbia River Gorge, Oregon

Steppe

True steppe, or grassland, occurs just below the Ponderosa Pines and just above the somewhat drier shrub steppe, and shares many of its plants and animals with one or both of those zones. Several species of bunchgrass give the steppe its form, but the flora is also rich in spring wildflowers. The open country supports populations of numerous birds and mammals that are found in no other habitat in the Pacific Northwest. There are few places to hide in such open country, so burrowing species such as ground squirrels, pocket gophers, American Badgers, and Burrowing Owls are well represented. Many animals such as Horned Larks and Short-horned Lizards are sandy-brown to match the prevailing dead-grass color.

Rocks and Cliffs

Rock outcrops, especially basalt cliffs, are widespread in the interior and support their own specialized flora and fauna. Rattlesnakes and Rock Wrens hide in crevices, and wide-ranging predators such as hawks and owls use rocks and cliffs for protected nest sites. Lichens, especially prominent on cliffs, become dormant when conditions are adverse—too dry, too hot, or too cold—and spring back to life when temperature and moisture are optimal.

Basalt cliffs, Washington

Desert shrub, Mann Lake, Oregon

Desert Shrub

Restricted to the saline soils of old lake beds in southeastern Oregon, this habitat resembles the shrub steppe but has different dominant shrubs. Greasewood, one such species, can tolerate high concentrations of salts in the soil by accumulating the salts in its own tissues; another is Spiny Hopsage, its spiny branches a common adaptation to desert conditions, where its succulent leaves are attractive to browsers such as deer and marmots. This hottest part of the Pacific Northwest is especially rich in reptiles, which depend on warmth for their activity; all become dormant during the cold plateau winters. Five species occur nowhere else in the region: Long-nose Leopard Lizard, Desert Horned Lizard, Mojave Black-collared Lizard, Western Whiptail, and Western Ground Snake. One of the most characteristic mammals, the White-tailed Antelope Squirrel, combats the heat by raising its reflective white tail over its back like a parasol.

Shrub Steppe

Shrub steppe, where annual precipitation averages less than 12 inches, is widespread in the Columbia Basin in south-central Washington and on the high plateau of eastern Oregon. It shares Bluebunch Wheatgrass and other herbaceous plants with the true steppe, but a

Shrub steppe, Succor Creek State Recreation Area, Oregon

half-dozen species of shrubs characterize it. Big Sagebrush dominates throughout a large part of its range, providing habitat for Sage Grouse, Sage Thrashers, Sage Sparrows, Sagebrush Lizards, and Sagebrush Voles—all use sagebrush for food or cover or both, highlighting the importance of even a single plant species to the animals of a habitat.

Freshwater Wetlands

Wetlands are widespread in this region, both as a network of rivers and streams and as a liberal sprinkling of lakes, ponds, marshes, and swamps. In their ecology and in many of their plants and animals, the wetlands west of the Cascades are much like those across forested parts of North America. On the other hand, the wetlands of the dry interior are especially rich. Their dense populations of freshwater invertebrates and plants feed large numbers of breeding and migratory waterbirds and attract much of the animal life to be seen in parts of the interior.

Hayes Lake, central Washington

Lakes and Ponds

Bodies of standing fresh water, from shallow ephemeral ponds to deep lakes, occur throughout the region, providing habitat for many aquatic animals such as muskrats, beavers, painted turtles, several duck species, Rough-skin Newts, Spotted and Red-legged Frogs, and introduced fishes such as Largemouth Bass and Bluegills. Plants of lakes and ponds may be submergent (entirely underwater), emergent (rooted but extending above the water, such as the Broad-leaved Cattail), or floating (also rooted but floating on the surface, such as the Yellow Pond Lily).

Freshwater Marshes

Marshes are shallow wetlands with low, emergent, soft-stemmed vegetation such as cattails and Tule and standing water throughout most of the year. The density of the vegetation distinguishes them from ponds and lakes, which have more open water. Marshes in the dry interior,

Marsh, Umatilla National WIldlife Refuge, Oregon

for example in the Columbia National Wildlife Refuge of eastern Washington and the Malheur and Klamath refuges of the high plateau of southern Oregon, are among the most productive habitats in North America. High summer temperatures and abundant nutrients support dense populations of algae and vascular plants, resulting in the emergence each summer of clouds of insects, among them many species of dragonflies, whose larvae are aquatic. These insects in turn feed large populations of blackbirds and waterfowl.

Alkaline Lakes

Salt flat, Summer Lake Wildlife Area, Oregon

In southeastern Oregon there are several large alkaline lakes —including Lake Abert and Summer Lake—that are evaporating remnants of a wetter period eons ago. In this very hot, dry climate, rains carry soil minerals downslope until they collect in the lowest basins; as the water evaporates, the minerals become more and more concentrated. These chemical soups support no higher plants and few animal species, but crustaceans such as brine shrimps are so abundant in alkaline lakes that tens of thousands of birds (including avocets, phalaropes, and Eared Grebes) feed and rest there in late summer to gain the energy to molt and migrate farther south.

Icicle Creek, Wenatchee National Forest, Washington

Rivers and Streams

The largest of the Northwest's myriad streams and rivers is the Columbia River, which drains a substantial part of the region but is so thoroughly dammed that many parts of it are now large reservoirs. Reservoirs that remain stable behind their dams become highly productive and support flora and fauna much like those of large lakes; those with a fluctuating water level become relatively sterile, with no permanent shallow water in which plants can take root and a very sparse food web. The Northwest's original rivers were richly endowed with fish, including the salmon (which migrate from marine waters upstream to breed in fresh water) and trout for which the region is famous. Most streams and smaller rivers retain their original life, not only the fishes but also many species of insects, such as stoneflies and mayflies, whose specially adapted sharp claws and flattened bodies allow them to live in swift-flowing waters.

Coastal Habitats

The Northwest has some 450 miles of coastline, most of which in Oregon and the southern half of Washington fronts the open Pacific Ocean. The northern Washington coast is enclosed in a series of straits and bays, with Puget Sound the most prominent. As shoreline flora and fauna are strongly affected by adjacent marine conditions, exposed and protected coastlines support different groups of marine plants and animals.

European Beachgrass, Oregon Dunes

Sand Dunes

Sand dunes, which occur behind many of the outer coast sand beaches, support a unique flora, with many species adapted to growing in the open sand. European Beachgrass spreads by a system of creeping underground stems called rhizomes and anchors the sand to provide better habitat for itself; by doing so, it actually expands the sand dunes on some beaches. Yellow Sand Verbena not only has a long taproot to reach the water level but also has hairy leaves that trap sand, holding the plant in place. Behind the dunes is usually a low area, where the sand surface lies at the level of the water table, that supports beach plants requiring higher moisture levels. A great variety of insects are attracted to dune vegetation, furnishing food for Savannah Sparrows and other birds of open country that nest among the grasses.

Salt Marshes

Salt marshes occur at many Northwest river mouths but reach their highest development in big protected bays such as Washington's Grays Harbor and Willapa Bay, the Columbia River estuary, and Coos Bay in Oregon. Salt-tolerant species dominate the distinctive plant communities; succulents such as American Glasswort actually incorporate salt into their leaves. Few animal species are found among the marsh vegetation; few birds nest here, perhaps because of the extreme tidal range. But the tidal saltwater channels that course through the marsh abound in invertebrates and fishes and the birds, such as shorebirds and herons, that prey on them.

Salt marsh, Willapa Bay, Washington

Manzanita Beach, Oregon

Sand Beaches

Much of the Oregon and southern Washington coasts are backed by sand beaches, where intense wave energy sifts the sand with each high tide. Inhabitants of these beaches must be adapted to this almost-fluid medium. Shorebirds such as Sanderlings and Snowy Plovers are quick runners, capturing invertebrates such as California Beach Fleas briefly exposed by receding waves. The "fleas" are actually crustaceans that live in burrows in the coarse sand, emerging under cover of darkness to scavenge organic matter.

Tidepool with sea star, Olympic National Park, Washington

Rocky Shores

Rocky shores, found from one end of the region to the other, are very distinct from the sand beaches with which they alternate. The rocky areas are usually steeper, with zones of plant and animal life sharply controlled by tidal levels. Species of acorn barnacles that can withstand desiccation colonize the highest levels; in a band below them live California Mussels, their upper limit set by the tidal height and their lower limit by the presence of the Ochre Sea Stars that prey on them. The intertidal zone (between high and low tide lines) in this region supports an exceptionally diverse community of marine organisms, including dozens of species of worms, snails, and other invertebrates that live in the interstices of the extensive mussel beds. The "seaweeds" that move rhythmically with each wave are representatives of three groups of algae: yellow-brown, green, and red. Unlike higher plants, they take their nutrients directly from the water.

Marine Habitats

Off the Northwest coast, cold currents running beneath the water cause massive upwelling of nutrient-rich particles and sediment from the bottom, making these waters as rich as any in the world. Marine invertebrates are especially abundant and diverse, and in some cases (octopuses, sea stars) the local species are the largest of their groups anywhere. Fish are also varied and plentiful in offshore waters, and other animal life is evident everywhere, the species changing with sea-bottom type, exposure, and distance from shore. Macroscopic plants such as kelps and eelgrasses are restricted to shallow inshore areas.

Seabirds with Gray Whale blowing in background

Offshore Waters

Off the coast and out of sight of land is a realm strikingly different from the same ocean close to shore. Pelagic animals—those that move across the ocean well away from land—dominate this habitat, especially over the very productive continental shelf, where upwellings are the strongest. These animals include birds such as albatrosses and storm-petrels, mammals such as Dall's Porpoises and Northern Fur Seals, and fishes such as Blue Sharks. Albatrosses use the winds to glide for days with scarcely a wingbeat, and fur seals float at the surface, their black flippers raised to absorb the sun's heat. One of the many offshore drifters is the By-the-wind Sailor, a relative of the jellyfishes with inflated pockets of gas that keep it afloat.

Inshore Waters

The extreme conditions of the outer coast—that part of the coast directly exposed to the Pacific Ocean and to the full power of the westerly winds and waves—lead to extreme adaptations. Seabirds such as gulls and loons that are common along

Dock Shrimp

Giant Pacific Octopus

the coast are strong fliers, and sessile (attached to the substrate) invertebrates such as barnacles and mussels are well attached. The complex shoreline of northern Washington has many deep channels and basins—Puget Sound, for example—that are less subject to wind and waves than locations on the outer coast, but are similarly bathed by nutrients. These protected inshore waters support a rich carpet of sessile invertebrates and algae, which feed a great diversity of predators and grazers; marine mammals such as California Sea Lions and seabirds such as Harlequin Ducks and Pigeon Guillemots are especially abundant.

Estuaries and Tidal Flats

The outer coast is interrupted by a series of large estuaries and bays at the mouths of the rivers that drain the region. Numerous rivers drain into the two very large bays in Washington, including the Chehalis into Grays Harbor and the Willapa into Willapa Bay. Bays such as Tillamook and Coos on the Oregon coast are smaller but similar, and the Columbia River has its own long estuary. The sand and silt deposited by these rivers, protected from the full force of Pacific waves, provides a rich substrate for burrowing invertebrates such as polychaete worms, beach fleas, and snails; these and the fish that feed on them are in turn prey for Harbor Seals and many shorebirds.

Tidal flat along Hood Canal, Washington

Disturbed Habitats

Although the Pacific Northwest comprises huge wilderness areas, much of the region has been modified by human activity. The most extreme changes come from agriculture and human settlement, both of which eliminate much natural habitat. Wheat farms and apple orchards support not only the human population of the region but a booming export business, and the moderate climate and beautiful scenery attract new residents from all over the world. Plants and animals that can adapt to these changes have increased in the region, while those that cannot have become rare. Nonetheless, disturbed areas are still habitats, and many species successfully find food and shelter in them.

Farmland, Palouse Hills, Washington

Farms and Orchards

The Columbia Basin irrigation project has turned much of this once-arid basin into a vast farmland. Much of the original steppe vegetation has disappeared, leaving virtually sterile croplands and orchards. Only one native bird, the Horned Lark, thrives in the wheat fields of the Palouse Hills of eastern Washington, along with the introduced Ring-necked Pheasant; both are able to survive on wheat and weed seeds. Apple orchards feature nesting Mourning Doves and American Robins but few other species. Livestock pastures, if not overgrazed, support a diversity of open-country animals such as Killdeers and moles, and many species colonize abandoned farms and orchards as varied vegetation cover develops.

Cities

The Pacific Northwest has few very large cities, but the region's urban areas, like its many croplands, represent an extreme of habitat destruction. Because they are very well adapted to human society, nonnative species such as European Starlings, Rock Doves, and

Black-capped Chickadee

Common Raccoons

Brown Rats abound in this much-altered environment. Many of the plants are also nonnative "weeds," but some primitive native plants are surprisingly resistant to disturbance and even soil pollution. For example, Common Horsetail is often the only plant growing in soils poisoned by industrial activities.

Suburbs

The suburbs around the larger cities sustain a substantial variety of flora and fauna, especially where ravines and hillsides are too steep to be developed. Parks and gardens, well-wooded backyards, and artificial ponds all contribute to suburban biodiversity, but the larger species of wildlife, as well as

Himalayan Blackberry

many of the smaller ones, are gone. Some species seem able to adapt readily to human-modified environments, and many of those species—some of them introduced, like the Rufous Garden Slug and Himalayan Blackberry—are certain to increase.

Feeder Birds

While in a strictly urban environment the nonnative European Starling and House Sparrow will likely be among the first visitors to a backyard birdfeeder, Black-capped Chickadees, House Finches, Song Sparrows, and Steller's Jays will soon arrive. In more suburban areas, wintering American Goldfinches, Dark-eyed Juncos, and White-crowned and other sparrows can be enticed. Occasionally a Sharp-shinned Hawk will quickly come through, searching for an avian meal. Black-chinned, Rufous, and Calliope Hummingbirds might stop by a special hummingbird feeder in the summer months. (See also the essay on attracting birds on page 306.)

Impact of Human Settlement

Species have always come and gone in the natural landscape, but the activities of humans speed up the process immensely. Plants and animals disappear along with their habitat, and habitat destruction is surely the most significant of the human effects changing the face of the earth. Each year Washington loses more than 30,000 acres of wildlife habitat to urban development. In the region overall, the following habitats are currently critically endangered (more than 98 percent in decline): prairies and oak savannas in the Willamette Valley, the foothills of the Coast Range of Oregon, the Palouse prairie of southeastern Washington, and ungrazed sagebrush steppe in the eastern parts of both states. Among those that are merely endangered (85 to 98 percent in decline) are old-growth forests, including old-growth Ponderosa Pine forests, native shrub and grassland steppes, marshes in the Coos Bay area, and large streams and rivers.

Purple Loosestrife

Introduced Plants

The Pacific Northwest has its complement of introduced species, the effects of which range from undetectable to minor nuisance to ecological disaster. Purple Loosestrife, introduced in this century as an ornamental plant, quickly spread throughout Northwest marshes, where it crowds out other marsh vegetation as well as wildlife. Loosestrife-eating leaf beetles are being brought in to control it. Saltmarsh Cordgrass threatens to strangle Washington's Willapa Bay and other estuaries, and Spotted Knapweed takes over as many as 6,000 acres per year of grassland wildlife habitat.

Canada Geese, Sun Lakes State Park, Washington

Introduced Animals

Little attempt has been made to control introduced animals in the region, including European Starlings, which outcompete native species for nest sites, and European Rabbits, which drastically alter landscapes. Canada Geese were introduced west of the Cascades in the 1950s for hunting; they are now ubiquitous in urban and suburban areas, where their abundant fecal deposits are detrimental to water quality and perhaps human health. They harass native water-

Grazing cattle with Wallowa Mountains in background, Oregon

fowl in nesting areas and are spreading rapidly into natural areas. Meanwhile, the Bullfrog is decimating native frog populations. Other introduced animals considered damaging include the Rufous Garden Slug (destroys garden plants) and the Black Rat (eats stored products and carries human diseases). Other creatures introduced for food or sport—such as the Giant Pacific Oyster, the Soft-shelled Clam, and the Ring-necked Pheasant—are considered benign.

Cattle Grazing

Livestock grazes on about 60 percent of the land used for agriculture in the Northwest. Moister grasslands can withstand considerable grazing, but drier shrub-steppe regions cannot. As a result, a wide variety of native shrub and grassland habitats, each associated with a specific soil type, have degenerated into simple communities dominated by invasive grasses, either Cheatgrass or Kentucky Bluegrass. The loss of native plants—the bunchgrasses that gave the habitat structure and the low, broad-leaved plants such as Arrowleaf Balsamroot and Long-leaved Phlox that gave it diversity—in turn reduces insect and bird diversity. Grazing has also devastated riparian communities, where the loss of deciduous woody vegetation has negatively affected aquatic species and migrant birds.

Orchard below Mount Adams, Washington

Farming

Agriculture occupies about one-third of the Pacific Northwest. In most areas in eastern Washington and northeastern Oregon, more than 50 percent of the natural shrub-steppe habitats of sagebrush and bunchgrasses have been lost to agriculture; in a few counties, the loss is close to 100 percent. Where irrigation is easily provided, as in the Columbia and Snake River valleys, field crops such as potatoes and alfalfa have now replaced vast areas of sagebrush steppe. At the eastern foot of the Washington Cascades, vast orchards of apples, cherries, and other fruits are expanding from the Columbia River up the steep slopes and eliminating the native sagebrush. Some of the state's rarest species, such as the Pygmy Rabbit and Sage Grouse, are restricted to ever-diminishing sagebrush communities. The moist prairies and oak savannas of the Willamette Valley of central Oregon and the formerly extensive natural grassland of the Palouse country of southeastern Washington now produce crops, especially grains; as a result, native grassland birds and mammals such as Sharp-tailed Grouse and White-tailed Jackrabbits are some of the rarest in the region.

Logging

Clearcut forest

The forests of the Pacific Northwest have a long history of logging. In the 1980s more than one-fourth of the softwood (coniferous) timber harvested in the United States came from Washington and Oregon, where combined harvest exceeded 10 billion board feet annually. At least 80 to 90 percent of the old-growth forests throughout the region have been cut; where not protected, the original wet forests are gone. With the felling of these forests, species such as Marbled Murrelets, Northern Goshawks, and Northern Spotted Owls, which depend upon old-growth forests for nesting habitat, have all declined sharply. In these complex, multilayered forests, sunlight penetrates to the ground, nurturing diverse shrubs and herbaceous plants that in turn provide food and habitat for many animals, whereas in the cultivated commercial forest plantations of today there is no penetration of sunlight and virtually no understory. Forests that shaded small streams have been cut, raising the water temperature to the lethal limit for salmon eggs, and the logging roads have caused erosion that deposits egg-killing silt on spawning gravel and also affects aquatic amphibians such as torrent salamanders and tailed frogs. Basic ecological links have been lost—snags (standing dead trees) that served as nest cavities, fallen trees that sheltered salamanders, and essential symbiotic associations between certain fungi and tree roots.

Extent of
Old-Growth Forests
▢ 1850   ▮ 1990

Commercial Fishing

Food fish landings in Washington and Oregon ports average about 10 percent of the nation's total. The majority of the catch is bottom fishes such as soles and rockfishes, but trawlers and gill netters bring in 25,000 tons of salmon each year. Present abundance notwith-

Salmon in net haul, Washington

standing, problems with overfishing are predicted; because of fishing pressures, loss of spawning grounds, and difficulties in moving through hydroelectric dams, salmon populations have decreased by more than 70 percent in the last few decades, and more than 200 salmon stocks adapted to particular streams are extinct or at risk. Some shellfish—oysters, for example—are now harvested primarily through aquaculture in estuaries. Pesticides sprayed in these estuaries to kill shrimp, whose burrows make oyster growth difficult, also kill young Dungeness Crabs, another very important species in the region's economy.

Water and Energy Resources

The Columbia and Snake Rivers are among the nation's great sources of hydroelectric power. The original free flow of these rivers in Washington and Oregon has been curtailed over much of their length by more than 60 dams. Wild salmon populations have been reduced dramatically, and many salmon runs—once extending over hundreds of miles of inland streams—have been destroyed entirely. The reservoir behind eastern Washington's Grand Coulee Dam— one of the world's largest producers of hydroelectric energy—waters large parts of the Columbia Basin. The overflow of water from such irrigation reservoirs and canals creates an array of productive wetlands in many low areas of Washington that were formerly bone-dry. However, most of the riparian groves of cottonwoods and willows, once full of songbirds and other terrestrial animals, are now submerged under deep reservoirs, and the free-flowing river with its diverse community of stream fishes no longer exists.

Coulee Dam National Recreational Area, Washington

Endangered, Threatened, and Recovering Species

Many factors have contributed to population decline in Northwest animals and plants: habitat destruction caused by logging, agricultural activity, wetlands drainage, and urbanization; pesticide use; transportation and storage of oil; overhunting and overfishing; hydroelectric dams on major rivers; and the introduction of alien species. Only in recent decades have regulatory agencies responded strongly to the decline of many species of plants and animals in the United States. The federal Endangered Species Act (1973) was enacted to protect the rarest species by imposing penalties on anyone who kills an endangered or threatened species or harms such a species by disturbing its nest or destroying its habitat. According to this act, an endangered species or subspecies is one in danger of extinction throughout all or a significant part of its range; a threatened species is one likely to become endangered within the foreseeable future. In recent years, some species (the Gray Whale and Sea Otter, for example) that had been reduced in number have begun to recover, showing increases in their populations.

Northern Spotted Owl

Endangered and Threatened Species

The old-growth forests of the Pacific Northwest are unique and valuable ecosystems that are at risk because they are also excellent sources of lumber. The region has therefore been the setting for one of the most significant chapters in the conservation movement: the attempt to maintain viable populations of the threatened Northern Spotted Owl by preserving these forests. Marked by lost jobs, acrimonious meetings, illegally logged forests, and millions of dollars on both owl research and lawsuits, this controversy will have consequences far into the future. Other species associated with old-growth forests that are listed as either endangered or threatened include the Oregon Chub (endangered because of the degradation of rivers), the Bald Eagle (threatened by pesticides and hunting), and the Marbled Murrelet (a seabird that nests in old-growth forests, and is threatened by habitat loss).

Trumpeter Swan

Recovering Swans

By 1900, extinction was predicted for the Trumpeter Swan, long decimated by hunting; its wild populations were restricted to a few birds that bred in Alaska and wintered in

Peregrine Falcon

the Northwest. However, since its protection by the Migratory Bird Treaty Act of 1918, this bird's numbers have increased steadily, and it is now not only not on any endangered- or threatened-species lists but is a common sight in western Washington.

Recovering Raptors

DDT, introduced as a pesticide just after World War II, becomes increasingly concentrated as it works its way up through the food chain, building up in birds that consume fish and other birds. The poison interferes with eggshell production, so that the birds crush their own eggs when they attempt to incubate them. Raptors, among the birds most affected by this, began to recover after the use of DDT was banned in 1972. Bald Eagles, Ospreys, and Peregrine Falcons are all much more common in the Northwest than they were two decades ago. Bald Eagle pairs in Washington and Oregon increased from 166 in 1974 to 573 in 1990, and the species was downlisted from endangered to threatened in 1995.

Conservation

No species that recently occurred in this region is extinct, although some species have disappeared locally. Gray Wolves and Grizzly Bears, absent from much of their former range in the lower 48 states, still wander into the northern Cascades of Washington, and there is talk of enhancing these peripheral populations with

Grizzly Bear

reintroductions. Parks, sanctuaries, and refuges abound, with both governmental and nongovernmental agencies attempting to set aside additional land containing rare and fragile ecosystems such as ungrazed steppe and undeveloped estuaries.

Overleaf: Arrowleaf Balsamroot, Okanogan County, Washington

Weather

The climate of the Pacific Northwest is profoundly affected by air masses from both the Pacific Ocean and the North American continent. Pacific air masses (mild in winter, cool in summer) dominate along the coast, while continental air (cold in winter, hot in summer) prevails east of the Cascade Mountains. However, the boundary between oceanic and continental air is always in motion, and at times the entire region can be engulfed by either kind of air.

Wind Patterns

Earth's atmosphere is driven into motion as hot tropical air rises and spreads toward the poles and cold polar air sinks and flows toward the equator. Earth's rotation warps this north–south exchange of warm and cold air into vast wind patterns, including the prevailing westerlies, a broad west-to-east air current that flows over most of the United States and southern Canada. Embedded in the prevailing westerlies are a succession of whirls and eddies: systems of high pressure (fair weather) and low pressure (cloudiness, high humidity, stormy weather) that form and dissipate along fronts, which are the boundaries between warm and cold air masses. Winds blow in a circular pattern around the center of weather systems: In the Northern Hemisphere they blow counterclockwise (as seen from above) in a low-pressure system and clockwise in a high-pressure system.

MOIST AIR

DRY AIR

UPSLOPE AND DOWNSLOPE WINDS: RAIN SHADOW EFFECT

The mountain ranges of the Northwest provide a formidable barrier to the flow of air across the region and profoundly influence local climates. When moist westerly winds are forced to ascend a ridge to get to the other side, the air cools to the condensation temperature (dew point), and clouds, rain, and snow develop. Because of this upslope effect, the western slopes of the Olympic, Coast, and Cascade Ranges are among the wettest spots in North America. As the westerlies, already reduced of moisture, descend the eastern slopes of the ranges, they warm up as a result of compressional heating, and humidity is even further reduced. These mild downslope winds, called "chinooks," create a rain shadow effect to the east of the larger ranges, and are responsible for the desert climate of parts of central and eastern Washington and Oregon.

Aleutian Low

During autumn, winter, and spring, a huge semi-permanent low-pressure system, the Aleutian Low, develops over the Gulf of Alaska. The counterclockwise flow around its southern perimeter intensifies the strength of the prevailing westerlies blowing into the Pacific Northwest coast, and the Aleutian Low spawns smaller low-pressure systems that come ashore with almost monotonous regularity.

North Pacific High

In summer, the Aleutian Low all but disappears, and the North Pacific High, a massive semi-permanent high-pressure system that occupies most of the Pacific Ocean north of the equator, expands northward, keeping Washington and Oregon in sunshine for days at a time as it shunts storms and cold fronts to the north. West of the Cascades, the ocean-cooled air keeps temperatures comfortable, but persistent sunshine farther inland can raise temperatures east of the Cascades into the 90s and 100s Fahrenheit. Occasionally, easterly winds send such heat into the Puget Sound and Willamette Valley areas. However, the humidity is usually quite low, making the heat bearable and virtually eliminating the chance of thunderstorms.

The Progress of a Storm

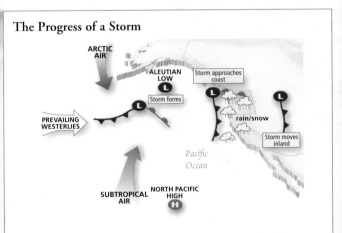

As a storm system spins off the Aleutian Low, a warm front, usually on the eastern side of the storm center, marks the leading edge of northbound warm air. As it rises over the colder, denser air to its north, the warm air produces moderate but steady rain. Meanwhile, west of the storm's center, arctic air plunges south behind a cold front, along which heavier air shoves like a wedge beneath the warm, and usually moist, air. Forced upward, the warm air expands and cools, its moisture condensing into clouds and rain. As the center of low pressure passes, generally to the east, the trailing cold front may sweep the entire region, setting off brief but heavy showers, squalls, and thunderstorms. After the storm departs, high pressure moves in, bringing clearing, cooler weather, perhaps a brief interval of fair skies, and eventually southerly winds ahead of the next storm.

Rain

For better or worse, the Northwest is famous for its rain, which may fall as an all-day soaker, a brief "sun shower," or a slow but steady drizzle. The region's average precipitation (which includes rain and melted snow) of 32 inches per year belies the extreme variation from place to place, ranging from 7 inches annually in the deserts of the east to 184 inches in the Olympic rain forest of northwestern Washington. Precipitation may vary greatly from year to year, with some wet years providing twice the amount of dry years. On occasion a substantial fraction of the annual precipitation falls in a one- or two-week spell of nearly continuous storms, resulting in widespread flooding, particularly if the rain falls on pre-existing snow cover.

Ice Storms and Sleet

When warm air aloft overruns a mass of cold air clinging to the ground, the result can be rain that falls as liquid but freezes on contact with everything it touches—grass, trees, roads, and wires; the resulting ice coating is called glaze. Minor ice storms, also know as freezing rain or "silver thaws," coat parts of the interior about ten times a year but are quite infrequent— occurring only once or twice a year—along the coast. If the cold air mass near ground level is deep enough, the falling rain may freeze solid before reaching the ground, resulting in sleet, tiny ice pellets that resemble small hailstones. Sleet, usually mixed with snow, rain, or freezing rain, occurs about eight times a year along the coast but only two to four times inland.

Record-setting Pacific Northwest Weather

HIGHEST TEMPERATURE 119° F at Pendleton, Oregon, August 10, 1898.

LOWEST TEMPERATURE –54° F at Seneca, Oregon, February 10, 1933.

WETTEST PLACE Wynoochee Oxbow, Washington. 184 inches of precipitation per year.

DRIEST PLACE Sunnyside, Washington. 6.9 inches of precipitation per year.

GREATEST SNOWSTORM 129 inches at Laconia, Washington, February 24–26, 1910.

SNOWIEST WINTER 1,122 inches at Paradise Ranger Station, Mount Rainier National Park, 1971–72.

HIGHEST WIND 170 mph at Tillamook Forest, Oregon, October 12, 1962.

Mount Hood, Oregon

Snow

Affected by elevation, latitude, and distance from the coast, snowfall in the Pacific Northwest ranges from infrequent to incredible. Along the Oregon coast, snowfall averages only 1 to 4 inches per year, and many winters pass with no snow at all; at higher elevations in the Olympics and Cascades, 400 to 600 inches of snow fall in an average year. Between these extremes, snowfall averages 6 to 12 inches in the Willamette Valley and around Puget Sound, and 20 to 60 inches across most of the interior east of the Cascades.

Tornadoes

On average, only two tornadoes per year touch down in the Northwest, making the region the least tornado-prone in the contiguous United States. Many (but not all) of the Northwest's tornadoes occur in winter, and because of the coolness, they are small, brief, and weak.

Lightning

Lightning is an electrical discharge between one part of a cloud and another, between two clouds, or between a cloud and earth. In a typical year, lightning strikes the Northwest about 250,000 times, and perhaps ten times as many flashes arc across the sky without touching the ground. Lightning is responsible for destroying 60 percent of the trees consumed annually by forest fires in the Northwest.

Seasons

The Pacific Northwest's location about midway between the equator and the North Pole makes it particularly sensitive to the changing angles of sunlight striking the ground over the course of a year, which is what causes the change of seasons. However, seasonal changes across the region, and especially along the coast, are moderated and slowed by the waters of the neighboring Pacific Ocean. As earth moves around its orbit, because of its 23½-degree tilt, half the year the Northern Hemisphere is inclined toward the sun and the sun's rays shine on it more directly, and half the year it is tilted away from the sun and the sun's rays are more oblique. The latitude that receives the greatest heat from the sun is farther north during the summer months (though earth's surface—land and sea—takes a while to warm up, so early August is actually hotter than late June). Atmospheric currents, such as the prevailing westerlies, in turn shift to the north. Higher sun angles and longer days in the Arctic during summer take the bite out of the polar air masses and decrease the heat difference between the tropics and the North Pole, weakening heat-driven currents.

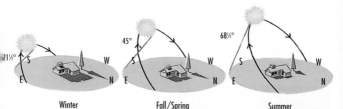

Winter	Fall/Spring	Summer

At 45° N (the latitude of Portland), the noontime sun at the winter solstice has an altitude above the horizon of only 21½°; at the spring and fall equinoxes its altitude is 45°; and at the summer solstice the noontime sun rises 68½° above the horizon.

Spring

Black-bellied Plover

Spring officially begins on or about March 21, called the spring (or vernal) equinox, when the sun appears directly overhead at noon at the equator. Held back by the slow-to-warm waters of the Pacific Ocean, spring-like weather arrives gradually in the Pacific Northwest. March is often wintry, with persistent clouds and rain (and heavy snow in the mountains), but April brings rain showers and increased sunshine. In May, one or two spells of warm, dry weather may engulf the region, providing a preview of the approaching summer.

Summer

The sun reaches its peak over the Northern Hemisphere around June 21 (the summer solstice), the longest daylight period of the year. As the sun's more direct rays heat the Arctic, the Aleutian Low all but disappears, and the North Pacific High expands northward and eastward. Slightly sunnier and warmer

Avalanche Lily

than May, June is a mix of dry, warm days and cool, wet days. By July, periods of long, sunny days may continue uninterrupted for a week or two (in July, Walla Walla, Washington, has more sunshine than Phoenix, Arizona). August brings continued near-perfect weather; on many summer days, the only clouds in the region are fog and stratocumulus along the immediate coast and a few puffy cumulus over mountains. Daytime temperatures average in the 70s Fahrenheit west of the Cascades and in the 80s inland.

Elk

Fall

As it does at the spring equinox, the sun "crosses" the equator again at the autumnal equinox, around September 22. However, September is quite summery and is often warmer, sunnier, and drier than June. But October brings the onset of autumn weather, as frequent

rains return to the coast, snow coats the mountains, and frost nips the apples in the east. October also brings spells of "Indian summer" (sunny, warm days after the first freeze), but November is not so kind. By Thanksgiving the wet season is in full gear, as a steady stream of storms spun off the Aleutian Low come ashore.

Winter

The winter solstice is around December 21. The gloom of the notably short days this far north is magnified by persistent clouds (December is the region's cloudiest month), frequent fog, and day-long storms. The prevailing westerlies keep the coast, Puget Sound, and Oregon's Willamette Valley areas

Douglas Fir cones

mild enough for most precipitation to fall as rain, but east of the Cascades snow is more likely. In the mountains, almost all the precipitation falls as snow. Several times a winter, arctic cold fills the Columbia Plateau, and nighttime temperatures may fall to zero degrees Fahrenheit or lower. On rarer occasions the arctic air crosses the Cascades into coastal areas, and heavy snow may fall if the arctic outbreak coincides with a storm approaching off the Pacific.

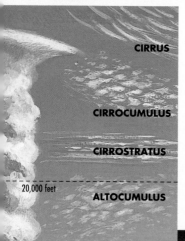

CIRRUS

CIRROCUMULUS

CIRROSTRATUS

20,000 feet

ALTOCUMULUS

ALTOSTRATUS

CUMULONIMBUS

6,500 feet

STRATOCUMULUS

TOWERING CUMULUS

STRATUS

CUMULUS

NIMBOSTRATUS

Typical Clouds

Clouds form when moist air is cooled, causing water molecules to condense into water droplets or ice crystals. While most types of clouds can be spotted over the Pacific Northwest, the ones described here are among the most common. The illustration at left shows the relative common altitudes of the different cloud types; distances are not shown to scale.

CUMULONIMBUS

Tallest of all cloud types; commonly called thunderheads. Lower part composed of water droplets; fuzzy, fibrous top—the "anvil"—made of ice crystals. Produce lightning, thunder, heavy rain, and sometimes hail, high winds, or tornadoes. Most common from May to September.

LENTICULAR CLOUDS

Stationary, smooth-edged clouds that form at crests of air currents over mountainous terrain. Indicate high winds at mountaintop level and turbulence above mountains. Also common are more ragged **cap clouds**, formed directly on summits of higher mountains.

CUMULUS

Water-droplet clouds formed at tops of rising air currents set in motion by uneven heating of ground by sun. Domed tops, like bright white heads of cauliflower. Typical clouds of fine summer days, but can occur any time of year. Can swell into **towering cumulus**, which may produce rain.

STRATOCUMULUS

Low, flat-based, white to gray water-droplet clouds, usually covering most of the sky and arranged in rows or patches, from which light rain may fall. Occurs all times of year, especially in maritime air west of the Cascades.

CIRRUS

High (5 miles or more), thin, wispy clouds made of ice crystals; may be seen in any season, anywhere in Northwest. In winter, cirrus thickening from west or south may signal approaching rain or snow; however, cirrus often come and go without bringing any lower clouds or rain.

ALTOSTRATUS

Middle-level clouds, mainly of water droplets; usually appear as featureless gray sheet covering sky. Thickening, low altostratus from west or south often bring steady widespread rain or snow within hours. May be seen in Northwest at any time of year; most common in winter.

FOG

Cloud formed at ground level; occurs up to 100 days per year in some areas. **Advection fog:** forms when humid air overruns cold surfaces like ocean water; common along coast, especially in summer. **Radiation fog:** caused by overnight cooling of still air; burns off as sun rises; more common inland.

STRATUS AND NIMBOSTRATUS

Stratus: low, indistinct, gray water-droplet clouds, usually covering sky in calm conditions; common in summer along coast; may become fog if close to ground. **Nimbostratus:** stratus clouds from which precipitation falls; almost always present during steady snow or rain.

Our Solar System

The sun, the nine planets that revolve around it, and their moons make up our solar system. Venus, Mars, Jupiter, and Saturn are easily visible to the naked eye; Mercury, Uranus, Neptune, and Pluto are more difficult to see. Other objects in our solar system are transient; the wide orbits of comets make them rare visitors near earth, and meteors flash brightly for only seconds before disappearing.

Observing the Sky in the Pacific Northwest

Contending with frequent clouds from late fall through early spring, stargazers in the Pacific Northwest have to take advantage of clear, dark nights when they occur. Turbulent air over mountains can affect the clarity of images seen in a telescope. In metropolitan areas (most notably the Seattle-Tacoma region), light pollution brightens the sky and obscures the Milky Way. But to the east of the Cascades, the clear, dry air and lack of light pollution make for great night-sky viewing from spring to fall.

FULL MOON

The full moon rises at sunset and sets at dawn. It is highest in the sky in December, up to 73 degrees above the horizon in northern Oregon (in summer, it rises only about 20 or 25 degrees). Some lunar features show up best when the moon is full: the dark "seas" (hardened lava flows) and "rays" of bright material splattered from craters. Craters and mountain ranges best seen before and after full moon, when the angle of sunlight throws them into relief; look especially near the terminator, the dividing line between the moon's day and night sides. Because the moon is locked in earth's gravitational grip, the same side of the moon always faces us.

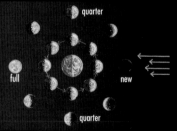

PHASES OF THE MOON

As the moon makes its monthly orbit around earth, the illuminated lunar surface area appears to grow (wax), shrink (wane), and even disappear (at new moon). The center of the illustration shows the phases, with sunlight coming from the right. The outer drawings show how the moon looks from our perspective on earth.

VENUS

Cloud-shrouded Venus alternates between being our "morning star" and "evening star," depending on where it is in its orbit. This brilliant planet usually outshines everything in the sky except for the sun and moon. As it circles the sun, Venus displays phases, which can be viewed through a small telescope or high-power binoculars.

Venus (left) and the moon

MARS

Every 25½ months, when earth is aligned between Mars and the sun, Mars is closest to us and at its brightest and most colorful, appearing orange-red to the naked eye. At this time, called opposition (opposite in the sky from the sun), Mars rises at sunset and remains in the sky all night. Bright, white polar caps and dusky surface markings may be glimpsed through a small telescope at opposition. Mars rivals Jupiter in brightness at opposition, but fades somewhat at other times.

JUPITER

Visible in our morning sky for about five months at a stretch and in our evening sky for five months, Jupiter appears brighter than any star in the night sky at all times. The largest planet in our solar system, it has a diameter of 88,850 miles, 11.2 times that of earth. Jupiter's four largest moons—Ganymede, Io, Europa, and Callisto—can be spotted with binoculars.

Jupiter (top) and moons

SATURN

Visible most of the year, Saturn appears to the naked eye as a slightly yellowish, moderately bright star. A small telescope reveals its rings, composed mainly of rocky chunks of ice, and the two largest (Titan and Rhea) of its more than 20 known moons.

METEORS

These "shooting stars" are typically chips ranging from sand-grain to marble size that are knocked off asteroids (tiny planets) or blown off comets and burn up as they strike our atmosphere. The strongest annual meteor showers are the Perseids, which peak around August 12, and the Geminids, which peak around December 13.

AURORA BOREALIS

Aurora borealis (northern lights) is a show of multicolored lights emitted 60 to 200 miles up in the atmosphere by oxygen and nitrogen atoms energized by flare-like eruptions on the sun's surface. Displays range from faint arcs to wildly flapping, colorful curtains to horizon-wide glows.

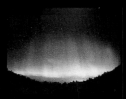

COMETS

Comet Hale-Bopp, 1997

Comets are irregular lumps of ice and rock left over from the formation of the solar system. Occasionally a notable comet approaches the sun as it travels in its far-ranging orbit. The sun's energy vaporizes the comet's surface, generating a tail of gas and dust that may be millions of miles long.

Stars and Deep-sky Objects

As earth orbits the sun in its annual cycle, our planet's night side faces in steadily changing directions, revealing different stars, constellations, and views of our own Milky Way. People in ancient times named constellations after mythological figures and familiar creatures whose shapes they saw outlined by the stars. The best known of these constellations lie along the ecliptic, the imaginary line that traces the apparent path of the sun through the sky. Earth, our moon, and other planets orbit in nearly the same plane, all traveling along a band roughly 16 degrees wide centered on the ecliptic and called the zodiac. (The zodiac is traditionally divided into 12 segments, but 13 constellations actually intersect it.)

Modern constellations are simply designated regions of the celestial sphere, like countries on a map. Most constellations bear little resemblance to their namesakes. Beyond the approximately 6,000 stars visible to the naked eye lie other fascinating deep-sky objects—star clusters, galaxies, nebulas (gas clouds)—that can be seen, some with the naked eye and others with binoculars or a small telescope.

The Zodiac

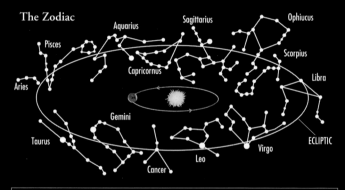

Seasonal Sky Maps

The following pages show star maps for each of the four seasons, drawn at a latitude of 45 degrees north for the specific times and dates given. (If you wish to observe at a different time or date, note that the same stars appear two hours earlier each month, or one hour earlier every two weeks.) The map for each season is divided into four quadrants: northeast, northwest, southeast, and southwest. Start by facing the direction in which you have the clearest view; if your best view is southeastward, use the southeast map. The maps plot the constellations and major stars; the wavy, pale blue areas represent the band of the Milky Way; the zenith, the point directly overhead, is indicated. The key to finding your way around the sky is to locate distinctive constellations or star groups (a few are described at right), and then use them to find others. The maps do not chart the planets of our solar system, whose positions change continually. Their locations are often listed in the weather section of newspapers.

galaxy. Many hot, young blue or white stars (such as Sirius, Rigel, and Procyon), along with some older, cooler yellow and reddish stars (Betelgeuse, Capella, and Aldebaran), dominate the sky. New stars are being born in the Orion Nebula, a mixture of young stars, gases, and dust visible to the naked eye or with binoculars as a fuzzy area in Orion's sword, which hangs from his belt.

SPRING: THE DIPPERS

The spring sky features the well-known Big Dipper, part of the constellation Ursa Major, the Great Bear. The two stars at the end of the Big Dipper's bowl point almost directly at Polaris, the North Star, a moderately bright star (part of the Little Dipper, or Ursa Minor) that lies slightly less than 1 degree from the true north celestial pole. Polaris sits above the horizon at an altitude equal to the observer's latitude (around 45 degrees in the Northwest).

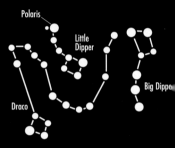

SUMMER: MILKY WAY

During the summer months, earth's dark side faces toward the bright center of the Milky Way, making that hazy band of light a dominant feature in the sky. A scan with binoculars through the Milky Way from Cygnus to Sagittarius and Scorpius reveals a dozen or more star clusters and nebulas. High to the northeast, the hot, white stars of the Summer Triangle—Vega, Deneb, and Altair—are usually the first stars visible in the evening.

FALL: ANDROMEDA GALAXY

On autumn evenings, earth's night side faces away from the plane of our galaxy, allowing us to see other, more distant ones. The Andromeda Galaxy can be found northeast of the Great Square of Pegasus, just above the central star on the dimmer northern "leg" of Andromeda. (On the Fall Sky Southeast map the galaxy is near the first D in Andromeda.) Appearing as an elongated patch of fuzzy light, it is more than 2.5 million light years away.

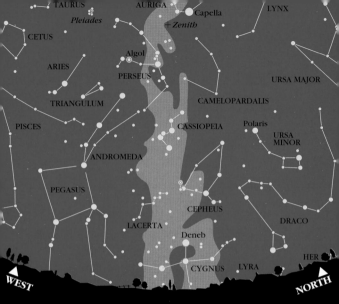

TAURUS   AURIGA   Capella   LYNX
Pleiades   + *Zenith*
CETUS
ARIES   Algol   URSA MAJOR
PERSEUS
TRIANGULUM   CAMELOPARDALIS
PISCES   CASSIOPEIA   Polaris   URSA MINOR
ANDROMEDA
PEGASUS   CEPHEUS   DRACO
LACERTA   Deneb
HER
WEST   CYGNUS   LYRA   NORTH

NORTHWEST

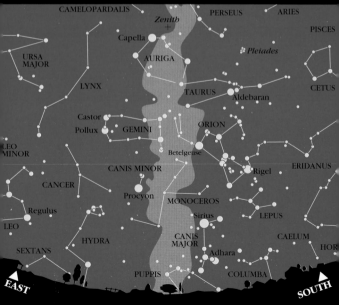

CAMELOPARDALIS   *Zenith* +   PERSEUS   ARIES
Capella   PISCES
URSA MAJOR   AURIGA   *Pleiades*
LYNX   TAURUS   CETUS
Castor   Aldebaran
Pollux   GEMINI   ORION
LEO MINOR   Betelgeuse   Rigel   ERIDANUS
CANIS MINOR
CANCER   Procyon   MONOCEROS   LEPUS
Regulus   Sirius   CAELUM
LEO   CANIS MAJOR   HOR
SEXTANS   HYDRA   Adhara
PUPPIS   COLUMBA
EAST   SOUTH

SOUTHEAST

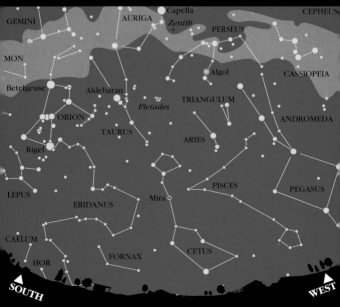

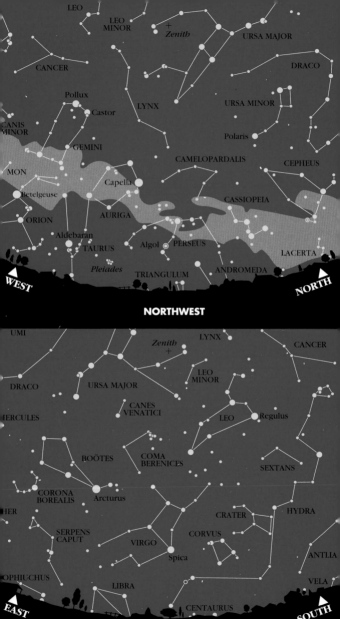

NORTHEAST

SOUTHWEST

SERPENS CAPUT
CORONA BOREALIS
HERCULES
+ *Zenith*
CYGNUS
DRACO
Arcturus
BOÖTES
VIRGO
CANES VENATICI
URSA MINOR
CEPHEUS
Polaris
COMA BERENICES
CAS
CAMELOPARDALIS
URSA MAJOR
LEO
LEO MINOR
WEST
Regulus
LYNX
AURIGA
Capella
NORTH

NORTHWEST

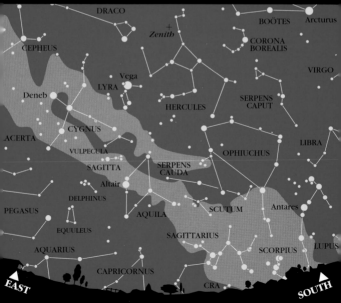

DRACO
BOÖTES
Arcturus
+ *Zenith*
CEPHEUS
CORONA BOREALIS
VIRGO
Vega
LYRA
Deneb
HERCULES
SERPENS CAPUT
CYGNUS
LIBRA
ACERTA
VULPECULA
OPHIUCHUS
SAGITTA
SERPENS CAUDA
Altair
SCUTUM
Antares
PEGASUS
DELPHINUS
AQUILA
EAST
EQUULEUS
SAGITTARIUS
AQUARIUS
SCORPIUS
LUPUS
CAPRICORNUS
CRA
SOUTH

SOUTHEAST

NORTHEAST

URSA MAJOR

HERCULES
+
Zenith

OPHIUCHUS

DRACO

SERPENS
CAUDA

URSA
MINOR

Vega

LYRA

VULPECULA

Altair

AQUILA

Polaris

CYGNUS

SAGITTA

Deneb

CAMELOPARDALIS

CEPHEUS

DELPHINUS

LYNX

LACERTA

EQUULEUS

CASSIOPEIA

PEGASUS

AQUARIUS

Capella

ANDROMEDA

PERSEUS

NORTH

EAST

SOUTHWEST

AQUILA

Zenith
+

DRACO

SERPENS
CAUDA

HERCULES

CORONA
BOREALIS

URSA MAJOR

CANES VENATICI

OPHIUCHUS

SERPENS
CAPUT

BOÖTES

Arcturus

COMA BERENICES

LIBRA

Antares

SCORPIUS

VIRGO

LEO

Spica

LUPUS

HYDRA

CORVUS

CRATER

SOUTH

WEST

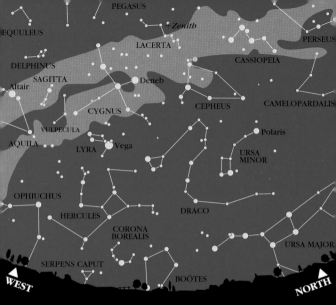

EQUULEUS
PEGASUS
Zenith
LACERTA
PERSEUS
DELPHINUS
CASSIOPEIA
SAGITTA
Deneb
Altair
CEPHEUS
CAMELOPARDALIS
CYGNUS
AQUILA
VULPECULA
LYRA Vega
Polaris
URSA MINOR
OPHIUCHUS
HERCULES
DRACO
CORONA BOREALIS
SERPENS CAPUT
URSA MAJOR
BOÖTES
◄ WEST
NORTH ►
NORTHWEST

CAMELOPARDALIS
LACERTA
CYGNUS
CASSIOPEIA
Zenith
DELPHINUS
ANDROMEDA
PEGASUS
EQUULEUS
Algol
AQUARIUS
PERSEUS
TRIANGULUM
ARIES
PISCES
Pleiades
CAPRICORNUS
TAURUS
PISCIS AUSTRINUS
Aldebaran
Mira
Fomalhaut
CETUS
ORION
GRUS
ERIDANUS
SCULPTOR
◄ EAST
SOUTH ►
SOUTHEAST

September 1, midnight (1 A.M. DST); October 1, 10 P.M. (11 P.M. DST); November 1, 8 P.M.; December 1, 6 P.M.

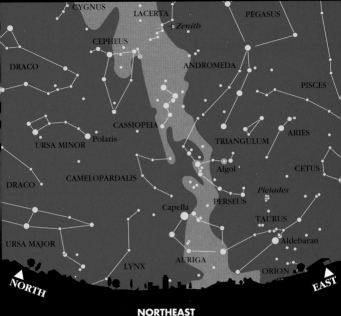

NORTHEAST

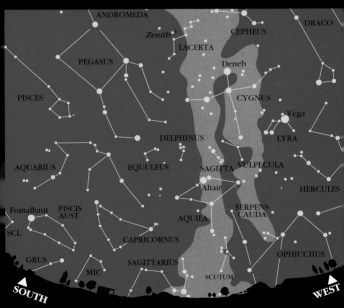

SOUTHWEST

Flora and Fauna

How to Use the Flora and Fauna Section

Part Two of this book presents 1,000 of the most common species found in the Pacific Northwest, beginning with mushrooms, algae, lichens, ferns, and other spore plants, and continuing with large and small trees, wildflowers, invertebrates (mostly seashore creatures and insects), fishes, amphibians, reptiles, birds, and mammals. Flora species are presented alphabetically by family name. Fauna species are sequenced according to their taxonomy, or scientific classification. The classification and the names of species in this guide are based on authoritative sources when these exist for a given group.

Introductions and Other Essays

Most major sections of Part Two—for example, trees, wildflowers, marine invertebrates, birds—have an introduction, and some groups within the larger sections are also described in brief essays. The introductions should be read along with the species accounts that follow, as they present information that is fundamental for understanding the plants or animals in question. For groups without introductory essays, shared features are sometimes given in the opening sentence of the first species in the sequence.

Names

Each account begins with the common name of the species. Common names can change and may differ in other sources; if a species has a widely used alternate name, that is also given, within quotation marks, directly below the common name. The scientific species name, shown below the common name, is italicized (alternate scientific names are also sometimes listed). In a few cases (some flowers and invertebrates), organisms are best known on the genus level and are presented as such here. For example, the earthworms are presented as a group: the *Lumbricus* species. Below the scientific name is the name of the group (class, order, or family) with which the species is most commonly associated. Note that common names of species appear capitalized throughout the guide, but common names of groups (genera, families) appear lower case.

Description

The species accounts are designed to permit identification of species in the field. An account begins with the organism's typical mature or adult size: length (L), height (H), width (W), diameter (D), tail length (T), and/or wingspan (WS). The size is followed by the species' physical characteristics, including color and distinctive markings. We use the abbreviations "imm." (immature) and "juv." (juvenile). The term "morph" describes a distinctive coloration or plumage that occurs in some individuals.

Other Information

For every species, the typical habitat is described. Other information may also be given, such as seasonality (bloom times of flowers or periods of activity for mammals) or the need for caution (species

Names

AMERICAN ROBIN
Turdus migratorius
THRUSH SUBFAMILY

Description

10″. Male breast and sides rufous-orange; back and wings gray-brown; head blackish, with broken white eye ring; throat striped; bill yellow; tail black, with tiny white corners; vent white. Female head and back duller brown. Tail fairly long. In spring and summer, an earthworm specialist; in fall and winter, roams in berry-searching flocks, forms large communal roosts. **VOICE** Song:

Other
Information

prolonged, rising and falling *cheery-up cheery-me*. Calls: *tut tut tut* and *tseep*. **HABITAT** Woodlands, shrubs, lawns. **RANGE** Resident in NW.

that can cause irritation, illness, or injury). Similar species are sometimes described at the end of an account. The range (the area in which the species lives) is not stated if the species occurs throughout the Pacific Northwest; the one exception to this rule is the birds, for which the range is always given. The term "local" means that a species occurs in spotty fashion over a large area, but not throughout the entire area. In describing the geographic range of species, we use the abbreviations e (east), w (west), n (north), s (south), c (central), and combinations of these (sc for south-central). For state names, we use the two-letter postal codes.

Readers should note that color, shape, and size may vary within plant and animal species, depending on environmental conditions and other factors. Bloom, migration, and other times can vary with weather, latitude, and geography.

Classification of Living Things

Biologists divide living organisms into major groups called kingdoms, the largest of which are the plant and animal kingdoms. Kingdoms are divided into divisions (for plants) or phyla (for animals); these are then divided into classes, classes into orders, orders into families, families into genera (singular: genus), and genera into species. The species is the basic unit of classification and is generally what we have in mind when we talk about a "kind" of plant or animal. The scientific name of a species consists of two Latin or Latinized words. The first is the genus name; the second is the species name, often describing the appearance or geographical distribution of the species. The scientific name of the House Mouse is *Mus musculus*. *Mus* is the genus, and *musculus* is the species.

Species are populations or groups of populations that are able to interbreed and produce fertile offspring themselves; they usually are not able to breed successfully or produce fertile offspring with members of other species. Many widespread species have numerous races (subspecies)—populations that are separated from one another geographically; races within a species may differ in appearance and behavior from other populations of that species.

Flora

The flora section of this guide includes flowering and nonflowering plants as well as algae and mushrooms, which are no longer considered part of the plant kingdom. Botanists are developing new classification systems that place most algae outside of the green plants group. Mushrooms are covered here because they are somewhat plant-like in appearance and are often found on plants or plant matter.

The first part of the Pacific Northwest flora section begins with mushrooms, followed by algae and lichens. The next group is the nonflowering spore plants such as liverworts, mosses, clubmosses, horsetails, and ferns. Trees follow, beginning with conifers, then large broadleaf trees, and finally small broadleaf trees and shrubs. Wildflowers, including flowering vines, grasses, and water plants in addition to terrestrial herbaceous plants, end the flora section.

In most of the flora subsections, species are grouped by family. The families are sequenced alphabetically by the English family name. The measurements given in the species accounts are typical mature sizes in the Pacific Northwest. Colors, shapes, and sizes may vary within a species depending on environmental conditions. Bloom times vary throughout the region—later northward and at higher elevations—and can also be affected by the weather conditions in a given year. The geographic range is specified only for those species that are not found throughout the entire Pacific Northwest region.

Users of this guide are warned against eating or otherwise consuming any plants or parts of a plant (including fiddleheads or berries or other fruits) or any mushrooms based on the information supplied in this guide.

Mushrooms

The organisms known as fungi—including molds, yeasts, mildews, and mushrooms—range from microscopic forms to mammoth puffballs. Unlike plants, they do not carry out photosynthesis, and thus must obtain food from organic matter, living or dead. The fungi in this book are of the type commonly known as mushrooms.

Most mushrooms that grow on the ground have a stalk and a cap. The stalks of different species vary in shape, thickness, and density. There is often a skirt-like or bracelet-like ring midway up or near the top of the stalk, and the stalk base is often bulbous or sometimes enclosed by a cup at or just below the surface of the ground. Bracket (or shelf) mushrooms, which grow on trunks or logs, are often unstalked or short-stalked. A mushroom's cap may be smooth, scaly, warty, or shaggy, and its shape may be round, flat, convex (bell- or umbrella-shaped), or concave (cup- or trumpet-shaped). The caps of many species change as they mature, from closed and egg-shaped to open and umbrella-like; the cap color may also change with age.

Fungi reproduce through the release of single-celled bodies called *spores*. Many mushrooms bear their microscopic, spore-producing structures on the underside of the cap, either on radiating blade-like gills or within tiny tubes that terminate in pores. In others, the spore-producing structures line the inside of a cup-shaped cap or are located in broad wrinkles or open pits on the sides or top of the cap. Puffball mushrooms produce their spores within a ball-shaped body; the spores are released when the mature ball breaks open at the top or disintegrates.

Mushroom seasons often begin earlier in wet areas than in dry ones. In the accounts that follow, sizes given are typical heights (for stalked species) and cap widths of mature specimens.

CAUTION
Of the many hundreds of mushroom species occurring in the Pacific Northwest, at least 10 are deadly poisonous to eat, even in small amounts, and many others cause mild to severe reactions. The brief descriptions and few illustrations in this guide are not to be used for determining the edibility of mushrooms. Inexperienced mushroom-hunters should not eat any species they find in the wild.

Parts of a Mushroom

FLY AMANITA
"Fly Agaric"
Amanita muscaria
AMANITA FAMILY
H 5"; W 5". Cap umbrella-shaped, bright red with white warts. Stalk white, cylindrical or tapered upward, has fragile skirt, bulbous base. Gills white. **CAUTION** Poisonous. **SEASON** July–Nov. **HABITAT** Under trees.

PANTHER AMANITA
Amanita pantherina
AMANITA FAMILY
H 5″; W 5″. Cap umbrella-shaped, tan to brown, with paler warts; edges finely lined. Stalk white, cylindrical or tapered upward, with skirt-like ring, bulbous base. Gills white, thin. **CAUTION** Deadly poisonous. **SEASON** Aug.–Oct. **HABITAT** Under conifers.

DEEP SPLASHCUP
Cyathus olla
BIRD'S-NEST FUNGUS FAMILY
H ½″; W ½″. A tiny, brown, wavy-edged, deep cup, with white flared lip; velvety outside. Spores contained in up to 10 white "eggs" held in cup, splashed out by rain. **SEASON** July–Oct. **HABITAT** Twigs, wood, organic debris in moist soil.

KING BOLETUS
Boletus edulis
BOLETUS FAMILY
H 10″; W 8″. Cap round, spongy, muffin-like, tawny brown, sticky when wet. Stalk stout, often pear-shaped, pale brown, partly covered with fine white netting. Cap underside white to green or yellow, with pores. **SEASON** July–Oct. **HABITAT** Under trees.

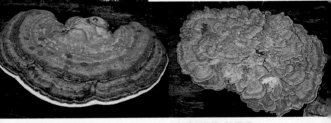

ARTIST'S FUNGUS
"Artist's Conk"
Ganoderma applanatum
BRACKET FAMILY
W 16″. Cap flat to convex, semicircular; shiny dark brown or gray, lighter and brighter at edge; wrinkled, hard, attached directly to wood. Underside white, bruises brown, with pores. **SEASON** Year-round. **HABITAT** Low on trunks of dead or dying trees.

SULPHUR SHELF
"Chicken Mushroom"
Laetiporus (Polyporus) sulphureus
BRACKET FAMILY
W 20″. Cap flat, fan-shaped; orange, with yellow lobed edge; wrinkled, attached directly to wood. Underside yellow, with pores. Forms large overlapping clusters. **SEASON** Late July–Oct. **HABITAT** Trunks of living or dead broadleaf trees.

GOLDEN CHANTERELLE
Cantharellus cibarius
CHANTERELLE FAMILY

H 5"; W 3". Entirely yellow-orange. Cap usu. trumpet-shaped, wavy-edged. Stalk tapers downward. Gills thick, ridge-like, forked; extend partway down stalk. **SEASON** Sept.–Nov. **HABITAT** Usu. under conifers.

CAULIFLOWER FUNGUS
Sparassis crispa (radicata)
CORAL FUNGUS FAMILY

H 10"; W 10". Large white to cream-white globe of curly, flat, noodle-like lobes; mildly spicy-fragrant, attached directly to wood. **SEASON** Sept.–Nov. **HABITAT** Conifer stumps or trunks near ground.

SHAGGY MANE
Coprinus comatus
INKY CAP FAMILY

H 8"; W 2½". Cap bell-shaped, white with brown tip, shaggy-scaly; edge turns black, dissolves upward. Stalk white, with ring; usu. hollow. Gills white to pink, then black and liquefying. **SEASON** May–June, Sept.–Oct. **HABITAT** Mostly urban, even through asphalt.

MEADOW MUSHROOM
Agaricus campestris
MEADOW MUSHROOM FAMILY

H 5"; W 4". Cap flat, white to brown, smooth to fibrous; edge often fringed. Stalk stout, silky white, with slight ring. Gills pink to brown. **SEASON** Aug.–Sept. **HABITAT** With grasses.

YELLOW MOREL
Morchella esculenta
MOREL FAMILY

H 3"; W 1½". Cap conical to egg-shaped, honeycombed with deep pits, yellow-brown to grayish, hollow. Stalk hollow, enlarged at base, whitish. Spores produced in pits on cap. **SEASON** Apr.–May. **HABITAT** Under hardwoods, esp. cottonwoods and in old apple orchards.

GIANT PUFFBALL
Calvatia gigantea
PUFFBALL FAMILY

H 14"; W 14". Large white to light brown ball, smooth to warty to cracking and flaking. Attached to ground by thick, root-like cord. Top breaks apart to release spores. **SEASON** May–mid-July, Sept.–Oct. **HABITAT** Pastures, other open areas.

GEMMED PUFFBALL
Lycoperdon perlatum (gemmatum)
PUFFBALL FAMILY

H 2"; W 1¾". Pear-shaped, white to light brown body with tiny conical spines that fall off, leaving slight bumps. Top becomes nipple-like, opens to release spores. **SEASON** July–Oct. **HABITAT** Various, from lawns to forests.

EMETIC RUSSULA
Russula emetica
RUSSULA FAMILY

H 6"; W 4". Cap umbrella-shaped to flat, with sunken center; brittle; skin deep red, shiny; flesh pure white. Stalk fragile, hollow, white. Gills deep, white, brittle. Mildly fragrant. **CAUTION** Poisonous. **SEASON** Aug.–Oct. **HABITAT** Under conifers.

HONEY MUSHROOM
Armillariella (Armillaria) mellea
TRICHOLOMA FAMILY

H 3"; W 3". Cap convex, cream to rusty, sticky; hairy-scaly, esp. in center. Stalk slender; white above thick cottony ring, brown below. Gills white; become dingy. Forms large clusters, with caps overlapping. **SEASON** Aug.–Nov. **HABITAT** Bases of trees or stumps.

WHITE MATSUTAKE
"Pine Mushroom"
Armillaria ponderosa (Tricholoma magnivelare)
TRICHOLOMA FAMILY

H 5"; W 6". Cap convex to flat; white to pale tan, becoming brown-scaly in center; firm. Stalk white above thick ring, scaly and dirty below; tapers downward. Gills broad; white to creamy, bruise pinkish brown. Strange fragrance. **SEASON** Sept.–Nov. **HABITAT** Usu. under pines in montane or coastal forests.

FAIRY RING MUSHROOM
Marasmius oreades
TRICHOLOMA FAMILY

H 3″; W 2″. Cap tan, umbrella-shaped, with central bump. Stalk slender, yellowish brown, finely velvety. Gills white. Grows in radiating rings or arcs. **SEASON** May–Oct., after rain. **HABITAT** Pastures, lawns.

OYSTER MUSHROOM
Pleurotus ostreatus
TRICHOLOMA FAMILY

H 4″; W 8″. Bracket. Cap fan-shaped, white to yellowish. Stalk absent or very short, attached to one side of cap. Gills whitish. In overlapping clusters. **SEASON** Apr.–Oct. **HABITAT** Logs, dead trees.

Algae

Algae are a diverse array of organisms ranging from microscopic unicellular forms to large seaweeds. Three groups of algae are included in this guide: red algae, yellow-brown algae, and green algae. (In this section, the species are presented in these large groupings rather than by family or order.) Red algae and yellow-brown algae occur almost exclusively in salt water. Green algae most often live in fresh water but are also found in salt water and on land. In fact, land plants evolved from certain kinds of green algae.

The selected algae in this guide are all sizable marine plants commonly known as seaweeds. All have stalks, leaf-like structures called *fronds* (sometimes with air bladders that keep them afloat), and a pad-, disk-, or root-like structure called a *holdfast* with which they attach to a substrate such as sand, rock, shell, a pier, or some other surface. Some species tend to become detached from the substrate and float freely. In the accounts that follow, sizes given are lengths of mature specimens, unless otherwise noted.

GREEN RIBBON ALGAE
"Green Thread Algae"
Enteromorpha species
GREEN ALGAE

24″. Clusters of bright green, translucent, ruffled, ribbon-like strips or flat tubes that taper toward base. Attached to pebbles and docks. **HABITAT** Muddy gravel in estuaries and tidepools; also in fresh or septic seeps in spray zone.

SEA LETTUCE
Ulva fenestrata
GREEN ALGAE
W 3'. Light green, shiny, thin, round to irreg. ruffled sheets. Attached to rocks or pilings, often detached and free-floating. **HABITAT** Oceanside rocks in low to mid-intertidal zone; pilings, mudflats.

PACIFIC LAVER
"Red Laver"
Porphyra perforata
RED ALGAE
W 3'. Olive green to purplish gray, rubbery sheets with ruffled, often perforated edges; deep purple when dry. Usu. attached to rocks. **HABITAT** Mid- to high intertidal zone.

WINGED KELP
Alaria marginata
YELLOW-BROWN ALGAE
13'. Brown to olive-green. Fronds narrow, with raised midrib and flat ruffled edges; in spring–summer each has 2 rows of several smooth, oblong, 5" fruiting blades at base. Attached to rocks. **HABITAT** Offshore kelp beds in lower intertidal zone.

PACIFIC ROCKWEED
Fucus distichus
YELLOW-BROWN ALGAE
12". Greenish brown. Fronds thick, flat, with raised midrib; repeatedly branched; inflated branch tips pop when stepped on. Attached to rocks. Abundant in spring and summer. **HABITAT** Exposed rocky shores in upper intertidal zone.

SUGAR WRACK
Laminaria species
YELLOW-BROWN ALGAE
5'. Rich yellow-brown. Fronds oblong smooth blades, each with 2 rows of blister-like swellings. Attached to wharves, rocks, shells by root-like holdfast. **HABITAT** Low intertidal zone, quiet waters.

GIANT KELP
Macrocystis pyrifera
YELLOW-BROWN ALGAE
40'. Brown. Fronds long tubular stalks with many crinkly, toothed, leaf-like blades, each attached to stalk by pear-shaped air bladder. Attached to various rocky substrates by large, conical, root-like holdfast. **HABITAT** Large offshore kelp beds.

BULL KELP
Nereocystis luetkeana
YELLOW-BROWN ALGAE
40'. Brown. Long, bullwhip-like
stalk, with bulbous, 4" air bladder
and many strap-like 7' blades trailing from top of bulb. Dies off in
winter, washes onto beaches. Attached to various rocky substrates by
root-like holdfast. **HABITAT** Large offshore kelp beds.

SEA PALM
Postelsia palmaeformis
YELLOW-BROWN ALGAE
H 12". Green to chocolate-brown.
Palm-tree-shaped, with ribbon-like
fronds flopping from cylindrical
stalk. Small clumps share fibrous,
knot-like holdfast attached to exposed rocks. **HABITAT** High intertidal
zone with strong wave action.

Lichens

A lichen is a remarkable dual organism made up of a fungus and a
colony of microscopic green algae or cyanobacteria ("blue-green
algae"). Such a relationship—dissimilar organisms living in intimate
association—is known as *symbiosis* and may be detrimental to one
of the participants (parasitism) or beneficial to both (mutualism). In
a lichen, the fungus surrounds the algae and absorbs water, minerals, and organic substances from the substrate (soil, rock, tree bark)
it is growing on; the algae supply carbohydrates produced by photosynthesis. It is not definitely known whether symbiosis in lichens
is mutually beneficial or mildly to wholly parasitic.

Lichens occur in a wide range of habitats, including some of the
harshest environments on earth, such as deserts and the Arctic
(where they serve as the primary food of reindeer and caribou), and
can also be found in forests, along roadsides, on buildings and other
man-made structures, and on mountaintops. They can withstand
extreme variations in temperature and other harsh conditions. During droughts they dry up but do not die; they rapidly absorb water
when it does become available, springing back to life. Lichens range
widely in color, occurring in white, black, gray, and various shades
of red, orange, brown, yellow, or green. Their color often varies dramatically with moisture content.

Most lichens grow very slowly, about ⅟₂₅ inch to ½ inch per year,
and can have extremely long lifetimes; specimens estimated to be at
least 4,000 years old have been found. Many lichens have special
structures for vegetative reproduction—tiny fragments that break
off easily or powdery spots that release powdery balls of algae
wrapped in microscopic fungal threads. In others, the fungal component produces spores carried on conspicuous fruiting bodies,
which may be cup-like, disk-like, or globular.

Lichens are an important food source and nesting material for many mammals and birds. Humans have used lichens as food, medicine, dye, and fiber, and as natural tools for monitoring the environment, as lichens are sensitive indicators of air quality and ecosystem continuity.

In the accounts that follow, sizes given are typical heights, lengths, or widths of mature specimens.

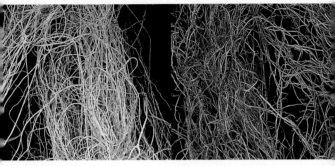

WITCH'S HAIR
Alectoria sarmentosa
L 12″. Conspicuous draping clumps of pale yellowish to greenish strands with tiny raised white markings. Fruiting bodies brown, disk-like, uncommon. **HABITAT** Trunks and branches of conifers, esp. in old-growth forests. **RANGE** Mainly west of Cascade crest.

HORSEHAIR LICHEN
Bryoria fremontii
L 15″. Dense clumps of hanging, branched, somewhat twisted brown strands, sometimes with yellow powdery spots. Fruiting bodies inconspicuous, rare. **HABITAT** Conifers, esp. pines and Douglas Firs. **RANGE** Mainly east of Cascade crest.

WESTERN BRITISH SOLDIERS
Cladonia bellidiflora
H 1″. Clusters of pale yellowish-green stalks with bare white patches and ruffled scales; usu. topped with globular, bright red fruiting bodies. **HABITAT** Mossy rocks, decaying wood, soil. **RANGE** Mainly west of Cascade crest.

OAKMOSS LICHEN
Evernia prunastri
W 2½″. Soft tufts of pale yellowish to greenish forking branches with white undersides. Often has scattered powdery patches, esp. on edges of branches. No fruiting bodies. **HABITAT** Twigs and branches mainly of broadleaf trees and shrubs. **RANGE** Mostly west of Cascades.

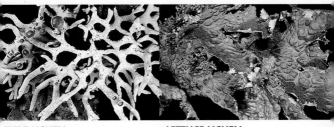

TUBE LICHEN
Hypogymnia imshaugii
W 2½". Tufts of antler-like, forked, hollow branches; pale gray to greenish or bluish gray (often brown near branch tips), with tiny black dots on upper surface; underside black, wrinkled. Fruiting bodies round, brown. **HABITAT** Branches, twigs, and trunks of trees, esp. conifers.

LETTUCE LICHEN
"Oregon Lungwort"
Lobaria oregana
W 8". Rosettes lettuce-like, yellowish to pale green lobes crisscrossed with network of ridges; edges frilly, with tiny, easily shed lobelets. **HABITAT** Usu. high in old-growth conifers; seen on ground as forest litter. **RANGE** West of Cascade crest.

VEINED LICHEN
Peltigera membranacea
W 8". Loose rosettes of large gray to brown lobes with down-turned edges; underside felt-like, with distinct, raised veins and long, slender, root-like strands. Fruiting bodies on extended lobe tips. **HABITAT** On soil, rocks, mosses, or rotting wood in humid forests. **RANGE** Throughout NW, esp. west of Cascades.

BULL'S-EYE LICHEN
Placopsis gelida
W 1½". Thick tan to gray or greenish crust with scalloped edges, round brown growths in center, and tan or green powdery spots. Fruiting bodies round, tan to pink. **HABITAT** Rocks in rainy areas, road cuts. **RANGE** Mainly west of Cascade crest.

OLD MAN'S BEARD
Usnea longissima
L 12". Yellowish strands with short perpendicular side branches; shape resembles tinsel garlands hung at Christmas. No fruiting bodies. Very sensitive to air pollution. Do not collect. **HABITAT** Tree branches, esp. overhanging or near creeks and rivers. **RANGE** West of Cascade crest.

Spore Plants

Spore plants are green land plants such as liverworts, mosses, club-mosses, horsetails, and ferns (ferns are introduced separately on page 91) that reproduce from spores rather than seeds. Among the earliest evolved land plants still present on earth, these plants do not produce flowers or fruits. The most conspicuous part of their reproduction is the *spore,* a reproductive cell that divides and eventually develops the structures producing the sperm and egg, which fuse to form a new adult plant.

Liverworts and mosses are mat-forming plants typically found in shady, damp to wet habitats; they typically absorb water and nutrients directly from the environment, as they lack a sophisticated vascular system for conducting water and nutrients internally. When "fruiting," their spores are released from a lidded capsule often elevated on a *fertile stalk.* Some liverworts consist of flat green lobes, while other liverworts are feathery-looking and thus easily mistaken for mosses.

Like ferns and trees, clubmosses and horsetails have well-developed vascular systems. Clubmosses often look like upright green pipe cleaners or tiny conifers rising from the ground in shady woodlands. When fruiting, their spores are produced in tiny but visible sacs, called *sporangia,* between the leaves. In some species the leaves and sporangia are densely clustered into a long, narrow, cone-like structure. Horsetails have conspicuously jointed stems with whorls of tiny, scale-like leaves and branches at most joints. Sporangia are produced along the edges of umbrella-like structures clustered into a cone-like configuration atop a brownish, whitish, or green stem.

In the accounts that follow, the size given is the typical height of a mature specimen unless otherwise noted; sizes are not given for very low, mat-forming species.

LUNG LIVERWORT
Marchantia polymorpha
LIVERWORT CLASS
Bright green, flat, leathery, ½" lobes with close rows of pale, bubble-like bumps, often with tiny cups. Fertile stalks each topped with flat disk (male) or star-shaped organ. **HABITAT** Streamsides; wet, disturbed, or burned ground.

OREGON BEAKED MOSS
Eurhynchium (Kindbergia, Stokesiella) oreganum
MOSS CLASS
Gold-green, feathery mats of branched strands that lie flat. Fertile stalks along branches bear spore cases, each with curved "beak." Most abundant moss on old-growth forest floors along coast and in w foothills. **HABITAT** Logs, tree bases, soil of moist lowland forests.

FERN MOSS
"Step Moss"
Hylocomium splendens
MOSS CLASS

Gold- to brownish-green mats. Each year's growth is tapering, fern-frond-like, 2"; grows stepwise from mid-point of previous year's "frond." Fertile stalks red, each topped by horizontal spore case. **HABITAT** Soil and logs in low to montane forests. **RANGE** West of Cascades.

ICICLE MOSS
"Mousetail Moss" "Cattail Moss"
Isothecium myosuroides (stoloniferum)
MOSS CLASS

Shiny, pale green, stringy masses (may hang down 10"). Fertile stalks dark red, each topped by up-tilted spore case. **HABITAT** Tree limbs (esp. maples) in deep moist forests; boulders, cliffs. **RANGE** West of Cascades, ne WA.

WAVY-LEAVED COTTON MOSS
Plagiothecium undulatum
MOSS CLASS

Shiny, whitish-green mats of thin, flat, few-branched shoots with wavy leaves. Fertile stalks each topped by slender, up-tilted spore case. **HABITAT** Logs, rocks, or soil in forests. **RANGE** West of Cascades, Blue Mtns.

HAIRCAP MOSS
"Narrow-leaved Moss"
Polytrichum juniperinum
MOSS CLASS

Green carpet of bottlebrush-like, erect, wiry stems with narrow, hair-pointed leaves. Fertile stalks reddish, each topped by golden-brown, cylindrical capsule. **HABITAT** Forests or open areas; esp. on disturbed or burned ground.

BIG SHAGGY MOSS
"Pacific Forest Moss"
Rhytidiadelphus loreus
MOSS CLASS

Light green mats of narrow, sprawling, irreg. branches; leaves tiny; stems red-brown. Fertile stalks rarely seen, each topped by short, thick, horizontal spore case. **HABITAT** Low to mid-elev. forest floors. **RANGE** West of Cascades.

RUNNING CLUBMOSS
"Staghorn Clubmoss"
Lycopodium clavatum
CLUBMOSS FAMILY

4″. Erect, branched stems from sporadically rooting runners with tiny, crowded, needle-like leaves. Fertile stalks topped by 2–4 slender, erect, straw-colored, 1″ spore cones. HABITAT Forest openings, swamp edges, roadsides. RANGE West of Cascades.

COMMON HORSETAIL
"Field Horsetail"
Equisetum arvense
HORSETAIL FAMILY

H 24″. Dense clusters of green, jointed, hollow stalks with many whorls of narrow jointed branches. Fertile stalks pale brown, unbranched, each topped by 1″ spore cone. HABITAT Woods, fields, swamp edges, cities.

SCOURING RUSH
Equisetum hyemale
HORSETAIL FAMILY

4′. Clusters of green, jointed, hollow, usu. unbranched stalks, each topped by sharp ¾″ spore cone; evergreen. HABITAT Streamsides, ditches, seeps, old wet pastures.

GIANT HORSETAIL
Equisetum telmateia
HORSETAIL FAMILY

8′. Dense clusters of green, jointed, hollow stalks with many whorls of narrow jointed branches. Fertile stalks pale brown, unbranched, each topped by 2″ spore cone. HABITAT Ditches, marshes, seeps, streamsides. RANGE West of Cascades.

Ferns

Ferns, the largest group of seedless vascular plants still found on earth, are diverse in habitat and form. In the Pacific Northwest they occur mainly in shady forests and near fresh water, but several fern species thrive in open sunny areas. Most ferns grow in soil, often in clumps or clusters; some grow on rocks or trees, and a few float on water.

Ferns have a stem called a *rhizome* that is typically thin and long and grows along the surface or below the ground. The rhizome bears the roots and leaves, and lives for many years. Fern leaves, called *fronds,* are commonly compound and may be *pinnate* (divided into *leaflets*), *bipinnate* (subdivided into *subleaflets*), or *tripinnate* (divided again into *segments*); they are often lacy or feathery in appearance.

Frond Types

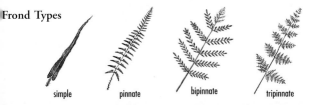

| simple | pinnate | bipinnate | tripinnate |

Ferns reproduce through the release of spores from tiny sacs called *sporangia,* which commonly occur in clusters *(sori)* on the underside of the frond. The sori may cover the entire frond underside, may form dots or lines, may occur only beneath the frond's curled-under edges, or may be covered by specialized outgrowths of the frond. Fronds that bear sporangia are called fertile fronds; those that do not are called sterile fronds. In some species the sterile and fertile fronds differ in size and shape.

Some ferns are evergreen, but the foliage of most Pacific Northwest ferns dies back each year with the autumn frosts. Each spring the rhizome gives rise to coiled tender young fronds called *fiddleheads.* Fiddleheads of some ferns are popular delicacies, but identification is difficult: the shoots of some deadly poisonous flowering plants (including various poison hemlocks) can be mistaken for fern fiddleheads, and many fiddleheads are edible at certain stages and poisonous at others. Only local experts should collect fiddleheads for consumption.

In the accounts that follow, sizes given are typical mature heights. For illustrations of leaf shapes, see page 128.

Parts of a Fern

segment
sori
leaflet
subleaflet
stalk
fiddlehead
rhizome

BRACKEN
Pteridium aquilinum
BRACKEN FAMILY

5'. Stalks robust, longer than fronds. Fronds divided into 3 broadly triangular, stalked, bi- or tripinnate leaflets, each with many pinnate subleaflets. Sori dot curled-under leaflet edges. **HABITAT** Open areas, forest clearings.

DEER FERN
Blechnum spicant
CHAIN FERN FAMILY

24". Stalks dark brown, in big clumps. Fronds pinnate, slender, tapered at both ends. Fertile fronds have widely-spaced, narrow, nearly tubular leaflets. Sterile fronds shorter, shiny, with broad-based leaflets; evergreen. **HABITAT** Deep moist forests. **RANGE** West of Cascades.

WESTERN MAIDENHAIR FERN
Adiantum aleuticum (pedatum)
MAIDENHAIR FERN FAMILY

H 18". Stalks black to dark red, shiny, wiry. Fronds bipinnate, fan-shaped; leaflets lobed along one side. Sori under rolled lobe tips. **HABITAT** Seeps, streamsides, wet cliffs. **RANGE** West of Cascades, n edge of WA.

LICORICE FERN
Polypodium glycyrrhiza
POLYPODY FERN FAMILY

12". Stalks greenish, straw-colored. Fronds evergreen, pinnate, with shiny, fine-toothed, broad-based leaflets. Sori in 2 rows. **HABITAT** Mostly on broadleaf trees and rocks in lowlands. **RANGE** West of Cascades; Columbia R. Gorge.

LADY FERN
Athyrium filix-femina
WOOD FERN FAMILY

4'. Stalks blackish, scaly. Fronds arch outward, bi- or tripinnate, tapered at both ends, with lobed, fine-toothed leaflets. Sori kidney-shaped. **HABITAT** Wet ground.

FRAGILE FERN
"Brittle Bladder Fern"
Cystopteris fragilis
WOOD FERN FAMILY

2". Stalks smooth, delicate, straw-colored. Fronds usu. bipinnate, tapered at both ends, with fine-toothed leaflets. Sori partly covered by translucent pouch that soon withers. **HABITAT** Rocky areas.

SPINY WOOD FERN
"Shield Fern"
Dryopteris expansa (austriaca)
WOOD FERN FAMILY

3'. Stalks brown-scaly. Fronds tri-pinnate, triangular, with spiny-toothed leaflets. Sori horseshoe-shaped. **HABITAT** Moist forests. **RANGE** West of Cascades; Columbia R. Gorge.

WESTERN SWORD FERN
Polystichum munitum
WOOD FERN FAMILY

4'. Stalks light brown, scaly, robust. Fronds pinnate, tapered at both ends, coarsely cut into finely toothed leaflets, evergreen. Sori covered by round shields, in 2 rows. **HABITAT** Low to mid-elev. forests.

ROCKY MOUNTAIN WOODSIA
Woodsia scopulina
WOOD FERN FAMILY

8". Stalks reddish brown. Fronds bipinnate, tapered at both ends; leaflets white-hairy underneath. Sori surrounded by star-shaped mem-branes. **HABITAT** Rocky slopes. **RANGE** Mainly mtns. east of Cascade crest.

Trees and Shrubs

Trees and shrubs are woody perennial plants. Trees typically have a single trunk and a well-developed crown of foliage, and grow to at least 16 feet tall; some attain heights of more than 300 feet. Shrubs are usually less than 20 feet tall and often have several woody stems rather than a single trunk. This book covers two major categories of trees and shrubs. Conifers begin on page 95. Broadleaf trees and shrubs begin on page 102.

Individual tree sizes vary according to age and environmental factors. The heights given in the following sections are for average mature individual trees on favorable sites in the Pacific Northwest; younger trees and those exposed to harsh conditions are smaller; older specimens may attain greater heights in optimal conditions. Trunk diameter, which also varies greatly within a species, is cited only for very large species.

Identifying a Tree

Trees can be identified by three key visual characteristics: crown shape, bark color and texture, and leaf shape and arrangement (illustrated on page 128). Below are common crown shapes for mature conifers and broadleaf trees. These shapes are idealized and simplified for illustrative purposes.

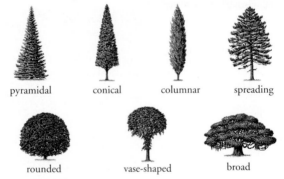

| pyramidal | conical | columnar | spreading |

| rounded | vase-shaped | broad |

The roots, trunk, and branches of most trees and shrubs are covered in bark, a protective layer consisting mainly of dead cells. The bark of young trees often differs in color and texture from mature bark. As a tree grows, the bark splits, cracks, and peels. In some trees, such as birches, the bark peels horizontally. In cedars the bark shreds in vertical strips. In many trees the bark may develop furrows, ridges, or fissures, may break up into plates, or may flake off. The species accounts describe mature bark unless otherwise noted.

Beneath the bark is the wood, most of which is dense, dark, dead tissue (heartwood) that provides structural support for the plant. Between the heartwood and the bark are many pale, thin layers of living tissue (including sapwood) that transport water and minerals, and produce new wood and bark. Concentric rings, each representing a period (often a year) of growth, are visible in cut trunks and branches.

Conifers

Gymnosperms ("naked seeds") are trees and shrubs that produce exposed seeds, usually in cones, rather than seeds enclosed in an ovary, as in the angiosperms (flowering plants). Conifers, ginkgos, and cycads are all gymnosperms. The Pacific Northwest's native gymnosperms are all conifers.

Conifers (also known as "softwoods") have leaves that are needle-like (long and slender) or scale-like (small and overlapping), typically evergreen, and well adapted for drought and freezing temperatures, thanks to a thick waxy coating and other protective features.

The distinctive cone is a reproductive structure comprised of a central axis with spirally arranged scales bearing pollen or seeds. A single tree usually has both pollen-bearing (male) and seed-bearing (female) cones; males are usually carried on lower branches, or lower down on the same branches as females. Male cones appear in spring, shed pollen, and soon fall from the tree. Female cones are larger, more woody, and have scales that protect the seeds until the cones expand to release them. Cones described in this guide are female.

Most conifer species in the Northwest belong to the pine family (Pinaceae). In our area, those commonly known as pines (genus *Pinus*) bear long needles in bundles of two to five. Other pine family members have much shorter needles. Larches (genus *Larix*) bear needles in brush-like clusters that are deciduous (shed seasonally) and that turn yellow in autumn; cones are stalked and round to egg-shaped. Hemlocks (genus *Tsuga*) bear needles on woody cushions and have small cones at the branch tips. Spruces (genus *Picea*) have rough twigs, hanging cones, and sharp, four-sided needles borne on tiny, raised, woody pegs. Douglas firs (genus *Pseudotsuga*) also have hanging cones and flat needles, but the needles grow directly from the branches. True firs (genus *Abies*) have upright cones that shed their scales and seeds while still on the tree, and needles arising from tiny depressions on the branches.

Other conifers in the Northwest include those of the cypress family (such as cedars and junipers) and the yew family. Most members of the cypress family (Cupressaceae) have narrow, scale-like leaves covering their branches; their small cones are round and bell-shaped or (in the junipers) fleshy and berry-like. Yews (family Taxaceae) have needles in two opposite rows and bear seeds not in cones but individually and surrounded by a fleshy, cup-shaped, berry-like structure called an aril.

In our area, conifers are usually part of a continuous forest canopy in which the shapes of individual trees cannot be discerned. Most conifers are pyramidal in shape when young, especially if they grow in an open area; they mature to a ragged columnar shape with a conical (commonly broken) top and a limbless lower half. The following species accounts give overall shape only if it differs from this description. Leaf shapes, including the needles and scale-like leaves of conifers, are shown on page 128. Unless otherwise noted in the individual species account, needle or scale color is green, fading to yellowish or brown when shedding, and cone color is brown.

INCENSE CEDAR
Calocedrus (Libocedrus) decurrens
CYPRESS FAMILY
H 140'; D 5'. Crown dense. Scales tiny, in whorls of 4; cover flat twigs. Cones 1", oblong, with 6 scales; hang down. Bark reddish brown, deeply furrowed. **HABITAT** Dry forests, lower mtn. slopes. **RANGE** OR Cascades, Siskiyous, their foothills.

PORT ORFORD CEDAR
Chamaecyparis lawsoniana
CYPRESS FAMILY
H 200'; D 6'. Scales tiny, with whitish X below, in opposite pairs; cover flat twigs. Cones ½", round, knobby, in clusters. Bark deeply furrowed, silvery reddish where stripped. **HABITAT** Lowland to mid-elev. conifer forests. **RANGE** sw OR.

ALASKA CEDAR
"Yellow Cedar"
Chamaecyparis nootkatensis
CYPRESS FAMILY
H 130'; D 5'; shrubby above tree line. Scales tiny; point outward in opposite pairs. Cones ½", round, knobby. Bark silvery gray, flaking in smooth strips. Wood fragrant. **HABITAT** Avalanche tracks, mixed forests at high elevs.

COMMON JUNIPER
Juniperus communis
CYPRESS FAMILY
3'. Usu. sprawling, mat-forming shrub. Needles ½", whitish above, sharp, crowded. Cones tiny, berry-like, green to blue-black, resinous. Bark reddish, shreddy. **HABITAT** Dry rocky areas from sea level to alpine elevs.

WESTERN JUNIPER
Juniperus occidentalis
CYPRESS FAMILY

30′. Dense pyramidal tree or low shrub. Scales tiny, gray-green, in whorls of 3. Cones tiny, berry-like, blue-black, resinous. Bark reddish brown, shreddy. **HABITAT** Forms open forests in steppe regions. **RANGE** e OR, se WA.

REDWOOD
Sequoia sempervirens
CYPRESS FAMILY

H 325′; D 12′. Trunk base flared, buttressed. Needles ¾″, whitish below, flat, in 2 rows. Cones 1″, elliptical, reddish; hang down. Bark red-brown, furrowed, thick. **HABITAT** Slopes just above river bottoms. **RANGE** Extreme sw OR.

WESTERN RED CEDAR
Thuja plicata
CYPRESS FAMILY

H 210′; D 10′. Trunk base flared, buttressed; branches droop. Scales tiny, in opposite pairs; cover flat twigs. Cones ½″, elliptical, in upright clusters. Bark gray to reddish, fibrous. **HABITAT** Lowland to mid-elev. moist to wet forests.

PACIFIC SILVER FIR
Abies amabilis
PINE FAMILY

H 180′; D 4′. Needles 1¼″, flat or up-curved; shiny above, whitish below; upswept or in 3 rows. Cones 5″, cylindrical, purple, upright. Bark light gray, smooth, blistered. **HABITAT** Conifer forests, mostly at mid-elevs. **RANGE** Coastal ranges to just east of Cascade crest.

male cones

GRAND FIR
Abies grandis
PINE FAMILY

H 200′; D 4′. Needles 1½″, white-striped below, flat, in 2 rows. Female cones 3″, cylindrical, greenish, upright. Bark gray-brown, smooth to furrowed, blistered. **HABITAT** Moderately dry lowland to mid-elev. forests.

SUBALPINE FIR
Abies lasiocarpa
PINE FAMILY

115′. Spire-shaped; low shrub above tree line. Needles 1½″, white-striped, flat, usu. up-curved. Cones 4″, cylindrical, purplish, upright. Bark gray, smooth to fissured. **HABITAT** Subalpine slopes, highest forests. **RANGE** c to e Cascades and Olympics, e WA and OR.

NOBLE FIR
Abies procera
PINE FAMILY

H 220'; D 5'. Crown rounded. Needles 1¼", blue-green, white-striped, flat, usu. up-curved. Cones 7", cylindrical, upright; scales have pointed papery bracts. Bark gray to red-brown, smooth to furrowed. Largest true fir. **HABITAT** Mid-elev. mtn. forests. **RANGE** South of Glacier Peak, WA, mainly on west slope of Cascades.

WESTERN LARCH
Larix occidentalis
PINE FAMILY

H 170'; D 4'6". Needles 1½", yellow-green, soft; in bundles of 15–30, or single near branch tips; deciduous, turn yellow. Cones 1½", elliptical, upright; scales have long-pointed bracts. Bark red-brown, scaly, furrowed. Largest larch. **HABITAT** Mid-elev. mtns. **RANGE** East of Cascade crest.

ENGELMANN SPRUCE
Picea engelmannii
PINE FAMILY

H 160'; D 3'. Tree with drooping branches; dense low shrub above tree line. Needles 1¼", blue-green, white-striped, sharp, stiff, 4-sided. Cones 2½", cylindrical, with papery thin scales; hang down. Bark grayish, thin, scaly. **HABITAT** High-elev. conifer forests. **RANGE** Mainly east of Cascade crest.

SITKA SPRUCE
Picea sitchensis
PINE FAMILY

H 225'; D 7'6". Needles 1", stiff, flat, sharp. Cones 3½", cylindrical, with papery thin scales; hang down. Bark gray, thin, scaly. **HABITAT** Lowland forests. **RANGE** Coast and up river bottoms to WA Cascades.

WHITEBARK PINE
Pinus albicaulis
PINE FAMILY

65'. Tree with spreading irreg. crown and multiple trunks; dense shrub above tree line. Needles 2½", yellow-green; in bundles of 5, concentrated near branch tips. Cones 3", egg-shaped, purplish; disintegrate at maturity. Bark whitish gray, smooth to scaly. **HABITAT** High-elev. open forests. **RANGE** ne Olympics, east of Cascade crest.

male cones

LODGEPOLE PINE
Pinus contorta
PINE FAMILY

115'. Tall with dense, conical crown inland; small, contorted, known as Shore Pine at coast. Needles 2", yellow-green, flat, in bundles of 2. Female cones 2", egg-shaped, asymmetrical at base. Bark red-brown to gray, thin, scaly. **HABITAT** Coastal forests, dunes, mid- to high-elev. dry forests; often dominant after fires.

SUGAR PINE
Pinus lambertiana
PINE FAMILY

H 180′; D 4″. Needles 4″, blue-green, white-striped, stiff, in bundles of 5. Cones 18″, cylindrical; hang down. Bark red-brown, deeply furrowed, scaly. Longest conifer cones. **HABITAT** Dry forests on lower mtn. slopes. **RANGE** sw OR.

WESTERN WHITE PINE
Pinus monticola
PINE FAMILY

H 200′; D 3′6″. Needles 4″, blunt, blue-green with white-striped inner surfaces, in bundles of 5. Cones 9″, cylindrical, usu. curved, reddish to silvery; hang down. Bark gray, square-plated. **HABITAT** Mid-elev. forests to tree line in s OR; Puget lowlands.

PONDEROSA PINE
"Yellow Pine"
Pinus ponderosa
PINE FAMILY

H 170′; D 4′. Needles 8″, yellow-green; in bundles of 3, concentrated near branch tips. Cones 5″, egg-shaped, reddish. Bark yellow-brown, thick, scaly. **HABITAT** Lowland to mtn. forests. **RANGE** East of Cascades; local in Willamette Valley, Puget lowlands.

DOUGLAS FIR
Pseudotsuga menziesii
PINE FAMILY

H 150′; D 4′. Needles 1¼″, flat. Cones 3½″, egg-shaped; scales have protruding, paper-thin, 3-pointed bracts. Bark reddish brown, deeply furrowed. Region's most ubiquitous and commercially valuable tree. **HABITAT** Lowland to mid-elev. forests.

WESTERN HEMLOCK
Tsuga heterophylla
PINE FAMILY

H 210'; D 4'. Treetop and branch-tips droop. Needles ½", white-striped below, flat with rounded tip. Cones 1", elliptical; hang down. Bark reddish, scaly, finely furrowed. **HABITAT** Lowland to mid-elev. wet forests.

MOUNTAIN HEMLOCK
Tsuga mertensiana
PINE FAMILY

H 115'; D 3'. Asymmetrically branched tree; low shrub above tree line. Needles ¾", blue-green, white-striped, blunt. Cones 2", cylindrical, purplish; hang down. Bark gray to brown, deeply furrowed. **HABITAT** Subalpine parklands and forests.

PACIFIC YEW
Taxus brevifolia
YEW FAMILY

35'. Shrub or tree with broad crown. Needles ¾", soft, flat, in 2 rows. Fruit (aril) tiny, red, cup-shaped, berry-like, juicy. Bark brown, purple, and red; smooth, flaky. **CAUTION** Fruit deadly poisonous. **HABITAT** Lowland to mid-elev. wet forests.

Broadleaf Trees and Shrubs

Trees belonging to the angiosperm (flowering plant) group are called broadleaf trees because their leaves are generally broad and flat, in contrast to the needle-like leaves of most conifers. Whereas the seeds of conifers and other gymnosperms are exposed, those of angiosperms are enclosed in an ovary that ripens into a fruit. The fruit may take the form of an edible drupe or berry, such as a cherry or mulberry, a hard-cased nut, the paired winged key of a maple, or a dried-out seedpod, such as that of a locust tree.

In warmer regions of North America, many broadleaf species (known in the timber industry as "hardwoods") maintain active green leaves year-round, but in the Pacific Northwest most flowering trees and shrubs are deciduous, shedding their leaves for the winter because the leaves cannot survive freezing weather.

The individual species descriptions in this guide note leaf color only if it is not green. The term "turn" indicates the fall color of the leaves. The various types of leaf arrangements and shapes mentioned in the species descriptions are illustrated on page 128. As most broadleaf trees bear their leaves in an alternate arrangement, only exceptions are noted in the species descriptions. Leaf measurements indicate length unless otherwise stated. Leaflet measurements are given for compound leaves.

Illustrations of flower types and parts, and a discussion of flower structure and function, are given on pages 129–131. Because the flowers of many trees are inconspicuous, only prominent ones are emphasized in the species accounts. In the Pacific Northwest, trees generally flower in the spring, from March through May (later at higher elevations); fruits of broadleaf trees mature mainly from July to October. Months of maturation are given only for edible fruit.

To facilitate identification, descriptions of large broadleaf trees (which begin on page 104) are grouped separately from small broadleaf trees and shrubs (which begin on page 107).

Fall Foliage

The Pacific Northwest has a remarkable preponderance of evergreen conifers, and its most abundant broadleaf trees—the Bigleaf Maple, alders, and oaks—are, at best, unexciting in fall. On the coast, only some understory trees—Vine and Douglas Maples, and dogwoods—stand out from the greenery, with leaves that turn scarlet, russet, and magenta. The mountains, however, offer unsurpassed fall panoramas. Subalpine parklands become exquisite heathery patchworks in September, when the leaves of the low Cascades Blueberry burst into fiery red, contrasting with the gold Sitka Mountain Ash, and the deep green foliage of Pink Mountain Heather. East of the Cascades, slopes are cloaked in the luminous yellows of larch, cottonwood, and aspen. The leaves of aspens—sometimes ranging to orange or red—stand out against the distinctive white trunks.

Each blaze of color represents a change in leaf chemistry. In late summer, leaves begin forming layers of cells at the leafstalk base that help the leaf detach and heal the resulting scar on the branch. As these layers grow, the veins of the leaves become clogged. The dominant pigment of the green leaf, chlorophyll, is no longer renewed and disintegrates quickly, revealing the yellow and orange pigments that had been masked by the chlorophyll. Under the right conditions, some species convert colorless compounds in their leaves into new red, scarlet, and purple pigments. Because these red pigments require high light intensity and elevated sugar content for their formation, the colors appear after a period of bright autumn days and cool nights, which prevent accumulated sugar from leaving the dying leaf. The best autumn leaf colors accompany relatively dry and warm autumn weather. Incessant rains may brown the leaves, while heavy winds and early frosts may cause premature leaf drop.

GOLDEN CHINQUAPIN
"Giant Chinquapin"
Chrysolepis (Castanopsis)
chrysophylla
BEECH FAMILY

40′ (100′ in sw OR valleys). Tree with broad rounded crown, or tall shrub. Leaves 5″, lanceolate; shiny above, scaly and golden below; evergreen. Bark gray to reddish brown, furrowed. Fruit 1″ spiny brown bur; contains edible nut, ripe in fall. **HABITAT** Lowland to mid-elev. moist forests. **RANGE** w OR, sw WA (local).

OREGON WHITE OAK
Quercus garryana
BEECH FAMILY

80′. Crown broad, rounded; sometimes shrubby. Leaves 6″, elliptical; deeply, bluntly 5- to 7-lobed; turn brown, stay on tree. Bark pale gray, furrowed. Acorns 1¼″, elliptical; cap shallow. **HABITAT** Dry lowland forests. **RANGE** Mostly west of Cascade crest.

RED ALDER
Alnus rubra
BIRCH FAMILY

110′. Crown pointed or rounded. Leaves 6″, ovate, coarse-toothed, pale gray below. Bark smooth, mottled white and gray with lichens. Male flowers in 5″ yellowish catkins, females in ½″ reddish cones; bloom Mar.–Apr. **HABITAT** Lowland wet forests, streamsides, disturbed areas. **RANGE** Mainly west of Cascades.

WHITE ALDER
Alnus rhombifolia
BIRCH FAMILY

70′. Crown open, rounded; trunk tall. Leaves 3″, ovate, fine-toothed; yellow-green above, pale gray below. Bark reddish brown, fissured. Male flowers in 3″ yellowish catkins, females in ½″ reddish cones; bloom Jan.–Feb. **HABITAT** Riparian forests, foothills. **RANGE** Mainly east of Cascades; sw OR.

PACIFIC DOGWOOD
Cornus nuttallii
DOGWOOD FAMILY

40′. Crown rounded. Leaves 5″, opposite, elliptical, wavy-edged, with curved veins; turn russet to magenta. Bark reddish brown, smooth to scaly. Flowers 5″, each made up of 4–7 white, petal-like bracts around dense greenish flower cluster; bloom Apr.–June, sometimes again in Sept. Berries ½″, bright red, elliptical, in 1½″ clusters. **HABITAT** Lowland wet forests. **RANGE** West of Cascades.

PACIFIC MADRONE
Arbutus menziesii
HEATH FAMILY

80′. Crown irreg. or rounded. Leaves 6″, oblong, thick, evergreen (dead leaves red). Bark green to reddish brown, smooth, peeling. Flowers tiny, white, in branched 4″ clusters; bloom Apr.–May. Berries ½″, orange-red, warty, in clusters. **HABITAT** Rocky coasts, hot rocky slopes. **RANGE** West of Cascade crest.

BIGLEAF MAPLE
Acer macrophyllum
MAPLE FAMILY

70'. Crown spreading. Leaves 8", opposite, long-stalked, deeply palmately 5-lobed; turn yellow. Bark brown, furrowed; often heavily draped with mosses, ferns, lichens. Fruit 1½" narrowly V-shaped keys. **HABITAT** Mainly lowland wet forests; moist areas, dry hillsides in some areas. **RANGE** West of Cascades.

OREGON ASH
Fraxinus latifolia
OLIVE FAMILY

80'. Leaves 10", opposite, pinnately compound, with 5–7 elliptical 5' leaflets; hairy-pale below; turn yellow or brown. Bark gray, furrowed in forking ridges. Fruit light brown, 1-winged, 2" keys, in clusters. **HABITAT** Lowland wet forests, moist areas. **RANGE** West of Cascades.

BITTER CHERRY
Prunus emarginata
ROSE FAMILY

50'. Tree with rounded crown, or thicket-forming shrub. Leaves 3½", elliptical, fine-toothed, with 1–2 knobby glands at base. Bark bronze to silvery with horizontal markings; shrub form has purplish stems. Flowers ½", white 5-petaled, in branched clusters; bloom Apr.–June. Cherries ½", red to blackish. **HABITAT** Wet and riparian forests, lowlands.

BLACK COTTONWOOD
Populus balsamifera (trichocarpa)
WILLOW FAMILY

H 90'; D 24". Crown open to vase-shaped. Leaves 6", ovate; shiny above, dull gray below; turn yellow. Bark gray, deeply furrowed. Flowers in 3" reddish-purple catkins; bloom Apr.–May. Fruit tiny brown capsules; contain cottony seeds. **HABITAT** Streamsides and wet forests to mid-elevs.

QUAKING ASPEN
Populus tremuloides
WILLOW FAMILY

50'. Crown narrow, rounded. Leaves 2½", heart-shaped to rounded, fine-toothed; turn yellow. Bark greenish white, smooth. Flowers in 2" brownish catkins; bloom May. Fruit tiny green capsules in 4" catkins. **HABITAT** Lowland to mid-elev. streamsides, wet meadows and slopes, avalanche tracks. **RANGE** Mostly east of Cascades.

PACIFIC WILLOW
Salix lucida (lasiandra)
WILLOW FAMILY

30'. Tree with open irreg. crown, or thicket-forming shrub. Leaves 5", lanceolate, fine-toothed. Bark gray or brown, furrowed. Flowers in yellow catkins; males 3", females 5"; bloom Apr.–May. **HABITAT** Low-elev. streamsides.

Small Broadleaf Trees and Shrubs

To facilitate identification, we have separated most small broadleaf trees and shrubs from the large broadleaf trees. The species in this section generally reach an average mature height of 40 feet or less.

Trees typically have a single woody trunk and a well-developed crown of foliage, whereas shrubs usually have several woody stems growing in a clump. Many of the Pacific Northwest's small trees and shrubs have beautiful and conspicuous spring flowers and/or colorful late-summer or autumn fruits. Flower and leaf arrangements and shapes are illustrated on pages 128–129. The majority of species covered here are deciduous; evergreens are noted as such.

BIG SAGEBRUSH
Artemisia tridentata
ASTER FAMILY

6'. Rounded gnarled shrub. Leaves 1½", narrowly oblanceolate, with 3-lobed tip; fuzzy, gray-green, spicy-aromatic. Stems brown, shreddy. Flowers tiny, drab yellow, in loose spikes; bloom Sept.–Oct. **HABITAT** Steppes to high-elev. dry meadows.

GRAY RABBITBRUSH
Chrysothamnus nauseosus
ASTER FAMILY

6'. Dense, broom-like shrub. Leaves 3", linear, soft, gray-hairy. Stems shreddy; twigs hairy. Flowers tiny, yellow, in rounded clusters; bloom Aug.–Oct. **HABITAT** Steppes.

TALL OREGON GRAPE
Berberis (Mahonia) aquifolium
BARBERRY FAMILY

7'. Usu. erect shrub. Leaves 8", pinnately compound, with 5–9 elliptical, spiny-edged, 3" leaflets; dark, glossy, evergreen. Bark light brown, heavily ridged. Flowers ½", yellow, with petal-like parts in concentric whorls; in 3" clusters; bloom Mar.–May. Berries ½", blue, clustered; edible (tart), ripe Aug.–Sept. OR state flower. **HABITAT** Semi-open lowland forests.

CASCADE OREGON GRAPE
Berberis (Mahonia) nervosa
BARBERRY FAMILY

30". Shrub. Leaves 10", pinnately compound, with 9–19 lanceolate, spiny-edged, 2" leaflets; evergreen. Flowers ½", yellow, with petal-like parts in concentric whorls; in 8" clusters; bloom Mar.–June. Berries ½", blue; edible, ripe in fall. **HABITAT** Lowland wet forests. **RANGE** West of Cascades.

SITKA ALDER
Alnus viridis (crispa)
BIRCH FAMILY

13′. Small tree or thicket-forming shrub. Leaves 4″, ovate, doubly toothed, wavy-edged. Bark gray-green, warty. Male flowers 4″ yellowish catkins, females ¾″ reddish cones; bloom May–July. **HABITAT** Mid-elev. to subalpine streamsides and valleys.

WATER BIRCH
Betula occidentalis
BIRCH FAMILY

30′. Tall shrub, or tree with rounded crown. Leaves 2″, ovate, doubly toothed; shiny above, pale and dotted below; turn yellow-brown. Bark shiny red-brown, smooth with horizontal slits. Flowers in 1½″ catkins; males drooping and yellowish, females upright and greenish; bloom Feb.–June. **HABITAT** Lowland to mid-elev. streamsides. **RANGE** East of Cascades.

BEAKED HAZEL
Corylus cornuta
BIRCH FAMILY

15′. Multi-stemmed shrub. Leaves 4″, ovate, doubly toothed, usu. asymmetrical at base. Bark tawny brown, smooth, with horizontal slits. Flowers 2¾″ yellowish catkins; bloom Jan.–Mar. Fruit paired, bristly, green, ½″ husks each contain tiny, edible nut in heavy shell. **HABITAT** Lowland to mid-elev. wet forests (esp. regrowth) with some sun.

REDSTEM CEANOTHUS
"Buckbrush"
Ceanothus sanguineus
BUCKTHORN FAMILY

8′. Erect shrub. Leaves 3″, ovate, toothed. Stems usu. purplish. Flowers tiny, white, with musky fragrance, in dense, oblong, 3″ clusters on leafless branchlets; bloom May–July. **HABITAT** Open forests, burned areas, clearings at low mtn. elevs.

SNOWBRUSH
"Sticky Laurel" "Tobacco Brush"
Ceanothus velutinus
BUCKTHORN FAMILY

6′. Thicket-forming shrub. Leaves 3½″, ovate, fine-toothed, curled, fragrant; shiny, sticky above; evergreen. Flowers tiny, creamy, in conical 5″ clusters; bloom June–Aug. **HABITAT** Clearings in mtns. to mid-elev. **RANGE** Mainly east of Cascade crest; sw OR.

CASCARA
Rhamnus purshiana
BUCKTHORN FAMILY

35′. Many-branched tree or large shrub. Leaves 6″, elliptical, fine-toothed. Bark gray or brown, smooth to scaly. Flowers tiny, greenish, clustered in leaf axils; bloom Apr.–May. Berries ½″, red to black. **CAUTION** Berries poisonous. **HABITAT** Lowland wet forests, mostly second growth. **RANGE** Throughout (local east of Cascades).

WHITE VIRGIN'S BOWER
"Western White Clematis"
Clematis ligusticifolia
BUTTERCUP FAMILY

L variable. Prolific climbing, woody vine. Leaves 6″, pinnately compound, with 5–7 coarse-toothed, 2″ leaflets. Flowers ¾″, creamy, with 5 petal-like sepals; in open 2″ clusters; bloom June–July. Seeds 2″, with white plumes. **HABITAT** Streamsides, disturbed areas. **RANGE** w OR valleys, east of Cascades.

WESTERN POISON OAK
Toxicodendron (Rhus) diversilobum
CASHEW FAMILY

H 4′ or L 16′. Shrub or climbing vine. Leaves 6″, divided into 3 ovate, reddish-green, 3″ leaflets, usu. toothed or lobed; turn crimson. Stems grayish. Flowers tiny, greenish white, clustered; bloom Apr.–June. Berries tiny, white, striped, clustered. **CAUTION** Do not touch; even indirect contact (via clothes, pets, smoke) with any part can cause severe rash. **HABITAT** Dry lowland forests and clearings. **RANGE** West of Cascades (local in WA), Columbia R. Gorge.

STINK CURRANT
Ribes bracteosum
CURRANT FAMILY

8′. Straggly shrub. Leaves 8″, fragrant, deeply palmately 5- or 7-lobed. Bark reddish. Flowers tiny, greenish white, in loose 12″ clusters; bloom May–June. Berries ⅜″, blue-black. **HABITAT** Lowlands to mtn. streamsides, seeps, wet thickets, avalanche basins. **RANGE** Mostly west of Cascade crest.

Poisonous Plants

Poisonous plants are those that contain potentially harmful substances in high enough concentrations to cause injury if touched or swallowed. Determining whether a plant species is "poison" or "food" requires expertise. The information in this guide is not to be used to identify plants for edible or medicinal purposes.

Sensitivity to a toxin varies with a person's age, weight, physical condition, and individual susceptibility. Children are most vulnerable because of their curiosity and small size. Toxicity can vary in a plant according to season, the plant's different parts, and its stage of growth; and plants can absorb toxic substances, such as herbicides, pesticides, and pollutants from the water, air, and soil. Among the potentially deadly plants in Pacific Northwest are Death Camas and Poison Hemlock. The berry-like fruits of the Pacific Yew are deadly poisonous; those of the Cascara and the Pacific Red Elderberry are mildly toxic.

Physical contact with plants that contain irritating resinous compounds causes rashes in many individuals. The main offenders in the Pacific Northwest are well-known members of the cashew family: Poison Ivy and Poison Oak. All parts of these plants contain the irritating compounds. Stinging Nettle and Devil's Club have needle-like hairs or spines that release stinging substances when touched.

REDFLOWER CURRANT
Ribes sanguineum
CURRANT FAMILY

8′. Spindly shrub. Leaves 2½″, palmately 5-lobed. Bark reddish. Flowers ¾″, red to pink, tubular; 5 outer sepals brighter than 5 petals; in dense hanging clusters; bloom Mar.–May. Berries ⅓″, blue-black. **HABITAT** Semi-open lowland forests, clearings, rocky slopes.

RED OSIER DOGWOOD
Cornus stolonifera (sericea)
DOGWOOD FAMILY

10′. Spreading, thicket-forming shrub. Leaves 5″, opposite, elliptical, with curved veins; turn purple to russet. Stems red to purple, smooth. Flowers tiny, white, in dense flat clusters; bloom May–July. Berries tiny, pale blue-green, in clusters. **HABITAT** Lowland to mtn. streamsides, swampy forests.

DEVIL'S CLUB
Oplopanax horridum
GINSENG FAMILY

9′. Gnarly, sparsely branched shrub with cane-like stems. Leaves 14″, toothed, palmately 7- to 9-lobed, with spiny stalks and veins; lie flat near stem tips. Stems light brown, spiny. Flowers ¼″, whitish, in terminal 10″ clusters; bloom May–July. Berries ¼″, bright red, in terminal 10″ clusters. **CAUTION** Spines carry a skin irritant. **HABITAT** Wet ground in mature lowland to mid-elev. forests. **RANGE** West of Cascade crest; east only in wet mtns.

SPINY HOPSAGE
Grayia (Atriplex) spinosa
GOOSEFOOT FAMILY

4′. Rounded shrub. Leaves 1″, oblanceolate, rough-hairy, gray-green. Bark gray, shreddy; twig tips spiny. Flowers tiny, drab; females green to red-tinged, in clusters; bloom Apr.–June. Fruit tiny, reddish, winged disks. **HABITAT** Saline deserts, sagebrush steppes.

GREASEWOOD
Sarcobatus vermiculatus
GOOSEFOOT FAMILY

8′. Dense shrub. Leaves 1½″, linear, fleshy. Bark pale gray, smooth. Flowers tiny, greenish, in catkin-like 1¼″ spikes. **HABITAT** Deserts (dry lake beds), sagebrush steppes. **RANGE** East of Cascades.

HAIRY MANZANITA
Arctostaphylos columbiana
HEATH FAMILY

10′. Gnarled shrub. Leaves 2″, elliptical, gray-green, hairy below, evergreen. Bark red, smooth, with peeling gray flakes. Flowers tiny, pinkish to white, jug-shaped, in 1″ clusters; bloom May–July. Berries ⅓″, red, dry. **HABITAT** Hot rocky sites, areas of poor soil in wet forests. **RANGE** West of Cascade crest.

KINNIKINNICK
"Bearberry"
Arctostaphylos uva-ursi
HEATH FAMILY

H 6″; L 10′. Prostrate spreading shrub. Leaves 1¼″, obovate, rounded, shiny, evergreen. Bark red, smooth, with peeling gray flakes. Flowers tiny, pinkish, jug-shaped, in 1″ clusters; bloom Apr.–June. Berries ⅓″, bright red, dry. **HABITAT** Sunny rocky areas from lowlands to alpine elev.

SALAL
Gaultheria shallon
HEATH FAMILY

5′. Spreading shrub. Leaves 3½″, ovate, fine-toothed, evergreen. Flowers tiny, white to pink, bell-shaped, in long clusters; bloom May–July. Berries ½″, purplish black, sticky-hairy; edible, ripe Aug.–Sept. **HABITAT** Dry to moist forests (esp. with poor soil), coasts. **RANGE** West of Cascade crest.

WESTERN BOG LAUREL
Kalmia microphylla (polifolia)
HEATH FAMILY

20″. Mat-forming shrub. Leaves 1½″, opposite, elliptical, grayish below, evergreen. Flowers ¾″, pink, bowl-shaped, 5-lobed; 10 stamens spring free when pollinated; bloom June–Aug. **HABITAT** Bogs. **RANGE** Cascades and west.

TRAPPER'S TEA
"Western Labrador Tea"
Ledum glandulosum
HEATH FAMILY

3′. Gnarled shrub. Leaves 2½″, ovate, white-wooly below, evergreen. Flowers ½″, white, 5-petaled, in broad clusters; bloom July–Aug. Fruit tiny, brown, hairy capsules. **CAUTION** Poisonous. **HABITAT** Lowland to mid-elev. moist to boggy areas. **RANGE** Cascades and e mtns.

PINK MOUNTAIN HEATHER
Phyllodoce empetriformis
HEATH FAMILY

15″. Thick, mat-forming shrub. Leaves ½″, needle-like. Flowers ⅓″, pink, bell-shaped, 5-lobed, single or in clusters; bloom June–Aug. Fruit tiny, round, brown. **HABITAT** Subalpine meadows and forest edges.

WHITE RHODODENDRON
"Cascades Azalea"
Rhododendron albiflorum
HEATH FAMILY

6′. Erect shrub. Leaves 3½″, elliptical, glossy, bumpy, bronze-tinged; turn yellow. Bark shreddy; twigs red-hairy. Flowers ¾″, white, bowl-shaped, 5-lobed, in small clusters. Fruit tiny, woody, brownish pods. **HABITAT** Thickets in mid- to high-elev. forests. **RANGE** WA, n OR.

PACIFIC RHODODENDRON
Rhododendron macrophyllum
HEATH FAMILY
12'. Gnarled shrub. Leaves 8", elliptical, leathery, evergreen; edges roll under in summer. Flowers 1½", pink, bell-shaped, 5-lobed, in rounded 6" clusters; bloom May–June. Fruit ½", reddish-brown, woody pods. WA state flower. **HABITAT** Forests with poor soil, lowlands (higher in OR). **RANGE** w OR, w WA (local).

CASCADES BLUEBERRY
Vaccinium deliciosum
HEATH FAMILY
24". Dwarfed or erect shrub. Leaves 2", obovate, stiff, pale bluish below, partly fine-toothed; turn scarlet. Flowers tiny, pinkish, jug-shaped; bloom May–June. Berries ½", bright blue with whitish coating; edible, ripe Aug.–Sept. **HABITAT** Mid-elev. to subalpine meadows, forests.

BLACK HUCKLEBERRY
Vaccinium membranaceum
HEATH FAMILY
5'. Erect shrub. Leaves 2½", elliptical, thin, fine-toothed; turn red. Bark shreddy. Flowers tiny, pinkish, jug-shaped; bloom Apr.–June. Berries ½", purple to reddish black; edible, ripe June–Sept. **HABITAT** Mid-elev. to subalpine meadows, forests, burned areas.

EVERGREEN HUCKLEBERRY
Vaccinium ovatum
HEATH FAMILY
6'. Stout spreading shrub. Leaves 2", ovate, fine-toothed, evergreen. Flowers tiny, pink, bell-shaped, in drooping clusters; bloom Apr.–Aug. Berries tiny, black; edible, ripe July–Dec. **HABITAT** Coastal forests and dunes.

RED HUCKLEBERRY
Vaccinium parvifolium
HEATH FAMILY

10′. Erect shrub with angled branches. Leaves 1″, elliptical. Bark bright green. Flowers tiny, pinkish, jug-shaped; bloom Apr.–June. Berries tiny, red; edible, ripe July–Sept. **HABITAT** Lowland wet forests. **RANGE** West of Cascade crest.

TWINBERRY
"Inkberry"
Lonicera involucrata
HONEYSUCKLE FAMILY

8′. Erect shrub. Leaves 5″, opposite, elliptical. Bark shreddy, light brown. Flowers ¾″, pale yellow, tubular, 5-lobed; in pairs, with 4 green bracts that turn magenta; bloom Apr.–Aug. Berries tiny, black, paired. **HABITAT** Lowland to high-elev. streamsides, moist forests.

BLUE ELDERBERRY
Sambucus mexicana (cerulea)
HONEYSUCKLE FAMILY

20′. Tall shrub, or tree with rounded crown. Leaves 6″, opposite, pinnately compound, with 5–9 lanceolate, fine-toothed, 3″ leaflets. Bark gray, furrowed. Flowers tiny, white, in flattish, branched, 8″ clusters; bloom May–July. Berries tiny, blue or white, in flattish 8″ clusters; edible, ripe Aug.–Sept. **HABITAT** Clearings, thickets; mostly in dry forests to mid-elevs. **RANGE** More common east of Cascades.

PACIFIC RED ELDERBERRY
Sambucus racemosa
HONEYSUCKLE FAMILY

20′. Tree or tall, weak-stemmed shrub. Leaves 10″, opposite, pinnately compound, with 5–7 lanceolate, fine-toothed, 5″ leaflets. Flowers tiny, white, in 4″ conical clusters; bloom Mar.–July. Berries tiny, red (mtn. variety black), in 4″ conical clusters; used for jam and wine, ripe Aug.–Sept. **CAUTION** Raw berries mildly toxic. **HABITAT** Wet thickets, clearings, woods.

COMMON SNOWBERRY
Symphoricarpos albus
HONEYSUCKLE FAMILY

5′. Erect shrub. Leaves 1″, opposite, elliptical, irregularly lobed. Flowers tiny, white to pink, bell-shaped, clustered; bloom May–Aug. Berries ½″, white, in tight, popcorn-like clusters; persist through winter. **HABITAT** Lowlands to mid-elev. open forests, hillsides.

MOCK ORANGE
Philadelphus lewisii
HYDRANGEA FAMILY

8'. Erect shrub. Leaves 3", opposite, ovate. Flowers 1¼", white, with 4 petals, many yellow stamens; fragrant, clustered; bloom May–July. Fruit ⅓" woody capsules. **HABITAT** Sunny areas in lowlands. **RANGE** Mainly east of Cascades.

VINE MAPLE
Acer circinatum
MAPLE FAMILY

30'. Shrub or sprawling tree with vine-like branches. Leaves 4", opposite, palmately 7- or 9-lobed, toothed; turn red. Bark gray, smooth. Flowers tiny, with 4 or 5 purple sepals, in small clusters; bloom Mar.–June. Fruit reddish 2" keys with wings at wide angle. **HABITAT** Wet forests, avalanche chutes. **RANGE** West of Cascade crest.

ROCKY MOUNTAIN MAPLE
Acer glabrum
MAPLE FAMILY

30'. Shrub or small tree. Leaves 4", opposite, palmately 3- or 5-lobed; turn red-orange. Bark gray to reddish, smooth. Flowers tiny, greenish, saucer-shaped, in branched clusters; bloom Apr.–June. Fruit reddish 1" keys with wings at right angle. **HABITAT** Open forests, thickets. **RANGE** Throughout; more common east of Cascade crest.

PURPLE SAGE
Salvia dorrii
MINT FAMILY

20″. Broad round shrub; branches rigid, spine-tipped. Leaves 1¼″, opposite to whorled, oblanceolate, silvery, aromatic. Flowers ½″, blue-violet, tubular, with 6 odd lobes; in whorled clusters; bloom May–June. **HABITAT** Sagebrush steppes. **RANGE** Local.

BITTERSWEET
Solanum dulcamara
NIGHTSHADE FAMILY

8′. Vine-like climber or shrub. Leaves 3″, variably shaped (ovate, heart-shaped, 3-lobed, or 3-parted). Flowers ¾″, with 5 bent-back, blue to violet petals around yellow cone of fused stamens; in sparse branched clusters; bloom May–Sept. Berries ½″, bright red. **CAUTION** Leaves and berries poisonous. **HABITAT** Lowland thickets, disturbed areas.

RUSSIAN OLIVE
Elaeagnus angustifolia
OLEASTER FAMILY

30′. Crown dense, rounded. Leaves 4″, lanceolate, untoothed, sage-green above, silvery below. Bark gray-brown, shreddy in strips. Flowers ½″, yellow, bell-shaped, 4-lobed; single or paired in leaf axils; bloom May–June. Berries ½″, yellow to brown; pulp edible; ripe Aug.–Oct. Planted as windbreak. **HABITAT** Steppe areas where water table has been raised by irrigation.

SCOTCH BROOM
Cytisus scoparius
PEA FAMILY

8′. Broom-like shrub with greenish angled branches. Leaves 1½″, obovate or divided into 3 leaflets, sparse. Flowers ¾″ bright yellow pea-flowers; bloom Apr.–June. Fruit 3″ blackish flat pods that pop open. **HABITAT** Lowland roadsides, prairies, clearings, neglected fields. **RANGE** West of Cascades.

YELLOW BUSH LUPINE
Lupinus arboreus
PEA FAMILY

5'. Bushy shrub. Leaves 3", palmately compound, with 6–12 leaflets, each 2½". Flowers ¾" yellow pea-flowers in 6" spikes; bloom May–Sept. Fruit 2" hairy green pods. **HABITAT** Coastal dunes.

GORSE
Ulex europaeus
PEA FAMILY

8'. Dense shrub with spiny branches and angled stems. Leaves tiny, few, hidden among green spines. Flowers ¾" yellow pea-flowers; bloom Apr.–Sept. Fruit 1", flat, hairy, blackish pods. **HABITAT** Disturbed lowland areas. **RANGE** Mainly coasts.

WESTERN SERVICEBERRY
"Saskatoon"
Amelanchier alnifolia
ROSE FAMILY

15'. Broad shrub or small tree. Leaves 1¾", elliptical, partly toothed. Bark gray-brown, smooth or lined. Flowers 1¼", white, with 5 narrow petals, clustered; bloom Apr.–July. Berries ½", purple to black; edible, ripe Aug.–Sept. **HABITAT** Rocky slopes, forest openings, shrub swamps; lowlands in west, all elevs. in east.

CURL-LEAF MOUNTAIN MAHOGANY
Cercocarpus ledifolius
ROSE FAMILY

15'. Shrub, or tree with rounded crown and twisted branches. Leaves 1¼", lanceolate, with rolled edges; resinous, aromatic, evergreen. Bark reddish, furrowed. Flowers ½", yellowish, funnel-shaped, hairy; bloom Apr.–June. Fruit tiny seed with white-hairy, twisted, 3" tail. **HABITAT** Mid-elev. dry slopes. **RANGE** Blue Mtns. and south, to e and sw OR.

BLACK HAWTHORN
"River Hawthorn"
Crataegus douglasii
ROSE FAMILY

15'. Thicket-forming shrub, or tree with rounded crown. Leaves 2½", ovate, toothed, slightly lobed. Bark gray or brown, scaly; twigs red, with 1" spines. Flowers ½", with 5 white petals, pink stamens; in rounded clusters; bloom May–June. Berries ½", reddish black, in drooping clusters. **HABITAT** Lowland streamsides, roadsides, shrub swamps.

OCEAN SPRAY
Holodiscus discolor
ROSE FAMILY

10'. Many-branched shrub. Leaves 3", ovate, toothed, slightly lobed. Bark reddish, flaking. Flowers tiny, creamy; in upright to drooping, conical, 7" clusters; bloom June–Aug. **HABITAT** Open forests to mid-elevs.

PACIFIC CRABAPPLE
Malus (Pyrus) fusca
ROSE FAMILY

35'. Tree with rounded crown, or thicket-forming shrub. Leaves 3", ovate, fine-toothed, lobed on one or both sides. Bark smooth to scaly, gray. Flowers 1", white or pink, with 5 round petals, in broad clusters; bloom May–June. Apples ½", yellow to reddish; edible, ripe fall–winter. **HABITAT** Lowland moist forests, wetland edges. **RANGE** West of Cascades.

INDIAN PLUM
"Osoberry"
Oemleria cerasiformis
ROSE FAMILY

10'. Shrub or small tree. Leaves 5", elliptical, aromatic. Bark purplish, smooth. Flowers ½", greenish white, funnel-shaped, in hanging clusters; bloom Feb.–Apr. Plums ½", blue-black; edible, ripe June–July. **HABITAT** Open lowland forests, roadsides. **RANGE** West of Cascades.

SHRUBBY CINQUEFOIL
Pentaphylloides floribunda
ROSE FAMILY
24″. Rounded to mat-forming shrub. Leaves 1½″, pinnately compound, with usu. 5 linear, hairy, ¾″ leaflets. Stems red, smooth to shreddy. Flowers 1″, yellow, 5-petaled; bloom July–Aug. Fruit tiny, white-hairy seedpods. **HABITAT** Alpine to subalpine outcrops.

CHOKECHERRY
Prunus virginiana
ROSE FAMILY
20′. Thicket-forming shrub or rounded to straggly tree. Leaves 4″, elliptical, fine-toothed; turn yellow. Bark gray-brown, smooth. Flowers ½″, white, 5-petaled, in drooping 4″ clusters; bloom Apr.–June. Cherries ½″, red to blackish; flesh bitter, used for jam, ripe June–Aug. **CAUTION** Pits poisonous. **HABITAT** Lowland riparian forests, thickets.

BITTERBRUSH
Purshia tridentata
ROSE FAMILY
7′. Stiff bushy shrub. Leaves ¾″, oblanceolate, with 3-lobed tip, rolled-under edges, white-hairy underside. Flowers ¾″, yellow, funnel-shaped, with 5 flat petals; bloom Apr.–June. Fruit ¾″ green seedpods. **HABITAT** Steppes, forests.

NOOTKA ROSE
Rosa nutkana
ROSE FAMILY
7′. Many-stemmed shrub. Leaves 5″, pinnately compound, with 5–7 ovate, toothed, 2½″ leaflets. Stems reddish brown, thorny. Flowers 3″, pink, 5-petaled; bloom May–July. Fruit ¾″, purplish, round to pear-shaped rose hips. **HABITAT** Lowland to mid-elev. clearings, sea bluffs, roadsides, shrub prairies.

HIMALAYAN BLACKBERRY
Rubus discolor (procerus)
ROSE FAMILY

10′. Thicket-forming. Leaves 10″, palmately compound, with 5 ovate, fine-toothed, 4″ leaflets. Stems red, prickly, arching. Flowers 1″, white, 5-petaled, clustered; bloom June–Aug. Berries 1″, red to black; edible, ripe July–Sept. **HABITAT** Roadsides, disturbed areas. **RANGE** Throughout, but very local in east.

THIMBLEBERRY
Rubus parviflorus
ROSE FAMILY

5′. Shrub. Leaves 6″, 5-lobed, toothed, hairy. Stems green to light brown. Flowers 2″, white, with 5 rounded, crinkly petals; bloom May–July. Berries ¾″, crimson, cup-shaped; edible, ripe June–Aug. **HABITAT** Lowland to high elev. roadsides, open forests, clear-cuts, burned areas.

SALMONBERRY
Rubus spectabilis
ROSE FAMILY

8′. Cane-like shrub. Leaves 6″, compound, with 3–5 ovate, fine-toothed, 3″ leaflets. Stems orange-brown, flaky, spiny. Flowers 1″, fuchsia to red, 5-petaled; bloom Mar.–June. Berries 1″, crimson to yellow, cup-shaped; edible, ripe July–Aug. **HABITAT** Coastal forests, swamps, creek bottoms, moist clear-cuts. **RANGE** West of Cascade crest; very local in east.

TRAILING BLACKBERRY
Rubus ursinus
ROSE FAMILY

H 8″; L 15′. Prostrate trailing shrub. Leaves compound, with usu. 3 ellipti-cal, toothed, 2″ leaflets. Stems slender, spiny. Flowers 1″, white, 5-petaled; bloom Apr.–July. Berries 1″, red to black, cup-shaped to conical; edible, ripe July–Aug. **HABITAT** Open forests, clear-cuts, prairies.

SITKA MOUNTAIN ASH
Sorbus sitchensis
ROSE FAMILY

10′. Shrub with rounded crown. Leaves 6″, pinnately compound, with 7–11 oblong, partly toothed, 2″ leaflets; turn yellow or orange-yellow. Bark gray, smooth. Flowers ½″, white, 5-petaled, in flat dense clusters; bloom June–July. Berries ½″, red to orange, clustered. HABITAT Drier subalpine and alpine areas, mid-elev. clearings.

SUBALPINE SPIRAEA
Spiraea densiflora
ROSE FAMILY

3′. Sometimes prostrate shrub. Leaves 3″, ovate, partly toothed. Flowers tiny, pink to red, with many stamens; in fuzzy, flat to rounded, 2″ clusters; bloom July–Aug. HABITAT Mid-elev. to subalpine thickets, rocky slopes, wet areas.

HARDHACK
Spiraea douglasii
ROSE FAMILY

6′. Thicket-forming shrub. Leaves 3″, oblong, partly toothed. Bark dark brown. Flowers tiny, rose-pink; in fuzzy, branching, 8″ conical clusters; bloom June–Aug. HABITAT Lowland to mid-elev. streamsides, lakesides, bogs.

SHRUBBY PENSTEMON
Penstemon fruticosus
SNAPDRAGON FAMILY

16″. Low bushy shrub. Leaves 2½″, opposite, elliptical to linear, semievergreen. Flowers 2″, pale blue-purple, tubular, with 2 upper lobes, 3 lower lobes; hairy inside; bloom May–Aug. **HABITAT** Rocky clearings in mtn. forests. **RANGE** East of Cascade crest.

ROCK PENSTEMON
Penstemon rupicola
SNAPDRAGON FAMILY

6″. Mat-forming shrub. Leaves ¾″, opposite, ovate, leathery, fine-toothed, semievergreen. Flowers 1¼″, pink to red-lavender, tubular, with 2 upper lobes, 3 lower lobes; hairy inside; 2–5 per stem; bloom May–Aug. **HABITAT** Mid-elev. (sea level in Columbia R. Gorge) to alpine rock crevices. **RANGE** Cascades from Snoqualmie Pass south, Klamaths.

PACIFIC WAX MYRTLE
"Bayberry"
Myrica californica
WAX MYRTLE FAMILY

20′. Tree with rounded crown, or many-branched shrub. Leaves 4″, oblanceolate, toothed; yellow with black dots below; evergreen. Bark gray-brown, smooth. Flowers ¾″ yellowish catkins; bloom Mar.–Apr. Berries tiny, purple-brown, warty, waxy. **HABITAT** Coastal sand dunes and spruce forests. **RANGE** Grays Harbor, WA, and south.

SCOULER WILLOW
Salix scouleriana
WILLOW FAMILY

35′. Thicket-forming shrub or multi-stemmed tree. Leaves 3″, obovate, dark green above, white- or rusty-hairy beneath. Bark gray to brown, fissured, aromatic. Flowers tiny, in 2″ blackish catkins; appear before leaves. **HABITAT** River bars; dry clear-cuts and burned areas in e mtns.

Leaf Shapes

scales

needles in bundle

needles in cluster

linear

oblong

lanceolate

oblanceolate

obovate

ovate

rounded

heart-shaped

arrowhead-shaped

elliptical

toothed

lobed

palmately lobed

pinnately lobed

palmately compound

pinnately compound

bipinnately compound

Leaf Arrangements

axil
alternate

opposite

whorled

basal

clasping

sheathing

Flower Types

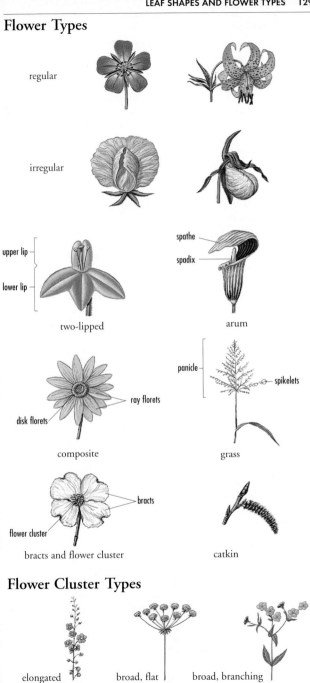

regular

irregular

upper lip
lower lip

two-lipped

spathe
spadix

arum

disk florets
ray florets

composite

panicle
spikelets

grass

bracts
flower cluster

bracts and flower cluster

catkin

Flower Cluster Types

elongated

broad, flat

broad, branching

Wildflowers

The Pacific Northwest has more than 3,900 species of flowering plants in more than 130 families. This section covers a broad selection of common and interesting wildflowers, including vines, grasses, and water plants.

The term "wildflower" has many connotations: one person's wildflower is another person's weed—a plant growing where it's not wanted. For the purposes of this field guide, wildflowers are defined as relatively small, noncultivated flowering plants that die back after each growing season.

The wildflowers included here are mainly herbaceous (nonwoody); some are woody but too small to be placed with the shrubs; a few have a woody base with herbaceous stems. These plants come in many forms. Many have a single, delicate, unbranched, erect stem terminated by a single flower or a flower cluster. Some have very robust stems, others are many-branched and shrubby. In some, the stems trail along the ground, sometimes spreading by runners. Those known as "vines" have long, slender, often flexible stems that either trail on the ground or climb, sometimes with tendrils to hold them in place. Plants of the grass family have erect, jointed stems and blade-like leaves; some other plants, such as rushes and sedges, are described as grass-like because they have narrow leaves and slender stems. Aquatic plants are adapted to life in or along water.

Wildflowers are most often identified by features of their flowers. The flowers or flower clusters may be borne in the leaf axils along the main stem or on branches off the stem. Modified leaves called *bracts* are often situated at the base of the flower or flower cluster. Flowers are typically composed of four sets of parts. The outermost set in a "complete" flower is the typically green, leaf-like *sepals* (known collectively as the *calyx*) that protect the often colorful second set—the *petals*. The next set is the *stamens,* the "male" part of the flower, each consisting of pollen sacs *(anthers)* typically on a stalk *(filament)*. The innermost set is the "female" part of the flower, with one or more *pistils,* each of which typically has a swollen base, the *ovary* (containing the ovules that after fertilization become the seeds), and a stalk *(style)* topped by the pollen-collecting *stigma.* The fruit develops from the ovary, forming a covering for the seed or seeds. The form of the fruit varies from species to species.

Parts of a Flower

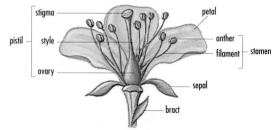

Although many plants have flowers with both stamens and pistils, some species have unisexual flowers that may occur on the same or separate plants. Many wind-pollinated species, such as grasses, sedges, and cattails, have reduced flowers that lack petals and/or sepals. These wind-pollinated flowers tend to be inconspicuous, unlike flowers that need to attract insects for pollination. Seed dispersal is often aided by animals: migrating birds and other animals eat fruit or seeds whole and disperse seeds in their droppings; fruits that are bur-like or covered with various kinds of sticky hairs attach to animals on contact and later fall off or are shed along with fur. Plants such as dandelions bear tiny fruits that have parachute-like tops and are carried by the wind far from the parent plant.

Flowers of a few representative types are illustrated on page 129. The buttercup and the lily are *regular* flowers; their parts radiate in a wheel-like (radially symmetrical) fashion. Pea and orchid flowers are commonly encountered flowers of *irregular* shape. Many plants in the lobelia, mint, and snapdragon families have tubular, *two-lipped* flowers. The tiny flowers of the arum family are clustered on a club-like *spadix,* which is usually enfolded by a leaf-like *spathe.* The *composite* "flower" of the daisy or aster is actually a head of many flowers; tiny tubular *disk florets* form a disk in the center, encircled by petal-like *ray florets.* (Dandelions have flower heads made up of all ray florets; true thistles have all disk florets.) Grasses have tiny, reduced florets enclosed in scale-like bracts; these are organized in overlapping arrangements called *spikelets,* which typically form a larger, often plume-like arrangement called a *panicle.*

Dogwood "flowers" in fact consist of a dense head of tiny flowers encircled by several large, petal-like *bracts.* The tiny unisexual flowers of oaks and many other species of trees and shrubs are clustered into slender spikes called *catkins.* Many plants bear flowers in clusters along or atop the stems or branches. Flower clusters take many forms, such as small round bunches, elongated spikes, feathery plumes, and broad, flat-topped, or branching arrangements.

In the accounts that follow, sizes given are typical heights of mature specimens unless otherwise noted.

YELLOW SKUNK CABBAGE
Lysichiton americanum
ARUM FAMILY

12″. Flowers minute, yellow, on thick 4″ spadix hooded by 8″, yellow, parallel-veined spathe; skunky-smelling. Leaves huge, ovate, net-veined, to 5′. **BLOOMS** Mar.–June. **HABITAT** Wet ground, bogs, swamps.

YARROW
Achillea millefolium
ASTER FAMILY

24″. Flowers ½″, with 3–5 white to pink rays around yellow disk; in dense, flat or slightly rounded, 3″ clusters. Single stem. Leaves fern-like, finely cut, narrow, sharply fragrant when crushed. **BLOOMS** Apr.–Aug. **HABITAT** Sunny dry sites.

PATHFINDER
"Trail Plant"
Adenocaulon bicolor
ASTER FAMILY

22″. Flowers tiny, white, rayless, in sparse branched sprays on slender stalks. Leaves 5″, triangular, fuzzy-white underneath, long-stalked. **BLOOMS** June–July. **HABITAT** Lowland to mid-elev. forests. **RANGE** Cascades and west.

ORANGE MOUNTAIN DANDELION
Agoseris aurantiaca
ASTER FAMILY

15″. Flowers 1″, dandelion-like, with burnt-orange rays that dry purplish; 1 per stem. Stems unbranched, with milky juice. Leaves to 12″, very slender, with few pairs of slight lobes. **BLOOMS** July–Aug. **HABITAT** Mid-elev. to alpine meadows.

PALE MOUNTAIN DANDELION
Agoseris glauca
ASTER FAMILY

17″. Flowers ¾″, with pale, waxy, yellow rays that dry pinkish; 1 per stem. Stems unbranched, with milky juice. Leaves lanceolate, sometimes wavy-edged. Seed heads dandelion-like. **BLOOMS** May–Sept. **HABITAT** Alpine and subalpine meadows; grass steppes.

PEARLY EVERLASTING
Anaphalis margaritacea
ASTER FAMILY

22". Slender erect stems end in roundish clusters of tiny globular flowers, each with many papery white bracts that persist indefinitely and smell rather rancid. Leaves linear, wooly underneath. **BLOOMS** Aug. **HABITAT** Disturbed clearings to high elevs.

WOOLY PUSSYTOES
Antennaria lanata
ASTER FAMILY

7". Clump-forming. Flowers tiny, whitish-wooly tufts of minute bristles, in rounded ½" clusters. Leaves elliptical to linear, whitish-wooly. **BLOOMS** July–Sept. **HABITAT** Alpine and subalpine meadows.

MAYWEED
"Stinking Dogfennel"
"Chamomile"
Anthemis cotula
ASTER FAMILY

14". Flowers daisy-like, ¾", with 10–20 white rays around yellow disk; several per stem. Leaves fern-like, lacy (bi- or tripinnately compound), bad-smelling when crushed. **BLOOMS** June–Aug. **HABITAT** Disturbed ground.

MOUNTAIN ARNICA
Arnica latifolia
ASTER FAMILY

14". Flowers 1½", yellow, with 8–15 rays around disk. Stem leaves ovate, toothed, stalkless; 4 or 5 opposite pairs per stem; basal leaves long-stalked, triangular to heart-shaped. **BLOOMS** May–Aug. **HABITAT** Open forests, subalpine meadows.

COMMON CALIFORNIA ASTER
Aster chilensis
ASTER FAMILY

24″. Often sprawling. Flowers ¾″, with 15–40 white to lilac or blue rays around yellow disk; cupped in green bracts. Leaves narrowly oblanceolate. BLOOMS Aug.–Sept. HABITAT Lowland brush; dry open plains, bluffs.

DOUGLAS'S ASTER
Aster subspicatus
ASTER FAMILY

26″. Patch-forming. Flowers 1½″, with violet to blue rays around yellow disk, cupped by green, translucent-edged bracts. Leaves narrowly lanceolate, mostly toothed. BLOOMS Aug.–Sept. HABITAT Lowlands, esp. beaches, salt marshes, ditches, streamsides.

ARROWLEAF BALSAMROOT
Balsamorhiza sagittata
ASTER FAMILY

20″. Forms robust clumps. Flowers 3″, yellow, with 8–25 rays around disk; 1 per stem. Leaves arrowhead-shaped, silvery, with felt-like wool when young. BLOOMS Apr.–June. HABITAT Grasslands, steppes, Ponderosa Pine forests.

ENGLISH DAISY
Bellis perennis
ASTER FAMILY

4″. Flowers 1″, with many white to pink or purplish rays around yellow disk; 1 per stem. Leaves spoon-shaped to round, fine-toothed. BLOOMS Feb.–Sept. HABITAT Disturbed ground. RANGE Mainly west of Cascades.

SPOTTED KNAPWEED
Centaurea maculosa (biebersteinii)
ASTER FAMILY

24″. Flowers 1½″, pink to purple, thistle-like, with large, 5-lobed outer "rays"; cupped by black-tufted, bulbous, green ½″ base. Stems stiff, many-branched. Leaves narrowly pinnately lobed. BLOOMS July–Aug. HABITAT Disturbed ground. RANGE East of Cascades.

CHICORY
"Blue Sailors"
Cichorium intybus
ASTER FAMILY
3'. Flowers 1½", bright blue (rarely white), with rays toothed at tips. Stem juice milky. Leaves deeply pinnately lobed, to 10"; midrib often red. **BLOOMS** July–Oct. **HABITAT** Disturbed areas. **RANGE** Mainly west of Cascades.

CANADA THISTLE
Cirsium arvense
ASTER FAMILY

3'. Prickly, white-hairy. Flowers ½" pink to purple disk on ¾" green base. Leaves irregularly shaped, with curling, very spiny lobes. **BLOOMS** July–Aug. **HABITAT** Disturbed areas.

BULL THISTLE
Cirsium vulgare
ASTER FAMILY
3'. Flowers 2" pink to purple disk on spiny, green, 1¼" base. Stems spiny-winged. Leaves irregularly shaped, with spiny lobes. **BLOOMS** July–Aug. **HABITAT** Disturbed areas.

SUBALPINE DAISY
Erigeron peregrinus
ASTER FAMILY

16". Flowers 1½", with 30–60 pink or lavender to pale blue rays around yellow disk. Leaves lanceolate, to 6". **BLOOMS** June–Aug. **HABITAT** Mid-elev. to alpine meadows.

WOOLY SUNFLOWER
"Oregon Sunshine"
Eriophyllum lanatum
ASTER FAMILY
14". White-wooly. Flowers 1¼", daisy-like, yellow, with about 13 rays around disk. Leaves linear or divided into finger-like lobes. **BLOOMS** Apr.–July. **HABITAT** Steppes, rocky or grassy areas.

NARROW-LEAVED GOLDENWEED
Haplopappus stenophyllus
ASTER FAMILY

4½". Flowers 1", daisy-like, yellow, with 6–8 rays around disk with protruding tubes. Stems woody. Leaves tiny, needle-like, rough; densely cover stem. **BLOOMS** May. **HABITAT** Steppes, grasslands.

COMMON SUNFLOWER
Helianthus annuus
ASTER FAMILY

4'. Bristly-hairy. Flowers 5", with yellow rays around brown disk. Stems branched. Lower leaves heart-shaped, upper leaves elliptical. **BLOOMS** June–Sept. **HABITAT** Roadsides, steppes. **RANGE** Mainly east of Cascades.

HAIRY CAT'S-EAR
Hypochaeris radicata
ASTER FAMILY

15". Flowers 1½", yellow, dandelion-like. Stems wiry. Leaves lanceolate, pinnately lobed, hairy; most flattened on ground. The common "dandelion" of late summer. **BLOOMS** May–Oct. **HABITAT** Lawns, fields, roadsides. **RANGE** Mainly west of Cascades.

WALL LETTUCE
Lactuca muralis
ASTER FAMILY

2'6". Flowers ½", with 5 yellow rays; in loose sprays on wiry branched stems. Leaves deeply pinnately lobed, with terminal lobe largest; contain milky juice. **BLOOMS** July–Sept. **HABITAT** Disturbed forest understory and edges.

OXEYE DAISY
Leucanthemum vulgare
ASTER FAMILY

16". Blooms profusely. Flowers 1½", daisy-like, with white rays around yellow disk. Basal leaves obovate, deeply lobed; stem leaves oblanceolate, toothed. Introduced; takes over meadows. **BLOOMS** May–Aug. **HABITAT** Disturbed ground, ex. steppes.

PALMATE COLTSFOOT
Petasites frigidus (palmatus)
ASTER FAMILY

12″. Flowers ½″, with white rays around yellow disk; in round clusters; bloom before leaves emerge. Stems have linear leaf-like bracts. Leaves palmately lobed, on stout stalks. **BLOOMS** Feb.–Apr. **HABITAT** Wet areas.

CANADA GOLDENROD
"Meadow Goldenrod"
Solidago canadensis
ASTER FAMILY

3′. Patch-forming. Pyramidal clusters of many tiny golden flowers form dense branching plume atop each hairy stem. Leaves lanceolate, prominently 3-veined, crowded. **BLOOMS** July–early Sept. **HABITAT** Roadsides, meadows, rock outcrops, disturbed fields.

COMMON TANSY
Tanacetum vulgare
ASTER FAMILY

3′6″. Many tiny, button-like, yellow flowers in dense clusters; rays minute, barely visible around large disk. Leaves dark green, fern-like, tripinnately compound, aromatic when crushed. **CAUTION** Poisonous. **BLOOMS** Aug.–Sept. **HABITAT** Roadsides.

DANDELION
Taraxacum officinale
ASTER FAMILY

11″. Flowers 1″, yellow, from rosette of leaves at stem base. Stems unbranched, hollow, with milky juice. Leaves lanceolate, lobed, toothed; flattened near ground. Seed heads globular; seeds windborne on umbrella-shaped bristles. **BLOOMS** Feb.–May. **HABITAT** Lawns, fields, roadsides.

YELLOW SALSIFY
Tragopogon dubius
ASTER FAMILY

21″. Flowers 2″, yellow, dandelion-like, with narrow, long-pointed bracts; fold up in midday heat. Seed heads huge, dandelion-like. Stems branched. Leaves grass-like, clasping. **BLOOMS** May–June (some to Sept.). **HABITAT** Roadsides, dry fields. **RANGE** East of Cascades, Columbia R. Gorge, San Juan Is.

NORTHERN MULE'S EARS
Wyethia amplexicaulis
ASTER FAMILY

21″. Flowers 4″, yellow, with 13–21 rays around disk. Leaves elliptical, with varnish-like sheen and thick yellow midrib. **BLOOMS** May–June. **HABITAT** Dry slopes to mid-elevs. **RANGE** East of Cascade crest.

VANILLA LEAF
Achlys triphylla
BARBERRY FAMILY

10″. Many minute, cream-white flowers form dense 1½″ spikes that poke up between leaflets. Stems wiry, straight. Leaves divided into 3 fan-shaped leaflets; vanilla-scented when dried. **BLOOMS** Apr.–July. **HABITAT** Lowland to mid-elev. forests. **RANGE** Cascades and west.

NORTHERN INSIDE-OUT FLOWER
Vancouveria hexandra
BARBERRY FAMILY

1″. Flowers ¾″, pointed, white; petals and sepals bent sharply backward; in sparse clusters. Leaves divided into slightly 3-lobed leaflets; mostly in 3s. **BLOOMS** May–July. **HABITAT** Forests. **RANGE** West of Cascade crest, south of Puget Sound.

HAREBELL
"Bluebells-of-Scotland"
Campanula rotundifolia
BELLFLOWER FAMILY

18″. Bell-shaped, pale blue, 1″ flowers nod on thread-like stalks. Stem leaves linear; basal leaves stalked, round to heart-shaped. **BLOOMS** June–Aug. **HABITAT** Diverse open habitats to sub-alpine elevs.

LONG-TAILED WILD GINGER
Asarum caudatum
BIRTHWORT FAMILY

4″. Single cup-shaped, purple-brown, 3″ flower on ground; 3 triangular sepals with very long, curling tails. Leaves dark green, leathery, heart-shaped, hairy-stalked. Pollinated by ants. **BLOOMS** Apr.–June. **HABITAT** Lowland to mid-elev. forests. **RANGE** West of Cascade crest.

SULPHUR BUCKWHEAT
Eriogonum umbellatum
BUCKWHEAT FAMILY

7″. Tiny cream, sulphur-yellow, or red flowers in tight balls that form domed clusters. Stems wooly, unbranched. Leaves ovate, in whorls, usu. gray-wooly on lower or both sides. **BLOOMS** June–Aug. **HABITAT** Rocky mtn. slopes, sagebrush steppes. **RANGE** Mainly east of Cascade crest.

MOUNTAIN SORREL
Oxyria digyna
BUCKWHEAT FAMILY

11″. Flowers minute, greenish, in dense spikes from leaf rosette at stem base; swell and become reddish when in seed. Leaves reddish, kidney-shaped to heart-shaped. Round, reddish, papery husks enclose seeds. **BLOOMS** July–Aug. **HABITAT** Moist rocky areas at alpine and subalpine elevs.

WATER SMARTWEED
Polygonum amphibium (coccineum)
BUCKWHEAT FAMILY

4″ (flower cluster stalks). Sprawling; afloat or on watersides; forms pink "fields" in water. Flowers tiny, deep pink, in 1 or 2 dense, egg-shaped, 1″ clusters. Leaves elliptical to oblong, with whitish midvein. **BLOOMS** June–Sept. **HABITAT** Fresh water.

WESTERN BISTORT
Polygonum bistortoides
BUCKWHEAT FAMILY

20″. Tiny white to pinkish flowers in fuzzy 1″ balls atop slender, unbranched, reddish stems. Leaves lanceolate, mostly at stem base. **BLOOMS** June–Aug. **HABITAT** Moist subalpine meadows.

GIANT BUR-REED
Sparganium eurycarpum
BUR-REED FAMILY

3′. Grass-like, with several spherical, bur-like, ½″ heads, upper ones with greenish flowers (male), lower ones with bristly white flowers (female). Leaves 32″, light green, linear. **BLOOMS** July–Sept. **HABITAT** Marshes, wet meadows.

WESTERN MONKSHOOD
Aconitum columbianum
BUTTERCUP FAMILY

4′. Tall spike of 1″ blue-purple flowers with 5 petal-like sepals, uppermost sepal forming a large, helmet-shaped hood. Leaves deeply palmately 5-lobed, long-toothed. **CAUTION** Poisonous, esp. roots. **BLOOMS** June–Aug. **HABITAT** Mtn. streamsides, moist forests, subalpine meadows.

WESTERN PASQUEFLOWER
Anemone occidentalis
BUTTERCUP FAMILY

8″. Clump-forming. Single, white, cup-shaped, 1″ flower with 5–8 crinkled, petal-like sepals. Stem single, hairy. Leaves lacy, fern-like, bi- or tripinnately compound. Seeds have long, silky, light green plumes. **BLOOMS** June–July. **HABITAT** Subalpine meadows.

OREGON ANEMONE
"Blue Anemone"
Anemone oregana
BUTTERCUP FAMILY
8". Single, flat, 1½" flower, blue to lavender, with usu. 5 petal-like sepals and many white stamens; on single stem from rhizome. Leaves divided into 3 elliptical, few-toothed leaflets; in whorl of 3. BLOOMS Apr.–June. HABITAT Open forests, brushy slopes. RANGE WA and n OR Cascades, n OR Coast Range.

RED COLUMBINE
Aquilegia formosa
BUTTERCUP FAMILY

24". Bushy. Flowers 1½"; 5 red to orange, spreading, petal-like sepals; 5 tubular yellow petals with rearward spurs; many yellow stamens. Stems branching. Leaves repeatedly divided into round-lobed leaflets. BLOOMS May–July. HABITAT Forest openings.

WHITE MARSH MARIGOLD
Caltha leptosepala
BUTTERCUP FAMILY
5". Succulent, patch-forming. Flowers 1", white, bowl-shaped, with 6–11 petal-like sepals, many yellow stamens; usu. 1 per stem. Leaves oblong, notched at base. CAUTION Poisonous. BLOOMS June–July. HABITAT Mainly subalpine streams, seeps, marshes.

NUTTALL'S LARKSPUR
Delphinium nuttallianum
BUTTERCUP FAMILY

10". Flowers 1", with 5 blue sepals (upper 1 spurred) around 4 smaller, white petals; in 1 loose spike per delicate stem. Leaves deeply divided into many narrow lobes. CAUTION Poisonous. BLOOMS Mar.–July. HABITAT Gravelly slopes with Ponderosa Pine or sagebrush. RANGE East of Cascades.

SAGEBRUSH BUTTERCUP
Ranunculus glaberrimus
BUTTERCUP FAMILY
5". Flowers 1", saucer-shaped, with 5 or more glossy yellow petals, many stamens. Leaves elliptical to shallowly 3-lobed. BLOOMS Mar.–June. HABITAT Ponderosa Pine forests, sagebrush steppes. RANGE East of Cascade crest.

WESTERN BUTTERCUP
Ranunculus occidentalis
BUTTERCUP FAMILY

15". Flowers 1", with 5 glossy yellow petals, many stamens, hairy, bent-back sepals. Stems branched. Leaves 3-lobed, toothed. **BLOOMS** Apr.–June. **HABITAT** Moist meadows from sea level to mid-elevs. **RANGE** Mainly west of Cascades.

FRAGILE PRICKLY PEAR
Opuntia fragilis
CACTUS FAMILY

8". Spiny clump. Flowers 1½", yellow to greenish, with many petals and red-stalked stamens. Stems form flattish joints; upper ones break off easily. **CAUTION** Barbed spines. **BLOOMS** May–June. **HABITAT** Dry areas. **RANGE** East of Cascades, San Juan Is.

SIMPSON'S HEDGEHOG CACTUS
Pediocactus simpsonii
CACTUS FAMILY

3". Clump of spiny spherical stems topped with several 1¼" rose-pink or purple flowers. **CAUTION** Sharp spines. **BLOOMS** May–July. **HABITAT** Rocky ridges in steppes. **RANGE** East of Cascades.

YELLOW BEE PLANT
Cleome lutea
CAPER FAMILY

3'. Fuzzy, rounded clusters of ½" yellow flowers with 4 petals and very long stamens atop bluish-waxy stems that grow tall as slender seedpods mature. Leaves palmately compound, with lanceolate leaflets. **BLOOMS** May–July. **HABITAT** Sandy areas. **RANGE** East of Cascades.

SEASIDE ANGELICA
Angelica hendersonii
CARROT FAMILY

3'6". Flowers tiny, white, 5-petaled, in small, ball-like clusters, grouped to form flat to rounded 4" clusters. Stems thick, succulent. Leaves bipinnately compound, with rounded toothed leaflets; wooly below. **BLOOMS** June–July. **HABITAT** Coastal bluffs and dunes. **RANGE** OR, s WA.

POISON HEMLOCK
Conium maculatum
CARROT FAMILY
6'. Broad, domed, 2" clusters of tiny white flowers. Stems purple-blotched, smooth, thick, hollow. Leaves 12", bipinnately compound, fernlike. **CAUTION** All parts deadly poisonous. **BLOOMS** May–Aug. **HABITAT** Moist disturbed ground. **RANGE** Mainly west of Cascades.

QUEEN ANNE'S LACE
Daucus carota
CARROT FAMILY
3'. Flat, lacy, 3" clusters of tiny white flowers. Branches of old clusters curl inward, resemble bird's nests. Leaves bipinnately compound, lacy, fern-like. **BLOOMS** July–Sept. **HABITAT** Disturbed ground.

COW PARSNIP
Heracleum sphondylium (lanatum)
CARROT FAMILY
6'. Domed 7" clusters of tiny white flowers atop thick, succulent, strong-smelling stems. Leaves compound, hairy, not fern-like, 16" long and wide; leaflets palmately lobed. **BLOOMS** May–July. **HABITAT** Moist forests and clearings.

FERN-LEAVED DESERT PARSLEY
Lomatium dissectum
CARROT FAMILY
3'4". Lacy bush. Minute, dark purple-brown or yellow flowers in globular 4" clusters that form loose groups. Stems often purple. Leaves large, fern-like. **BLOOMS** Apr.–June. **HABITAT** Roadsides, dry slopes. **RANGE** East slope of Cascades, w OR valleys, Columbia R. Gorge.

NARROW-LEAVED DESERT PARSLEY
Lomatium triternatum
CARROT FAMILY
20". Minute yellow flowers in flat-topped, 3" clusters. Leaves hairy, bi- or tripinnately compound, with linear to elliptical leaflets. **BLOOMS** Apr.–July. **HABITAT** Steppes, Ponderosa Pine forests, meadows. **RANGE** Mainly east of Cascades.

SPRING GOLD
"Fineleaf Desert Parsley"
Lomatium utriculatum
CARROT FAMILY

10". Fern-like, ground-hugging to erect. Minute yellow flowers in flat-topped, 1½" clusters. Leaves tripinnately compound, very lacy. **BLOOMS** Mar.–May. **HABITAT** Dry meadows, rocky slopes. **RANGE** West of Cascades.

WATER PARSLEY
"Water Celery"
Oenanthe sarmentosa
CARROT FAMILY

24". Sprawling. Flowers tiny, white, in flat-topped, 4" clusters. Leaves 12", bipinnately compound; resemble Italian parsley. **BLOOMS** June–Aug. **HABITAT** Lowland wet areas. **RANGE** West of Cascades.

BROAD-LEAVED CATTAIL
Typha latifolia
CATTAIL FAMILY

6'. Minute flowers in dense, 2-part spike: tapering light-brown male part (fluffy, then withered) above dense, dark brown, cylindrical female part; each part to 6"; female part releases fluffy seeds. Leaves sheathing, as tall as stem. Cause sediment to collect, making water shallower, turning lakes into marshes. **BLOOMS** June–July. **HABITAT** Marshes, ditches.

SPREADING DOGBANE
Apocynum androsaemifolium
DOGBANE FAMILY

18". Shrub-like. Tiny, fragrant, pinkish, bell-shaped flowers in loose clusters. Stems have milky juice. Leaves ovate, drooping. Fruit long, slender, paired seedpods. **CAUTION** Foliage poisonous. **BLOOMS** June–Sept. **HABITAT** Dry forests, orchards to mid-elevs. **RANGE** Mainly east of Cascade crest.

BUNCHBERRY
"Ground Dogwood"
Cornus canadensis
DOGWOOD FAMILY

5". Flowers 2½", each made up of 4 white, petal-like bracts around dense greenish flower cluster. Stems erect, from creeping rootstock. Leaves ovate, whorled. Berries bright red-orange, densely clustered. **BLOOMS** June–July. **HABITAT** Forests.

EELGRASS
Zostera marina
EELGRASS FAMILY

Long (4'), limp, tape-like leaves, submerged to floating. Flowers inconspicuous. One of very few flowering plants adapted to ocean water. **BLOOMS** June–Aug. **HABITAT** Ocean bays, from just above to below low-tide line. **RANGE** Coast.

DEERHORN CLARKIA
"Pink Fairies" "Ragged Robin"
Clarkia pulchella
EVENING-PRIMROSE FAMILY

12". Flowers 1½", brilliant pink, with 4 petals, each divided into 3 long lobes, side petals often twisted. Leaves linear. **BLOOMS** May–July. **HABITAT** Steppes. **RANGE** East of Cascades.

FIREWEED
Epilobium angustifolium
EVENING-PRIMROSE FAMILY

5'. Flowers 1½", with 4 pink to purple, round petals; in conical spikes. Leaves narrow, linear. Seedpods 3", reddish, slender; release fluffy white seeds. **BLOOMS** June–July. **HABITAT** Clear-cuts, burned areas, avalanche tracks, river bars, subalpine meadows.

PALE EVENING PRIMROSE
Oenothera pallida
EVENING-PRIMROSE FAMILY

12". Flowers 2", saucer-shaped, white aging to pink, 4-petaled, with sepals bent back and sideways. Stems have whitish flaky "bark." Leaves linear. **BLOOMS** May–June. **HABITAT** Dunes, sandy steppes.

WESTERN BLUE FLAX
Linum perenne
FLAX FAMILY

18". Flowers 2", sky blue, with 5 flat petals around yellow center. Leaves linear. **BLOOMS** May–July. **HABITAT** Steppes to alpine slopes. **RANGE** East of Cascades.

WESTERN GROMWELL
"Puccoon"
Lithospermum ruderale
FORGET-ME-NOT FAMILY

16″. Clump-forming, finely hairy. Tiny, bell-shaped, fragrant, pale yellow flowers crowded together with leaves at stem ends. Leaves linear, stalkless. **BLOOMS** Apr.–June. **HABITAT** Dry sites from foothills to mid-elevs. **RANGE** Mainly east of Cascade crest.

TALL BLUEBELL
Mertensia paniculata
FORGET-ME-NOT FAMILY

3′. Forms lush clumps. Flowers ½″, blue (initially pink-tinged), narrowly bell-shaped, 5-lobed, in hanging clusters. Leaves stalked, ovate or heart-shaped. **BLOOMS** May–Aug. **HABITAT** Streamsides, moist meadows in mtns.

YELLOW SAND VERBENA
Abronia latifolia
FOUR-O'CLOCK FAMILY

4″. Sticky creeper. Many hemispheric clusters of 1″, yellow, trumpet-shaped, 5-lobed, fragrant flowers. Stems long. Leaves fleshy, roundish. **BLOOMS** May–Aug. **HABITAT** Beaches.

MOUNTAIN BOG GENTIAN
"Explorer's Gentian"
Gentiana calycosa
GENTIAN FAMILY

8″. Flowers 1″, deep blue, vase-shaped, 5-lobed, with 2–4 pointed fringes in notches. Leaves ovate, clasping. **BLOOMS** Aug.–Oct. **HABITAT** Moist subalpine to alpine areas.

STORKSBILL
"Filaree"
Erodium cicutarium
GERANIUM FAMILY

6″. Flowers ½″, deep pink, 5-petaled; 2–10 per cluster. Stems red, usu. prostrate. Leaves pinnately compound, mostly prostrate at stem base. Fruits have 1–2″ protruding "bills." **BLOOMS** Mar.–June. **HABITAT** Disturbed ground. **RANGE** Mainly east of Cascades.

STICKY GERANIUM
"Cranesbill"
Geranium viscosissimum
GERANIUM FAMILY
24". Flowers 1", bright pink to purple, 5-petaled, in loose clusters. Leaves deeply 5- to 7-lobed, toothed. Fruits have 5-tipped, 1–2" "bills." BLOOMS May–Aug. HABITAT Open forests, meadows. RANGE East of Cascades.

AMERICAN GLASSWORT
"Pickleweed" "Saltwort"
Salicornia virginica
GOOSEFOOT FAMILY

7". Sprawling tangle of jointed succulent stems with minute green flowers in club-like spikes at branch tips. Leaves scale-like, barely visible. BLOOMS June–Sept. HABITAT Salt marshes.

RUSSIAN THISTLE
"Tumbleweed"
Salsola kali
GOOSEFOOT FAMILY
3'. Bushy, ferociously spiny. Flowers tiny, with 4 or 5 magenta or green petal-like sepals. Leaves thorn-like. Dies, turns rigid in fall, blows over open areas, scattering seeds. BLOOMS June–Aug. HABITAT Neglected croplands, overgrazed rangelands. RANGE East of Cascades.

WESTERN WILD CUCUMBER
"Manroot"
Marah oreganus
GOURD FAMILY

L variable. Sprawling or climbing vine. Flowers ½", bell-like, in loose clusters. Leaves large, rough-hairy, heart-shaped or palmately lobed. Fruit 2½", gourd-like, green, weakly spiny. BLOOMS Apr.–June. HABITAT Clearings, thickets, broadleaf forests. RANGE Mainly west of Cascades.

INDIAN RICEGRASS
Achnatherum (Oryzopsis) hymenoides
GRASS FAMILY
18". Forms thick clumps. Flowers in delicate, open, 4½" panicles of tiny white plumes (florets) on fine branchlets. Leaves tightly in-rolled. BLOOMS May–June. HABITAT Sandy or rocky grasslands. RANGE East of Cascades.

EUROPEAN BEACHGRASS
Ammophila arenaria
GRASS FAMILY

3'6". Stout, tufted, thicket-forming. Flowers in dense, light brown, 9" spikes that taper at both ends. Leaves stiff, narrow, with in-rolled edges. Introduced; planted for dune stabilization; becomes invasive, changes sand-accumulation patterns. **BLOOMS** June–Aug. **HABITAT** Sand beaches.

CHEATGRASS
Bromus tectorum
GRASS FAMILY

14". Forms small tufts. Flowers in loose, arching, reddish panicles of stiff-hairy, ¾" spikelets. Leaves flat. Introduced; permanently invasive in e OR and WA, even after grazing or disturbance. **BLOOMS** Apr.–June. **HABITAT** Disturbed ground. **RANGE** East of Cascades.

COMMON VELVETGRASS
Holcus lanatus
GRASS FAMILY

26". Forms small, fuzzy, grayish clumps. Flowers in compact, purplish 4" panicles. Leaves fairly short, wide, grayish. Aggressive introduced weed; spreads by surface runners. **BLOOMS** June–Sept. **HABITAT** Lawns, gardens, roadsides. **RANGE** Mainly west of Cascades.

FOXTAIL BARLEY
Hordeum jubatum
GRASS FAMILY

14". Forms small clumps. Flowers in brush-like, green to purplish-red, often curved, 3" spikes, with long stiff hairs. Leaves rough-feeling. **BLOOMS** June–Aug. **HABITAT** Roadsides, fields, open forests or mtn. meadows.

REED CANARY GRASS
Phalaris arundinacea
GRASS FAMILY

4'. Robust, bamboo-like, colony-forming. Flowers in purplish, compact to spreading, 6" panicles. Stems stout, from pinkish rhizomes. Leaves rough, broad; some horizontal. Planted for streambank stabilization, but becomes invasive. **BLOOMS** June–July. **HABITAT** Ditches, ponds, intermittently flooded ground.

TIMOTHY
Phleum pratense
GRASS FAMILY

30″. Thickly clumped grass. Flowering spikes dense, slender, yellowish, 4″ cylinders. Stems bulbous just above root crown. Leaves flat. Introduced; top U.S. crop hay; hay fever allergen. **BLOOMS** June–Aug. **HABITAT** Roadsides, fields.

KENTUCKY BLUEGRASS
Poa pratensis
GRASS FAMILY

24″. Sod-forming. Flowers purple, in open, delicate, conical or arching panicles, each comprised of 3–5 spikelets. Leaves slender, soft, abundant. Introduced; popular for lawns, but invades gardens, rangeland. **BLOOMS** May–Oct. **HABITAT** Lawns, gardens, roadsides, moist grasslands.

BLUEBUNCH WHEATGRASS
Pseudoroegneria (Agropyron) spicata
GRASS FAMILY

32″. Forms thick clumps; often bluish-coated. Hairy spikelets form 4½″ spikes spaced along stem tips. Originally a steppe dominant; now decimated where grazed, but still common. **BLOOMS** June–Aug. **HABITAT** Steppes, grasslands.

PIPSISSEWA
"Prince's Pine"
Chimaphila umbellata
HEATH FAMILY

6″. Flowers ½″, pink to white, nodding, with 4–5 petals spread flat around fat, knob-like pistil. Stems slender, woody. Leaves elliptical, fine-toothed, leathery, dark green, evergreen, mostly whorled. **BLOOMS** June–Aug. **HABITAT** Conifer forests.

INDIAN PIPE
Monotropa uniflora
HEATH FAMILY

6″. Whole plant fleshy, waxy white. Flowers ¾″, bell-shaped, 5-lobed, nodding to erect; 1 per stem. Stems thick, translucent. Leaves tiny, scale-like. Obtains all nutrients from soil fungi, which draw them from trees. **BLOOMS** June–July. **HABITAT** Old-growth forests.

PINK WINTERGREEN
"Heart-leaved Pyrola"
Pyrola asarifolia
HEATH FAMILY

11″. Narrow spike of bowl-shaped, pink to red, ½″ flowers with 5 petals and curved, off-center style. Leaves elliptical to heart-shaped, leathery, dark green, evergreen, in rosette at stem base. **BLOOMS** June–Aug. **HABITAT** Moist forests.

TWINFLOWER
Linnaea borealis
HONEYSUCKLE FAMILY

5" (flower stalks). Evergreen creeper. Flowers ½", pink to white, 5-lobed, bell-shaped, fragrant, paired. Stems woody, reddish. Leaves 1", obovate, fine-toothed, glossy dark green. **BLOOMS** June–Sept. **HABITAT** Old-growth forests.

ROCKY MOUNTAIN IRIS
"Western Blue Iris"
Iris missouriensis
IRIS FAMILY

18". Forms dense clumps. 1–4 pale blue or blue-violet, 3½" flowers with petal-like parts in 3s (down-curved sepals, erect petals, style branches). Leaves sword-like. **BLOOMS** May–June. **HABITAT** Sites that are wet in spring, dry in summer. **RANGE** East of Cascades, Whidbey Is.

OREGON IRIS
Iris tenax
IRIS FAMILY

9". Clumping, grass-like. Single, 3½", usu. violet flower, with petal-like parts in 3s (down-curved sepals, erect petals, style branches). Leaves tough, usu. taller than flower stalk. **BLOOMS** Apr.–June. **HABITAT** Grassy lowland clearings. **RANGE** West of Cascades, south of Puget Sound.

IDAHO BLUE-EYED GRASS
Sisyrinchium idahoense (angustifolium)
IRIS FAMILY

11". Grass-like. Flowers ¾", blue with yellow center, with 3 petals, 3 petal-like sepals, all spreading and tipped with thorn-like point. Stems flat. Leaves minute. **BLOOMS** May–July. **HABITAT** Sagebrush steppes and Ponderosa Pine forests that are wet in spring, to mid-elevs. **RANGE** East of Cascades.

NODDING ONION
Allium cernuum
LILY FAMILY

14″. Grass-like, onion-scented. Tiny pink to white flowers in round, nodding, 2″ clusters. Stems unbranched, tubular. Leaves linear, basal. **BLOOMS** June–July. **HABITAT** Dry forest clearings. **RANGE** Cascades, Coast Ranges, Okanogan Highlands.

DOUGLAS'S ONION
Allium douglasii
LILY FAMILY

10″. Onion-scented. Globular to hemispherical 2″ clusters of tiny pink flowers. Stems tubular, with 1 pair of 6″ narrow leaves. **BLOOMS** May. **HABITAT** Grasslands that are moist in winter. **RANGE** Columbia R. Basin of se WA, ne OR, and Columbia R. Gorge.

LYALL'S MARIPOSA LILY
Calochortus lyallii
LILY FAMILY

12″. Flowers 1½″, white; 3 petals with fringed edges and small purple crescent at base; 3 pointed, petal-like sepals. Leaves few, linear, grass-like. **BLOOMS** May–July. **HABITAT** Open forests. **RANGE** East slope of WA Cascades.

SAGEBRUSH MARIPOSA LILY
Calochortus macrocarpus
LILY FAMILY

14″. Flowers 3″, lavender or rose-purple; 3 broad, sharp-tipped petals, each with dark purple band and yellowish hairy base; 3 longer, pointed, petal-like sepals. Leaves linear, curled at tips. **BLOOMS** June–July. **HABITAT** Steppes.

COMMON CAMAS
Camassia quamash
LILY FAMILY

18″. Grass-like. Tall conical clusters of many 1½″, bright blue-violet flowers with nearly flat-spreading petals. Leaves linear, sheathing. **BLOOMS** Apr.–June. **HABITAT** Meadows moist in spring, to mid-elevs.

QUEEN'S CUP
"Bead Lily"
Clintonia uniflora
LILY FAMILY

3". Flowers 1", white, vase-shaped to nearly flat-spreading, with long petals. Single stem. Leaves oblong or elliptical, glossy, smooth. Berry ½", deep blue, firm. **BLOOMS** June–July. **HABITAT** Lowland to mid-elev. forests.

GLACIER LILY
Erythronium grandiflorum
LILY FAMILY

9". Flowers 2½", yellow, with 6 curved-back petals, 6 stamens protruding from center. Leaves and stalk tulip-like. Leaves pointed-elliptical. **BLOOMS** May–July. **HABITAT** Clearings in forests and meadows, often near melting snow. **RANGE** All NW, ex. se OR.

AVALANCHE LILY
"Glacier Lily"
Erythronium montanum
LILY FAMILY

9". Flowers 2½", white with yellow center, with 6 curved-back petals, 6 stamens protruding from center. Leaves and stalk tulip-like. Leaves pointed-elliptical. **BLOOMS** July, 1–2 weeks after snowmelt. **HABITAT** Subalpine meadows. **RANGE** Olympic Mtns., WA and OR Cascades.

CHOCOLATE LILY
"Checker Lily" "Rice-root"
Fritillaria affinis (lanceolata)
LILY FAMILY

20". Flowers 1", bell-shaped, hanging, purple-brown mottled with yellow-green. Leaves lanceolate, usu. in 1 or 2 whorls. **BLOOMS** Apr.–June. **HABITAT** Prairies, grassy forest openings, to mid-elevs.

COLUMBIA LILY
"Tiger lily"
Lilium columbianum
LILY FAMILY

3'. Flowers 2½", nodding, yellow-orange speckled with maroon, with 6 strongly curved-back petals, 6 long stamens. Leaves lanceolate, some whorled. **BLOOMS** June–Aug. **HABITAT** Open forests to near tree line.

CASCADE LILY
Lilium washingtonianum
LILY FAMILY

3'6". Easter-lily-like. Flowers 5", white (often purple-spotted) aging to pink, with 6 curved-back petals; fragrant. Leaves lanceolate, wavy-edged, mostly whorled. **BLOOMS** June–July. **HABITAT** Mid-elev. clearings. **RANGE** OR Cascades and Klamaths.

FALSE LILY-OF-THE-VALLEY
"May Lily"
Maianthemum dilatatum
LILY FAMILY

9". Single stem bears slender spike of tiny white flowers and 2 heart-shaped, parallel-veined, shiny leaves. Tiny berries speckled green; ripen to red in July **BLOOMS** May–June. **HABITAT** Lowland forests.

FALSE SOLOMON'S SEAL
Smilacina racemosa
LILY FAMILY

24". Minute, white, fragrant flowers form fuzzy, many-branched, 4" clusters. Stems arch out from rootstock. Leaves elliptical, parallel-veined. Berries speckled green; ripen red July–Aug. **BLOOMS** May–July. **HABITAT** Lowland to mid-elev. forests.

WESTERN TRILLIUM
Trillium ovatum
LILY FAMILY

11". Single 3" white flower opens flat, ages to dark red; 3 petals alternate with 3 green sepals. Leaves ovate, in flat whorl of 3. **BLOOMS** Mar.–Apr. **HABITAT** Lowland to mid-elev. forests.

DOUGLAS'S TRITELEIA
Triteleia (Brodiaea) douglasii
LILY FAMILY

18". Grass-like. Round clusters of ¾", bell-shaped, blue flowers; 6-lobed, inner 3 lobes ruffled. 1 or 2 narrow 20" leaves. **BLOOMS** Apr.–June. **HABITAT** Steppes, Ponderosa Pine forests. **RANGE** East of Cascades.

GREEN CORN LILY
"Green False Hellebore"
Veratrum viride
LILY FAMILY

5′. Many ¾″, green, 6-petaled flowers on drooping spikes below 1 erect terminal spike. Leaves 10″, elliptical, strongly pleated. **CAUTION** Poisonous. **BLOOMS** July–Sept. **HABITAT** Wet mtn. meadows.

BEARGRASS
"Indian Basket Grass"
Xerophyllum tenax
LILY FAMILY

4′. Flowers ½″, saucer-shaped, white to cream, 6-petaled, fragrant; in broad, dense, pointed cluster atop stout stalk. Leaves tough, grass-like, in massive basal bunch. **BLOOMS** June–Aug. **HABITAT** Dry high forests, subalpine meadows.

DEATH CAMAS
Zigadenus venenosus
LILY FAMILY

19″. Pointed 4″ cluster of ½″, cup-shaped, white to cream flowers with 6 petals (3 long, 3 short). Leaves grass-like, 16″. **CAUTION** Poisonous. **BLOOMS** Mar.–July. **HABITAT** Dry clearings, grasslands, sagebrush steppes.

PURPLE LOOSESTRIFE
Lythrum salicaria
LOOSESTRIFE FAMILY

5′. Erect, branching, squarish stems bear 12″ spikes of tiny, whorled, pinkish-purple flowers with tissue-like petals. Leaves lanceolate, with ear-like lobes at base. Introduced; invades wetlands, crowding out ecologically important native plants. **BLOOMS** July–Sept. **HABITAT** Lakeshores, marshes.

STREAMBANK GLOBE MALLOW
"Mountain Hollyhock"
Iliamna rivularis
MALLOW FAMILY

5′. Hollyhock-like. Flowers 1½″, pink to lavender, with 5 petals, 5 sepals, many stamens; in tall spikes. Leaves palmately 3- to 7-lobed. **BLOOMS** June–July. **HABITAT** Streamsides. **RANGE** East of Cascades.

SHOWY MILKWEED
Asclepias speciosa
MILKWEED FAMILY

3′6″. Gray-wooly. Flowers ½″, pink to maroon, with 5 sharply bent-back petals and 5 curved-in, horn-like stamens. Stem juice milky. Leaves 8″, lanceolate. Seedpods velvety, spiny; release silky white fluff. **BLOOMS** June–Aug. **HABITAT** Streamsides, roadsides. **RANGE** East of Cascades.

FIELD MINT
Mentha arvensis
MINT FAMILY

15″. Tiny pale pink flowers nearly hidden in leaf axils encircle weak, hairy, square stems. Leaves elliptical, sharp-toothed. **BLOOMS** July–Sept. **HABITAT** Wet areas; to mid-elevs.

GREAT HEDGE NETTLE
Stachys cooleyae
MINT FAMILY

3′6″. Open spike has whorls of pink to red-purple, tubular, 1″ flowers with long, rounded upper lip and 3-lobed lower lip. Leaves ovate, blunt-toothed, hairy. **BLOOMS** June–Aug. **HABITAT** Moist forests, roadsides, streamsides; to mid-elevs.

FIELD MORNING GLORY
"Hedge Bindweed"
Calystegia (Convolvulus) arvense
MORNING GLORY FAMILY

H/L variable. Aggressive twining vine. Flowers 1″, pink-tinged white, funnel-shaped, shallowly 5-lobed. Leaves triangular to arrowhead-shaped. Introduced; notorious pest; regrows from deep roots when pulled out. **BLOOMS** May–Oct. **HABITAT** Gardens, disturbed ground.

FIELD MUSTARD
Brassica campestris
MUSTARD FAMILY

24″. Spindly. Flowers yellow, ¾″, with 4 petals and 4 sepals, in round-topped clusters. Stems bluish-waxy. Upper leaves arrowhead-shaped, clasping; lower leaves pinnately lobed. **BLOOMS** Spring–late summer. **HABITAT** Fields, roadsides.

AMERICAN SEA-ROCKET
Cakile edentula
MUSTARD FAMILY

10″ (or prostrate). Straggly, succulent. Flowers pink, ½″; bloom a few at a time at tip of long cluster. Leaves fleshy, oblanceolate, scalloped to toothed. 1″ seedpods persist after leaves. **BLOOMS** July–Aug. **HABITAT** Beaches, in driftwood belt.

SAND-DUNE WALLFLOWER
Erysimum capitatum (asperum)
MUSTARD FAMILY

22". Foliage grayish. Flowers ¾",
with 4 petals; yellow, orange, or
reddish. Leaves narrowly lanceolate,
finely toothed. Seedpods slender,
square in cross section. **BLOOMS**
Apr.–June. **HABITAT** Sandy steppes,
mtn. meadows.

STINGING NETTLE
Urtica dioica
NETTLE FAMILY

5'. Covered with stinging hairs. Loose clusters of
minute green flowers dangle from leaf axils.
Stems spindly, square. Leaves opposite, ovate,
toothed. **CAUTION** Painful skin irritant; do not
touch. **BLOOMS** May–Sept. **HABITAT** Moist areas.

FAIRY SLIPPER
Calypso bulbosa
ORCHID FAMILY

5". Purple scaly stem topped with single 1" pink
flower with 5 narrow, ascending petals and sepals
above large, slipper-shaped lip mottled with orange, yellow, and white. 1 ovate leaf; grows in
fall, withers in summer. **BLOOMS** Mar.–May. **HABI-
TAT** Mature forests to mid-elevs.

SPOTTED CORALROOT
Corallorhiza maculata
ORCHID FAMILY

12". Fleshy. Seemingly leafless, dull reddish stem
bears tall spike of 1", brownish-purple flowers
with magenta and white lip petal. Obtains all
nutrients from soil fungi, which draw them from
trees. **BLOOMS** May–July. **HABITAT** Forests.

MOUNTAIN LADY'S SLIPPER
Cypripedium montanum
ORCHID FAMILY

12". Solitary flower has white, slipper-shaped, 1"
lip with yellow tongue surrounded by 4 slender,
twisted, bronze-purple, 2" petals and sepals. Single stem. Leaves elliptical. **BLOOMS** May–June.
HABITAT Open forests. **RANGE** East of Cascade
crest in WA; all OR.

RATTLESNAKE PLANTAIN
Goodyera oblongifolia
ORCHID FAMILY

8″. Single leafless stalk bears 1-sided spike of ½″, greenish-white, tubular flowers. Leaves elliptical, dark green with white midrib or white snake-skin-like pattern; in basal rosette. **BLOOMS** July–Aug. **HABITAT** Forests.

WHITE REIN ORCHID
"White Bog Orchid"
Platanthera (Habenaria) dilatata
ORCHID FAMILY

18″. Single, straight, hollow stem bears dense 8″ spike of ¾″, white, spicy-scented orchids; "rein" refers to long, strap-shaped lowest petal. Leaves lanceolate, sheathing. **BLOOMS** June–July. **HABITAT** Marshy forest openings, bogs.

WOOLYPOD MILKVETCH
"Woolypod Locoweed"
Astragalus purshii
PEA FAMILY

3″. Prostrate, matted, gray-hairy. Clusters of pink to purple or cream 1″ flowers. Leaves pinnately compound. Seedpod 1″, white-wooly. **BLOOMS** Mar.–Apr. **HABITAT** Sagebrush steppes.

BEACH PEA
Lathyrus japonicus
PEA FAMILY

20″. Sprawling or climbing. Clusters of 1″ purple to light blue pea-flowers. Stems angled. Leaves pinnately compound, with terminal tendrils and 6–12 leaflets, each elliptical or with 2 triangular basal appendages. Hairy pods contain edible peas. **BLOOMS** May–Sept. **HABITAT** Coastal dunes.

STEPPE SWEETPEA
"Few-flowered Pea"
Lathyrus pauciflorus
PEA FAMILY

18″. Climber. Angled stems bear clusters of pink to purple or blue, ¾″ pea-flowers. Leaves pinnately compound, with 8–10 linear to ovate, fleshy leaflets and terminal tendrils. **BLOOMS** Apr.–June. **HABITAT** Steppes, Ponderosa Pine forests. **RANGE** East of Cascade crest.

BIRD'S-FOOT TREFOIL
Lotus corniculatus
PEA FAMILY

11″. Wiry-stemmed creeper. Flowers yellow (age to red-tinged) ½″ pea-flowers in clusters of 3–15. Leaves clover-like, with 2 small appendages at leafstalk base, often hairy. **BLOOMS** June–July. **HABITAT** Moist disturbed places, e.g., ditches.

SEACOAST LUPINE
Lupinus littoralis
PEA FAMILY

8″. Silky-hairy. Upright stalks from prostrate stems bear conical clusters of many blue to purple ½″ pea-flowers in whorls. Leaves palmately compound, with 6–8 leaflets. **BLOOMS** May–Aug. **HABITAT** Sandy coastal areas.

SILKY LUPINE
Lupinus sericeus
PEA FAMILY

16″. Flowers ½″ blue (white in Asotin Co., WA) pea-flowers, whorled in conical clusters. Brownish silky hair on leaves, seedpods, sepals, back of upper petal. Leaves palmately compound, with 6–9 leaflets. **BLOOMS** May–July. **HABITAT** Steppes, Ponderosa Pine forests.

WHITE SWEET CLOVER
Melilotus alba
PEA FAMILY

5′. Wide-branched. Tiny white flowers in 3½″ spikes on most branches. Leaves divided into 3 oblong, fine-toothed leaflets. Sweet scent attracts bees. **BLOOMS** May–Oct. **HABITAT** Roadsides (esp. east of Cascades), lowland riverbanks.

BIG-HEAD CLOVER
Trifolium macrocephalum
PEA FAMILY

6″. Mat-forming. Globular 1½″ heads of tiny pink and white flowers. Stems hairy. Leaves thick, hairy, palmately compound, with 5–7 oblanceolate leaflets. **BLOOMS** Apr.–May. **HABITAT** Rocky steppes, Ponderosa Pine forests.

RED CLOVER
Trifolium pratense
PEA FAMILY

18″. Round 1″ heads of tiny, deep pink to red flowers. Stems sparsely hairy. Leaves divided into 3 oval to elliptical leaflets, each usu. marked with a pale V. **BLOOMS** June–Aug. **HABITAT** Lawns, pastures, roadsides.

WHITE CLOVER
Trifolium repens
PEA FAMILY

5″. Tiny white or pinkish flowers in ¾″ round heads. Leaves divided into 3 round, fine-toothed leaflets with slightly notched tips. Roots freely from runners. **BLOOMS** Apr.–Sept. **HABITAT** Disturbed ground.

WOOLY VETCH
Vicia villosa
PEA FAMILY

L 3′. White-hairy vine; climbs via tendrils. Long, 1-sided clusters of many red-purple, often partly white, ½″ flowers. Leaves pinnately compound, with 10–20 leaflets and terminal tendrils. Seedpods 1″, flat. **BLOOMS** June–Aug. **HABITAT** Roadsides, disturbed ground.

WESTERN PEONY
Paeonia brownii
PEONY FAMILY

16″. Flowers 2″, globular, drooping, maroon to brown, with 5–10 often yellow-edged petals, 5–6 reddish-green sepals. Stems fleshy; become floppy. Leaves thick, bluish-coated, divided into 3 segments, each with 3 lobed parts. **BLOOMS** Apr.–June. **HABITAT** Steppes, pine forests. **RANGE** East of Cascade crest, south of Lake Chelan.

SKYROCKET
"Scarlet Gilia"
Ipomopsis (Gilia) aggregata
PHLOX FAMILY

21″. Flowers 1″, trumpet-shaped, with 5 pointed lobes; scarlet, often white-speckled. Leaves finely pinnately lobed, skunky-smelling. Hummingbird favorite. **BLOOMS** May–July. **HABITAT** Dry rocky slopes to subalpine elevs.

LONG-LEAVED PHLOX
Phlox longifolia
PHLOX FAMILY

10″. Densely branched. Flowers 1″, with 5 lobes spread flat from tubular base; pink with white center, lilac, or pure white. Stems semiwoody. Leaves linear. **BLOOMS** Apr.–June. **HABITAT** Dry rocky places. **RANGE** East of Cascade crest.

SHOWY JACOB'S LADDER
"Sky Pilot"
Polemonium pulcherrimum
PHLOX FAMILY

10″. Flowers ½″, broadly bell-shaped, 5-lobed, blue to lavender with yellow center, densely clustered. Leaves pinnately compound, with 11–25 elliptical leaflets; often skunky-scented. **BLOOMS** May–Aug. **HABITAT** Mid- to alpine elev. forests and forest edges.

COMMON PLANTAIN
Plantago major
PLANTAIN FAMILY

16″. Dense 4″ spikes of minute, drab white flowers rise on wiry stems above basal rosette of ovate 5″ leaves. **BLOOMS** May–Aug. **HABITAT** Lawns, ditches, river flats.

FLOATING-LEAVED PONDWEED
Potamogeton natans
PONDWEED FAMILY

Scattered leaves float on shallow water atop long submerged stems. Flowers minute, greenish, whorled in dense 2″ spikes emerging from water. Some leaves ovate, copper-tinged, leathery; others tubular. **BLOOMS** May–Aug. **HABITAT** Ponds, backwaters.

WESTERN CORYDALIS
Corydalis scouleri
POPPY FAMILY

3′. Spikes of 1″, pink, long-spurred flowers. Leaves fern-like, tripinnately compound, with elliptical, often lobed leaflets. Seedpods explosively eject seeds. **BLOOMS** Apr.–July. **HABITAT** Seeps and streamsides in low-elev. forests. **RANGE** West of Cascades.

WESTERN BLEEDINGHEART
Dicentra formosa
POPPY FAMILY

14″. Clusters of 1″, pink, nodding, somewhat heart-shaped flowers. Leaves fern-like, elaborately pinnately compound, with finely cut leaflets. Green seedpod emerges from flower tip. **BLOOMS** Mar.–July. **HABITAT** Moist forests, streamsides. **RANGE** West of Cascade crest.

FEW-FLOWERED SHOOTING STAR
Dodecatheon pulchellum (pauciflorum)
PRIMROSE FAMILY

9″. Single stem bears deep pink, dart-like, 1″ flowers, each with 5 petals swept sharply upward from purplish to yellow point. Leaves lanceolate, in basal rosette. **BLOOMS** Apr.–Aug. **HABITAT** Moist meadows.

WESTERN STARFLOWER
"Broadleaf Starflower"
Trientalis latifolia (europaea)
PRIMROSE FAMILY

7″. Flowers ½″, star-shaped, pale pink, each on thread-like stalk from center of elevated whorl of 4–8 ovate leaves. **BLOOMS** Apr.–July. **HABITAT** Forests and prairies to mid-elevs. **RANGE** Mainly west of Cascades.

REDMAIDS
Calandrinia ciliata
PURSLANE FAMILY

4″. Sprawling succulent. Flowers ½″, shallowly bowl-shaped, 5-petaled, crimson to magenta with yellow stamens. Leaves linear to lanceolate, fringed with hairs. **BLOOMS** Apr.–May. **HABITAT** Weedy fields, gravel areas moist in spring. **RANGE** Common in OR.

WESTERN SPRING BEAUTY
Claytonia lanceolata
PURSLANE FAMILY

8″. Slightly succulent. Flowers ½″, 5-petaled, white to pinkish with fine red veins. 1 pair of oval or lanceolate leaves. **BLOOMS** May–July. **HABITAT** Meadows, esp. subalpine, esp. near snowbanks.

MINER'S LETTUCE
Claytonia (Montia) perfoliata
PURSLANE FAMILY

8″. Small cluster of white, 5-petaled, ½″ flowers emerges from center of round stem leaf. Other leaves basal, spoon-shaped. **BLOOMS** Mar.–Aug. **HABITAT** Forests and meadows to mid-elevs.

SIBERIAN MINER'S LETTUCE
Claytonia (Montia) sibirica
PURSLANE FAMILY

10″. Loose clusters of white to pink ½″ flowers with 5 notch-tipped petals. 1 pair of ovate leaves on stem; spoon-shaped leaves at base. **BLOOMS** Apr.–Sept. **HABITAT** Moist forests to mid-elevs.

BITTERROOT
Lewisia rediviva
PURSLANE FAMILY

5″. Pink to deep pink 2″ flowers with 10–18 petals top inconspicuous stems with linear fleshy leaves that wither at flowering. **BLOOMS** May–June. **HABITAT** Steppes, Ponderosa Pine forests. **RANGE** East of Cascade crest.

GOATSBEARD
Aruncus dioicus (sylvester)
ROSE FAMILY

5′. Bushy. Many minute, cream-white flowers in stringy, branched, 12″ clusters. Leaves bi- or tripinnately compound, with ovate, fine-toothed leaflets. **BLOOMS** May–July. **HABITAT** Lowland to low subalpine moist thickets. **RANGE** Cascades and west.

WOODLAND STRAWBERRY
Fragaria vesca
ROSE FAMILY

5″. Groundcover. Flowers ¾″, white to pinkish, with 5 rounded petals. Leaves divided into 3 elliptical toothed leaflets; on hairy stalks. Strawberries red, ½″; edible, delicious when ripe (June–July). **BLOOMS** May–June. **HABITAT** Lowland to mid-elev. clearings.

LARGE-LEAVED AVENS
Geum macrophyllum
ROSE FAMILY

24″. Hairy. Flowers ½″, yellow, saucer-shaped, with 5 petals, many stamens and pistils. Leaves 10″, pinnately compound, tipped with large, rounded-heart-shaped leaflet; other leaflets smaller, scattered. **BLOOMS** May–July. **HABITAT** Lowland to subalpine meadows, open forests.

PARTRIDGEFOOT
Luetkea pectinata
ROSE FAMILY

4″. Carpet-forming. Dense, round, ¾″ clusters of tiny cream-white flowers with many long stamens. Stems red, unbranched, somewhat woody, from runners. Leaves crowded, divided into 9 narrow lobes. **BLOOMS** July–Aug. **HABITAT** Subalpine and lower alpine meadows.

SILVERWEED
Potentilla (Argentina) anserina
ROSE FAMILY

7″. Silky-hairy creeper. Tip of each ascending stalk bears 1 saucer-shaped, yellow, ¾″ flower with 5 broad petals and many stamens and pistils. Leaves silky, pinnately compound, with elliptical toothed leaflets. **BLOOMS** May–July. **HABITAT** Wet meadows, streamsides. **RANGE** Mainly east of Cascades.

SLENDER CINQUEFOIL
Potentilla gracilis
ROSE FAMILY

18″. Spindly. Flowers ½″, yellow, with 5 petals, many stamens; in loose clusters. Leaves long-stalked, palmately compound, with 5–9 deeply toothed, elliptical leaflets, hairy on one or both sides. **BLOOMS** June–July. **HABITAT** Meadows, open forests. **RANGE** East of Cascade crest.

SOFT RUSH
"Common Rush"
Juncus effusus
RUSH FAMILY

24". Grass-like clumps of tubular pointed stems with spray-like, 4" clusters of green to deep brown flowers. Leaves are brown sheaths around stem bases. **BLOOMS** June–Aug. **HABITAT** Ditches, tidal flats, bogs; invasive in old wet pastures. **RANGE** Mainly west of Cascades.

ST.-JOHN'S-WORT
"Klamath Weed"
Hypericum perforatum
ST.-JOHN'S-WORT FAMILY

24". Flowers ¾", star-shaped, yellow, with 5 flat-spreading petals with black-speckled edges, very long stamens; in clusters at stem tips. Leaves lanceolate, black-speckled. Introduced; invasive. **BLOOMS** June–Aug. **HABITAT** Roadsides, dry fields.

TOLMIE'S SAXIFRAGE
Saxifraga tolmiei
SAXIFRAGE FAMILY

3". Mat-forming succulent. Each stem has 1–3 white ½" flowers with 5 petals and 10 red-tipped stamens. Leaves linear, thick. *Saxifraga* ("rock-breaker") refers to crevice habitat. **BLOOMS** July. **HABITAT** Alpine to subalpine wet gravels, crevices. **RANGE** Cascades, Olympics.

SLOUGH SEDGE
Carex obnupta
SEDGE FAMILY

4'. Grass-like, with tiny, dry, dark brown flowers in 5" drooping spikes. Stems triangular, clumping. Stems and leaves sharp-edged. **BLOOMS** Apr.–July. **HABITAT** Wooded or open wetlands, shorelines. **RANGE** West of Cascades.

TULE
"Hardstem Bulrush"
Scirpus acutus (lacustris)
SEDGE FAMILY

7'. Colony-forming. Thick, grass-like stems produce many brownish spikelets in loose sprays. Leaves are long sheaths around stem base. **BLOOMS** June–Aug. **HABITAT** Marshes, shallow lakes.

GIANT RED PAINTBRUSH
Castilleja miniata
SNAPDRAGON FAMILY

18". Usu. wooly. Flowers and brightly colored bracts form ragged scarlet "paintbrush" clusters. Leaves linear. This and other paintbrush species are partly parasitic, their roots connecting with those of other plants. **BLOOMS** May–July. **HABITAT** Clearings in foothills to mid-elevs.

SMALL-FLOWERED PAINTBRUSH
Castilleja parviflora
SNAPDRAGON FAMILY

9″. Dense clusters of magenta to crimson to white ¾″ flowers partly enclosed by bracts. Leaves arrowhead-shaped, 3- to 5-lobed. **BLOOMS** July–Aug. **HABITAT** Subalpine meadows. **RANGE** Olympics, Cascades from Three Sisters north.

FOXGLOVE
Digitalis purpurea
SNAPDRAGON FAMILY

4′. Fuzzy, patch-forming. Flowers 2″, tubular, white or purple, spotted inside, shallowly 5-lobed; nodding on tall, 1-sided spire. Leaves soft, ovate to lanceolate. **CAUTION** Poisonous. **BLOOMS** June–July. **HABITAT** Roadsides, clear-cuts, fields.

BUTTER-AND-EGGS
"Common Toadflax"
Linaria vulgaris
SNAPDRAGON FAMILY

20″. Dense spikes of 1″, pale yellow, 2-lipped flowers with deep yellow center and long straight rearward spur. Leaves linear. **BLOOMS** June–Sept. **HABITAT** Disturbed places.

COMMON MONKEYFLOWER
Mimulus guttatus
SNAPDRAGON FAMILY

16″. Flowers 2″, snapdragon-like, brilliant yellow, with hairy and usu. red-spotted throat. Leaves ovate, toothed. Variable in size, hairiness, branching. **BLOOMS** Mar.–Sept. **HABITAT** Seeps and streams from coast to mid-elevs.

PINK MONKEYFLOWER
Mimulus lewisii
SNAPDRAGON FAMILY

20″. Lush, sticky-hairy, clumping. Flowers 1½″, deep pink, with yellow throat; upper lip 2-lobed, lower lip 3-lobed. Leaves ovate to lanceolate. **BLOOMS** June–Aug. **HABITAT** Mid-elev. to subalpine streamsides.

BRACTED LOUSEWORT
"Wood Betony"
Pedicularis bracteosa
SNAPDRAGON FAMILY

20″. Dense tall spike of many ½″ beak-like flowers, usu. yellow (dark red in Olympics, purple on Mt. Adams). Leaves fern-like, pinnately compound, with lanceolate toothed leaflets. **BLOOMS** June–Aug. **HABITAT** Subalpine meadows, mid-elev. and subalpine forests.

ELEPHANT'S HEAD
Pedicularis groenlandica
SNAPDRAGON FAMILY

16″. Dense spike of many ¾″ pink flowers, each unmistakably shaped like an elephant's head with up-curved trunk. Leaves fern-like, pinnately lobed, toothed. **BLOOMS** July–Aug. **HABITAT** Wet subalpine meadows, bogs, shallow streams.

SHOWY PENSTEMON
Penstemon speciosus
SNAPDRAGON FAMILY

20″. Tall sparse spike of whorled, bright blue, tubular, wooly-throated, 1″ flowers; upper lip 2-lobed, lower lip 3-lobed. Leaves oblanceolate. **BLOOMS** May–July. **HABITAT** Open juniper or pine woodlands, sagebrush steppes.

WOOLY MULLEIN
Verbascum thapsus
SNAPDRAGON FAMILY

4′6″. Tall dense stalk of yellow, 5-lobed, ¾″ flowers. Leaves lanceolate, thick, gray-wooly; large (12″) at plant base, smaller up stem. **BLOOMS** June–Aug. **HABITAT** Roadsides, disturbed places. **RANGE** Mainly east of Cascades.

ALPINE SPEEDWELL
Veronica wormskjoldii
SNAPDRAGON FAMILY

5″. Flowers ½″, deep blue-violet, with 4 unequal lobes. Single stem. Leaves elliptical. **BLOOMS** July–Aug. **HABITAT** Alpine to subalpine wet areas.

SITKA VALERIAN
Valeriana sitchensis
VALERIAN FAMILY

2′6″. Round clusters of ½″, tubular, white flowers with 5 unequal lobes, 3 protruding stamens. Single stem. Leaves pinnately compound, with 3–7 toothed leaflets. Seeds have umbrella-shaped plumes. Young shoots red in July, rank-smelling in Aug. **BLOOMS** Aug. **HABITAT** Moist subalpine meadows, mtn. forests.

WESTERN BLUE VIOLET
Viola adunca
VIOLET FAMILY

3″. Flowers ½″, blue to violet, 5-petaled; lower 3 petals often white at base, lowest petal longest and with long, hooked, rearward spur. Leaves heart-shaped to ovate, finely hairy, scalloped. **BLOOMS** Apr.–July. **HABITAT** Dry to moist meadows and forests.

STREAM VIOLET
Viola glabella
VIOLET FAMILY

8″. Flowers ½″, yellow, 5-petaled; lower 3 petals purplish-lined, lowest petal longest and spurred. Multistemmed. Leaves heart-shaped with sharp tip, toothed. **BLOOMS** Apr.–July, soon after snowmelt. **HABITAT** Low forests to subalpine meadows.

SAGEBRUSH VIOLET
"Desert Pansy"
Viola trinervata
VIOLET FAMILY

4″. Flowers ½″, upper 2 petals deep red-violet, lower 3 paler, with bases streaked yellow to whitish. Multistemmed. Leaves fan-like, with usu. 5 leaflets, deeply narrow-lobed, bluish-coated, leathery. **BLOOMS** Mar.–May. **HABITAT** Sagebrush steppes. **RANGE** Columbia Plateau.

BALLHEAD WATERLEAF
Hydrophyllum capitatum
WATERLEAF FAMILY

7″. Flowers tiny, pale lavender, bell-shaped, 5-lobed, in fuzzy, globular, 1½″ clusters. Leaves few, pinnately compound, with 5–11 elliptical or deeply few-lobed leaflets. **BLOOMS** Mar.–July. **HABITAT** Lowland to mid-elev. open forests. **RANGE** East of Cascade crest.

SILKY PHACELIA
"Purple Fringe"
Phacelia sericea
WATERLEAF FAMILY

10″. Silvery. Fuzzy, dense, cylindrical clusters of tiny purple to deep blue flowers with very long, yellow-tipped stamens. Stems silky-hairy. Leaves deeply pinnately lobed. **BLOOMS** June–Aug. **HABITAT** Dry rocky mtn. sites.

YELLOW POND LILY
"Spatterdock"
Nuphar lutea (polysepalum)
WATER-LILY FAMILY

Flowers and leaves float on or emerge from water. Flowers 3½″, cup-shaped, yellow, with 5 thick, waxy, petal-like sepals around broad pistil and purplish stamens. Leaves massive (12″), heart-shaped. **BLOOMS** May–Aug. **HABITAT** Shallow lakes, ponds.

OREGON WOOD SORREL
Oxalis oregana
WOOD SORREL FAMILY

6″. Patch-forming. Flower solitary, 1″, 5-petaled, white to pink, usu. with fine red veins. Leaves divided into 3 heart-shaped leaflets; fold up in bright sun. Resembles Shamrock, its Irish relative. **BLOOMS** Apr.–June. **HABITAT** Moist forests to mid-elevs. **RANGE** Cascades and west.

Invertebrates

Biologists divide the animal kingdom into two broad groupings—vertebrates, animals with a backbone, and invertebrates, those without. While this distinction seems apt, perhaps because we are vertebrates ourselves, it is really one of mere convenience. Vertebrates are but a small subphylum of the animal kingdom, and invertebrates comprise the vast majority of animal life forms that inhabit water, air, and land. Invertebrates have thrived on earth for more than a billion years, with species evolving and disappearing through the eons; they include a fascinating spectrum of phyla with extraordinarily diverse life styles and evolutionary developments. This guide describes selected species from eight phyla found in marine, terrestrial, and freshwater environments:

Phylum Porifera	Sponges
Phylum Cnidaria	Hydrozoans, jellyfishes, sea pens, and sea anemones
Phylum Rhynchocoela	Unsegmented worms
Phylum Annelida	Segmented marine worms and earthworms
Phylum Mollusca	Chitons, gastropods, bivalves, and cephalopods
Phylum Arthropoda	Crustaceans, centipedes, millipedes, arachnids, and insects
Phylum Echinodermata	Sea stars, sea urchins, and sea cucumbers
Phylum Chordata	Tunicates (vertebrates belong to this phylum)

There are two basic invertebrate body structures. *Radially symmetrical* invertebrates like sea stars have a circular body plan with a central mouth cavity and a nervous system encircling the mouth. *Bilateral* invertebrates have virtually identical left and right sides like vertebrates, with paired nerve cords that run along the belly, not the back, and a brain (in species with a head). All invertebrates are cold-blooded, and become dormant or die in extreme temperatures.

In this guide, marine invertebrates are covered first, followed by freshwater and land invertebrates. Many of the groups covered below are described in more detail in separate introductions.

Plant or Animal?

Some marine invertebrates, such as sponges and sea anemones, are often mistaken for plants, but several key features place them in the animal kingdom. Plant cell walls, made of cellulose, are thick and strong, while those of animals are thin and weak. Plants have no nervous system, and therefore react slowly; almost all animals have a nervous system and can react quickly. Through the process called photosynthesis, most plants manufacture their own food from inorganic raw materials, while animals obtain energy by ingesting and metabolizing plants and/or other animals. Plants grow throughout their lives, while most animals stop growing at maturity (a few types, such as fish and snakes, keep growing but at a very slow rate). Finally, most plants are sedentary, while most animals move about. A sponge or sea anemone may be as immobile as a seaweed, but it qualifies as an animal on the basis of the above and other characteristics, such as the nature of its reproductive organs and its developmental pattern.

Marine Invertebrates

Northwest marine environments are home to a wide variety of clinging, digging, swimming, and scuttling invertebrates. This text covers representatives of classes from eight invertebrate phyla. Members of other invertebrate marine phyla are generally small or difficult to see.

The colorful and diverse sponges of the phylum Porifera are the simplest of multicellular creatures; they lack body organs and a mouth, and filter water through pores to obtain food and oxygen. Sponges are mainly sedentary; they vary in size from tiny cups to wide encrustations. In the phylum Cnidaria are the gelatinous sea anemones, jellyfishes, and hydrozoans. All are radially symmetrical; most possess tentacles armed with stinging cells that ensnare and paralyze tiny animals. Most Northwest species are harmless to humans, although some, like the Lion's Mane, can be extremely dangerous. Unsegmented worms of the phylum Rhynchocoela are generally slender, flattened, and brightly colored. They are quite elastic, capable of stretching to many times their relaxed body length. The phylum Annelida, or segmented worms, is divided into four classes. We cover the bristle worms of the class Polychaeta, which are either sedentary (living in a tube) or mobile. These worms have visible external segments covered with bundles of bristles that aid them in swimming, crawling, or digging; they are found in a wide range of habitats, from intertidal to abyssal depths. The phylum Mollusca, which includes many of the most familiar marine invertebrates, is discussed on page 172. Species of the phylum Arthropoda usually are identified by their rigid exoskeleton and jointed legs. Of the five marine arthropod classes, the most common is Crustacea. Crustaceans, including barnacles, shrimps, crabs, and lobsters, live chiefly in sunlit shallower waters. Their forms are so diverse that their single common characteristic is paired antennae. Crabs are discussed on page 180. Animals of the phylum Echinodermata, discussed on page 182, include sea stars, brittle stars, sea urchins, and sea cucumbers. Non-vertebrate species of the phylum Chordata are mostly small sedentary filter-feeders as adults, with free-swimming larvae.

The following accounts give typical adult lengths or heights, unless otherwise noted. Many species can survive in a wide range of water depths, which are noted in the accounts; the term *intertidal zone* refers to the area between the high- and low-tide lines.

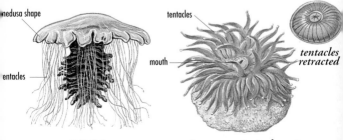

Jellyfish

Anemone, *tentacles out*

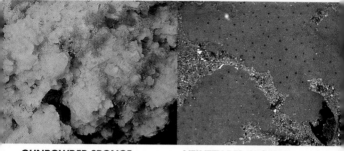

GUNPOWDER SPONGE
"Bowerbank's Crumb-of-bread Sponge"
Halichondria bowerbanki
SILICEOUS AND HORNY SPONGE CLASS
W 25". Body wide, thin, encrusting; tan, yellow, or greenish. Surface irregular, covered with volcano-like pores and needle-like ridges. Has strong gunpowder odor. **HABITAT** Low-tide line to 200' deep; on stones, wharves, pilings.

VELVETY RED SPONGE
Ophlitaspongia pennata
SILICEOUS AND HORNY SPONGE CLASS
W 25". Body flat, velvety, encrusting; bright coral red. Densely covered with small, star-like pores. **HABITAT** High-tide line to 10' deep; on rocks, in crevices. **RANGE** Puget Sound and south.

TUBULARIAN HYDROIDS
Tubularia species
HYDROZOAN CLASS
4". Body flower-like, with clusters of long, sparsely branched stems; pale brown. Stem heads have 2 whorls of pink feeding tentacles, 1 at base, 1 at top; feeds on plankton. Colonial. **HABITAT** Shallow water; on pilings, floats, boat bottoms.

MANY-RIBBED HYDROMEDUSA
Aequorea aequorea
HYDROZOAN CLASS
W 3". Body saucer-shaped, jelly-like, transparent; luminescent at night. 25–100 vertical radial canals, tinged bluish white (male) or rosy (female). Short feeding tentacles fringe outer edge. Washed ashore by storms. **HABITAT** Open ocean, along coast; floats at or below surface.

BY-THE-WIND SAILOR
Velella velella
HYDROZOAN CLASS
3". Body flat, oval, with gas-filled pockets; transparent blue. Triangular crest above acts as sail. Many blue stinging tentacles around rim, harmless to humans. Sometimes washed ashore in tremendous numbers. **HABITAT** Open ocean surface; warm waters. **RANGE** Outer coast.

OSTRICH PLUME HYDROID
Aglaophenia struthionides
HYDROZOAN CLASS

5″. Body feather-like; white, yellow, tan, or reddish. Branched plumes on jointed, flexible stems grow in clusters from creeping tube. Colonial. Washed ashore by storms. **HABITAT** Low-tide line to 525′ deep; on rocks, shells, seaweeds.

LION'S MANE
Cyanea capillata
JELLYFISH CLASS

W 20″. Body a smooth, saucer-shaped, yellowish-orange to reddish-brown bell. 150 long yellowish tentacles. World's largest jellyfish; can grow to 8′ wide, with tentacles to 60′ long in Arctic. **CAUTION** Highly toxic; causes severe burns, blisters; can be fatal. **HABITAT** Ocean surface.

MOON JELLYFISH
Aurelia aurita
JELLYFISH CLASS

W 16″. Body saucer-shaped, whitish, translucent. Many short, fringe-like tentacles. 4 round or horseshoe-shaped gonads near center: yellow, pink, or bluish (adults); white (imm.). Often washes ashore. **CAUTION** Causes mild rash. **HABITAT** Inshore ocean surface, large harbors.

GURNEY'S SEA PEN
Ptilosarcus gurneyi
CORAL AND SEA ANEMONE CLASS

14″. Body stout, plume-like; translucent orange, yellow, or tan. Base swollen; midrib has 15–30 leaf-like disks. Can retract quickly into tube in mud; emits greenish light when disturbed. Colonial. **HABITAT** Low-tide line to 100′ deep; soft, muddy bottoms.

ROSE ANEMONE
"Northern Red Anemone"
"Christmas Anemone"
Urticina crassicornis
CORAL AND SEA ANEMONE CLASS

7″. Body columnar, red, often green spotted. 100 thick, red, retractable tentacles around mouth; used to stun small fish. **HABITAT** Intertidal zone to 100′ deep; anchors to rocks; hangs limply at low tide.

AGGREGATING ANEMONE
Anthopleura elegantissima
CORAL AND SEA ANEMONE CLASS
8″ (solitary); 2″ (in colonies). Body cylindrical, thick; pale green or olive. About 100 tentacles around mouth; gray with pink, lavender, or blue tips. Often covered with sand, shells. Asexually reproduces to form aggregate colony. **HABITAT** Intertidal zone; in tidepools on rocks.

GIANT GREEN ANEMONE
Anthopleura xanthogrammica
CORAL AND SEA ANEMONE CLASS
6″. Body cylindrical, greenish brown. Many stubby, tapered, gray-green to bluish-white tentacles in 6 or more rings around yellow-brown mouth. Adhesive projections on column hold shell pieces, debris. Solitary. **HABITAT** Intertidal zone to 15′ deep.

FRILLED ANEMONE
"Plumose Anemone"
Metridium senile
CORAL AND SEA ANEMONE CLASS
10″. Body cylindrical, smooth; reddish brown to olive or lighter. Several white lobes around mouth, each with 100s of small pale tentacles giving "frilled" appearance. **HABITAT** Low-tide line to 50′ deep; on rocks, pilings.

POLYMORPHIC RIBBON WORM
Tubulanus polymorphus
RIBBON WORM CLASS
3′. Body slender, flattened, flexible, unsegmented; pencil-size when contracted. Bright red or orange-yellow. Head broad, rounded. Everts proboscis to capture prey at night. **HABITAT** Intertidal zone to 25′ deep; on rocky shores.

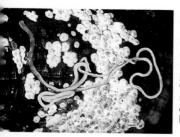

MUSSELBED RIBBON WORM
Emplectonema gracile
RIBBON WORM CLASS
3″. Body rounded, slender, unsegmented; above dark green, below pale yellow. Head small, colorless. Clusters together by day; feeds at night on barnacles, worms, snail eggs. **HABITAT** Rocky shores; among barnacles, in mussel beds.

EIGHTEEN-SCALED WORM
Halosydna brevisetosa
POLYCHAETE WORM CLASS
2″. Body thick, somewhat flattened; dull brown or gray. 18 pairs of oval scales on back, each with pale dot. Legs small, paired. Very aggressive. **HABITAT** Intertidal zone to 1,450′ deep; among mussels and algae, on rocks and pilings.

MUSSEL WORM
Nereis vexillosa
POLYCHAETE WORM CLASS
6″. Body long, flattened; gray with iridescent green and blue. More than 100 segments, each with 2 paddle-like legs. Black pincer-like jaws. Feeds on algae. Swims near surface to breed. **CAUTION** Bites. **HABITAT** Shallow bays; in mussel beds, under rocks and wood.

GIANT FEATHER DUSTERS
Eudistylia species
POLYCHAETE WORM CLASS
10″. Body cylindrical, somewhat flattened, tapered toward rear; tan. At head end, large whorl of retractable, feather-like, brown, orange, reddish, or maroon gills. Sedentary; lives in sturdy papery tube. **HABITAT** Low-tide line to 1,400′ deep; on rocks, pilings.

RED TUBE WORM
Serpula vermicularis
POLYCHAETE WORM CLASS
4″. Tube slender, sinuous, with funnel-shaped lid; tapers toward rear; pink. Pale pink or reddish worm inside has plume of 40 pairs of red or orange, white-banded gills. **HABITAT** Low-tide line to 300′ deep; rocks, pilings, tidepools.

LUGWORM
Abarenicola pacifica
POLYCHAETE WORM CLASS
12″. Body elongated, tapered at both ends; yellow, green, or brown. Midsection has side bristles. Burrows head-first; swallows mud and sand, extracting organic matter. Fecal castings form spirals on sand. **HABITAT** Near low-tide line to 15′ deep; muddy sand in shallow bays.

Marine Mollusks

Mollusks, of the phylum Mollusca, are amazingly numerous and diverse. Northwest species range in size from the near-microscopic to the Giant Pacific Octopus, which grows to 10 feet long. Worldwide, seven classes of mollusks inhabit land, freshwater, and marine environments; four are commonly found in inshore marine waters of the Pacific Northwest.

Chitons have eight-valved shells held together by a tough outer membrane (the girdle); they crawl about on rocks and pilings, scraping up algae. Gastropods, including snails, usually have a single calcium-carbonate shell whorled to the right, from which protrudes the fleshy foot; the nudibranchs (sea slugs) are shell-less. Gastropods feed on marine plants and animals, scraping up food as they crawl or swim about. Bivalves, which include clams and oysters, have two separate shells called valves; two siphons and a muscular foot protrude. Mollusks filter-feed on tiny plants and animals. Most bivalves attach to a hard substrate or burrow into sand, mud, or wood; some species, such as scallops, can also swim. Cephalopods, the most advanced mollusks, include the squids, which have a thin internal shell-like structure, and octopuses, which are shell-less. All have highly developed eyes and long tentacled arms. They move by swimming and water propulsion, and feed by grabbing and eating, with parrot-beak-like mouths, crabs, fish, and other mollusks.

Gastropods and bivalves can be easily observed at most coastal locations. Chitons are harder to see, as they reside under rocks and inside dead whelk shells. Cephalopods are generally found only in subtidal waters. The Northwest's inshore molluscan habitats include sand- and mudflats, coastal rocks, tidepools, and wooden structures, like piers and pilings. When exploring, remember to think small—many species are less than 1 inch at maturity. Rocky tidepools are home to chitons, periwinkles, dogwinkles, and mussels; shallow flats support snails, whelks, scallops, and oysters; wooden pilings harbor colorful nudibranchs within their algae and hydroid colonies. Very high tides and storms often bring up shells of unusual deepwater species.

Recreational shellfishing is tightly regulated in the Northwest, and most towns require a license. Environmental and seasonal conditions sometimes make local shellfish populations unsafe to eat, so always check with authorities before harvesting.

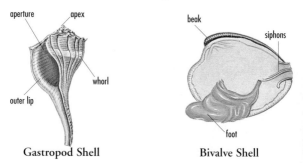

Gastropod Shell   **Bivalve Shell**

LINED CHITON
Tonicella lineata
CHITON CLASS

2″. Body oval, domed; red, blue, brown, black, or whitish. Shells shiny, with light wavy lines. Girdle thin, smooth, fringed. Clings to rocks by day; feeds on algae at night. HABITAT Low-tide line to 180′ deep; algae-covered rocks.

GUM BOOT CHITON
"Giant Chiton"
Cryptochiton stelleri
CHITON CLASS

10″. Body oblong, somewhat flattened; brick red to reddish brown. Girdle leathery, gritty, with blunt spines; completely covers shells. Rolls into ball when handled. World's largest chiton. HABITAT Low-tide line to 70′ deep; on rocks, in kelp beds.

MOSSY CHITON
Mopalia muscosa
CHITON CLASS

2″. Body an elongated oval. Shells dark gray to greenish brown. Girdle has yellow-brown bristles, giving mossy appearance. Often covered with algae, worm tubes. Nocturnal; returns to same rock after foraging. HABITAT Intertidal zone; exposed rocks, estuaries.

NORTHERN ABALONE
"Japanese Abalone"
"Pinto Abalone"
Haliotis kamtschatkana
GASTROPOD CLASS

5″. Shell oval, domed, thin; often corrugated. Reddish blue or brown; inside pearly white. 4–6 open holes near outer edge. Scrapes algae off rocks. Edible. HABITAT Shallow water to 50′ deep; on rocks.

FINGERED LIMPET
Collisella digitalis
GASTROPOD CLASS

1¼″. Shell oval from above, slightly conical; coarse radiating ribs form wavy edge; apex off-center. Brown to olive green, with many white lines and spots. Feeds on algae. HABITAT Intertidal zone; on rocks.

BLUE TOP SNAIL
Calliostoma ligatum
GASTROPOD CLASS

¾". Shell conical, with 3 wide convex whorls; apex bluntly pointed; base almost flat. Brown with fine, buffy bands. Opening round. Worn shells show pearly blue wash. **HABITAT** Intertidal zone; under rocks, among algae.

BLACK TURBAN SNAIL
Tegula funebralis
GASTROPOD CLASS

1". Shell triangular from side, thick, with 4 low whorls; apex bluntly pointed, often worn and white; base flat. Purplish black; white near round opening. Feeds on algae; clusters in crevices at low tide. **HABITAT** Intertidal zone; on rocks.

CHECKERED PERIWINKLE
Littorina scutulata
GASTROPOD CLASS

½". Shell moderately conical, sturdy, smooth, shiny, with 4 convex whorls; apex sharp. Reddish brown or slaty, with irregular whitish checkered spots; inside purplish brown. Clusters in crevices at low tide. **HABITAT** Intertidal zone; rocky shores.

LEWIS'S MOON SNAIL
Polinices lewisii
GASTROPOD CLASS

4". Shell round, thick, finely grooved; 3 whorls, 1st very large; apex blunt. Pale yellow; inside brown. Inner lip of opening straight. Fleshy foot can entirely cover shell. Drills into clamshells to feed. **HABITAT** Intertidal zone to 600' deep; sandy bottoms.

OREGON HAIRY TRITON
Fusitriton oregonensis
GASTROPOD CLASS

4". Shell spindle-shaped, elongated, covered with rows of dark brown bristles; 6 convex whorls with concentric and vertical ridges. Gray-brown to reddish brown; inside white. Canal short; opening oval. Feeds on urchins, barnacles. **HABITAT** Low-tide line to 400' deep; rocky bottoms.

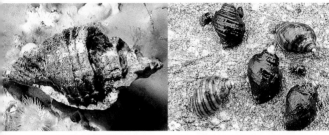

LEAFY HORNMOUTH
Ceratostoma foliatum
GASTROPOD CLASS

3″. Shell spindle-shaped, with 3 irregular vertical ridges; spire high. White, buff, or yellow-brown, sometimes banded dark brown. Opening small, oval; canal a sealed, twisted tube. Feeds on mollusks. **HABITAT** Low-tide line to 200′ deep; on rocks.

EMARGINATE DOGWINKLE
Nucella (Thais) emarginata
GASTROPOD CLASS

1″. Shell plump; 4–5 whorls with many rounded bumps; spire conical. White, buff, brown, or gray, sometimes with double bands of dark brown or orange. Opening wide, covered by brown lid; lips flared; canal short. **HABITAT** Intertidal zone; on rocks, among mussels, barnacles.

FRILLED DOGWINKLE
Nucella (Thais) lamellosa
GASTROPOD CLASS

2″. Shell spindle-shaped, with wavy vertical ridges, lower horizontal ridges; 3–4 indented whorls; spire conical. White or brown; some buffy with orange bands. Opening oval; canal fairly long, open. **HABITAT** Intertidal zone; on rocks, among barnacles.

FALSE SEA LEMON
"Monterey Doris"
Archidoris montereyensis
GASTROPOD CLASS

2″. Body oval; yellow, yellow-orange, or brownish. Covered with 100s of brown to black cone-shaped projections. Tentacles short, thick, comb-like. Feather-like yellowish gills surround anus. Feeds on sponges. **HABITAT** Low-tide line to 160′ deep; rocky areas.

ORANGE-TIPPED NUDIBRANCH
"Sea Clown Nudibranch"
Triopha catalinae
GASTROPOD CLASS

3″. Body nearly cylindrical, pointed at rear; translucent white or pale yellow. Scattered rounded projections, comb-like tentacles, 5 feathery gills all tipped bright orange. **HABITAT** Low-tide line to 110′ deep; tide-pools, kelp beds, rocky bottoms.

MANED NUDIBRANCH
"Shag-rug Nudibranch"
Aeolidia papillosa
GASTROPOD CLASS

3". Body oval; white, gray, or pale orange. 100s of pointed, nonrigid projections, with bare area down midline. Head square, with 4 thick tentacles. Feeds on sea anemones. **HABITAT** Low-tide line to 2,200' deep; rocks, pilings, mudflats.

OPALESCENT NUDIBRANCH
"Hermissenda Nudibranch"
Hermissenda (Phidiana) crassicornis
GASTROPOD CLASS

2". Body tapered at rear; pale bluish white with neon blue edges, yellow midline stripe. Many variably colored white-tipped projections. 4 tentacles, 1st pair widely spaced. Feeds on hydroids, sea anemones, from which stinging cells (nematocysts) pass to nudibranch's own projections for its defense. **HABITAT** Low-tide line to 110' deep; rocks, pilings, mudflats, tidepools.

RINGED NUDIBRANCH
Diaulula sandiegensis
GASTROPOD CLASS

3½". Body oval, flattened; creamy white to light gray, with few black or brown spots and open circles. Tentacles short, comb-like. Back gritty (but looks velvety). Gills on sides near rear. **HABITAT** Low-tide line to 110' deep; rocky shores.

PACIFIC PINK SCALLOP
Chlamys hastata
BIVALVE CLASS

2½". Shell nearly round, convex; 20 radiating ribs with tiny spines. Pale orange, pink, or purple, with darker rays and concentric rings. Many tiny stalked eyes along margin. Edible. **HABITAT** Intertidal zone to 500' deep; rock, sand, mud bottoms.

EDIBLE MUSSEL
"Blue Mussel" "Bay Mussel"
Mytilus edulis
BIVALVE CLASS

2". Shell thin, shiny; front beaked, rear rounded. Brown, blue-black, or black. Attaches to objects with bundles of hair-like threads (byssus); forms dense colonies. Edible. **HABITAT** Intertidal zone, estuaries; on rocks, pilings.

CALIFORNIA MUSSEL
Mytilus californianus
BIVALVE CLASS

5″. Shell teardrop-shaped, with several strong concentric grooves, weak radial lines. Brown, often eroded to dark purple-black. Attaches to rocks with strong, hair-like threads (byssus); occurs in large "beds." Edible. **CAUTION** Can be toxic May–Oct. **HABITAT** High-tide line to 80′ deep; on rocks, pilings of exposed coasts.

GIANT PACIFIC OYSTER
Crassostrea gigas
BIVALVE CLASS

8″. Shell irregularly triangular to almost rectangular; surface rough, with few strong radial ridges. Gray-white, sometimes with purplish streaks; inside white. Cements to solid objects. Edible. **HABITAT** Near low-tide line in bays, mudflats; on rocks, shells. **Native Pacific Oyster** *(Ostrea lurida),* 3″, lacks radial ridges; both are used in Puget Sound's mariculture industry.

HEART COCKLE
Clinocardium nuttallii
BIVALVE CLASS

3½″. Shell plump, almost round, with scalloped margin and about 35 radiating ribs. Grayish, mottled with brown or yellowish orange. Foot bright yellow, extensible, can flip shell. **HABITAT** Low-tide line to 600′ deep; soft bottoms of bays, estuaries.

PACIFIC LITTLENECK CLAM
Protothaca staminea
BIVALVE CLASS

2″. Shell oval, plump, with many fine radial ribs, fewer depressed concentric bands. Whitish to tan. Edible; a popular seafood; easily dug from burrow 1–3″ below surface. **HABITAT** Shallow water in bays, estuaries; sand or mud bottoms.

PACIFIC RAZOR CLAM
Siliqua patula
BIVALVE CLASS

5″. Shell a thin, flattish, elongated oval. Grayish white with thin brown "skin," dark concentric rings; inside whitish, tinged with purple. No permanent burrow; moves about in surf-pounded sand. Can quickly burrow to 12″. Edible; overharvested; only shells over 4½″ may be taken. **HABITAT** Intertidal zone; sandy open beaches.

GEODUCK
Panopea generosa
BIVALVE CLASS

8″. Shell oblong; front rounded, rear squarish; coarse, with raised concentric rings. Pale yellow to white, with yellow-brown "skin." Neck long, dark, not retractable. Burrows 2–4′ in sand, mud bottoms. Pronounced *Gooeyduck*. Largest N. Amer. bivalve; weighs up to 8 lb. Edible. **HABITAT** Intertidal zone to 50′ deep; protected bays.

SOFT-SHELLED CLAM
Mya arenaria
BIVALVE CLASS

3″. Shell thin, oval, rounded in front. Whitish, with fine concentric rings. Siphons fused into long neck, yellow at base. Shoots up jets of water at low tide. Burrows 8″ into sand, mud bottoms. Edible. **HABITAT** Intertidal zone to 30′ deep; also in brackish water.

OPALESCENT SQUID
Loligo opalescens
CEPHALOPOD CLASS

8″. Body cylindrical, tapered toward rear; whitish, mottled gold, brown, or red (color changeable). Head has 2 large blue eyes, 8 arms ½ body length, 2 tentacles ⅔ body length. Triangular fin on each side at rear. Edible; accounts for most squid sold. **HABITAT** Ocean surface to bottom; coastal waters.

GIANT PACIFIC OCTOPUS
Octopus dofleini
CEPHALOPOD CLASS

10′ (incl. arms). Body globe-shaped; skin very wrinkled; reddish brown with fine black lines (color changeable). 8 arms, each with 2 alternating rows of white suckers. Head broad with 2 high eyes. Feeds on shellfish, shrimp, crabs, fish. Edible. Fished commercially; largest recorded size 16′, 600 lb. **HABITAT** Intertidal zone to 1,650′ deep; rocky tidepools.

PACIFIC GOOSE BARNACLE
Mitella (Pollicipes) polymerus
CRUSTACEAN CLASS

3″. Body cylindrical, stalked; 6 large white plates, with many smaller plates near base. Stalk thick, tough, grayish, with fine spines. 6 pairs of feather-like feeding appendages extend through gape between plates. HABITAT Intertidal zone of outer coast; on rocks.

DALL'S ACORN BARNACLE
Chthamalus dalli
CRUSTACEAN CLASS

¼″. Body conical; 6 grayish-white plates on sides form cross on top when closed; 2 plates in center with gape between. Lacy feeding appendages extend through gape at high tide. Forms encrusting masses. HABITAT Near high-tide line; rocky shores, pilings.

GIANT ACORN BARNACLE
Balanus nubilis
CRUSTACEAN CLASS

3″. Conical; resembles a tiny volcanic crater; often encrusted. 6 whitish overlapping plates on sides; 4 central plates with gape between. Filter-feeds for plankton with feather-like appendages. HABITAT Low-tide line to 300′ deep; on rocks, pilings, hard-shelled invertebrates.

CALIFORNIA BEACH FLEA
Megalorchestia (Orchestoidea) californiana
CRUSTACEAN CLASS

1″. Body arched, stout, elongated; white. Head has 2 pairs antennae; 2nd pair rose-red, longer than body. 14 legs. Nocturnal; masses on beach above waves; eats washed-up seaweeds. HABITAT High-tide line and above; open sandy beaches.

DOCK SHRIMP
"Coon-stripe Shrimp"
Pandalus danae
CRUSTACEAN CLASS

4″. Body tapers to small "tail fan"; pale red or olive, with blue stripes, white spots. Head has forward-pointing appendages, long antennae. 8 brown and white legs. Edible. HABITAT Low-tide line to 600′ deep; bays, estuaries, Eelgrass beds.

BAY GHOST SHRIMP
Callianassa californiensis
CRUSTACEAN CLASS

4". Body elongated; pale, translucent orange. Abdomen 3 times carapace length. Pincers unequal, one of male's very large. Shares deep burrow with small fish, invertebrates. Feeds on organic waste, plankton. **HABITAT** Intertidal zone; bays, estuaries.

Crabs

Crabs, of the order Decapoda, fall into two categories: short-tailed decapods, or true crabs, and long-tailed decapods. As the name implies, all have ten legs. True crabs have a large cephalothorax, or fore-body, and a small abdomen tucked beneath their shells. They can move well in all directions, but usually walk sideways. Most species are scavengers, although some feed on living animals. Long-tailed decapods, such as lobsters and hermit crabs, are named for their elongated abdomens, or "tails." Hermit crabs have soft abdomens that they protect by hiding in empty gastropod shells. They are fascinating to observe as they carry their homes about, switching shells as they grow or as their domestic tastes change. Take care when handling crabs; some are aggressive and all can pinch. Measurements in accounts are of the carapace, the shell part that extends over the crab's head and thorax.

Parts of a Crab

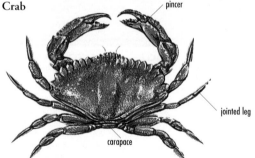

pincer

jointed leg

carapace

FLAT PORCELAIN CRAB
Petrolisthes cinctipes
CRUSTACEAN CLASS

1". Carapace flat, round; dark reddish brown or blue. Pincers large, equal; legs tipped white. Antennae long, angled backward. **HABITAT** Intertidal zone; among mussel beds, sponges, under rocks.

BLUE-HANDED HERMIT CRAB
Pagurus samuelis
CRUSTACEAN CLASS

1½". Body pear-shaped; olive-brown. Pincers unequal, with pale blue tips. Legs banded bright blue. Prefers Black Turban Snail shell, leaving only to switch to larger one. **HABITAT** Intertidal zone; rocky shores.

DUNGENESS CRAB
Cancer magister
CRUSTACEAN CLASS

8". Carapace fan-shaped; above dark gray-brown, below creamy. Pincers stout; walking legs short. Molts in shallow water; molted skeletons often wash ashore. Edible; important commercially. **HABITAT** Low-tide line to 300′ deep; sandy bottoms.

RED CRAB
Cancer productus
CRUSTACEAN CLASS

5". Carapace fan-shaped; above brick red, below yellowish white; imm. white, brown, blue, red, or orange, solid or patterned. Pincers stout; walking legs short. **HABITAT** Low-tide line to 260′ deep; sandy bottoms, among rocks in tidepools, bays, estuaries.

PURPLE SHORE CRAB
Hemigrapsus nudus
CRUSTACEAN CLASS

1½". Carapace round; above purplish black, sometimes mottled with reddish brown or greenish yellow; below white. Pincers paler with dark spots; walking legs flattened. Easily seen in intertidal zone. **HABITAT** Open rocky shores, bays, estuaries, among seaweeds.

SHIELD-BACKED KELP CRAB
Pugettia producta
CRUSTACEAN CLASS

3". Carapace shield-shaped, smooth; reddish, olive, or olive-brown (blending with kelp color); below paler. Pincers small; legs thin. Head spiny, projecting. Eats kelp; carnivorous in winter when kelp dies. **HABITAT** Low-tide line to 240′ deep; kelp beds.

Echinoderms

In the Northwest, the phylum Echinodermata is represented by sea stars, sea urchins, and sea cucumbers. *Echinoderm* means "spiny skin," and all species in this phylum are covered with spines or bumps of varying lengths. They are radially symmetrical and possess a unique water vascular system consisting of internal canals that pump fluids through the body. These canals end on the undersurface in tube feet, slender appendages that expand and contract to allow the animal to move and feed. Sea stars, named for their starlike shape, have varying numbers of arms radiating from a central disk; they feed mainly on mollusks and other echinoderms. Sea urchins, including sand dollars, feed on plankton, algae, and tiny organic particles in sand. The spines of the elongated sea cucumbers are actually embedded in the skin, which is outwardly smooth; these animals feed almost exclusively on plankton. Measurements given are diameters, including arms and spines, unless otherwise noted.

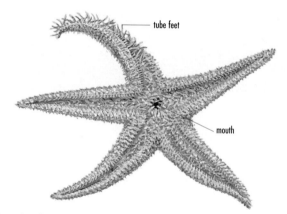

Underside of a Sea Star

ORANGE SUN STAR
"Stimpson's Sun Star"
Solaster stimpsoni
SEA STAR CLASS
8″. Disk fairly small; 9–11 slender pointed arms. Orange; sometimes red, rose, yellow, green, or blue. Blue-gray spot in center with radiating stripe on each arm. **HABITAT** Low-tide line to 200′ deep; rocky and sandy bottoms.

SUNFLOWER STAR
Pycnopodia helianthoides
SEA STAR CLASS

24". Disk convex, broad; up to 24 arms. Purple, red, pink, brown, orange, or yellow. Soft, flexible, with tiny spines, gills. Largest, fastest sea star on Pacific coast. **HABITAT** Low-tide line to 1,400' deep; rocky shores, soft bottoms.

SPINY SUN STAR
"Rose Star"
Crossaster papposus (roseus)
SEA STAR CLASS

11". Disk large, sunflower-like; 8–14 arms. Rosy, orange, or red, with concentric yellow, pink, or white bands. Covered with brush-like spines. **HABITAT** Low-tide line to 1,000' deep; rocky bottoms. **RANGE** South to Puget Sound.

PACIFIC BLOOD STAR
"Pacific Henricia"
Henricia leviuscula
SEA STAR CLASS

5". Disk very small; 5 long, slender, cylindrical arms. Red or orange with tiny pale spots. Covered with tiny blunt spines. **HABITAT** Low-tide line to 1,300' deep; on algae-covered rocks, sponges.

EQUAL SEA STAR
"Red Sea Star"
Mediaster aequalis
SEA STAR CLASS

5". Disk broad, flattened; 5 tapering slender arms, edged with plates. Red or orange. Covered with rosettes of blunt spines. Smells like gunpowder. **HABITAT** Low-tide line to 200' deep; rocky bottoms.

LEATHER STAR
Dermasterias imbricata
SEA STAR CLASS

8". Disk broad, high, leathery; 5 wide arms. Blue-gray with red or orange spots. Smells of sulfur or garlic. Feeds on sea anemones, sea cucumbers, sponges. **HABITAT** Low-tide line to 300' deep; rocky shores, pilings, seawalls.

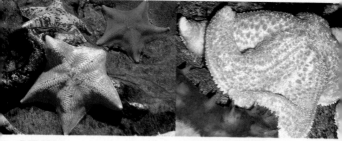

BAT STAR
Patiria miniata
SEA STAR CLASS

6″. Disk almost flat, not well demarcated; 5 short triangular arms. Red-orange; sometimes white, yellow, brown, purple, or mottled. Abundant in intertidal zone. **HABITAT** Intertidal zone to 960′ deep; rocks, sand bottoms, kelp forests, surfgrass.

SHORT-SPINED SEA STAR
Pisaster brevispinus
SEA STAR CLASS

16″. Disk medium-size; 5 thick arms. Pink or purplish; sometimes red, orange, brown, or tan. Spines large, rounded, blue with white tips. Feeds on clams, snails, dead fish. **HABITAT** Low-tide line to 300′ deep; rocky shores and bottoms.

OCHRE SEA STAR
Pisaster ochraceus
SEA STAR CLASS

12″. Disk fairly large; 5 stout tapering arms. Yellow, orange, brown, reddish, or purple. Tiny white spines form network on arms, star on disk. Feeds on mussels, barnacles, snails, limpets, chitons; most prey can detect sea star's scent and close up or escape. A keystone species; controls diversity and abundance of some

invertebrates in intertidal zone. Tolerant of air; often exposed up to 6 hours at low tide. **HABITAT** Above low-tide line; wave-washed rocky shores, pilings.

DAISY BRITTLE STAR
Ophiopholis aculeata
SEA STAR CLASS

8″. Disk small (¾″), flat, often spiny, with scalloped edges; 5 flexible slender arms edged with spines. Color very variable, arms with lighter and darker bands. **HABITAT** Low-tide line to 5,400′ deep; hides under rocks, among bases of kelps.

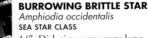

BURROWING BRITTLE STAR
Amphiodia occidentalis
SEA STAR CLASS
14″. Disk tiny; arms very long, slender, flexible, edged with spines. Gray or olive, often mottled; black dot at base of each arm. A fast burrower. **HABITAT** Low-tide line to 1,200′ deep; muddy sand, seagrass beds, under rocks in quiet bays.

DWARF BRITTLE STAR
*Amphipholis (Axiognathus)
squamata*
SEA STAR CLASS
2″. Disk tiny; 5 long, slender, flexible arms edged with spines. Gray, pale orange, tan, or lavender, with white spots on disk at base of arms. Emits light at night. **HABITAT** Intertidal zone to 2,700′ deep; crevices, sand, gravel, tidepools, under rocks.

GREEN SEA URCHIN
Strongylocentrotus droebachiensis
SEA URCHIN CLASS
3″. Body oval, with 100s of 1″ greenish spines. Spineless brownish-green bodies washed ashore show 10 ridged plates. Roe edible. **CAUTION** Spines pierce skin. **HABITAT** Low-tide line to 3,800′ deep; rocky shores, kelp beds, bays. **RANGE** South to Puget Sound.

PURPLE SEA URCHIN
Strongylocentrotus purpuratus
SEA URCHIN CLASS
3″. Body oval; domed above, flat below; covered with 2″ bright purple spines (imm. greenish). Feeds on red and brown algae. **HABITAT** Low-tide line to 525′ deep; rocky shores with moderate surf.

RED SEA URCHIN
Strongylocentrotus franciscanus
SEA URCHIN CLASS
5″. Body oval; domed above, flat below; covered with red, red-brown, or purple spines of varying lengths, some to 3″. Feeds on kelp. Ovaries a delicacy in Asia. **HABITAT** Low-tide line to 300′ deep; rocky shores.

ECCENTRIC SAND DOLLAR
Dendraster excentricus
SEA URCHIN CLASS

3". Circular, slightly convex, with tiny spines. Purplish-black; occ. gray or reddish brown; white when washed ashore. 5 petal-shaped loops radiate from center. Form dense beds. Traps plankton in mucus on surface. **HABITAT** Low-tide line to 130' deep in bays, coasts; sandy bottoms.

CALIFORNIA SEA CUCUMBER
Parastichopus californicus
SEA CUCUMBER CLASS

12". Body cucumber-shaped; brown or red; scattered pale orange or yellow conical projections with red tips. Moves like an inchworm, sifting nutrients from mud with tentacles around mouth. **HABITAT** Low-tide line to 300' deep; protected areas.

RED SEA CUCUMBER
Cucumaria miniata
SEA CUCUMBER CLASS

8". Body cylindrical, tapered toward rear; brick red, bright orange, pink, or purple. Head end has 10 branched orange to white retractable tentacles. Lives in crevice, exposing tentacles to moving water. **HABITAT** Low-tide line to shallow water; rocks, crevices.

SEA VASE TUNICATE
Ciona intestinalis
TUNICATE CLASS

5". Slender, vase-like tube, open at top; translucent pale yellow-green. Filters water into inlet tubes for food, oxygen; excretes wastes from exit tube. **HABITAT** Low-tide line to 1,650' deep; harbors, protected bays; on rocks, pilings.

Freshwater and Land Invertebrates

Tens of thousands of invertebrate species thrive in the Northwest's freshwater and terrestrial environments. Ponds and meadows are home to literally billions of invertebrates per acre, and even sheer rock faces and acidic bogs support a varied assortment. The most commonly seen Northwest invertebrates belong to three phyla.

Land and freshwater members of the phylum Mollusca are the generally small, drab species of slugs, snails, and clams. They are both aquatic, living amid vegetation or in bottom sediment, and terrestrial, found in leaf litter and under leaves, boards, and rocks. Some of these terrestrial species, like slugs, are our most annoying garden pests. The phylum Annelida includes the earthworms, which can occur at an average of 1,000 pounds per acre; they help fertilize and oxygenate soil by pulling vegetation underground. The phylum Arthropoda comprises the largest number of freshwater and land invertebrates, with four classes covered here: crustaceans, millipedes, arachnids, and insects. Crustaceans include the terrestrial pillbugs, commonly found under rocks and rotting logs. Terrestrial millipedes look like worms with legs—two per segment—and are vegetarian (the similar centipedes, not covered in this guide, have one leg per segment and are predatory). Arachnids—spiders, scorpions, daddy-long-legs (harvestmen), and ticks—are discussed on page 189. Insects, introduced on page 192, are comprised of many well-known invertebrate orders, including dragonflies, grasshoppers, beetles, flies, butterflies, and ants, wasps, and bees (see their separate introductions within the section).

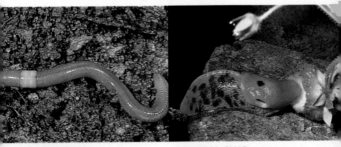

EARTHWORMS
"Night Crawlers"
Lumbricus species
EARTHWORM CLASS

L 5″. Body soft, cylindrical, legless; about 150 segments; purplish orange. Aerates moist soil; common on surface after heavy rains. Feeds on decaying plant matter. Used as fishing bait. **HABITAT** Moist soils in woodlands, meadows, yards.

BANANA SLUG
Ariolimax columbianus
GASTROPOD CLASS

L 5″ (to 10″). Body soft, cylindrical; yellow, often with black spots. Eyes stalked. Large breathing hole on side at front end. **HABITAT** Moist forest floors. **RANGE** West of Cascades.

LEOPARD SLUG
Limax maximus
GASTROPOD CLASS

L 4". Body cylindrical, leathery, with ridge on top at rear. Pale gray or brownish; above spotted and striped. Eyes on long stalks. A garden pest; imported from Europe. **HABITAT** Gardens, moist woodlands. **RANGE** Chiefly west of Cascades.

RUFOUS GARDEN SLUG
Arion ater
GASTROPOD CLASS

L 2". Body cylindrical, tapered toward rear; reddish. Eyes on retractable stalks. Covered with protective mucus; ejects jet of slime if disturbed. Mainly nocturnal; dried mucus trails glisten in sun. A garden pest. **HABITAT** Gardens, meadows, woodland edges.

COMMON PILLBUG
"Sowbug"
Armadillidium vulgare
CRUSTACEAN CLASS

L ⅓". Body convex, with gray, shrimp-like plates, 7 pairs of short legs; can roll into ball. Head has 2 short antennae. Feeds on decaying plant matter. **HABITAT** Common under rocks and logs.

MILLIPEDE
Harpaphe haydeniana
MILLIPEDE CLASS

L 3". Body gray, brown, or black. Anterior rounded; antennae short. Dozens of segments, each with 2 pairs of short legs. Slow-moving; rolls into spiral ball when threatened, releasing foul-smelling secretion. **HABITAT** Under leaves, stones, logs; often seen crawling.

Spiders and Kin

The class Arachnida includes spiders, ticks, daddy-long-legs (harvestmen), and scorpions. These generally dreaded invertebrates are much maligned; in fact, most species are harmless to humans, many are beneficial to the environment, and all have habits worthy of the naturalist's attention.

Spiders have two body parts and eight legs. Most also have eight simple eyes, the arrangement of which differs from genus to genus. On jumping spiders, which hunt without benefit of a web, two eyes are tremendously enlarged, a trait that enables them to judge accurately distances to their prey. All spiders extrude up to three or four types of silk from spinnerets on their undersides: one to make cocoons for their eggs; another, much finer, for lowering themselves; sturdy strands to construct radial web lines; and finally, the sticky silk they use to entrap prey.

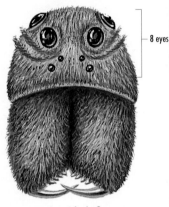
8 eyes

A spider's face

Spiders hunt by stalking, ambushing, or ensnaring their victims, then subduing or killing them with a poisonous bite. Their venom acts as a powerful digestive fluid, which liquefies their prey so they can suck it up. All spiders are venomous, but most are entirely harmless to humans, and indeed retreat quickly when we arrive on the scene. Spiders are not parasitic on humans or domesticated animals, nor do they transmit any diseases to humans. They can be incredibly abundant, especially in meadows, where hundreds of thousands can inhabit a single acre. Their hearty appetites help to control the insect population.

In addition to spiders, there are many other arachnids among us. Daddy-long-legs, also called harvestmen, are nonvenomous and have one body part and very long, fragile legs. They are normally solitary, but in winter they may huddle together in masses. Scorpions look like tiny lobsters but with stingers on the tips of their upturned "tails." Ticks are parasites with little foreclaws that grasp onto passing animals. To feed, they bury their heads under the skin and draw blood.

Arachnids in buildings may be active all year; those at higher elevations are active chiefly from April to October. The accounts below give typical lengths of females, not including legs; the rarely seen males are often much smaller.

WESTERN BLACK WIDOW SPIDER
Latrodectus hesperus
ARACHNID CLASS

¾″. Female black, glossy; abdomen bulbous, with red hourglass pattern below. Male and imm. appear paler, due to fine white, yellow, or red lines. Web irregular, with funnel-like exit. **CAUTION** Poisonous (mainly female). **HABITAT** Woodpiles, debris, crawl spaces. **SEASON** Year-round. **RANGE** e WA, much of OR.

GOLDENROD SPIDER
"Flower Spider"
Misumena vatia
ARACHNID CLASS

⅜″. Female yellow or white with red streaks on abdomen; legs thick. Male abdomen dark reddish with whitish and green mottling; rest of body and legs dark reddish brown. Hides in flowers snatching insects. **HABITAT** Flowers in gardens, meadows. **SEASON** Late April–early July.

BANDED GARDEN SPIDER
Argiope trifasciata
ARACHNID CLASS

1″. Abdomen large, smooth, egg-shaped; silvery white to yellow, with fine dark crossbands. Head/thorax has silver hair. Legs hairy, often banded. Web flat, with central zigzag pattern. Spins silken hemispherical egg sac. **HABITAT** Tall grass, gardens. **SEASON** Summer.

WOLF SPIDERS
Pardosa species
ARACHNID CLASS
⅖″. Body slender, hairy; dark, with lighter marks on sides. Legs long, banded light and dark. Active hunter by day; runs prey down. Female drags egg sac, carries hatched brood on back. **HABITAT** Coniferous forests; under logs and stones. **SEASON** June–Aug.

NORTHERN SCORPION
Paruroctonus boreus
ARACHNID CLASS
1¾″. Body cylindrical, broad, segmented; pale yellow to orange-brown. "Tail" long, segmented; stinger at tip curves up. Pincers crayfish-like. Preys on insects; harmless to humans. Nocturnal. **HABITAT** Rocky slopes. **SEASON** Year-round in warm soil. **RANGE** East of Cascades.

DADDY-LONG-LEGS
Phalangium opilio
ARACHNID CLASS
¼″. Head/thorax and abdomen joined in single body; yellowish brown, sometimes striped. Legs long, arching; 2nd pair longest, used like antennae. Feeds on tiny spiders, insects, plant juices. **HABITAT** Tree trunks, fields, buildings. **SEASON** Apr.–Nov. (year-round inside).

WOOD TICKS
"Dog Ticks"
Dermacentor species
ARACHNID CLASS
⅛″. Body oval. Female reddish brown with silvery shield near small orange head. Male gray with reddish-brown spots. **CAUTION** If bitten, be sure to remove tick head to prevent infection. **HABITAT** Brush, tall grass. **SEASON** Spring–fall.

Insects

Insects (class Insecta) bring out special feelings in people: they fascinate children with their forms and colors; they bewilder naturalists with their ecological intricacies; they cause rational adults to cringe at their mere presence. Their vast repertory of environmental adaptations is overwhelming, as are their sheer numbers and staying power. Try as we might (and we have tried mightily), we have not succeeded in exterminating any Pacific Northwest insect pests. Perhaps instead we should spend more time observing their beauty and variety.

All insects have three main body parts—head, thorax, and abdomen—to which various other organs are attached. The head has a pair of antennae, which may be narrow, feathery, pointed, short, or long (sometimes much longer than the body). The eyes are compound and the mouthparts are adapted to chewing, biting, piercing, sucking, and/or licking. Insect wings (usually four) and legs (six) attach at the thorax. The abdomen, usually the largest section, houses the reproductive and other internal organs.

A remarkable aspect of insect life is the transformation from egg to adult, known as metamorphosis. In complete metamorphosis, which includes a pupal stage and is unique to insects, the adults lay eggs from which the larvae are hatched. The larva feeds and grows, molting its skin several times, until it prepares for its immobile pupal state by hiding or camouflaging itself. Within the pupa, larval organs dissolve and adult organs develop. In incomplete metamorphosis, there is no pupal stage, and insects such as dragonflies, grasshoppers, and bugs gradually develop from hatched nymphs into adults. The metamorphic timetable varies widely; some insects complete the transformation in a matter of days while others, like cicadas, take up to 17 years.

The importance of insects to the ecological health of the planet cannot be overstated. In the Northwest and other temperate regions, insects pollinate approximately 80 percent of the flowering plants. They are a vital link in every ecosystem.

This book introduces representative species or genera of insects from many orders in a sequence from primitive to more advanced. We have placed the large butterfly and moth section last, although traditionally these insects precede the ants, bees, and wasps. For many insects, there is no commonly accepted English name at the species level. We give orders for all members of the class Insecta, except in the well-known butterfly and moth order, in which we give families. Descriptions and seasonal information refer to typical adult forms unless otherwise noted. Measurements indicate typical adult body lengths, except in the butterfly accounts, in which wingspan measurements are given.

Dragonflies

Dragonflies are large predatory insects, many of which specialize in killing mosquitoes. The order is 300 million years old and comprises two major groups—dragonflies and damselflies. Both have movable heads and large compound eyes that in dragonflies nearly cover the head and in damselflies bulge out from the sides. Their legs are attached to the thorax just behind their heads, a feature that makes walking all but impossible but greatly facilitates their ability to grasp and hold prey while tearing into it with sharp mouthparts. They have four powerful wings that move independently, allowing for both forward and backward flight. At rest, the wings are held horizontally by dragonflies, and together over the top of the abdomen by damselflies. Nymphs, called naiads, live among the vegetation and muck in ponds and streams and feed on mosquito larvae, other insects, tadpoles, and small fish. Many of the Northwest's colorful species have captured the interest of bird and butterfly enthusiasts. A few species are migratory, gathering in the fall for southbound flights. In the accounts that follow, all species not noted as damselflies are dragonflies. The size given for dragonflies is the typical adult body length (not the wingspread).

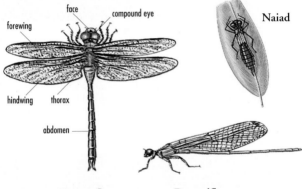

Naiad

Dragonfly   Damselfly

RIVER JEWELWING
Calopteryx aequabilis
DRAGONFLY ORDER
2″. Damselfly. Body metallic green; sometimes appears bluish. Wings dark brown or blackish at tips; clear, tinged with brown, at base; female's paler with white spot near tip. Slow fluttery flight. **HABITAT** Streams. **SEASON** June–Aug.

SPOTTED SPREADWING
Lestes congener
DRAGONFLY ORDER

1½". Damselfly. Male thorax bronzy with yellow spots; abdomen black with pale bands. Female reddish brown with yellow stripe on thorax. Wings clear. Perches with wings partially open. Flies late in season. **HABITAT** Ponds, marshy lakesides. **SEASON** July–Nov.

WESTERN RED DAMSEL
Amphiagrion abbreviatum
DRAGONFLY ORDER

1". Damselfly. Male thorax black with reddish sides; abdomen shortish, stout, mostly red, with black tip. Female dull reddish brown. Wings clear; extend almost to abdomen tip. Perches low amid vegetation. **HABITAT** Marshy ponds, sloughs. **SEASON** May–Sept.

VIVID DANCER
Argia vivida
DRAGONFLY ORDER

1¼". Damselfly. Male bright blue; abdomen has black bands, blue tip. Female duller blue or brown. Wings clear with black spot near tip. Dances above the ground. **HABITAT** Streamsides. **SEASON** Apr.–Sept. **RANGE** East of Cascades.

mating pair (left), male (right)

TULE BLUET
Enallagma carunculatum
DRAGONFLY ORDER

1¼". Damselfly. Male head black; thorax striped blue and black; abdomen mostly blue, with extensive black markings, blue tip. Female tan or pale bluish. Wings clear. **HABITAT** Ponds, lakes. **SEASON** May–Sept.

PACIFIC FORKTAIL
Ischnura cervula
DRAGONFLY ORDER

1⅛". Male thorax black above, with 4 pale blue spots; greenish below; abdomen black with bluish-green sides, blue tip. Female dark with pink thorax; sometimes like male. Wings clear. **HABITAT** Ponds, slow-moving streams. **SEASON** Apr.–Oct.

BLACK PETALTAIL
Tanypteryx hageni
DRAGONFLY ORDER

2¼". Body black with yellow spots on thorax and paired yellow spots on each abdominal segment. Wings clear. Eyes separated, unlike most dragonflies. **HABITAT** Moist mtn. meadows. **SEASON** June–Aug.

BLUE-EYED DARNER
Aeshna multicolor
DRAGONFLY ORDER

2¾". Body brown with blue stripes on thorax and blue spots on abdomen. Eyes blue. Wings clear. Strong flier; rarely perches. **HABITAT** Open lowlands; sometimes far from water. Breeds in still waters. **SEASON** June–Oct.

COMMON GREEN DARNER
Anax junius
DRAGONFLY ORDER

3". Thorax green. Abdomen blue (male) or reddish brown (female). Wings clear, tinged with amber with age. In late summer flies over open water, pairs in tandem; seldom perches. Many migrate south in winter. **HABITAT** Ponds, lakes, slow-moving streams. **SEASON** May–Oct.

GRAPPLETAIL
Octogomphus specularis
DRAGONFLY ORDER

2". Thorax yellow with wide black stripes on sides at front; abdomen black with yellow at base and tip. Wings clear. Perches on leaves over streams. **HABITAT** Lowland streams. **SEASON** June–July. **RANGE** West of Cascades.

PACIFIC SPIKETAIL
Cordulegaster dorsalis
DRAGONFLY ORDER

3". Body black with yellow bands. Wings clear. Nymph (naiad) rough, hairy, sometimes covered with green algae; lives in mud of stream bottoms. **HABITAT** Woodlands near streams. **SEASON** Summer.

MOUNTAIN EMERALD
Somatochlora semicircularis
DRAGONFLY ORDER

2". Body blackish; thorax metallic green with 2 yellowish spots on sides; abdomen has yellowish markings at base. Wings clear. Hovers above sedges. **HABITAT** Marshy bogs, shallow mtn. ponds. **SEASON** June–Sept.

female (left), male (right)

WESTERN PONDHAWK
Erythemis collocata
DRAGONFLY ORDER

1¾". Male uniformly light blue. Female and imm. thorax green; abdomen green with gray bands, black tip. Wings clear. Perches on ground or rocks. **HABITAT** Ponds. **SEASON** May–Sept.

DOT-TAILED WHITEFACE
Leucorrhinia intacta
DRAGONFLY ORDER

1⅓". Body black; abdomen, above, has 1 (male) or many (female) yellow spots toward rear. Face gleaming white. Female duller. Wings clear. **HABITAT** Ponds, lakes. **SEASON** June–July.

EIGHT-SPOTTED SKIMMER
Libellula forensis
DRAGONFLY ORDER

2". Thorax dark brown with yellow streaks; abdomen dark brown with yellow stripes, becoming gray with age. Wings clear, each with 2 black, 2 white patches (some females lack white). **HABITAT** Ponds, lakes. **SEASON** May–Sept.

COMMON WHITETAIL
"White-tailed Skimmer"
Libellula (Plathemis) lydia
DRAGONFLY ORDER

1¾". Male thorax brown with yellow streaks; abdomen wide, pale bluish white; wings clear with small black spot at base and broad black band on outer half. Female brown with whitish spots on sides of abdomen, 3 brown spots on each wing. **HABITAT** Ponds, lakes. **SEASON** May–Sept.

FOUR-SPOTTED SKIMMER
Libellula quadrimaculata
DRAGONFLY ORDER

1¾". Body olive-brown with narrow yellow stripe along sides; base of head and thorax yellow. Wings clear with yellowish leading edge, each with 2 black spots. **HABITAT** Ponds, lakes. **SEASON** May–Sept.

CARDINAL MEADOWHAWK
Sympetrum illotum
DRAGONFLY ORDER

1½". Head and thorax rusty red with 2 white spots on each side; abdomen bright red. Wings reddish with dark markings at base. Flies low over reedy pond edges. **HABITAT** Ponds, river backwaters, ditches. **SEASON** June–Sept.

STRIPED MEADOWHAWK
Sympetrum pallipes
DRAGONFLY ORDER

1⅜". Thorax tawny or reddish, with 2 indistinct white lines above, 2 broad, oblique, pale yellow stripes on sides; abdomen yellow-brown or red, with dark markings on sides. Wings clear. **HABITAT** Edges of ponds, lakes. **SEASON** July–Oct.

NORTHERN ROCK CRAWLER
Grylloblatta campodeiformis
ROCK CRAWLER ORDER

¾". Body hairy, wingless; amber-yellow. Antennae long, arched toward rear. 2 tails. Nocturnal; forages in snow for dead insects. Active in temperatures near freezing. Hibernates; matures over several years (8 nymphal molts). **HABITAT** Glaciers, snowfields. **SEASON** Summer.

PACIFIC DAMPWOOD TERMITE
Zootermopsis angusticollis
TERMITE ORDER
½″ (nymph), ¾″ (soldier), 1″ (reproductive). Soldier and nymph (worker) yellowish. Soldier head large, reddish brown, with black mandibles. Reproductive grayish, small, sometimes winged. **HABITAT** Moist woodlands; colonies in rotting wood, sometimes in buildings. **SEASON** July–Oct.

EUROPEAN EARWIG
Forficula auricularia
EARWIG ORDER
⅝″. Body slender; brownish to black; legs yellowish. Antennae bead-like. Pincers at abdomen tip curved (male) or straight (female). Female guards eggs, feeds young nymphs. **HABITAT** Decaying logs, leaf litter, trees, sheds. **SEASON** Apr.–Oct. **RANGE** West of Cascades.

Grasshoppers, Locusts, and Kin

Members of the order Orthoptera are beloved for their musical abilities and despised for their voracious appetites. All species have mouthparts designed to bite and chew, and straight, membranous wings. Grasshoppers, locusts, and crickets have greatly developed hindlegs for jumping. Females have long ovipositors, straight in most species but sickle-shaped in katydids; they lay eggs in soil or tree vegetation. While no insects have true voices, orthopterans manage to make themselves heard in a variety of distinctive ways; most melodies are produced by males trying to attract mates. Crickets and katydids raise their wings and rub together specialized parts to produce their well-known calls. Most crickets are "right-winged," rubbing their right wings over their left, while katydids are "left-winged." Grasshoppers rub their hindlegs and wings together, and also make rattling, in-flight sounds by vibrating their forewings against their hindwings.

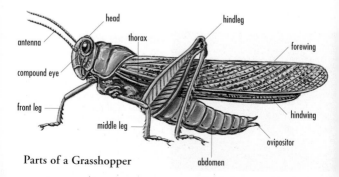

Parts of a Grasshopper

CAROLINA LOCUST
Dissosteira carolina
GRASSHOPPER ORDER

2″. Body and eyes cinnamon brown. Hindwings black with broad, light yellow border (visible in flight). Flies with purring, fluttering sound; often hovers. **HABITAT** Roadsides, meadows, shores. **SEASON** June–Sept.

KEELED SHIELD-BACK KATYDID
Neduba carinata
GRASSHOPPER ORDER

1″. Body light brown. Cape-like shield extends from head over back. Female has stout upcurved ovipositor. Antennae long, hair-like; hindlegs long; wings inconspicuous, nonfunctional. Nocturnal. **CAUTION** Bites. **HABITAT** Trees, shrubs. **SEASON** Summer.

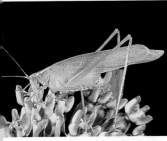

FORK-TAILED BUSH KATYDID
Scudderia furcata
GRASSHOPPER ORDER

1½″. Body green. Hindlegs, antennae long, thin. Wings extend past abdomen. Female has stout upcurved ovipositor; male has forked "tail." Nocturnal. **HABITAT** Meadows, marshes, woods. **SEASON** Summer.

MEADOW SPITTLEBUG
"Froghopper"
Philaenus spumarius
CICADA ORDER

⅜″. Adult body long, pear-shaped; gray, green, yellow, or brown; spotted. Antennae and wings short. Nymph oval, pale yellow; emits bubbly protective froth. Adult hops about on leaves like a tiny frog. **HABITAT** Brushy meadows, roadsides. **SEASON** May–Sept.

GREEN LACEWINGS
Chrysopa species
NERVEWING ORDER

⅝″. Body elongated, pale green; head narrow; eyes large; antennae long. Wings clear, veined, at least ¼ longer than body; fold together over back. Adult and larva eat aphids, mealybugs. **HABITAT** Gardens, woodland edges. **SEASON** May–Sept.

SNAKEFLIES
Agulla species
NERVEWING ORDER

¾″. Body elongated, dark brown. Long head and thorax give serpentlike appearance. Female ovipositor long, thin. Wings transparent with dark veins. Voracious; eats destructive aphids, bark beetles, caterpillars. **HABITAT** Forests, orchards; larva lives under bark. **SEASON** Spring–summer.

WATER BOATMEN
Arctocorixa species
TRUE BUG ORDER

⅓″. Body oval; gray and black, finely crossbanded. Forelegs short, hindlegs paddle-shaped for rowing. Aquatic; carries air bubble underwater; can remain submerged for long periods. **HABITAT** Ponds, puddles, and slow-moving streams; can be abundant in sewage lagoons. **SEASON** Spring–summer.

COMMON BACKSWIMMERS
Notonecta species
TRUE BUG ORDER

½″. Body boat-shaped; blackish or dark green with white patches. Rear legs large, paddle-shaped. Swims on back, with abdomen tip just above surface. Eats water insects, tiny fish. **CAUTION** Bites. **HABITAT** Ponds, puddles, slow-moving streams. **SEASON** Summer– winter.

GIANT WATER BUG
"Toe-biter"
Belostoma flumineum
TRUE BUG ORDER

1″. Body oval, flattish, light brown. Forelegs have hooked pincers; middle and hindlegs longer, paddle-like. Hides among floating vegetation, muddy bottoms; eats fish, tadpoles. Male carries eggs on back. Nocturnal. **CAUTION** Bites. **HABITAT** Muddy ponds. **SEASON** May–Oct.

COMMON WATER STRIDERS
Gerris species
TRUE BUG ORDER

⅝″. Body slender, blackish with pale sides. Middle and hindlegs very long, slender, spider-like. Skates over water using surface tension; eats mosquito larvae and small insects. **HABITAT** Slow-moving streams, ponds. **SEASON** May–Oct.

Beetles

There are more species of beetles, order Coleoptera, than any other animals on earth (not all are called beetles: June bugs and fireflies are in this order). Beetles' forewings are hardened dense sheaths known as *elytra,* which meet in a straight line down the back. Their hindwings underneath function as the organs of flight. Beetle legs and antennae vary from long and straight to stout and angled. Both adults and larvae, known as grubs, have mouthparts adapted for biting and chewing. They are vegetarians, predators, scavengers, and in a few instances parasites. Some, like lady beetles, are highly prized by gardeners because they eat aphids and other garden pests, while others are nuisances at best. They range in size from microscopic organisms to some of the largest insects in the world.

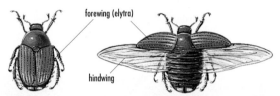

forewing (elytra)

hindwing

OREGON TIGER BEETLE
Cicindela oregona
BEETLE ORDER
½". Head and thorax narrow, abdomen wide; dark brown. Forewings have white spots. Adult quick, ferocious, runs down prey; in flight resembles a fly. Larva ambushes from burrows. **HABITAT** Open areas, incl. beaches. **SEASON** Late spring–fall.

SMALL WHIRLIGIG BEETLES
Gyrinus species
BEETLE ORDER
¼". Body oval, flattened. Above shiny black, below and sides black to yellowish brown. 2 pairs of eyes. Legs reddish; rear legs paddle-shaped for swimming. Swims in circles on surface. **HABITAT** Ponds, slow-moving streams. **SEASON** June–Sept.

DARKLING GROUND BEETLES
Eleodes species
BEETLE ORDER
¾". Body oval, shiny; black, sometimes with reddish above. Forewings fused; flightless. Runs with rear end raised 45 degrees; sprays foul-smelling secretion if disturbed. Mainly nocturnal. **HABITAT** Steppes, deserts. **SEASON** Year-round.

CALIFORNIA PRIONUS
Prionus californicus
BEETLE ORDER
2″. Body elongated; dark brownish black. Thorax has 3 large spines on each side. Antennae long, segmented; legs long. Nocturnal; crashes against lighted windows. Larva in burrow whitish; eats dead wood. **HABITAT** Coniferous forests. **SEASON** July–Aug. **RANGE** West of Cascades.

BANDED ALDER BORER
Rosalia funebris
BEETLE ORDER
1¼″. Body elongated, rectangular. Head black; thorax white with black central spot; forewings and very long antennae banded black and white. Larva eats dead wood of broadleaf trees. **HABITAT** Broadleaf woodlands. **SEASON** Apr.–Sept.

MILKWEED BORER
Tetraopes femoratus
BEETLE ORDER
½″. Body cylindrical; above red with black dots, below black. 4 eyes. Antennae long, blackish with thin gray bands. Adult and larva eat milkweeds (tolerant of its poison); poisonous to birds. **HABITAT** On or near milkweeds. **SEASON** Summer.

TEN-LINED JUNE BEETLE
Polyphylla decimlineata
BEETLE ORDER
1″. Body oval; brown with white stripes on head, thorax, and forewings: each wing has 1 short and 4 long stripes. Eats conifer needles. Larva white; eats shrub and tree roots; serious pest in nurseries. **HABITAT** Woodlands. **SEASON** June–Aug.

TWO-SPOTTED LADY BEETLE
Adalia bipunctata
BEETLE ORDER
¼″. Body oval, rounded. Forewings reddish orange with 1 black spot on each. Adult and larva feed on aphids, soft-bodied insects. Overwinters in houses and under bark. **HABITAT** Fields, gardens. **SEASON** May–Oct.

CONVERGENT LADY BEETLE
Hippodamia convergens
BEETLE ORDER
¼″. Body oval. Thorax has converging white stripes. Forewings reddish orange with many black spots. Adult and larva eat aphids, soft-bodied insects. In fall, large masses migrate to overwinter in mtn. canyons. **HABITAT** Gardens, meadows, woodlands. **SEASON** Mar.–Oct.

Flies and Mosquitoes

Flies and mosquitoes, some of humankind's least favorite insects, are nonetheless worthy of a second glance. All species have two wings and mouthparts formed for sucking, or piercing and sucking combined. The larvae, which are legless and wingless, undergo complete metamorphosis. Terrestrial larvae, called maggots, are almost always whitish or grayish in color. Aquatic larvae have various names; those of mosquitoes are called wrigglers. Adults fly with a wingbeat frequency in the range of 100 to 300 beats per second, and in tiny species this can be even faster. This incredible speed produces the familiar in-flight buzzing sounds. Flies feed on decomposing matter, nectar, other insects, and in the case of biting flies, blood. Mosquitoes' lower lips form a proboscis with six knife-sharp organs, some smooth and some saw-toothed, that cut into skin.

GIANT CRANE FLY
Holorusia rubiginosa
FLY ORDER
1¼″. Looks like a giant mosquito. Body long, slender; usu. reddish brown, with white stripes on thorax. Wings clear, slender, long. Legs fall off easily. Larva aquatic. Does not bite. **HABITAT** Woodlands near water, forest edges. **SEASON** Summer.

COMMON MIDGE
Chironomus attenuatus
FLY ORDER
¼″. Looks like a mosquito. Body pale green or brown. Wings pale brown. Rests with forelegs up, wings spread out to sides. Forms large swarms when mating. Does not bite. **HABITAT** Near water. **SEASON** Summer.

MOSQUITOES
Aedes and *Culex* species
FLY ORDER
½″. Body black, brown, or striped. Wings narrow, scaly; banded, black, or clear. Sharp proboscis; female sucks blood; male, plant juices. Male antennae feathery, female's threadlike. **CAUTION** Bites. **HABITAT** Woodlands, towns, watersides. **SEASON** Apr.–Sept.

BLACK FLIES
Simulium species
FLY ORDER
⅛″. Body black; head pointed down. Wings clear. Larvae pupate in cocoons that coat rocks in streams. **CAUTION** Bites; female sucks bird and mammal blood. **HABITAT** Woodlands, watersides. **SEASON** May–July.

DEER FLIES
Chrysops species
FLY ORDER
½″. Head small. Body dull gray-brown to black. Wings have brownish-black patches. **CAUTION** Circles target, gives quick nasty bite on landing. **HABITAT** Woodlands, roadsides near water. **SEASON** May–Sept.

BLACK HORSE FLY
Tabanus atratus
FLY ORDER
1″. Body black with bluish sheen on abdomen; thorax hairy. Wings brownish. Eyes large. Male drinks nectar; female sucks blood, esp. of livestock. **CAUTION** Bites. **HABITAT** Fields, pastures. **SEASON** Summer.

DRONE FLY
Eristalis tenax
FLY ORDER
½″. Thorax brownish black with orangish sides, golden hairs; abdomen black and yellow. Wings clear. Lacks Honey Bee's narrow waist. Feeds on nectar, pollen. **HABITAT** Flowering fields. **SEASON** June–Aug.

HOUSE FLY
Musca domestica
FLY ORDER
¼″. Body gray with dark stripes. Wings clear. Eyes large, red-brown; legs hairy. Egg hatches in 10–24 hours; matures to adult in 10 days; lives 15 (male) to 26 (female) days. Sucks liquid sugars from garbage; spreads disease. **HABITAT** Buildings, farms. **SEASON** Chiefly May–Oct.

BLUE BOTTLE FLIES
Calliphora species
FLY ORDER
⅜″. Thorax gray, hairy; abdomen metallic blue. Wings clear. Eyes red, cheeks orange. Larvae (maggots) infest dead animals, excrement; spread disease. **HABITAT** Pastures, barnyards, houses, garbage dumps. **SEASON** Summer.

Ants, Wasps, and Bees

The insects of the order Hymenoptera include narrow-waisted bees, wasps, and ants. Hymenopterans have two pairs of membranous, transparent wings, mouthparts modified to chew and lick, and, in adult females, an ovipositor. All species undergo complete metamorphosis.

The narrow-waists are divided into two broad groupings. The first, parasitic wasps, includes the large and varied assemblage of nonstinging ichneumon wasps, which live as parasites during their larval stage. Some ichneumons are greatly feared by humans for their astonishingly long ovipositors, which are used not for stinging but to probe about in woody vegetation for suitable insects on which to lay eggs. The second group of narrow-waists are stinging insects, with ovipositors that have been modified into stinging organs. These include vespid wasps (such as hornets and yellow jackets), bees, and many ants.

carpenter ant colony

Ants and some wasps and bees are highly social creatures, while other species in this order live solitary lives. Their nests vary in complexity from a single-celled hole in the ground to the Honey Bee's elaborate comb structure. Many ant species excavate in soil or wood, building multi-chambered homes mostly hidden from sight. Bumble bees, yellow jackets, and some hornets build similar homes. Unlike ants, though, they build a separate six-sided chamber for each of their young, made of a papery material that consists of wood or bark and adult saliva. Bald-faced Hornets often construct their nests in open situations, while Honey Bees utilize man-made hives or hollow trees or logs. The Honey Bees' two-sided, vertically hanging beeswax combs can contain more than 50,000 cells.

Bees and flowering plants have developed a great many interdependencies over the eons as they have evolved together. We would lose too many of our flowers and fruits were we to let our bees be poisoned out of existence. We would also lose some of the greatest known examples of animal industry.

The following species accounts give the typical body lengths of the commonly seen workers; queens are generally larger.

wasp nest

CARPENTER ANTS
Camponotus species
ANT, WASP, AND BEE ORDER
½". Body black; abdomen has long brownish hairs. Antennae elbowed. Tunnels into soft wood, but does not eat it; causes structural damage to buildings. **CAUTION** Bites. **HABITAT** Dying trees, logs, wooden structures. **SEASON** Apr.–Nov.

WESTERN THATCHING ANT
"Red Ant"
Formica obscuripes
ANT, WASP, AND BEE ORDER
¼". Head and thorax rusty red; abdomen and legs blackish. Constructs large mounds of twigs, pine needles, grass. Eats larvae, flower nectar, aphid honeydew (a sugar-rich secretion). Tends herds of aphids; enslaves larvae of other *Formica* species. **HABITAT** Woodlands, steppes. **SEASON** Summer.

HARVESTER ANTS
Pogonomyrmex species
ANT, WASP, AND BEE ORDER
¼". Body red. Head, thorax hairy; abdomen shiny. Builds underground nests with gravel mound near entrance; clears vegetation around burrow. **CAUTION** Bites and stings. **HABITAT** Steppes, grasslands. **RANGE** East of Cascades. **SEASON** Apr.–Sept.

WESTERN YELLOW JACKET
Vespula pennsylvanica
ANT, WASP, AND BEE ORDER
⅝". Body stout, wider than head; yellow, with heavy black bands and spots. Antennae long, curving. Aggressively defends nests in burrows, logs. Raids picnic food, trash cans. **CAUTION** Stings. **HABITAT** Open areas. **SEASON** Spring–fall; workers swarm in late summer.

BALD-FACED HORNET
Vespula maculata
ANT, WASP, AND BEE ORDER
¾". Body rotund, black. Yellowish-white spots on short head, base of wings, waist, and tip of abdomen. Builds football-size paper nest under branch or overhang. **CAUTION** Stings nest visitors. **HABITAT** Woodland edges, gardens. **SEASON** May–Sept.

HONEY BEE
Apis mellifera
ANT, WASP, AND BEE ORDER

½". Body rounded. Thorax hairy, brown; abdomen banded black and golden. Wings dusky. Makes honey; pollinates crops; nests in tree holes. Introduced from Eurasia. **CAUTION** Stings, but is not aggressive; if stung, remove stinger immediately. **HABITAT** Fields, orchards. **SEASON** Apr.–Oct.

YELLOW-FACED BUMBLE BEE
Bombus vosnesenskii
ANT, WASP, AND BEE ORDER

½". Body robust, hairy. Mainly black with yellow bands, bright yellow face. Wings dark. Queen overwinters; starts new colony in spring; nests in underground burrow. **CAUTION** Stings, but is not aggressive. **HABITAT** Open areas. **SEASON** Early spring–fall. **RANGE** Chiefly west of Cascade crest.

Butterflies and Moths

The order Lepidoptera comprises the familiar groups of moths and butterflies. *Lepidoptera* means "scale-winged," and refers to the minute scales that cover the four wings of all butterfly and moth species. All lepidopterans share the same generalized life cycle—egg to larva to pupa to adult. Eggs are laid singly, or in rows, stacks, or masses, depending on the species. The emergent larva, usually referred to as a caterpillar, feeds on plant life, and grows through several stages, or instars, shedding its skin each time. When fully grown, the caterpillar prepares to pupate by spinning a silken cocoon (moth) or finding a secure hiding place (butterfly). Then the caterpillar sheds its last larval skin, revealing the pupa, an outer shell with no head or feet, within which the wings and other adult features fully develop. Finally, the pupal skin breaks open and the winged moth or butterfly emerges. The time required for this process is different for each species. Many have only one emergence of adults per year; others have two or three. Most Northwest lepidopterans live out their entire lives within the region, although a few species, like the world-famous Monarch, migrate south in the fall.

Metamorphosis of a Monarch

The hundreds of species that stay behind survive the winter as eggs, larvae, or pupae, although a few species overwinter as adults.

Several key differences distinguish moths and butterflies. Moths' antennae are either feather-like or wiry, and lack the clubbed tip of butterflies' antennae. Moths rest with their wings outstretched or at an angle above the body; butterflies rest with their wings outstretched or held together vertically, like a sail. Moths may fly by day or night, while butterflies fly only by day. Color and size are poor general distinguishing features between the two groups.

Butterflies and especially night-flying moths use scents called pheromones to find and attract mates. Many male butterflies have special scent scales on their wings that form visible markings called stigma. Uniquely shaped stigma help identify some skippers.

When trying to identify a species, pay special attention to the wing colors, shape, and pattern. Most of the characteristic wing markings on moths are found on the uppersides. In butterflies, look at the upperside of those species that rest with outstretched wings and on the underside of those that rest with their wings folded up.

Butterflies drink nectar from many species of wildflowers and shrubs. Among the best wild nectar plants in the Northwest are Spreading Dogbane and most members of the aster family, for example, thistles and fleabanes. Excellent garden flowers that attract butterflies and moths include Butterfly Bush, Red Valerian, lavenders, hollyhocks, and, again, most asters. Nocturnal moths are also drawn to lights.

Each larva, or caterpillar, species has its own select food plants, and the accounts that follow list several of these. Measurements given are typical wingspans for adult forms, from tip to tip.

CLODIUS PARNASSIAN
Parnassius clodius
SWALLOWTAIL FAMILY

2¾". Translucent chalky white above and below; forewings have 3 short black bars in front, 2 wide gray bars along outer margin; hindwings have red-orange spots. Caterpillar black with rows of reddish or yellow spots. **HABITAT** Mtn. openings, forest edges. **FOOD PLANTS** Bleedingheart. **SEASON** June–Aug.

ANISE SWALLOWTAIL
Papilio zelicaon
SWALLOWTAIL FAMILY

2¾". Black above and below, with broad yellow band on each wing; hindwings have small blue spots, orange eyespot, tail. Caterpillar green with yellow-spotted black bands. **HABITAT** Diverse open areas. **FOOD PLANTS** Carrot family. **SEASON** Mar.–Sept.

INDRA SWALLOWTAIL
Papilio indra
SWALLOWTAIL FAMILY

2¾″. Mostly black above and below, with 2 narrow bands of pale yellow spots; hindwings have row of blue spots, orange eyespot, very short tail. Caterpillar banded yellow and black, with orange spots. **HABITAT** Meadows, woodland openings. **FOOD PLANTS** Carrot family. **SEASON** Apr.–Aug. **RANGE** Chiefly east of Cascades.

WESTERN TIGER SWALLOWTAIL
Papilio rutulus
SWALLOWTAIL FAMILY

3½″. Bright yellow above, with black "tiger" stripes, black, yellow-spotted margins; hindwings have several blue and 2 orange spots near long black tail. Paler yellow below; hindwings have blue line along outer margin. Second largest NW butterfly. Caterpillar green with 2 large yellow eyespots. **HABITAT** Parks, backyards, streamsides. **FOOD PLANTS** Willows, poplars, alders, orchard trees. **SEASON** May–Sept.

PALE SWALLOWTAIL
Papilio eurymedon
SWALLOWTAIL FAMILY

3½″. Pale cream above, with black stripes, broad black borders, long twisted tails. Below paler, with distinct black veins. Masses on hilltops to mate. Caterpillar pale green with yellow and black eyespots. **HABITAT** Hills, mtns., canyons. **FOOD PLANTS** Snowbrush, Deerbrush, alders. **SEASON** May–Aug.

PINE WHITE
Neophasia menapia
WHITE AND SULPHUR FAMILY

2″. White above, with black markings at tip and leading edge of forewings; female hindwings have black line near outer margin. Below, hindwings veined with narrow (male) or broad (female) lines; female's outlined with orange. Caterpillar dark green with white stripes. **HABITAT** Coniferous forests. **FOOD PLANTS** Pines, true firs, Douglas Fir. **SEASON** July–Sept.

WESTERN WHITE
Pontia occidentalis
WHITE AND SULPHUR FAMILY

1¾". Male white above, with scattered grayish checkering, more obvious near forewing tip; female similar, but spots extend onto hindwings. Below, hindwings veined with greenish lines. Caterpillar light green with fine bands. **HABITAT** Meadows, mountaintops. **FOOD PLANTS** Mustard family. **SEASON** July–Sept.

CABBAGE WHITE
Pieris rapae
WHITE AND SULPHUR FAMILY

1⅝". White above; forewings have slaty tip, 1 black spot (male) or 2 (female). Yellowish white below. Introduced from Europe; abundant. Caterpillar green with yellow stripes; feeds heavily on commercial crops. **HABITAT** Fields, gardens. **FOOD PLANTS** Mustard family. **SEASON** Apr.–Oct.

LARGE MARBLE
Euchloe ausonides
WHITE AND SULPHUR FAMILY

1¾". Creamy white above; forewings have black markings near tip, black patch along leading edge. Below, hindwings white with extensive yellow-green marbling. Caterpillar dark green with yellowish stripes, black projections. **HABITAT** Open woodlands, mtn. openings, trails. **FOOD PLANTS** Mustard family. **SEASON** May–June.

SARA ORANGETIP
Anthocharis sara
WHITE AND SULPHUR FAMILY

1½". White above (female sometimes yellow); forewings have bright orange tip. Below, hindwings have dark gray marbling; forewing tip paler orange. Unmistakable as it bounces along trails in spring. Caterpillar dull green. **HABITAT** Open slopes, streamsides, meadows. **FOOD PLANTS** Mustard family. **SEASON** Mar.–Aug.

ORANGE SULPHUR
Colias eurytheme
WHITE AND SULPHUR FAMILY

2". Orange-yellow above; black margins (female's spotted yellow), black spot on forewings. Below, olive or yellow; silver spots ringed red or black. Caterpillar green, white, and red. **HABITAT** Fields. **FOOD PLANTS** Clovers, vetches, Alfalfa. **SEASON** Apr.–Oct.

WESTERN SULPHUR
Colias occidentalis
WHITE AND SULPHUR FAMILY

2″. Bright yellow above (female paler); outer wings black (male) or grayish (female); forewings have central black spot; male hindwings have central orange spot. Below, hindwings yellow with pink-rimmed white spot. **HABITAT** Streamsides, roadsides. **FOOD PLANTS** Pea family. **SEASON** June–Aug.

RUDDY COPPER
Lycaena (Chalceria) rubidus
GOSSAMER-WING FAMILY

1¼″. Male bright red-orange above, with narrow white fringe; female dull orange with small black spots, brownish shading. Both sexes pale yellow or white below; forewings have black spots. **HABITAT** Open dry meadows, shrub steppes. **FOOD PLANTS** Docks, Wild Rhubarb. **SEASON** July–Aug.

PURPLISH COPPER
Lycaena (Epidemia) helloides
GOSSAMER-WING FAMILY

1¼″. Coppery orange above (male has purplish wash) with black spots (larger on female), narrow brown outer margins; hindwings have wavy orange line at rear margin. Below, forewings ocher with black spots; hindwings dull pinkish tan to grayish tan with fine black spots, scalloped red submarginal band. Caterpillar green with yellow stripes. **HABITAT** Marshes, yards, roadsides, mtn. meadows. **FOOD PLANTS** Knotweeds, docks, Sheep Sorrel. **SEASON** May–Sept.

SYLVAN HAIRSTREAK
Satyrium sylvinus
GOSSAMER-WING FAMILY

1⅛″. Plain rust and gray above, with bluish tinge; hindwings have tiny tail. Below, grayish white with single band of small black spots; single orange and blue spot near base of tail. Caterpillar green with white side stripes. **HABITAT** Streamsides in foothills. **FOOD PLANTS** Willows. **SEASON** July–Aug.

SHERIDAN'S HAIRSTREAK
Callophrys sheridani
GOSSAMER-WING FAMILY

⅞". Gray above; green below, with prominent white line across wings. Tail-less. Caterpillar green or pink, with rows of white spots. **HABITAT** Hillsides, canyons, shrub steppes. **FOOD PLANTS** Buckwheats. **SEASON** Apr.–May.

GRAY HAIRSTREAK
Strymon melinus
GOSSAMER-WING FAMILY

1⅛". Dark gray above, with white trailing edges; hindwings have orange spot, 2 black tails. Below, paler gray, with distinct black, orange, and white line. Often rests with wings open. **HABITAT** Fields, coasts, roadsides. **FOOD PLANTS** Pea family, oaks, mints, corn and strawberry plants. **SEASON** May–Oct.

WESTERN TAILED-BLUE
Everes amyntula
GOSSAMER-WING FAMILY

1". Pale blue above (female darker), with narrow dark margins. Whitish below, lightly marked with thin dark lines and spots; hindwings have orange spot over small thin tail. Low-flying. Caterpillar yellow-green with transverse maroon stripe. **HABITAT** Streamsides, openings, mtn. meadows. **FOOD PLANTS** Pea family. **SEASON** Mar.–Aug. **Eastern Tailed-Blue** (*E. comyntas*) occurs sparingly in OR; only other tailed blue butterfly.

SPRING AZURE
Celastrina ladon
GOSSAMER-WING FAMILY

1". Male entirely pale blue above; female with black borders. Below, grayish white with small dark spots. Caterpillar variable: often creamy-rose with green side slashes. **HABITAT** Woodland openings. **FOOD PLANTS** Dogwoods, viburnums, blueberry bushes. **SEASON** Apr.–June.

SILVERY BLUE
Glaucopsyche lygdamus
GOSSAMER-WING FAMILY

1⅛". Brilliant silvery blue above (female darker), with blackish border. Below, gray with white-ringed black dots along margins. Caterpillar green or tan with dark back stripe. **HABITAT** Fields, open woodlands. **FOOD PLANTS** Pea family. **SEASON** Apr.–July (varies with elevation).

BOISDUVAL'S BLUE
"Common Blue"
Plebejus icarioides
GOSSAMER-WING FAMILY

1¼". Male blue above, with narrow black borders; female brownish, sometimes with blue at base. Below, light gray with white-ringed black spots, larger on forewings. Caterpillar green with fine white hairs. **HABITAT** Woodland openings, meadows, shrub steppes. **FOOD PLANTS** Lupines. **SEASON** May–Aug.

ACMON BLUE
Plebejus (Icaricia) acmon
GOSSAMER-WING FAMILY

¾". Male lilac-blue above, with thin black margins; hindwings have iridescent pink trailing edge with black spots; female duller blue or brown, with orange trailing edge. Below, white with many small black spots; hindwings have row of red-orange crescents. Caterpillar yellow with green back stripe. **HABITAT** Open areas. **FOOD PLANTS** Pea family, buckwheats. **SEASON** Apr.–Sept.

GREAT SPANGLED FRITILLARY
Speyeria cybele
BRUSHFOOT FAMILY

female (left), male (right)

2½". Male orange above, brownish near body, with black dots and crescents; female brown with wide yellow band across wingtips. Below, shades of brown; forewings have black crescents; hindwings have many silvery-white spots, wide yellow band. Caterpillar black with orange-based spines. **HABITAT** Moist broadleaf woodlands, meadows. **FOOD PLANTS** Violets. **SEASON** July–Aug.

HYDASPE FRITILLARY
Speyeria hydaspe
BRUSHFOOT FAMILY

2⅛". Orange-brown above, with black spots and bars. Below, darker orange with purplish wash; large, black-ringed cream spots. Caterpillar blackish with branching spines. **HABITAT** Moist mtn. meadows, roadsides. **FOOD PLANTS** Violets. **SEASON** July–Aug.

SILVER-BORDERED FRITILLARY
Boloria selene
BRUSHFOOT FAMILY

1⅝". Orange above, peppered with black spots; black borders have small orange dots. Below, cream and orange-brown with silver patches and row of black dots. Caterpillar blackish, mottled with yellow or gray; covered with branching spines. **HABITAT** Moist meadows, bogs. **FOOD PLANTS** Violets. **SEASON** June–Aug.

PACIFIC FRITILLARY
"Western Meadow Fritillary"
Boloria epithore
BRUSHFOOT FAMILY

1⅝". Orange above (brownish at base), with blackish spots. Below, paler orange with irregular dark mottling; basal two-thirds of forewings have blackish spots. **HABITAT** Meadows, open woodlands. **FOOD PLANTS** Violets. **SEASON** May–Aug.

NORTHERN CHECKERSPOT
Chlosyne palla
BRUSHFOOT FAMILY

1⅝". Male orange-red with black checks above; female blackish with creamy patches, orange spots on margins. Below, male forewings orange with black marks; hindwings cream, checkered with black and orange; female chalky with pale orange checkering. Caterpillar black with white dots, orange dashes, spines. **HABITAT** Meadows, open woodlands. **FOOD PLANTS** Asters, goldenrods. **SEASON** Apr.–July. **RANGE** East of Cascade crest; Klamaths.

MYLITTA CRESCENT
Phyciodes mylitta
BRUSHFOOT FAMILY

1¼". Mostly orange above, with evenly spaced wavy dark lines, blackish borders. Below, yellowish brown with complex darker brown markings. Caterpillar black with yellow marks, spines. **HABITAT** Agricultural fields, roadsides. **FOOD PLANTS** Thistles. **SEASON** Mar.–Oct.

VARIABLE CHECKERSPOT
Euphydryas chalcedona
BRUSHFOOT FAMILY

1⅝". Dark brown above, with creamy patches, red-orange spots along margins. Below, forewings mostly orange with tiny white spots near outer margin; hindwings have alternating red and cream bands. Caterpillar black with orange stripes, spines. **HABITAT** Open woodlands, steppes, tundra, clearings. **FOOD PLANTS** Snapdragon family, Snowberry. **SEASON** May–July.

SATYR COMMA
"Satyr Anglewing"
Polygonia satyrus
BRUSHFOOT FAMILY

2". Bright rusty orange above, with black patches, ragged margins. Below, mottled rich brown; hindwings have white "comma." Adult overwinters; flies on warm days. Caterpillar black with greenish yellow above. **HABITAT** Canyons, woodland edges, roadsides. **FOOD PLANTS** Stinging Nettle, Hop. **SEASON** Mar.–Sept.

MOURNING CLOAK
Nymphalis antiopa
BRUSHFOOT FAMILY

3". Mainly dark mahogany brown above, with wide creamy edges beyond blue-spotted black borders. Below, blackish brown with pale borders. Adult overwinters; first butterfly to appear in spring. Caterpillar dark purple with reddish spots on back. **HABITAT** Woodlands, fields, parks. **FOOD PLANTS** Willows, elms, cottonwoods. **SEASON** Mar.–Oct.

MILBERT'S TORTOISESHELL
Nymphalis (Aglais) milberti
BRUSHFOOT FAMILY

2". Dark chocolate brown above, with outer band of yellow blending to orange; dark borders. Below, dark brown, lighter toward wingtips. Caterpillar greenish yellow, spiny. **HABITAT** Riversides, roadsides, mtn. meadows. **FOOD PLANTS** Nettles. **SEASON** May–Sept.; hibernates.

WEST COAST LADY
Vanessa annabella
BRUSHFOOT FAMILY

2". Orange above, with dark markings; forewings tipped with white spots; hindwings have 4 black-ringed blue eyespots near margin. Below, marbled olive, beige, and whitish. Caterpillar tan or black with yellow lines. Population fluctuates. **HABITAT** Open areas, mtn. canyons. **FOOD PLANTS** Mallows. **SEASON** May–Oct.

SMALL WOOD-NYMPH
Cercyonis oetus
BRUSHFOOT FAMILY

1½". Dark brown above and below; forewings have 1–2 yellow-ringed black eyespots. Caterpillar striped green, white, and yellow. **HABITAT** Open grassy areas in mtns., shrub steppes. **FOOD PLANTS** Grasses. **SEASON** July–Aug.

COMMON RINGLET
Coenonympha tullia
BRUSHFOOT FAMILY

1½". Orange above and below; hindwings, below, washed with gray. Caterpillar olive-brown with stripes, tails. **HABITAT** Meadows. **FOOD PLANTS** Grasses. **SEASON** May–Sept. **RANGE** All NW, ex. Olympic Peninsula.

RED ADMIRAL
Vanessa atalanta
BRUSHFOOT FAMILY

2". Brownish black above, with semicircular orange band; forewing tips spotted white. Below, mottled brown, black, and blue; pale orange band on forewings. Caterpillar black with yellow spots. **HABITAT** Meadows, woodland edges. **FOOD PLANTS** Nettles, Hop. **SEASON** May–Oct.

GREAT ARCTIC
Oeneis nevadensis
BRUSHFOOT FAMILY

2¼". Mostly tawny or orange-brown above, with small black eyespots: 2 on each forewing, 1 on each hindwing. Below, forewings pale tawny, with single eyespot; hindwings mottled gray and brown. Adults more common in even-numbered years. **HABITAT** Woodland openings, rocky slopes, hilltops. **FOOD PLANTS** Grasses. **SEASON** June–Aug.

VIDLER'S ALPINE
Erebia vidleri
BRUSHFOOT FAMILY

2". Dark chocolate brown above. Fore-wings and top of hindwings have orange band with blue-centered black eyespots, less conspicuous on hindwings. Below, gray-brown; forewings have jagged pale orange band, hindwings have grayish-white band. **HABITAT** Subalpine and alpine meadows. **FOOD PLANTS** Grasses. **SEASON** July–Aug. **RANGE** n WA.

MONARCH
Danaus plexippus
BRUSHFOOT FAMILY

3¾". Orange above, with black veins, orange- and white-spotted blackish margins; male has black spot on vein of hindwing. Below, yellow-orange. Head and body black with white spots. Glides with wings held at an angle. Caterpillar banded black, white, and yellow. Adult and caterpillar poisonous to predators. Migrates south in fall to overwinter in coastal c CA. **HABITAT** Fields, gardens. **FOOD PLANTS** Milkweeds. **SEASON** May–Oct.; migratory.

DREAMY DUSKYWING
Erynnis icelus
SKIPPER FAMILY

1¼". Dark brown above; outer forewings have silvery patches, narrow dark bands; hindwings dotted with tiny pale spots. Usu. seen with wings spread. Caterpillar light green with white specks, black head. **HABITAT** Woodland paths and openings, along streams. **FOOD PLANTS** Aspens, willows, poplars. **SEASON** May–July.

TWO-BANDED CHECKERED-SKIPPER
Pyrgus ruralis
SKIPPER FAMILY

1". Brown-black above, with 2 irregular bands of white spots on each wing. Below, duller; hindwings also white-spotted, often with reddish tint. Body stout, blackish. **HABITAT** Open meadows, mtn. openings. **FOOD PLANTS** Cinquefoils. **SEASON** May–July.

ARCTIC SKIPPER
Carterocephalus palaemon
SKIPPER FAMILY

1". Dark brown above, with bright orange patches. Below, hindwings rusty orange with large silver spots. Resembles a small fritillary. Caterpillar dark green with yellow side stripe. **HABITAT** Bogs, meadows, swamps. **FOOD PLANTS** Grasses. **SEASON** Late May–June.

JUBA SKIPPER
Hesperia juba
SKIPPER FAMILY

1¼". Wings pointed. Orange above, merging in zigzag with broad black border; male forewings have black line. Below, hindwings yellow-olive with white patches. Caterpillar dull green with black head. **HABITAT** Shrub steppes, grasslands, open woodlands. **FOOD PLANTS** Grasses. **SEASON** May–June, Aug.–Sept.

WOODLAND SKIPPER
Ochlodes sylvanoides
SKIPPER FAMILY

1". Male bright reddish brown above, with dark borders, ragged edges; forewings have narrow black stigma (streak of scent-producing scales) that extends to border. Female duller; lacks stigma. Below, variably ocher to brown with indistinct markings. **HABITAT** Open areas; common in urban areas. **FOOD PLANTS** Grasses. **SEASON** July–Sept.

TENT CATERPILLAR MOTHS
Malacosoma species
TENT CATERPILLAR MOTH FAMILY

1½". Wings yellowish (male) or red-brown (female), with dark band on forewings. Body brown. Nocturnal. Caterpillar brownish with blue stripes, dots; hairy; groups build dense silken tents in branches. Denudes trees; rarely kills them. **HABITAT** Oak woodlands. **FOOD PLANTS** Oaks, willows, fruit trees. **SEASON** July–Aug.

POLYPHEMUS MOTH
Antheraea polyphemus
GIANT SILKWORM MOTH FAMILY

4¾". Wings orange with black and white line near trailing edges; each has yellow-ringed eyespot, surrounded on hindwings with red and blue to startle predators. Body orange-brown; antennae feathery. Nocturnal. Caterpillar green with red spines. **HABITAT** Broadleaf and mixed forests. **FOOD PLANTS** Many broadleaf trees. **SEASON** June–Sept.

CEANOTHUS SILK MOTH
Hyalophora euryalus
GIANT SILKWORM MOTH FAMILY

4½". Wings reddish brown with black-edged white median line; large white comma shape on each wing. Nocturnal; sometimes seen near lights in morning. Caterpillar powdery green with yellow spines; plump; occurs throughout summer. **HABITAT** Brush. **FOOD PLANTS** Snowbrush, Bitterbrush, willows, alders. **SEASON** Apr.–June.

NUTTALL'S DAY MOTH
"Nuttall's Sheep Moth"
Hemileuca nuttalli
GIANT SILKWORM MOTH FAMILY

2½". Wings bright pink and orange with large black dots and crossbands. Body banded black and orange; antennae plume-like. Flies by day. Caterpillar brown with red stripes, whorled rows of barbed spines; causes rash if touched. **HABITAT** Shrub steppes. **FOOD PLANTS** Bitterbrush, Snowberry. **SEASON** Summer.

WHITE-LINED SPHINX
Hyles lineata
SPHINX MOTH FAMILY

3″. Forewings brown with white veins, white stripe; hindwings rose, edged with brown. Body brown with white stripes, black and white bars. Active day and night. Caterpillar green with orange rear horn. **HABITAT** Meadows, gardens, roadsides. **FOOD PLANTS** Many low-growing plants, esp. bedstraws. **SEASON** July–Sept. **RANGE** Mainly lowlands.

TOBACCO HORNWORM
Manduca sexta
SPHINX MOTH FAMILY

4¼″. Wings gray-brown with lighter mottling. Body gray-brown with row of 6 orange spots on sides of abdomen. Mainly nocturnal. Caterpillar large (to 4″), green with white diagonal stripes on sides, large orange rear horn. **HABITAT** Gardens, crops. **FOOD PLANTS** Tomato and potato plants. **SEASON** June–Sept.

CERISY'S SPHINX
"Eyed Sphinx"
Smerinthus cerisyi
SPHINX MOTH FAMILY

3″. Forewings grayish with light and dark patches; hindwings rose, black and blue eyespot. Nocturnal. Caterpillar green, streaked yellow; rear horn. **HABITAT** Streamsides. **FOOD PLANTS** Willows, cottonwoods. **SEASON** June–Aug.

ORNATE TIGER MOTH
Apantesis ornata
TIGER MOTH FAMILY

1½″. Forewings black with white crosshatching; hindwings pink or red with black patches. Body black; white markings on thorax. Nocturnal. Caterpillar mostly black; yellow midline stripe. **HABITAT** Roadsides, fields. **FOOD PLANTS** Herbs. **SEASON** Spring–summer.

WOOLLY BEAR CATERPILLAR MOTH
Isia isabella
TIGER MOTH FAMILY

1¾″. Forewings rusty orange with rows of small black spots; hindwings lighter. Body rusty orange with black central stripe. Nocturnal. Caterpillar distinctive; hairy, reddish brown, black at both ends; often

crosses roads, paths by day in Sept., Oct. **HABITAT** Shrubby fields, roadsides. **FOOD PLANTS** Grasses, plantains, low-growing weeds. **SEASON** June–Aug.

Vertebrates

There are approximately 43,000 vertebrate species on earth. The evolution of a variety of anatomical structures has made them extraordinarily successful for half a billion years. Today vertebrates are one of the most widespread groups of animals, inhabiting every corner of the globe, from ocean depths to mountaintops, deserts, and polar regions.

Vertebrata is one of three subphyla of the phylum Chordata. All members of Chordata possess an internal stiffening rod called a notochord during their embryonic development. The sac-like, marine sea squirts, salps, and their relatives (members of the subphylum Urochordata, the most primitive of the Chordata) lose their notochord completely as they develop, and in the file-shaped, marine lancelets (of the subphylum Cephalochordata) the notochord remains an unsegmented rod. In vertebrates the notochord is replaced during the animal's development by a series of cartilaginous or bony disks, known as vertebrae, that run along the back.

The evolution of the vertebrates stemmed from an invertebrate sea squirt–like animal, passed through a "missing link" invertebrate-to-vertebrate stage with the lancelets, and reached the beginnings of the vertebrate stage some 500 million years ago (mya) with the appearance of the first jawless fishes. During the following 350 million years, the various classes of vertebrates evolved. The ancestors of modern fishes developed from their jawless ancestors about 400 mya; 100 million years further into vertebrate development, amphibians evolved from fishes crawling about in search of water during the droughts of the Devonian period. Reptiles first appeared about 250 mya and flourished because of their ability to reproduce on land. Mammals and birds, warm-blooded and able to successfully live in places too cold for fishes, amphibians, and reptiles, spread across the world's environments, mammals beginning about 170 mya and birds about 150 mya.

Today's vertebrates share a number of characteristics that separate them from the estimated 50 million or so invertebrate species with which they share the earth. Virtually all vertebrates are bilaterally symmetrical; that is, their left and right sides are essentially mirror images of one another. The strong but flexible backbone, composed of vertebrae, protects the spinal cord and serves as the main structural component of the internal skeletal frame and the segmented muscles that attach to it.

Vertebrates are well-coordinated runners, jumpers, swimmers, and/or fliers because of this unique combination of skeletal and muscular development. Other shared characteristics of nearly all vertebrates include one pair of bony jaws (with or without teeth), one or two pairs of appendages, a ventrally located heart (protected by a rib cage), and blood contained in vessels.

The subphylum Vertebrata includes several classes: three classes of living fishes, the amphibians, the reptiles, the birds, and the mammals.

Fishes

Living fishes fall into three major groups: the primitive lampreys and hagfishes (rarely seen deepwater fishes, hagfishes are not covered in this book), the cartilaginous fishes (sharks, skates, and rays), and the bony fishes. Aquatic, mostly cold-blooded vertebrates with fins and internal gills, fish are typically streamlined and have a muscular tail. Most move through the water by weaving movements of their bodies and tail fins, using their other fins to control direction. The skin of a fish is coated with a slimy secretion that decreases friction with the water; this secretion, along with the scales that cover most fish, provides their bodies with a nearly waterproof covering. The gills are located in passages that lead from the throat usually to a pair of openings on the side, just behind the head. With rare exceptions, fish breathe by taking water in through the mouth and forcing it past the gills and out through the gill openings; the thin-walled gills capture oxygen from the water and emit carbon dioxide.

The body shapes of fishes vary from cylindrical eels and elongated, spindle-shaped mackerels (rounded in the middle, with tapered ends) to vertically compressed (flattened) sunfishes to horizontally compressed skates and rays. Body colors can vary within a species due to season, sex, age, individual variation, and water temperature, and the color normally fades or otherwise changes after death. Most fishes have one or more dorsal (back) fins that may be spiny or soft (a few fishes, such as trout and salmon, have an additional fleshy fin behind the dorsal fins, called an adipose fin); a tail (caudal) fin, usually with an upper and a lower lobe; and an anal fin, just in front of the tail along the edge of the ventral (belly) side. They also have a pair of pectoral fins, usually on the sides behind the head, and a pair of pelvic fins, generally under the middle of the body. Some fishes lack one or more of these fins.

The mouths and snouts of fishes may be disk-shaped, pointed, tubular, or sword-like; depending on the species, the upper jaw (the snout) projects beyond the lower, the two parts of the jaw are of equal length, or the lower jaw projects beyond the upper. Some species have sensory barbels, whisker-like projections of the skin, usually on the lower jaw, that detect objects, especially in muddy or murky water. Most fish are covered with scales, but some species lack scales altogether, and some lack scales on the head or other areas; in other species, scales have been modified into bony plates. Some fishes have a conspicuous lateral line, a sensory organ beneath the skin that responds to vibrations in the water and often looks like a thin stripe along the side.

Some fish species are solitary, some live in small groups, and others are found mainly in enormous schools, in which members respond as a unit to stimuli while feeding or migrating.

Lengths given (from tip of snout to tip of tail) are for typical adults, although, as fish grow throughout their lives, larger individuals may be seen. The icon ![icon] denotes fishes that can be found in both salt and fresh water (see box, page 238).

PACIFIC LAMPREY
Lampetra tridentata
LAMPREY FAMILY

16–20″. Eel-like, scaleless. Marine: steel-blue above, silvery below. Freshwater: reddish brown above; buffy below. 2 wavy dorsal fins; tail fin small, diamond-shaped; no other fins. No jaws; mouth round, sucker-like. Filter-feeds in fresh water to age 6, then enters ocean; for 1–2 years sucks fluids of large fish, then (Apr.–July) returns far up rivers to breed and die. **HABITAT** Ocean, rivers.

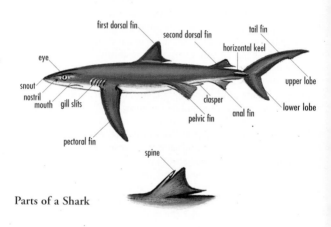

first dorsal fin
second dorsal fin
tail fin
horizontal keel
eye
upper lobe
snout
nostril
mouth   gill slits
clasper
lower lobe
pelvic fin   anal fin
pectoral fin
spine

Parts of a Shark

Cartilaginous Fishes

The cartilaginous fishes have skeletons of somewhat flexible cartilage and several (usually five) pairs of conspicuous external gill slits. This group includes, in waters off the Pacific Northwest, a chimaera, sharks, and skates. Chimaeras have a single gill opening on each side and a long ribbony tail. Sharks typically have an elongated shape that tapers toward each end; one or two triangular dorsal fins, sometimes with a fin spine on the leading edge; two large pectoral fins; two smaller pelvic fins; a tail fin of which the upper lobe is usually larger than the lower; and sometimes an anal fin and a pair of horizontal keels at the base of the tail. The skates and rays (collectively called batoids) have flattened bodies, usually round or diamond-shaped, with greatly enlarged pectoral fins that are attached to the side of the head, forming "wings" with which they "fly" through the water. The mouth is located on the underside of the head. Sharks have several rows of sharply pointed teeth; when a tooth breaks off or is worn down, a new tooth takes its place. The skin is rough and sandpapery, studded with tiny, tooth-like scales called denticles. Because cartilaginous fishes lack the swim bladder that keeps the bony fishes buoyant, and the efficient "gill pump" of bony fishes that keeps water moving over their gills, many sharks must swim constantly. Most live in ocean waters, although a few may enter large rivers. The male shark has a pair of external copulatory organs called claspers, modifications of the pelvic fins that are used to internally fertilize the female. Depending on the species, the female lays eggs enclosed in a horny case, retains the eggs internally until they hatch, or gives birth to live young that have been nourished in the womb.

SPOTTED RATFISH
Hydrolagus colliei
CHIMAERA FAMILY
24–30". Elongated; tail very long; skin smooth. Bronzy brown above, with large bluish-white spots; silvery below. Head large; snout bulky, rounded; small mouth below large eye. Male has club-shaped knob before eyes. Long poisonous spine before 1st dorsal fin; 2nd dorsal fin low, merges with tapered tail fin. Lateral line wavy. Most often seen at night. **HABITAT** Soft bottoms to 3,000' deep.

SIXGILL SHARK
Hexanchus griseus
COW SHARK FAMILY
6–10'. Elongated. Gray. 1 dorsal fin, located far back; pelvic fins far back, near anal fin; tail fin's upper lobe long, swept-back, notched. 6 gill slits. Sluggish, lethargic, usu. docile. Strong teeth and jaws cause havoc when tangled in fishing gear. Gives birth to as many as 100 fully formed young up to 16" long. **HABITAT** Ocean waters.

BLUE SHARK
Prionace glauca
REQUIEM SHARK FAMILY

7–10′. Very slender; snout pointed, longer than width of mouth. Dark blue above; sides light blue; white below. 1st dorsal fin smallish, rounded; pectoral fins long, crescent-shaped; tail fin's upper lobe long, very swept-back. Teeth curved, triangular. Follows boats, waiting for offal. **CAUTION** Rarely bites beachgoers, but attacks people swimming at sea. **HABITAT** Usu. open ocean, occ. near shore.

SPINY DOGFISH
Squalus acanthias
REQUIEM SHARK FAMILY

2–3½′. Snout rounded. Slaty brown above, shading to dirty white below. 2 pointed dorsal fins equal in size, each with spine in front, notched at rear; trailing edge of pectoral fins notched; upper lobe of tail fin long, without notch; no anal fin. Imm. has conspicuous white spots on sides. May swarm in schools of thousands. **CAUTION** Slightly poisonous spines. **HABITAT** Surf zone to deep water.

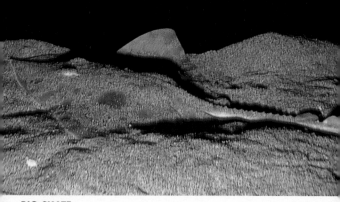

BIG SKATE
Raja binoculata
SKATE FAMILY

4–6′. Flat, diamond-shaped, concave in front; pectoral fins (wings) pointed. Olive-brown or gray above; 2 dark brown, multi-ringed false eyes on pectoral fins; whitish below. Small eyes set well back from pointed snout; mouth on underside. Tail long with spines on top; flanked by horizontal pelvic fins. Usu. rests hidden on bottom. Empty black egg case, with 4 curled extensions, called mermaid's purse. **HABITAT** Over sandy and silty bottoms to 360′.

Bony Fishes

Bony fishes normally have harder, less flexible bony skeletons than cartilaginous fishes, as well as a gas- or fat-filled swim bladder that keeps them buoyant. Most bony fishes have overlapping scales embedded in flexible connective tissue, though some lack scales entirely. There is a single gill opening on each side protected by a hard gill cover.

More than 99 percent of all living fishes are ray-finned bony fishes; a few bony fishes (none of which occur in Northwest waters) are classified as lobe-finned fishes. The fins of ray-finned bony fishes consist of a web of skin supported by bony rays (either segmented soft rays or stiffer spines), each moved by a set of muscles, which makes the fins very flexible. The tail fin is typically symmetrical.

Most bony fishes reproduce by spawning: males directly fertilize eggs after the females release them from their bodies into the water. The eggs may float at mid-levels, rise to the surface, or sink to the bottom. A few fish species guard nests or incubate eggs in a pouch or the mouth. Newborn fish are called larvae; within a few weeks or months, a larva develops to resemble a miniature adult, and is called a juvenile or fry.

This section is presented in two categories—saltwater fishes (starting on page 222) and freshwater fishes (starting on page 238). Most fish species live strictly in either salt water or fresh water. Other species are frequently found in brackish water, where fresh and salt water mix, and some primarily saltwater species breed in fresh water but return to spend most of their lives at sea. Species are placed in the category where they spend most of their time or are most likely to be seen. The icon ⬛ denotes those that live in both types of water (see box, page 238).

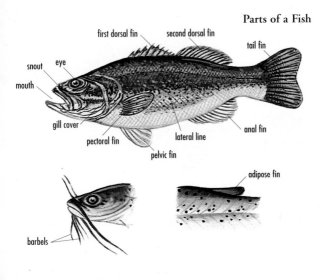

Parts of a Fish

first dorsal fin · second dorsal fin · tail fin · snout · eye · mouth · gill cover · pectoral fin · pelvic fin · lateral line · anal fin · adipose fin · barbels

WHITE STURGEON
Acipenser transmontanus
STURGEON FAMILY

6–10′. Elongated; round in cross section. Dark gray above, paler below. Back and sides have rows of raised bony scales. 1 dorsal fin, set far back; tail fin's upper lobe long, swept-back. Snout long, flattened, pointed, with 4 barbels near tip. Spawns in rivers in spring. May live 100 years. **HABITAT** Soft-bottomed coastal waters, deep pools of large rivers. **RANGE** All NW coasts and estuaries, Columbia and larger rivers.

AMERICAN SHAD
Alosa sapidissima
HERRING FAMILY

18–24″. Back rounded. Dark blue-green above; sides silvery, with 6–10 small black spots, largest one above gills; belly whitish. Dorsal fin small, triangular; tail fin deeply forked. Head scaleless; eyes yellow. **HABITAT** Bays, estuaries; rivers when spawning. **RANGE** Puget Sound, sw WA, Columbia River, sw OR.

PACIFIC HERRING
Clupea pallasi
HERRING FAMILY

10–11″. Elongated; back slightly rounded; large scales on body. Silvery, washed greenish above. Triangular dorsal fin above small pelvic fin; tail fin deeply forked, lobes equal. No scales on head; eyes large; lower jaw projects. Deposits eggs on kelp, sea grass, rocks. Vast schools appear as silvery masses at sea surface; some leap out of water. Numbers reduced by overfishing. **HABITAT** Inshore waters.

EULACHON
Thaleichthys pacificus
SMELT FAMILY

5–7″. Elongated, compressed. Olive green or brown above; long lateral line; whitish below. 1 midback dorsal fin, behind start of pelvic fin; rounded adipose fin; tail fin forked, lobes equal. Lives in schools; spawns in large silty rivers in spring. **HABITAT** Inshore ocean waters, rivers. **RANGE** All NW coasts, lower Columbia River, Puget Sound area rivers.

PACIFIC COD
Gadus macrocephalus
COD FAMILY

20–29″. Front-heavy, tapered toward rear. Dark brown above; sides gray, speckled brown; pale lateral line; pale gray below. 3 dorsal fins, last 2 mirror 2 anal fins; tail fin squared. Upper jaw projects; long barbel on lower jaw; eyes large. Often in schools. **HABITAT** Deep water over soft bottoms.

PACIFIC TOMCOD
Microgadus proximus
COD FAMILY

7–9″. Elongated, tapered toward rear. Olive green above; sides gray; dark lateral line; pale gray below. 3 dorsal fins, last 2 mirror 2 anal fins; tail fin squared; fin tips dusky. Upper jaw projects; short barbel on lower jaw; eyes large. Often in schools near piers and wharves. **HABITAT** Shallow water over soft bottoms.

WALLEYE POLLOCK
Theragra chalcogramma
COD FAMILY

22–28″. Elongated, tapered toward rear. Dark slaty green above; sides gray; dark lateral line; pale gray below. 3 dorsal fins, last 2 mirror 2 anal fins; tail fin slightly notched. Lower jaw projects; very short barbel on lower jaw; eyes large. Often in schools. **HABITAT** Shallow to moderate depths over soft bottoms.

PLAINFIN MIDSHIPMAN
Porichthys notatus
TOADFISH FAMILY

9–12″. Elongated, tapered toward rear. Purplish bronze above, with dark brown blotches; pale yellow below. Spots on head and in rows on sides emit light. 1st dorsal fin tiny; 2nd dorsal fin and anal fin very long-based, extend to small rounded tail fin. Head flattened; eyes bulge; lower jaw projects. Often lies buried in silt by day; active at night. Male guards eggs. **HABITAT** Over sand and mud bottoms to 1,200′ deep.

Scorpionfishes

Sixty-two species in the scorpionfish family occur off the Pacific Coast of America north of Mexico, making it one of the largest fish families in the region. Scorpionfish bodies are deep, and tapered at both ends. They have large mouths, and ridges and spines on the bony plate that covers much of the head; most are brightly colored. The first dorsal, pelvic, and anal fins have sharp spines. Most Northwest members of the family are rockfish of the genus *Sebastes*. Rockfish are colorful species with mildly toxic fluids in their fin spines. They occur at all water levels, and bear live young.

BROWN ROCKFISH
Sebastes auriculatus
SCORPIONFISH FAMILY

12–16″. Olive-brown above; lateral line and sides pale orange, sides with dark brown mottling; whitish below. Dorsal fins continuous, 1st very spiny, 2nd rounded; tail fin rounded; fins on underside pink. Heavy spine near eye; dark spot on gill cover. Usu. sedentary. **HABITAT** Shallow, weedy, rocky areas; around wharves, jetties; to 400′ deep.

COPPER ROCKFISH
Sebastes caurinus
SCORPIONFISH FAMILY

13–17″. Body coppery above, with pale orange, pink, or yellow blotches; rear half of lateral line whitish; whitish below. Head pale with darker, angled stripes; 5 pairs of head spines. Dorsal fins continuous, 1st very spiny, longer-based, 2nd rounded; tail fin rounded. **HABITAT** Rocks and kelp beds in inlets; around pilings, jetties; to 600′ deep.

YELLOWTAIL ROCKFISH
Sebastes flavidus
SCORPIONFISH FAMILY

16–20″. Brown above; lateral line curved, white; whitish below; tiny reddish speckles on each scale. Fins yellow-green. 1st dorsal fin spiny, long-based, 2nd rounded; back of anal fin vertical; tail fin forked. Head spineless; chin ends in knob. Schools with other rockfish. HABITAT Over rocks and soft bottoms to 900′ deep.

QUILLBACK ROCKFISH
Sebastes maliger
SCORPIONFISH FAMILY

14–18″. Dark brown above, with large yellow or orange blotches; buffy below, with tiny brown speckles. Cheeks yellowish orange; 5 pairs of spines on head; eyes large. Dorsal fins continuous, 1st deeply notched, longer-based, pale (all other fins black), 2nd dorsal fin rounded; back edge of anal fin vertical; tail fin rounded. Solitary. HABITAT Over rocky bottoms, caves, to 900′ deep.

CHINA ROCKFISH
Sebastes nebulosus
SCORPIONFISH FAMILY

10–14″. Head and body black, with many tiny, pale blue dots; yellow-orange blotches on head and sides; wide yellow stripe from 1st dorsal fin along lateral line to tail; lips blue; patterning variable. Dorsal fins continuous, 1st spiny, longer-based, 2nd rounded; tail fin rounded. All fins black with blue dots at base. 5 pairs of spines on head. Solitary. HABITAT Over rocky bottoms, caves, to 400′ deep.

TIGER ROCKFISH
Sebastes nigrocinctus
SCORPIONFISH FAMILY

14–18″. Body pale orange, pink, or gray, with 5 wide, dark red to black vertical bars. Head pale; dark stripes radiate from eye; lower jaw projects. Dorsal fins whitish, continuous, 1st spiny, 2nd rounded; tail fin rounded, whitish; other fins reddish. Solitary. HABITAT Over rocky bottoms, caves, to 900′ deep.

CANARY ROCKFISH
Sebastes pinniger
SCORPIONFISH FAMILY

16–20″. Body orange above; gray stripe along curved lateral line; gray below, speckled with orange. Head pale with 3 orange stripes; lower jaw projects. Dorsal fins continuous, 1st spiny, 2nd straight-edged; tail fin notched; pelvic and anal fins pointed. Active in small, loosely organized groups. HABITAT Over rocky bottoms to 1,200′ deep.

YELLOWEYE ROCKFISH
"Red Snapper"
Sebastes ruberrimus
SCORPIONFISH FAMILY

22–26". Dark orange above, paler orange below; white line from eye to tail along curved lateral line; less distinct white line below. Dorsal fins continuous, 1st very spiny, 2nd straight-edged; tail fin rounded. Head has ridge of spines; eyes yellow; throat white. **HABITAT** Over rocky bottoms, caves, to 1,800' deep.

SABLEFISH
Anoplopoma fimbria
SABLEFISH FAMILY

26–30". Elongated; round in cross section. Brownish black above; faint lateral line; sides speckled green and bronze; whitish below. 2 well-spaced, spineless dorsal fins; tail fin

forked. Eyes fairly large. Young common near piers, jetties in summer; adults in deep water. Swift swimmer. **HABITAT** Over soft bottoms to 6,000' deep.

KELP GREENLING
Hexagrammos decagrammus
GREENLING FAMILY

14–18". Elongated, slightly compressed. Male grayish brown with many small black spots and larger iridescent, black-edged blue spots. Female gray or blue with reddish-brown spots. 1 long-based dorsal fin notched in middle; tail fin squared. Lips fleshy; thread-like projections behind eyes. Often follows divers. **HABITAT** Rocky coastal waters to 150' deep.

LINGCOD
Ophiodon elongatus
GREENLING FAMILY

34–38". Elongated; round in cross section. Gray-brown above with dark brown speckling on sides; straight lateral line; whitish below. 1 long-based dorsal fin notched in middle; tail fin squared. Snout

pointed; lower jaw projects; jaws heavily toothed. Voracious predator. Territorial. **HABITAT** Over soft and rocky bottoms to 6,600' deep.

PAINTED GREENLING
Oxylebius pictus
GREENLING FAMILY

5–6". Elongated. Male all blackish when spawning (winter), like female in summer. Female buffy with 6–7 reddish-orange vertical bars; colors run onto fins. 1 long-based dorsal fin notched in middle; tail fin squared. Snout pointed; lips fleshy; bushy projections behind eyes. Male guards eggs. **HABITAT** Shallow rocky waters, piers.

Sculpins

A typical sculpin is a bizarre-looking, partly scaled fish with a large, flattened, spiny head, eyes placed high on the head, a tapered body, and a fan-like tail fin. The pectoral fins are also fan-like, with stiff spines that are used like legs to hold on to bottoms in swift currents. Sculpins often live in rocky areas between the high- and low-tide lines, although some live only in fresh water. The male guards eggs at the nest site. It is wise to avoid handling members of this family, as the sharp spines on the head and fins can inflict nasty wounds. There are dozens of species of sculpins in inland and maritime waters of the Pacific Northwest.

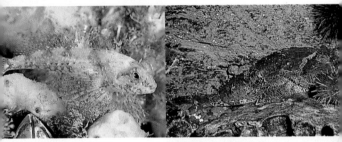

SCALYHEAD SCULPIN
Artedius harringtoni
SCULPIN FAMILY

2½–3½". Elongated, tapered, with broad bands of scales on back. Brownish olive above, with 5–7 dark brown saddles; large round white spots on sides merge into white belly. 1st dorsal fin spiny, 2nd longer-based; pectoral fins fan-like; tail fin squared. All these fins banded. Red bars radiate from eye; fleshy projections on head. **HABITAT** Shallow rocky waters, pilings, to 80′ deep.

BUFFALO SCULPIN
Enophrys bison
SCULPIN FAMILY

9–11". Elongated, heavily armored. Head large, bony; long barbed spine projects from gill cover; snout steep. Dark brown, mottled and blotched with buff; sharp bony plates on lateral line. 2 dorsal fins banded; tail fin rounded, banded; pectoral fins fan-like, spotted. Well camouflaged; awaits passing prey in rocks, seaweeds. **HABITAT** Rocky and sandy coasts to 65′ deep.

RED IRISH LORD
Hemilepidotus hemilepidotus
SCULPIN FAMILY

9–12". Elongated; round in cross section; wide band of scales on back, another below lateral line. Reddish, with 4 brown saddles and white mottling above; whitish below. Dorsal fin long, notched twice; tail fin rounded; both fins transparent with red stains. Head large, spiny. Blends in with surroundings; sedentary. **HABITAT** Rocky shorelines, piers, to 160′ deep.

PACIFIC STAGHORN SCULPIN
Leptocottus armatus
SCULPIN FAMILY

8–10″. Elongated, scaleless. Gray or olive green above, pale yellow below. Dorsal fins separate, 1st short, with large black spot at rear, 2nd long; tail fin rounded; pectoral fins fan-shaped; all fins banded. Head gently sloping, pointed, fairly smooth; spine over gill cover ragged, antler-like. Often lies partly buried in silt; slow-swimming. **HABITAT** Bays, inlets over sandy bottoms, to 300′ deep.

SAILFIN SCULPIN
Nautichthys oculofasciatus
SCULPIN FAMILY

5–7″. Elongated, slender. Body buffy with few brown spots. Head concave behind large yellow eyes; dark line from eye to throat. Fins buffy, banded brown; 1st dorsal fin very high, 2nd long; tail fin rounded. Skin sandpapery. Active mainly at night. **HABITAT** Rocky and sandy bottoms, piers, to 360′ deep. **RANGE** All NW coasts, but mainly Puget Sound and north.

TIDEPOOL SCULPIN
Oligocottus maculosus
SCULPIN FAMILY

2½–3″. Elongated, smooth (no scales or prickles). Color varies: reddish to greenish, with darker saddles above; creamy below. 2 separate dorsal fins and rounded tail fin lightly banded. Hair-like projections on head. Abundant in tidepools. **HABITAT** Tidepools, surf-drenched rocky areas.

GRUNT SCULPIN
Rhamphocottus richardsoni
SCULPIN FAMILY

2–3″. Deep, compressed, odd-looking. Creamy yellow with brown bars and streaks. Small separate dorsal fins, rounded tail fin, and free-rayed pectoral fins bright red. Snout long, narrow; mouth tiny; eyes camouflaged. Walks along bottom on finger-like pectoral fin rays; hides in shells, bottles, cans; often waves tail; grunts when removed from water. **HABITAT** Shallow rocky shorelines.

CABEZON
Scorpaenichthys marmoratus
SCULPIN FAMILY

22–26″. Elongated, slightly compressed, scaleless. Marbled red, green, and brown, with large dark and light blotches. Head large; spine on snout. 1st of 2 dorsal fins notched in middle; tail fin rounded; pectoral fins fan-shaped; all fins heavily patterned. Sedentary. Males often seen guarding eggs. **CAUTION** Roe is highly toxic. **HABITAT** Shallow rocky areas, piers, to 250′ deep.

STURGEON POACHER
Podothecus acipenserinus
POACHER FAMILY

7–9″. Elongated, slender, very tapered. Scales modified into rows of fused bony plates. Brown above, whitish below. Head thicker than body; eyes large, yellow; 2 short spines on snout; mouth on underside of head; bushy yellow whiskers below snout and jaw. 2 small dorsal fins; tail fin rounded. **HABITAT** Soft bottoms to 180′ deep.

PACIFIC SPINY LUMPSUCKER
Eumicrotremus orbis
SNAILFISH FAMILY

3–4″. Stocky, covered with spiny round cones. Male orange or yellowish above; female pale green above; both pale brown or purplish below. 1st dorsal fin well separated from 2nd; 2nd dorsal, tail, and anal fins rounded. Underside has large sucking disk with fringing margin, formed by modified pelvic fins. Attaches to rocks, kelp, sunken logs. Moves fins rapidly, but swims slowly. **HABITAT** Tidepools, rocky shores, to 500′ deep. **RANGE** Puget Sound, nw WA.

STRIPED BASS
Morone saxatilis
TEMPERATE BASS FAMILY

22–28″. Elongated, moderately compressed, streamlined, with small fins. Pale; olive or slaty blue above; sides silvery, with 6–9 blackish side stripes; belly white. 2 dorsal fins triangular; tail fin notched. Lower jaw projects slightly. Introduced to San Francisco Bay in 1879; spread north to Brit. Col. **HABITAT** Ocean; rivers when spawning (early summer). **RANGE** All NW coasts, esp. coastal OR.

SHINER PERCH
Cymatogaster aggregata
SURFPERCH FAMILY

4–5″. Elongated, compressed. Greenish yellow above; sides silvery gray; curved lateral line; horizontal rows of blackish spots on sides; whitish below. Female and winter male have 3 yellow bars on sides; male dark in summer. Fins transparent; dorsal fins continuous; tail fin forked. Head concave above yellow eyes. Occurs in loose schools. Bears live young. **HABITAT** Shallow quiet waters in summer; piers, kelp beds, coastal rivers, to 480′ deep in winter.

STRIPED SEAPERCH
Embiotoca lateralis
SURFPERCH FAMILY

9–11". Deep, very compressed. Body reddish orange with many thin, bright blue horizontal stripes that look gray in water; curved lateral line. Bright blue spots on head and gill covers; mouth small; upper lip black, lower white. Fins reddish orange with dark edges; dorsal fins continuous; tail fin forked. Bears live young. **HABITAT** Rocky shores, piers, kelp beds, to 70' deep.

PILE PERCH
Rhacochilus vacca
SURFPERCH FAMILY

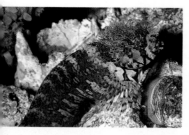

10–12". Deep, very compressed. Body silvery with indistinct broad blackish bar at mid-side; curved lateral line; breeding male dark overall. Spiny part of dorsal fin low; soft part high, pointed at front; tail fin deeply forked. Dark spot behind lips; upper lip dark, lower white. Occurs in schools. **HABITAT** Rocky shores, pilings, kelp beds, to 150' deep.

MOSSHEAD WARBONNET
Chirolophis nugator
PRICKLEBACK FAMILY

3–4". Elongated, eel-like. Brown above, round white spots below. 1 dorsal fin long, low, continuous, with about 13 evenly spaced, eye-like black spots ringed in white. Tail fin tiny, rounded; anal fin long, low. Head small, with moss-like growths on top; cheeks barred. Often hides in crevices, old shells, bottles, with just head showing. **HABITAT** Rocky shores to 265' deep.

ROCKWEED GUNNEL
Apodichthys fucorum
GUNNEL FAMILY

5–6". Elongated, eel-like. Uniformly yellow-green, brown, or red, depending on algae color where it lives. Long, low dorsal and anal fins joined to rounded tail fin; tiny pectoral fins; no pelvic fins. Head and mouth small. **HABITAT** Tidepools, bottoms with rocks or algae, to 30' deep.

WOLF-EEL
Anarrhichthys ocellatus
WOLFFISH FAMILY

4½–5½'. Very elongated, eel-like. Male grayish, female darker reddish brown; both have dark brown spots with light halos; all blackish toward tapered rear. Low, continuous, fringing dorsal and anal fins join at pointed tail; no pelvic fins. Head blunt; mouth large. Predator; lurks in crevices. **CAUTION** Beware of teeth. **HABITAT** Rocky bottoms, debris, to 750' deep.

BLACKEYE GOBY
Coryphopterus nicholsi
GOBY FAMILY

6". Elongated, scales large. Pink to orange; faint brown speckling. 1st dorsal fin rounded, black top edge; 2nd dorsal fin high, same length as anal fin; tail fin rounded; pelvic fins fused to form bottom-anchoring cone. Large black eyes on top of head. **HABITAT** Quiet sandy bottoms near rocks, shallows to 350'.

Flatfishes

Flatfish is the group name for three fish families (lefteye flounders, righteye flounders, and soles) with an unusual body form adapted to life on the seafloor. The larval fish starts life swimming normally, with an eye on each side. Soon one eye "migrates" to join the other on one side (right or left, depending on the species). The spineless, continuous dorsal fin and anal fin become fringing horizontal fins, and for the rest of the fish's life it swims on one side. Flatfish can change the color and pattern of their top (eyed) side to match their backgrounds, but their undersides are normally white. They usually lie partially buried in soft mud or sand bottoms, and dart quickly upward to seize passing small fish, crustaceans, and squid.

Parts of a Flatfish

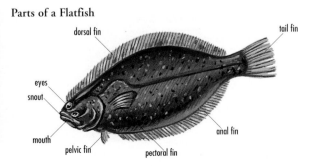

dorsal fin

tail fin

eyes

snout

mouth

pelvic fin

pectoral fin

anal fin

SPECKLED SANDDAB
Citharichthys stigmaeus
LEFTEYE FLOUNDER FAMILY

4½–5½". Flat oval disk. Brown, tan, or gray (color matches sea bottom), with many small and few large blackish speckles; lateral line straight; white below. Fringing dorsal and anal fins; tail fin rounded; all fins speckled. Eyes close to pointed mouth. **HABITAT** Over sandy bottoms to 1,800' deep.

PACIFIC HALIBUT
Hippoglossus stenolepis
RIGHTEYE FLOUNDER FAMILY

4–5'. Flat, diamond-shaped disk. Dark brown to blackish, with blackish marbling and white spots; lateral line arched; white below. Fringing dorsal and anal fins; tail fin crescent-shaped at rear; all fins speckled. Eyes close to large pointed mouth. Small ones (10 lb) called chicken halibut; huge old ones (can reach 500 lb) called whale halibut. **HABITAT** Over soft and rocky bottoms to 3,600' deep.

STARRY FLOUNDER
Platichthys stellatus
RIGHTEYE FLOUNDER FAMILY

18–22". Flat, square-shaped disk; eyes and color on right or left side of body; scales on eyed side star-shaped. Brown or gray with blackish marbling and white spots; lateral line slightly curved; white below. Fringing dorsal and anal fins, middle ones longer, forming square body shape; tail fin fan-shaped; all fins boldly striped blackish. Eyes close to pointed mouth. **HABITAT** Over soft bottoms, bays, to 900' deep; also rivers near coast (to 75 miles up Columbia R.).

ROCK SOLE
Pleuronectes (Lepidopsetta) bilineatus
RIGHTEYE FLOUNDER FAMILY

14–18". Flat oval disk; scales rough. Brown, tan, or gray (color matches sea bottom), with many small white and few large blackish spots; lateral line arched with short dorsal branch; white below. Fringing dorsal and anal fins; tail fin rounded; all fins boldly spotted. Eyes close to pointed mouth. Rarely on bottom; more active, swims free more often than other flatfish. **HABITAT** Over soft or pebbly bottoms to 1,200' deep.

ENGLISH SOLE
Pleuronectes (Parophrys) vetulus
RIGHTEYE FLOUNDER FAMILY

13–17″. Flat oval disk; upper eye visible from blind side; scales smooth on fore half of body; rough on rear half. Brown with few darker spots; lateral line straight with short dorsal branch; white to pale yellow-brown below. Fringing dorsal and anal fins; tail fin square; all fins boldly spotted. Snout pointed; jaws twisted. **HABITAT** Over soft bottoms to 1,800′ deep.

C-O SOLE
Pleuronichthys coenosus
RIGHTEYE FLOUNDER FAMILY

9–11″. Flat round disk. Brown with light and dark spots; some have large dark spot at midbody; lateral line straight with long dorsal branch; white below. Fringing dorsal and anal fins; 1st 6 rays of dorsal fin begin on blind side. Tail fin rounded; whitish "C" and "O" on brown rays. Snout rounded; small mouth almost hidden by bulging eyes. **HABITAT** Shallows with soft bottoms, kelp beds; also to 1,150′ deep.

OCEAN SUNFISH
Mola mola
MOLA FAMILY

4–6′. Round, massive, compressed; snout short; rounded, flap-like tail fin looks cut off; scaleless. Back gray-blue; sides and belly silvery. Mirror-image single dorsal fin and anal fin huge, shark-like, far back on body; no pelvic fins. Eyes large, well back from mouth; mouth and gill openings small. Young round, covered with spines; drifts on ocean currents. Strong swimmer; lies on side at surface, siphoning in jellyfish, squid, fish larvae. **HABITAT** Warm ocean surface waters, mainly in warmer months.

COMMON CARP
Cyprinus carpio
CARP AND MINNOW FAMILY

18–22″. Oval; back high, rounded. Dark olive above, shading to yellowish gray below. Dorsal fin long, begins at high point of back, has thickened forward spine; tail fin forked, lobes rounded. 2 pairs of barbels on upper lip. Native to Eurasia; destroys bottom plants needed by native NW fish as cover for eggs, fry. **HABITAT** Clear or turbid rivers, lakes, reservoirs; sometimes brackish waters. **RANGE** Columbia Basin, Willamette Valley, se OR, w WA.

PEAMOUTH
Mylocheilus caurinus
CARP AND MINNOW FAMILY

9–11″. Elongated. Back dark gray-brown; thick black line from gill to tail; whitish below, with 2nd black line along ½ of body. 1 midback dorsal fin; tail fin forked. Head and mouth small; small barbel at corner of jaw. Mature male has red lips, red stripe on gill covers and ventral fin bases. **HABITAT** Vegetated small rivers, lakes, brackish waters. **RANGE** Columbia and Willamette Valleys; fringes of Puget Sound, Lake Washington.

NORTHERN SQUAWFISH
Ptychocheilus oregonensis
CARP AND MINNOW FAMILY

13–15″. Elongated, slender. Gray-green above; sides silver; lateral line arches downward. Head and snout long, flattened; mouth large; jaws of equal length; lacks barbels. 1 triangular dorsal fin; tail fin forked; ventral fins reddish in old males. **HABITAT** Lakes, pools, rivers. **RANGE** Puget Sound rivers, Lake Washington, Columbia, Snake, and Willamette tributaries.

Fishes That Live in Both Fresh and Salt Water

A number of Northwest fish species spend occasional to great parts of their lives moving between salt and fresh water. As adults, the American Shad, Eulachon, and Striped Bass leave the sea every year, travel up a river to breed, and return to the sea, repeating this pattern for a number of years. All salmon (except those that are land-locked) and some trout species are born in fresh water but spend most of their lives in the sea; they return to the rivers of their birth once, breed, and usually die there. Some freshwater fishes occasionally visit brackish estuaries, while some marine fishes sometimes forage far up an estuary.

Salmon

Pacific salmon live most of their lives at sea, but they ascend rivers and streams to breed. The upstream journey is arduous, as the fish encounter waterfalls and predators and, now, dams. Chinooks may go upriver more than 1,000 miles to spawn in tributaries so shallow their backs are exposed. Males of most species become brightly colored in preparation for breeding and develop hooked jaws to threaten one another as they compete for spawning sites. Females dig depressions in gravel beds, where the eggs are fertilized. The adults soon die. The eggs hatch quickly, but the young remain in the gravel for some time before emerging as fry less than an inch long. They grow rapidly but remain in fresh water from a few weeks to several years, depending on the species. Salmon bring nutrients from the sea far inland, nourishing many other animals, including humans.

PINK SALMON
"Humpback"
Oncorhynchus gorbuscha
TROUT FAMILY

18–22″. Elongated; scales small. Silvery blue above, with large oval spots; whitish below. 1 midback dorsal fin; small adipose fin; tail fin forked, lobes equal; all these fins spotted black. Spawning male reddish pink; develops hump on back and hooked jaws. Spawns in even-numbered years a short distance up coastal rivers. Most abundant NW salmon. **HABITAT** Ocean, coastal rivers. **RANGE** All NW coasts, nearby rivers.

CHUM SALMON
"Dog Salmon"
Oncorhynchus keta
TROUT FAMILY

22–28″. Elongated. Silvery blue above, usu. with few or no spots; whitish below. Fins unspotted, with dark edges; 1 midback dorsal fin; small adipose fin; tail fin forked, lobes equal. Spawning male greenish with dark reddish bars on sides; jaws slightly hooked. Spawns short distances up coastal rivers. **HABITAT** Ocean, coastal rivers. **RANGE** All NW coasts, nearby rivers.

adult (left), spawning adults (right)

COHO SALMON
"Silver Salmon"
Oncorhynchus kisutch
TROUT FAMILY

22–28″. Elongated. Silvery blue above, sparsely black-spotted; whitish below. 1 midback dorsal fin; small adipose fin; tail fin forked, lobes equal; all these fins spotted except lower lobe of tail fin. Jaws of equal length, with needle-like teeth. Spawning male greenish above, reddish orange on sides; jaws hooked. Spawns medium distances up rivers; some inland to ID. **HABITAT** Ocean, rivers. **RANGE** All NW coasts, rivers of Cascades.

SOCKEYE SALMON
"Red Salmon"
Oncorhynchus nerka
TROUT FAMILY

20–26″. Elongated. Silvery blue above, with fine speckles; whitish below. 1 unspotted midback dorsal fin; small adipose fin; tail fin plain, forked, lobes equal. Spawning male has humped back, green head, red back and sides; spawning female slaty; both have hooked jaws. Spawns long distances up rivers that end in lakes, where fry spend 2 years before returning to sea. 2nd most common NW salmon after Pink Salmon. **HABITAT** Ocean surface, rivers. **RANGE** All NW coasts, rivers east to ID.

CHINOOK SALMON
"King Salmon"
Oncorhynchus tshawytscha
TROUT FAMILY

32–40″. The largest salmon. Elongated. Silvery blue above, with heavy black spotting; whitish below. 1 midback dorsal fin; small adipose fin; tail fin forked, lobes equal; all these fins heavily black-spotted. Lower jaw projects. Spawning male's back humped, greenish; sides pinkish orange; jaws hooked. Spawns spring and fall, long distances up rivers; inland to ID. **HABITAT** Ocean surface, rivers. **RANGE** All NW coasts, rivers east to ID.

CUTTHROAT TROUT
Oncorhynchus (Salmo) clarki
TROUT FAMILY

14–18″. Elongated, head large. Inland form: olive above; sides orange with faint red stripe, black spotting; bright red slash mark on throat. Marine form: green above; sides silver-blue to olive; pink mark on throat. 1 triangular dorsal fin, small adipose fin, and crescent-shaped tail fin greenish with black spotting. Mouth large; jaws extend behind eyes. Adult marine forms return up coastal rivers to spawn Apr.–June; return to sea July–Aug. (later from Puget Sound streams); young remain inland 2–8 years. **HABITAT** Gravel-bottomed rivers and streams, lakes; ocean near estuaries. **RANGE** West of Cascades, far e WA.

RAINBOW TROUT
Oncorhynchus mykiss
TROUT FAMILY

18–24". Elongated; head large; straight lateral line. Inland form: olive above; sides have wide red stripe, black spotting; yellowish to white below. Marine form (Steelhead): silvery blue above with black spotting; sides silvery; pink wash on fore half of sides. 1 triangular dorsal fin, small adipose fin, and crescent-shaped tail fin with black spotting. Mouth large; jaws extend to below eyes. Steelheads return up coastal rivers to spawn Feb.–June; return to sea in 1–3 years. Formerly known as *Salmo gairdneri*. **HABITAT** Gravel-bottomed rivers and streams, lakes, ocean.

BROOK TROUT
Salvelinus fontinalis
TROUT FAMILY

8–12". Elongated. Olive green above, with dark wavy lines; sides olive, with many large yellowish spots and few small red spots with blue halos; belly white (reddish in adult male). Dorsal fin spotted, triangular; tail fin squared or lightly forked; ventral fins reddish, with white and black leading edges. Large jaws extend well behind eyes. **HABITAT** Lakes, cool clear headwater ponds, spring-fed streams in mtns. **RANGE** WA Cascades, ne and se WA, ne OR.

THREESPINE STICKLEBACK
Gasterosteus aculeatus
STICKLEBACK FAMILY

2–3". Tapered at both ends; sides have bony plates. Olive-brown above, silver below; breeding male red below. 3 stout spines, widely separated, on back before dorsal fin; tail fin rounded. Lower jaw projects. Male territorial; builds cylindrical nest from water plants. **HABITAT** Lakes, streams, brackish waters, ocean. **RANGE** All NW coasts; inland mainly w of Cascades and Columbia Basin.

PRICKLY SCULPIN
Cottus asper
SCULPIN FAMILY

4–5". (See essay on Sculpins on page 231.) Elongated, tapered; body often prickly. Brown above, with many dark brown blotches; pale yellow below. 1st dorsal fin spiny; 2nd longer-based, mirrors anal fin; tail fin rounded; pectoral fins fanlike. Head sloping; eyes high on head. **HABITAT** Sandy pools in quiet rivers, lakeshores, brackish estuaries. **RANGE** West of Cascades, Columbia Basin.

BLUEGILL
Lepomis macrochirus
SUNFISH FAMILY
6–8″. Oval, compressed. Olive above, with 5–9 vertical dusky green bands; breeding male orange below, with blue gill covers; female whitish below. Dark spot on rear of single dorsal fin; tail fin slightly forked. Introduced from e U.S. **HABITAT** Shallow vegetated lakeshores, stream pools. **RANGE** WA, w and se OR.

SMALLMOUTH BASS
Micropterus dolomieu
SUNFISH FAMILY
13–17″. Elongated. Brown above; sides greenish yellow with diffuse, brownish bands; belly whitish. 1st dorsal fin spiny; 2nd rounded; tail fin notched, lobes rounded. Mouth extends to point below front of eye. Introduced from e U.S. **HABITAT**

Deep lakes, cool clear streams over rocks. **RANGE** West and east of Cascades.

LARGEMOUTH BASS
Micropterus salmoides
SUNFISH FAMILY
16–18″. Elongated; head large. Dark green above; sides olive green with brownish mottling; belly whitish. Dark lateral stripe disappears with age. 1st dorsal fin spiny; 2nd dorsal fin rounded; tail fin slightly forked. Mouth extends to point below rear of eye. Introduced from e U.S. **HABITAT** Warm shallow waters with vegetation. **RANGE** West and east of Cascades.

WHITE CRAPPIE
Pomoxis annularis
SUNFISH FAMILY
8–12″. Oval, very compressed. Back rounded, dark green; sides silvery green with many blackish spots. Dorsal fins continuous, rounded; tail fin forked; anal fin high; all fins have wavy black lines. Forehead

concave; lower jaw projects. Introduced from e U.S. **HABITAT** Streams, rivers, ponds, lakes. **RANGE** West and east of Cascades, ex. se OR.

YELLOW PERCH
Perca flavescens
PERCH AND DARTER FAMILY
9–11″. Oblong, somewhat compressed. Olive green or brownish, with 5–8 blackish vertical bars on back and sides. 2 separated dorsal fins dusky; 1st dorsal fin and first 2 rays of anal fin have sharp spines. Head small, pointed. Introduced from e U.S. **HABITAT** Clear streams, lakes with vegetation. **RANGE** West and east of Cascades.

Amphibians

The ancestors of today's amphibians began evolving from fish about 300 million years ago. Members of the class Amphibia typically start life in fresh water and later live on land. Most undergo metamorphosis (a series of developmental stages) from aquatic, water-breathing larvae to terrestrial or partly terrestrial, air-breathing adults. The most primitive of terrestrial vertebrates, amphibians lack claws and external ear openings. They have thin, moist, scaleless skin and are cold-blooded; their body temperature varies with that of their surroundings. In winter, they burrow deep into leaf litter, soft soils, and the mud of ponds, and maintain an inactive state. Unlike reptiles, amphibians can become dehydrated in dry environments and must live near water at least part of the year and for breeding. Their eggs lack shells, and most are laid in water.

Salamanders

Salamanders, order Caudata, have blunt heads, long slender bodies, short legs, and long tails. Most lay eggs in fresh water that hatch into four-legged larvae with tufted external gills; after several months or years, the larvae typically lose their gills and go ashore. A few species, such as the Ensatina and the Western Redback Salamander, lay eggs on land and skip the gilled larval stage. Western newts remain tied to water their whole lives, but adults feed on land in wet periods. Adult lungless salamanders lack lungs and breathe through their thin moist skin; mostly terrestrial, they live under bark, wood, or stones, sometimes near streams. Mole salamanders, which breathe through lungs, burrow into soft soil. Giant salamanders, the world's largest land salamanders, start out as aquatic larvae and usually become land dwellers as adults. During all life stages, salamanders eat small animal life. They are generally hard to see, as they feed under wet leaves and logs; they are easiest to see at night in early spring, when they congregate to mate and lay eggs at temporary pools created by the thaw and rains. Inactive in winter, they reside in decaying logs, between tree roots, and in soil. Salamanders differ from lizards, which are reptiles, in having thin, moist, unscaled skin and four toes on the front feet (lizards have five), and in their lack of claws and external ear openings. Salamanders are fast declining in number worldwide, due to habitat destruction and perhaps acid rain, pesticides, and increasing ultraviolet light.

The size given for salamanders is the typical length from the tip of the nose to the end of the tail.

ROUGHSKIN NEWT
Taricha granulosa
NEWT FAMILY

7". Slender. Warty above, light brown to blackish; yellow or orange below, some with dark blotches; tail vertically compressed. When threatened, curls head and tail up; skin secretions toxic to predators. **HABITAT** Lakes, ponds, wet woodlands, open valleys. **ACTIVITY** Day and night, year-round; hides in logs, burrows on hot days May–Sept.; easily seen in breeding ponds. **RANGE** Cascades and west.

egg mass

NORTHWESTERN SALAMANDER
Ambystoma gracile
MOLE SALAMANDER FAMILY

7″. Robust; snout rounded; large swollen gland behind eye; tail vertically compressed, with round glandular ridge on top; glands secrete irritating milky substance. Rich brown above, grayish brown below; grooves on sides. Adult terrestrial, secretive. **HABITAT** Under logs in woodlands, wetlands, to 10,200′. **ACTIVITY** Mainly nocturnal, year-round. **RANGE** Cascades and west.

LONG-TOED SALAMANDER
Ambystoma macrodactylum
MOLE SALAMANDER FAMILY

western race (left), sw Oregon race (right)

5½″. Slender; toes long; neck narrow. Dark brown or blackish, with tiny white dots on sides; belly brownish; grooves on sides. Dorsal colors vary; west of Cascades: green or yellow stripe on back; east of Cascades: yellow-green stripe on head and back; sw OR: yellow spots above. **HABITAT** Wet coniferous forests, alpine meadows, sagebrush deserts. **ACTIVITY** Day and night, year-round at low elevs., Apr.–Sept. in mtns.

PACIFIC GIANT SALAMANDER
Dicamptodon ensatus (tenebrosus)
GIANT SALAMANDER FAMILY

11″. Robust; skin smooth. Light brown above, with darker brown mottling; belly light brown to pale yellow. Adults mainly terrestrial, though some remain aquatic; deep burrowers. Most live under rocks, logs, leaf litter; some climb bushes and trees. **HABITAT** Rivers, wet coniferous forests. **ACTIVITY** Day and night, Feb.–Nov. **RANGE** Cascades and west.

ENSATINA
Ensatina eschscholtzii
LUNGLESS SALAMANDER FAMILY

5″. Slender; legs long; tail constricted at base. Plain reddish brown above; belly pale pink. **HABITAT** Streamside Douglas Fir and Vine Maple woodlands. **ACTIVITY** Mainly spring and fall, when ground is moist; hides in burrows, crevices, caves when hot and dry or cold. **RANGE** Cascades and west.

WESTERN REDBACK SALAMANDER
Plethodon vehiculum
LUNGLESS SALAMANDER FAMILY

4″. Slender; legs short. Color varies: top of head, back stripe that extends to tail tip, and tops of limbs usu. orange, less often yellow, green, or tan; sides blackish; blue-gray below. Hides under rocks, logs, leaf litter. **HABITAT** Rock slides, ravines, woodlands. **ACTIVITY** Day and night, year-round. **RANGE** Cascades and west.

Frogs

Adult frogs and toads (order Anura) have large heads and eyes, and wide, usually toothless mouths; they appear neckless, and most lack tails. Many can rapidly extend a long tongue for capturing insects. They have two long muscular hindlegs and two smaller front legs. All must keep their skin moist and avoid drying out in the sun. All Northwest frogs pass the winter in a state of torpor, burying themselves in mud at the edge of a pond or crawling between the bark and trunk of a large tree. In the spring, the male vocalizes to attract the larger female, and clings to her while fertilizing eggs as she lays them, usually in water. The eggs hatch into round-bodied, long-tailed aquatic larvae called tadpoles or pollywogs, which begin life with external gills that are soon covered with skin. The tadpole later transforms into a tail-less ground, tree, or marsh dweller with air-breathing lungs. Male members of the tailed frog family (Ascaphidae) have a tail-like copulatory organ, found only in this group. Members of the spadefoot family (Pelobatidae) have a hard spade on their hindlegs to facilitate burrowing; they breed in puddles after very heavy rains, and develop from egg to tadpole to frog in only two weeks. Toads are a family (Bufonidae) of frogs that have shorter legs for hopping and warty skin, which secretes poisons that

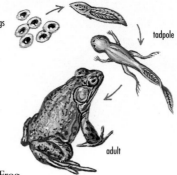

eggs

tadpole

adult

Life Cycle of a Frog

cause irritations. In the treefrog family (Hylidae), tadpoles live in water and adults live in trees; treefrogs have disks on their toes for clinging. The true frogs (Ranidae) are large, with slim waists, long legs, pointed toes, and webs on their hindfeet; most live in or near water and are good jumpers. Like salamanders, frogs are declining in number worldwide, partially because of environmental pollution.

Frogs and toads have well-developed ears (the eardrum is the conspicuous round disk behind each eye) and good vocal capabilities. In spring or summer, most male frogs and toads announce their presence with loud vocalizations that vary from species to species. When calling, the animals rapidly inflate and deflate balloon-like vocal sacs on the center or sides of the throat that amplify the sound. Calls are primarily used during the breeding season to attract mates, some by day, some at night; other species give calls to defend feeding territories long after breeding. Most Northwest frogs have rather soft voices, but the calls of the Pacific Treefrog and Bullfrog are conspicuous in spring and summer, respectively.

The size given for frogs is the typical length from the tip of the nose to the end of the body.

TAILED FROG
Ascaphus truei
TAILED FROG FAMILY
2″. Brown above, with irreg. blackish spots; skin covered with small warts; black line from snout past eye; yellow triangle on top of head; toes long, slender. Male has pear-shaped, tail-like copulatory organ. **VOICE** Quiet; lacks vocal sacs. **HABITAT** Cold clear mtn. streams, nearby woodland floors to near timberline. **ACTIVITY** Mainly nocturnal, Apr.–Sept. **RANGE** Cascades and west.

GREAT BASIN SPADEFOOT
Spea intermontana
SPADEFOOT FAMILY

2″. Olive-brown to gray-green with minute brown or red warts; indistinct creamy stripes on back and sides; whitish below. Snout blunt, rounded, upturned; eyes large, bulbous; glandular hump between eyes. Black, sharp-edged spade on inside of hindlegs. **VOICE** Loud, low, hoarse, repeated *kwaah*. **HABITAT** Sagebrush, pinyon-juniper woodlands. **ACTIVITY** Mainly nocturnal in spring and fall; in winter and summer, emerges from burrow on rainy nights. **RANGE** East of Cascades.

WESTERN TOAD
Bufo boreas
TOAD FAMILY

4″. Grayish green or brown above; raised warts blackish with red dots; bold yellow stripe on back from eyes to rump; whitish below, with black blotches. Oval gland behind eye. Tends to walk rather than hop. Lives in burrows when not foraging. **VOICE** Weak peeps; lacks vocal sacs. **HABITAT** In and near fresh water; woodlands, grasslands, gardens. **ACTIVITY** Mainly nocturnal in warm areas, by day in higher mtns. Feb.–Nov. near coast, Apr.–Oct. in mtns., inland.

PACIFIC TREEFROG
Hyla regilla
TREEFROG FAMILY

2″. Plain green, reddish, or light brown, with dark brown spots and irreg. stripes; thin dark line from nostril to eye; thick, dark brown stripe from eye to shoulder; yellowish below. Skin rough. Toes lack webbing. NW's most widespread frog. **VOICE** High musical *kree-eek*. **HABITAT** Rocks and shrubs near water. **ACTIVITY** Day and night, year-round west of Cascades, Apr.–Sept. east of Cascades.

RED-LEGGED FROG
Rana aurora
TRUE FROG FAMILY

4″. Reddish brown to gray-brown above, with small blackish blotches. Snout rounded; yellowish line on sides of upper jaw; dark brown mask behind eye. Legs banded black above, undersides red. **VOICE** Weak guttural *uh-uh-uh-uh-uh-unh* for 2–3 seconds, at night. **HABITAT** Woodlands, marshes; watersides during droughts. **ACTIVITY** Day and night, year-round. **RANGE** Cascades (low elevs.) and west.

CASCADES FROG
Rana cascadae
TRUE FROG FAMILY

2″. Pale yellowish brown; many round black spots on head and back; irreg. brown spots on sides and legs; yellowish below. Snout fairly pointed; yellowish line on sides of upper jaw; brown mask behind eye. 2 ridges on back. Swims away on surface rather than diving. **VOICE** Low raspy trill. **HABITAT** Wet meadows, marshes, pond edges, above 2,600′. **ACTIVITY** By day, Apr.–Oct. **RANGE** Cascades, Olympics.

BULLFROG
Rana catesbeiana
TRUE FROG FAMILY

6″. Yellowish green above, with dark mottling; pale yellow below. Head large, rounded. Ridge from eye to large eardrum, but not along sides of back. Legs long, dark-banded; feet mainly webbed. Tadpoles develop into adults in 1–3 years. NW's largest frog; introduced from e U.S.; wiping out native frogs. **VOICE** Deep resonant *jug-o-rum*, day or night. **HABITAT** Marshes, ponds, slow rivers. **ACTIVITY** Day and night; feeds mainly at night.

SPOTTED FROG
Rana pretiosa
TRUE FROG FAMILY

3″. Brown above, with light-centered blackish spots; yellow to orange below, with dark mottling on throat; yellowish stripe on upper jaw. Ridges on back; legs fairly short; eyes slightly upturned. Toes fully webbed. Exterminated in most areas west of Cascades by introduced Bullfrog and predatory fish. **VOICE** 6–9 short rapid croaks; calls from water. **HABITAT** Ponds, lakes, streams. **ACTIVITY** By day, Mar.–Oct. **RANGE** All NW, though mainly Cascades and east.

Reptiles

Members of the class Reptilia are cold-blooded, like amphibians. Their body temperature varies with that of their surroundings and their activities come to a halt in cold weather, when they hibernate alone or in communal dens. Reptiles are scarce on the Pacific Northwest coast due to the cool summers there. Many coastal species bear live young; on rare sunny days, pregnant females bask in the sun to aid in incubating the developing eggs. Of the four orders of living reptiles, the Northwest has two: turtles and scaled reptiles; the latter order includes both snakes and lizards. The reptilian body is low-slung and has a long tail and, except for the snakes, four short legs. Unlike the thin-skinned amphibians, reptiles are covered with protective scales (some are modified into plates in turtles) that waterproof their bodies and help keep them from becoming dehydrated. They breathe via lungs. All breed on land and mate by internal fertilization. Their eggs have brittle or leathery shells. Newborns and young look like miniature adults. Reptiles grow throughout their lives, though growth rates are much slower after an animal reaches maturity.

Turtles

Members of the order Testudines, turtles are the oldest living group of reptiles, dating back to the time of the earliest dinosaurs. The upper part of their characteristic bony shell is the *carapace,* the lower part the *plastron;* both parts are covered with hard plates called *scutes.* Some species have ridges, called *keels,* on the carapace and tail. Most can withdraw the head and legs inside the shell for protection. Aquatic species have flipper-like legs. Turtles are the only

Parts of a Turtle

toothless reptiles, but their horny beaks have sharp biting edges. The exposed skin of turtles is scaly and dry. Most spend hours basking in the sun. From October or November to March or April, turtles in the Northwest hibernate. All turtles lay eggs; most dig a hollow, lay the eggs, cover them up, and leave them alone. When the eggs hatch, the young claw their way to the surface and fend for themselves. Lengths given are for the carapace of a typical adult.

PAINTED TURTLE
Chrysemys picta
POND TURTLE FAMILY

8″. Carapace oval, fairly flat, smooth; 3 rows of smooth black or olive scutes edged in yellow or red; some have yellow stripe down middle; outer scutes lined with red. Plastron red; black in middle with radiating dark lines. Head, neck, legs, and tail black, with longitudinal yellow or red lines. **HABITAT** Marshy ponds, slow streams, river backwaters. **ACTIVITY** Groups bask on logs in water. In winter, hibernates in mud at water's edge. **RANGE** n Willamette Valley and ne OR, e WA, w WA (local).

WESTERN POND TURTLE
Clemmys marmorata
POND TURTLE FAMILY

6″. Carapace smooth, fairly flat; olive or brown; scutes have radiating blackish lines or mottling. Plastron pale yellow, often with black blotches on margins of scutes. Neck, legs, and short tail flecked black, coarsely scaled. Jaws yellowish. **HABITAT** Marshy ponds, slow streams. **ACTIVITY** Basks alone on logs in water. In winter, hibernates in mud with air pocket at edge of pond bottom. **RANGE** s Puget Sound area (rare), lower Columbia R., w OR.

Lizards

Lizards (suborder Sauria of the scaled reptile order, Squamata) generally have long tails; most species have legs and are capable of running, climbing, and clinging, though in some the legs are tiny or lacking. Typical lizards resemble salamanders but can be distinguished from them by their dry scaly skin, clawed feet, and external ear openings. Lizard species vary greatly in size, shape, and color; in many, color and patterns differ among adult males, adult females, and young. Most lizards are active by day, and many are particularly active in the midday heat. Most do not swim in water. Fertilization is internal; most lay eggs rather than give birth to live young. The size given for lizards is the length from the tip of the snout to the end of the tail.

MOJAVE BLACK-COLLARED LIZARD
Crotaphytus bicinctores
IGUANA FAMILY

11". Head large; neck narrow; tail long, thin. Head brown with network of white lines; 2 black collars separated by white collar; brown above, with many white spots (male) or crossbands of orange dots (female); feet yellowish; tail buffy. Male has blue and black throat. HABITAT Rocky desert canyons and hills. ACTIVITY By day; often basks on large boulders. RANGE se OR: Malheur and se Harney counties.

SHORT-HORNED LIZARD
"Horned Toad"
Phrynosoma douglassii
IGUANA FAMILY

3". Head small, plain; fan of short spines behind eyes. Body squat, flat. Brown or bluish gray above (color matches local soil); 2 dark blotches at back of neck; smaller dark spots with pale rear edges along either side of back; sides and short tail edged with whitish spines. HABITAT Rocky to sandy open areas, open juniper and pine woodlands. ACTIVITY By day, Apr.–Oct. RANGE East of Cascade crest.

SAGEBRUSH LIZARD
Sceloporus graciosus
IGUANA FAMILY

5½". Male striped brown and grayish white above; throat pale blue; belly bright blue with irreg. white line down middle; reddish-orange spot on sides. Female has faint or no blue below. Skin has small spiny scales. Feeds on ground. HABITAT Sagebrush deserts, open juniper and pine woodlands. ACTIVITY By day, Apr.–Sept. RANGE e WA, e and sw OR.

WESTERN FENCE LIZARD
Sceloporus occidentalis
IGUANA FAMILY

8″. Male has triangular pattern of light and dark brown and grayish white above; throat and belly dark blue with irreg. dark line down middle. Legs partly orange below. Female has faint or no blue on belly. Skin has coarse spiny scales. **HABITAT** Desert canyons, woodlands, boulders, old buildings, log piles. **ACTIVITY** By day; basks in morning sun; Mar.–Nov. west of mtns., May–Sept. east of mtns. **RANGE** Puget Sound area, e slope of WA Cascades, se WA, all OR.

SIDE-BLOTCHED LIZARD
Uta stansburiana
IGUANA FAMILY

5½″. Head and body gray to brown; white-edged, dark brown spots on back and tail; male sides and tail blue-speckled. Scales small. Fold of skin on neck; large black blotch on side behind forelegs. Often bobs head. **HABITAT** Cliffs, sagebrush deserts, juniper scrub. **ACTIVITY** By day, Apr.–Oct. **RANGE** Columbia Plateau of sc WA, e of Cascades in OR.

WESTERN SKINK
Eumeces skiltonianus
SKINK FAMILY

8″. Adult brown above, with wide buff and blackish stripes from face to base of tail; gray below; tail gray-brown. Body scales smooth and shiny, small; head scales large. Juv. stripes more black and white; tail bright blue. Hides under bark, logs, rocks. **HABITAT** Grasslands, woodlands, rocky streamsides. **ACTIVITY** By day, May–Sept. **RANGE** e WA, all OR.

NORTHERN ALLIGATOR LIZARD
Elgaria (Gerrhonotus) coerulea
ALLIGATOR LIZARD FAMILY

11″. Brown above with black speckles; fold of skin along sides; grayish below with dark stripes. Head large; eyes dark. Scales rough. Forages in grass, leaves; rests under wood, bark, logs, rocks. **HABITAT** Wet coniferous forest edges, talus slopes. **ACTIVITY** By day, Apr.–Sept. **RANGE** w and ne WA, w OR. **Southern Alligator Lizard** (*E. multicarinata*) 15″; eyes yellow; back and tail banded black; lives in grasslands, oak woodland of Willamette Valley to sc WA.

Snakes

Snakes (suborder Serpentes of the scaled reptile order, Squamata) have elongated scaly bodies without limbs, eyelids, or external ear openings. They grow throughout their lives, shedding their skin from snout to tail several times each year. Snakes are carnivorous, and they swallow their prey whole. The flicking, forked tongue serves as an organ of smell, collecting information on potential prey and dangers. Snakes usually mate in the fall, before their winter hibernation, which usually begins in November and ends in March or April. Most species lay eggs in June that hatch in September; a few give birth to live young in late summer. Most snakes in the Northwest are nonpoisonous, but beware of the Western Rattlesnake east of the Cascades and in southwestern Oregon. In the accounts below, the size given is the length of a typical adult.

RUBBER BOA
Charina bottae
BOA FAMILY

24″. Thick; looks rubbery; tail short, scales smooth, shiny. Plain brown above, yellowish below. Climbs trees; good burrower and swimmer. Feeds mainly at night and on warm overcast days; constricts mice, shrews, birds. **HABITAT** Woodlands, grasslands, sandy watersides. **RANGE** All NW, ex. Columbia Basin of e WA.

RACER
Coluber constrictor
COLUBRID SNAKE FAMILY

3′4″. Slender; body scales small, smooth. Adult solid olive green to grayish olive above; below yellowish (east of Cascades; pictured) or whitish (to west). Young yellowish with many brown spots on back, smaller spots on sides. Alert; active by day; moves fast, often with head off ground; climbs trees. Not a constrictor. **CAUTION** Bites hard, thrashes violently if handled (but not poisonous). **HABITAT** Woodland edges, grasslands, sagebrush deserts. **RANGE** East of Cascades, w OR.

CALIFORNIA MOUNTAIN KINGSNAKE
Lampropeltis zonata
COLUBRID SNAKE FAMILY

33″. Medium girth; scales smooth, shiny. Snout and head black with white ring behind eye; rest of body banded with wide red and narrower white rings, separated by black rings. Near streams with rotting logs nearby. Feeds on other snakes, lizards, birds. Locally called Coral King Snake. Active mainly by day. **HABITAT** Oak, pine, and chaparral to 3,000′. **RANGE** sc WA (very local), sw OR.

STRIPED WHIPSNAKE
Masticophis taeniatus
COLUBRID SNAKE FAMILY

5′. Slender; tail long, thin; scales smooth. Back slaty; sides finely striped in black and white; white on throat, buffy below at midbody, pinkish below tail; scales atop small head large, slaty, white-edged. Alert; moves fast, with head held off ground; often rests and hunts in bushes. Active by day. **HABITAT** Grasslands, sagebrush flats, dry canyons, to 5,000′. **RANGE** Columbia Plateau of e WA, e OR.

GOPHER SNAKE
Pituophis catenifer
COLUBRID SNAKE FAMILY

4′. Stocky to medium; head yellowish brown with dark line across top. West of Cascades: striped brown and yellowish gray above; stripes may be long blotches. East of Cascades (pictured): buffy with round, dark brown blotches; dark line on sides of neck. If threatened, puffs up, hisses, strikes; mimics rattlers by rustling dead leaves with tail. Active by day, warm nights. **HABITAT** Woodlands, grasslands, farms, sagebrush deserts. **RANGE** East of Cascades, west of Cascades in OR.

WESTERN TERRESTRIAL GARTER SNAKE
Thamnophis elegans
COLUBRID SNAKE FAMILY

30″. Top of head plain brown; head slightly larger than body; buffy yellow stripe from nape to tail on midback, another on lower sides; rest of upperparts brown with squarish dark brown spots. Active by day; basks in sun; feeds in water and on land. **HABITAT** Watersides and nearby woodlands and grasslands, to 8,400′.

NORTHWESTERN GARTER SNAKE
Thamnophis ordinoides
COLUBRID SNAKE FAMILY

24″. Extremely variable in color and pattern: may be striped, spotted, or plain. Back stripe, when present, may be red, orange, yellow, blue, or white; side stripe often yellow; rest of upperparts usu. dark brown with indistinct blackish spots; belly often reddish. Head small; scales keeled. Active by day; feeds on slugs, earthworms. **HABITAT** Wet grassy areas, forests, thickets, to 5,500′. **RANGE** West of Cascades.

COMMON GARTER SNAKE
Thamnophis sirtalis
COLUBRID SNAKE FAMILY

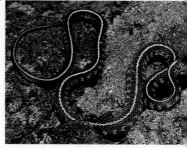

3′. Extremely variable in color and pattern. Head wider than body; scales keeled. All races have yellowish back stripe; most have side stripe. Red-spotted race of nw OR (pictured): black, with wide red spots on sides; wide yellow back stripe; top of head red. Puget Sound race of w WA: similar, but with narrow greenish back and side stripes; top of head black; few or no red spots. Valley race of interior and sw OR: brownish or gray; top of head blackish; back stripe wide; tiny red spots near side stripe. Active by day nearly year-round. Feeds on frogs, toads, salamanders, even newts (highly toxic to other creatures). **CAUTION** If handled, bites and expels musk and feces. **HABITAT** Woodlands, meadows, watersides, to 6,000′.

Poisonous Snakes and Snakebites

The Pacific Northwest has one poisonous snake—the Western Rattlesnake, found mainly to the east of the Cascades and in southwestern Oregon. This rattler has retractable fangs that can deliver blood-destroying venom, but it will flee from footsteps. If you encounter one, freeze to let it withdraw, then step away. While bites sting, they are rarely fatal. However, for any poisonous snakebite the best course of action is to get to medical care as soon as possible, with the dead snake or positive identification, so the proper antivenin can be administered. Meanwhile, the victim should avoid moving, as movement helps the venom spread through the system, and keep the injured body part motionless just below heart level. The victim should be kept warm, calm, and at rest while on the way to medical care. If you are alone and on foot, start walking slowly toward help, exerting the injured area as little as possible. If you run or if the bite has delivered a large amount of venom, you may collapse, but a snakebite seldom results in death.

WESTERN RATTLESNAKE
Crotalus viridis
VIPER FAMILY

4′. Stout; head wide, triangular; long hollow fangs; rattles on tail. Northern Pacific race of e WA and most of OR (pictured): gray-brown, with large, dark, diamonds on back edged with narrow whitish lines; top of head solid brown. Great Basin race of se OR: grayish buff with dark brown bands equal to interspaces; top of head variegated. Excitable and aggressive; gives warning by rattling tail and holding ground. Joins communal dens to overwinter. Feeds on ground squirrels, other rodents, rabbits; locates prey with heat sensors. Active day and night. **CAUTION** Poisonous; bites can be fatal. **HABITAT** Grasslands, sagebrush, rocky woodlands, canyonsides. **RANGE** East of Cascades, sw OR.

Birds

Members of the class Aves, birds are the only animals that have feathers, and most are capable of flight. Like their reptile ancestors, they lay eggs; like mammals, they are warm-blooded. They generally have excellent sight and hearing, but few have a good sense of smell. The bird skeleton is adapted for flight: the bones are lightweight, with a sponge-like interior. The forelimbs have become wings, with strong pectoral muscles attached to a keeled breastbone, and the hindlimbs are modified for running, grasping, or perching. Wing shapes vary among types of birds, ranging, for example, from the long broad wings of the soaring raptors to the narrow, fast-moving wings of hummingbirds.

While all Steller's Jays in one area look the same regardless of their age or gender or the time of year, this is not the case for most birds. Plumages may vary from immature to adult, from male to female, and from breeding to nonbreeding seasons (summer and winter, respectively). (If both sexes have a summer plumage distinct from nonbreeding plumage, we note this as "summer adult." If only the male has such a summer plumage, we note "summer male.") In some species, groups living in different geographic areas (subspecies, or races) have slightly or distinctly different plumages. Some birds within a given species have different colorations (called morphs or phases) that have nothing to do with where they live. Some birds have ornamental plumes, often developed in the breeding season. This guide describes the plumages most often seen in the Pacific Northwest. The photograph shows the male or the adult (if adults look alike) unless otherwise noted.

Flight allows birds to migrate great distances, though some are resident year-round in one region. Many birds who spend the winter in warmer, southern climes migrate north to breed, taking advantage of the abundant animal life in the summertime Northwest. Other birds breed to the north, in Canada or Alaska, and pass through the Northwest only in migration. Cold and snow rarely kill birds directly but may reduce the amounts of food (insects, animals, berries) they can obtain to maintain their ideal body temperature. Many of our breeding species winter in the southwestern United States, Mexico, or beyond. Most individuals return to the same breeding and wintering grounds throughout their lives.

Northbound migration occurs from March to early June, southbound from July to November. Migrants often wait until the wind is at their backs before beginning the journey. In spring, warm southerly winds help migrants return from southern regions to the Northwest. In autumn, winds from the north aid southbound migrants on their journey south. For more about bird migration, see the essay on bird-watching on page 257.

In bird species that do not nest in colonies, a male who is ready to breed stakes out and defends a nesting territory from other males. The female chooses a male in part on the quality and size of his territory, the presence of a secure nest site, and the quality of his plumage and song. The avian life cycle typically starts with the female laying one or more eggs in a nest, which, depending on the species, may be a scrape in the sand, a cup of rootlets and fibers, a woven basket, a stick platform, or another type of structure. After an incubation period of roughly two to four weeks, the young are hatched and fed by their parents for a period varying from a few days (shorebirds) to a few weeks (most species) to many months (raptors). Smaller birds tend to breed the year following their birth, while many larger birds remain immature for several years before breeding. During the breeding season, many male birds exhibit more colorful and elaborate plumages and courtship displays and rituals in order to attract a mate. Most species mate in solitary pairs, the males competing for breeding territories; other species nest colonially. In this section of the guide, assume a bird is a solitary nester unless the description notes that it nests in colonies. Space limitations prevent us from giving descriptions of nests in this guide.

Birds use their voices in many ways. In many species, contact and alarm call notes are given year-round by both sexes. The more musical songs, usually given only in spring and summer by the male, attract mates and define territory. Once the young are born, many birds stop singing; the Northwest woodlands and fields are much quieter in August than in June.

This section's descriptions give the length of the bird from the tip of the beak to the end of the tail. For some large species, both length and wingspan are given.

Parts of a Bird

For suggestions on attracting birds to your yard, see page 306. In this section, the icon ⚡ denotes species that will come into a yard to a feeder. The icon 🏠 indicates species that might use a nestbox in a yard.

Bird-Watching

Bird-watching, or birding, as it is often termed, can be a casual activity, develop into a hobby, or become a passion. Some observers enjoy generally keeping track of birds they come across in their daily activities or while hiking, driving, or boating, while others become intent on seeing as many different types of birds as possible. It's possible to see 300 or more species a year in the Pacific Northwest.

In breeding season, many birds tend to live in only one habitat and are active at certain times of day. Freshwater marsh birds (rails and bitterns) are most often calling and active at dawn and dusk. Until mid-morning on hot days, songbirds search woodlands, fields, and thickets for food; from mid-morning to late afternoon, they tend to be quiet; they forage again late in the day. Birds that live near beaches, lakes, and other aquatic habitats (herons, cormorants, ducks, sandpipers) may be active all day. Make an after-dark visit to a forest or wooded swamp to listen for owls, which may respond to taped or imitated calls and can be viewed with spotlights. The greatest variety of birds can be seen during the migration seasons. In early spring (March and April), larger birds such as nonwintering hawks and waterfowl return to the Northwest, while many wintering birds begin moving northward. Most songbirds migrate north to and through the region during the latter half of April and the month of May; males arrive a week or so before females in order to stake out territories. When the land bird migration tapers off in late May, sandpipers and plovers are still flying through. While larger birds migrate by day, most species, especially smaller, insect-eating ones, fly at night, resting and feeding during the day, tending to gather in quiet places where food is easy to find. In a light woodland along a stream, where there are newly opened leaves and plenty of small insects, it is possible to see a half-dozen or more species of migrant songbirds in a single spring morning.

Fall migration is underway by July, when the first southbound sandpipers and plovers reappear; adults in these groups migrate a week to a month before their offspring. From August into October, most of the dabbling ducks and songbirds pass through. The migration of diving ducks, geese, and raptors starts in September and continues into November. During severe winters, many birds may shift farther southward or come to the coast at any time.

For the serious birder, at least one good field guide is essential; many excellent ones are available, including the *National Audubon Society Field Guide to North American Birds (Western Region)*. Binoculars (7-, 8-, 9-, or 10-power) are a must; a close-focusing pair is especially helpful. A 15-, 20-, or 30-power telescope with a wide field of view, mounted on a sturdy, collapsible tripod, is invaluable for viewing waterfowl, shorebirds, and raptors.

While many species are rather tame, others are shy or secretive. Learn to move slowly and quietly, and avoid wearing brightly colored or patterned clothing and making loud noises. Please respect local laws, do not unduly frighten birds, and take great care not to disrupt nesting or resting birds.

RED-THROATED LOON
Gavia stellata
LOON FAMILY

26″. Appears slender, snake-like in water. Winter: back dark gray with fine white dots; white below; more white on neck than other loons. Bill slightly up-turned, blackish, thinner than in other loons. Lifts off water in shorter distance than other loons. **VOICE** Silent in NW. **HABITAT** Ocean and bays. **RANGE** Oct.–May: coast.

PACIFIC LOON
Gavia pacifica
LOON FAMILY

25″. Body stout, duck-like. Winter: back blackish, faintly scaled in 1st winter; white below; crown and hindneck blackish, sharply demarcated in straight edge from white throat and foreneck. Bill straight, blackish, thinner than Common Loon's. **VOICE** Silent in NW. **HABITAT** Ocean and bays. **RANGE** Oct.–May: coast.

COMMON LOON
Gavia immer
LOON FAMILY

summer (left), winter (right)

32″. Summer: back black with large white spots; head, neck, and bill black; white bands on neck. Winter: slaty above, white below; crown and hindneck blackish, sharply demarcated in zigzag edge from white throat and foreneck. Bill heavy, pointed. **VOICE** Quavering laughter, yodeling, mainly on spring and summer nights. **HABITAT** Summer: lakes. Migration: lakes, large rivers. Winter: large lakes, bays. **RANGE** Apr.–Aug.: mtn. lakes (rare). Aug.–May: all NW.

HORNED GREBE
Podiceps auritus
GREBE FAMILY

14″. Winter: back and hindneck slaty; crown black; throat and foreneck white. Summer: black above; neck and underparts chestnut; head black; yellowish stripe over eye. Neck thin; bill slender; eyes red. **VOICE** Croaks and chatters in summer. **HABITAT** Summer: lakes. Winter: lakes, coastal waters. **RANGE** Apr.–Aug.: east of Cascades (local). Sept.–May: all lowlands.

PIED-BILLED GREBE
Podilymbus podiceps
GREBE FAMILY

summer (left), winter (right)

13″. Summer: body brown; chin black; black ring on white bill. Winter: body brown; chin white; bill yellow or gray, lacks ring. Bill short, conical. Dives frequently for small fish. **VOICE** Series of 8 *cow* notes. **HABITAT** Summer: freshwater marshes, ponds. Winter: also inner coastal waters. **RANGE** All lowlands.

RED-NECKED GREBE
Podiceps grisegena
GREBE FAMILY

19″. Crown, back, and hindneck blackish; whitish below. Bill long, slender, black above, yellow below; eyes brown. Summer: foreneck reddish; cheeks and throat white. Winter: foreneck gray or buffy; white crescent from throat to nape. **VOICE** Wails and trills; summer only. **HABITAT** Summer: ponds, lakes. Winter: coastal waters. **RANGE** May–Aug.: ne WA; sc OR (local). Aug.–Apr.: entire coast.

EARED GREBE
Podiceps nigricollis
GREBE FAMILY

13″. Slaty above, whitish below; undertail coverts white, often fluffed. Forehead high; bill short, slender, black, slightly upturned; eyes red. Summer: sides rusty; head and neck black; sides of face streaked yellow. Winter: neck gray; head black ex. white throat and nape patch. **VOICE** Soft, frog-like *poo-eep*. **HABITAT** Summer: ponds, marshes. Winter: bays. **RANGE** May–Sept.: east of Cascades. Sept.–Apr.: entire coast (local).

WESTERN GREBE
Aechmophorus occidentalis
GREBE FAMILY

27″. Dark gray above, white below. Top half of head (to below eye) and hindneck black; throat and foreneck white; bill greenish yellow. Neck long, thin, snake-like; eyes red. Nests in colonies, on floating reed platforms in marsh. **VOICE** Rolling *kerr-rick, kerr-rick*. **HABITAT** Summer: lakes. Winter: coastal waters, lakes. **RANGE** Apr.–Oct.: east of Cascades. Sept.–May: entire coast, Columbia R. west of Cascades.

Tubenoses

Tubenoses—albatrosses, shearwaters, and storm-petrels—spend most of their lives beyond even the sight of the shore, coming to land only to breed. All are able to drink seawater and internally extract the salt, which exits as a briny liquid from tubes on the bill. They feed on fish, squid, and carrion at the sea's surface or make short dives from the surface. Tubenoses are opportunistic, feeding on smaller fish that large fish have forced to the surface. All but storm-petrels fly with long glides on stiff bowed wings; in a strong breeze they seem to fly sideways with one wing held high, the other below the body. Tubenoses sometimes follow fishing boats at sea; parties of ocean birders can attract them with cut-up fish and other animal matter. Albatrosses are very large, shearwaters roughly gull-size, storm-petrels the size of large swallows.

BLACK-FOOTED ALBATROSS
Diomedea nigripes
ALBATROSS FAMILY

L 34"; WS 7'. Body, head, and wings blackish brown. Bill long, thick, black; front of face and teardrop behind eye white. Wings very long, narrow. In light wind, makes long glides near surface, with stiff drooped wings. Nonbreeding visitor from c Pacific. **VOICE** Squeals at food fights. **HABITAT** Ocean; rarely seen from shore. **RANGE** Apr.–Oct.: outer coast, offshore.

PINK-FOOTED SHEARWATER
Puffinus creatopus
SHEARWATER FAMILY

20". Back and upperwing grayish brown; whitish below, incl. underwing. Head brownish; bill pink with dark tip. Legs pink. Nonbreeding visitor from s S. Amer. **VOICE** Silent at sea. **HABITAT** Ocean; rarely seen from shore. **RANGE** May–Oct.: outer coast (not Puget Sound), offshore. **Northern Fulmar** *(Fulmarus glacialis)* bill short, heavy, yellow; head large; back and wings gray; resident offshore as nonbreeder.

SOOTY SHEARWATER
Puffinus griseus
SHEARWATER FAMILY

17". Entirely sooty brown above and below; contrasting silvery-white underwing linings; bill narrow, black. Flies near surface on very stiff wings with fast flaps, long glides. Nonbreeding visitor from s S. Amer. and New Zealand. **VOICE** Usu. silent in NW. **HABITAT** Ocean; often seen from shore. **RANGE** Apr.–Oct.: outer coast.

Oceanic Bird-Watching

Thousands of seabirds and dozens of marine mammals can be seen from chartered boats that leave Northwest ports to cruise offshore waters. There are as many as 15 trips per year out of Westport, Washington, mostly from May to October; these popular day trips must be arranged well in advance. The goal is usually Grays Canyon, a popular feeding ground 20 to 30 miles offshore, although a few trips each year go farther offshore. Boats also leave from several Oregon ports, including Garibaldi, Depoe Bay, and Brookings. On these cruises, thousands of shearwaters and gulls accompany lesser numbers of albatrosses, storm-petrels, jaegers, terns, phalaropes, auklets, and puffins, most of which are only rarely seen from shore. Near-shore birds are also seen in large numbers as the boats traverse their home waters. Marine mammals sometimes spotted on these trips include Gray and Killer Whales, Dall's Porpoises, Northern Fur Seals, and Harbor Seals; many other rarer species are occasionally sighted. Blue Sharks and Ocean Sunfishes may be spotted in summer.

AMERICAN WHITE PELICAN
Pelecanus erythrorhynchos
PELICAN FAMILY

L 5'2"; WS 8'. All white at rest; bill long, flat, with orange-yellow pouch. Neck long; tail short. Legs short; feet wide, webbed; both orange-yellow. Flight reveals black primaries. Dips bill and pouch into water for small schooling fish. Rests on sandbars. Often flies in V formation or wheels high in sky on midday thermals; does not dive from air. Nests in colonies on islands. **VOICE** Grunts at nest. **HABITAT** Large inland lakes. **RANGE** Apr.–Sept.: mainly se OR; sc WA (local).

BROWN PELICAN
Pelecanus occidentalis
PELICAN FAMILY

L 4'2"; WS 7'. Body and wings grayish brown; head white, with yellowish wash on crown; neck mainly chestnut brown in summer, all white in winter; bill long, flat, gray (tipped red in summer); pouch black. Neck long; tail short. Legs short; feet wide, webbed; both slaty. Feeds on fish, alone or in groups; makes spectacular dives, bill-first, into water. Rests on seaside rocks, piers, beaches, ocean surface. Flies with slow regular wingbeats in V formation; glides long distances, skimming tops of waves. Nonbreeding visitor from CA and Mexico. **VOICE** Usu. silent. **HABITAT** Ocean, bays, estuaries. **RANGE** July–Nov.: coastal OR, outer coast of WA.

DOUBLE-CRESTED CORMORANT
Phalacrocorax auritus
CORMORANT FAMILY

33″. Black (may appear greenish); back and wings brownish; breeding crest (small tufts on either side) hard to see. Bill narrow, hooked, pale; orange skin on throat. Swims with bill angled upward; spreads wings to dry while resting. Flies with neck kinked. Nests in colonies, in platform nest of sticks and seaweeds in trees and on islands. Only inland cormorant in NW. **VOICE** Usu. silent; croaks at nest. **HABITAT** Coastal waters, lakes, rivers. **RANGE** Year-round: coast, Columbia Basin. Mar.–Sept.: se OR.

PELAGIC CORMORANT
Phalacrocorax pelagicus
CORMORANT FAMILY

28″. Summer adult: glossy blackish; white patch on flanks (Feb.–June). Winter adult: lacks white patch. Bill thin, hooked, black; neck long. Flies with straight neck. Nests in colonies, on saucers of moss and seaweed on cliff ledges by sea. **VOICE** Groans at nest; silent at sea. **HABITAT** Ocean, bays, rocky cliffs. **RANGE** Resident on NW coast.

BRANDT'S CORMORANT
Phalacrocorax penicillatus
CORMORANT FAMILY

34″. Adult glossy blackish; throat buffy brown; throat skin blue when breeding. Imm. brown, chest and throat buffy. Bill narrow, hooked, black; neck long. Flies with straight neck. Nests in colonies, on saucers of seaweed on cliffs by sea. **VOICE** Croaks at nest; silent at sea. **HABITAT** Ocean, bays, rocky cliffs. **RANGE** Resident on NW coast; in winter, common in WA.

adult (left), immature (right)

GREAT EGRET
Ardea alba
HERON FAMILY

L 3′3″; WS 4′3″. All white. Bill long, yellow; feet and long legs black. Neck long, thin. During breeding, long, lacy, white plumes on back; facial skin green. Nests in colonies, with other species. **VOICE** Deep croak. **HABITAT** Marshes; bays (in fall). **RANGE** Apr.–Aug.: east of Cascades (mainly OR). Sept.–Apr.: sw OR.

GREAT BLUE HERON
Ardea herodias
HERON FAMILY

L 4'; WS 6'. Adult back and wings blue-gray; black patches on side of breast and belly; crown black with white center; black plumes from back of head; face white; most of neck gray; underparts striped gray and white. Legs very long, dark; bill yellow. Imm. crown all black. Nests in colonies. **VOICE** Deep squawk. **HABITAT** Freshwater and saltwater shorelines. **RANGE** Resident in NW; in winter, local east of Cascades.

SNOWY EGRET
Egretta thula
HERON FAMILY

24". All white. Bill slender, black; lores yellow. Neck long. Legs long, black; feet yellow. During courtship, long, lacy, white plumes on back, chest, and crown. Imm.: back of legs yellow-green. Nests in colonies. **VOICE** Harsh *aah*. **HABITAT** Marshes, coastal bays. **RANGE** Apr.–Sept.: se OR.

AMERICAN BITTERN
Botaurus lentiginosus
HERON FAMILY

28". Adult brown, paler below, with brown streaks on underparts; thin white eyebrow stripe; black stripe partway down neck. Neck thick; legs greenish. Imm. lacks black neck stripe. Shy; points bill skyward if disturbed. **VOICE** Loud, pumping *uunk-KA-lunk*. **HABITAT** Marshes. **RANGE** May–Oct.: east and west of Cascades. Sept.–May: coastal marshes.

GREEN HERON
Butorides virescens
HERON FAMILY

19". Adult body slaty green; cap black; neck chestnut. Legs shortish; orange-yellow; bill dark. Imm. brownish; neck pale with heavy dark brown streaks; legs yellow-green. Often feeds by leaning over water from logs, rocks; also wades. **VOICE** Harsh *keyow*. **HABITAT** Wooded streams, ponds. **RANGE** Apr.–Sept: west of Cascades. Sept.–Apr.: sw OR.

adult (left), immature (right)

BLACK-CROWNED NIGHT-HERON
Nycticorax nycticorax
HERON FAMILY

26″. Adult crown and back black; wings gray; lores and underparts white; eyes red. Neck thick; legs shortish, yellow. Imm. back and wings brown, with large whitish spots; brown and white streaked below. Nests in colonies. **VOICE** Low *kwock*. **HABITAT** Ponds, marshes. **RANGE** Apr.–Sept.: most of OR, e WA. Sept.–Apr.: west of Cascades (local).

WHITE-FACED IBIS
Plegadis chihi
IBIS FAMILY

24″. Summer: glossy chestnut with glossy green wings; white line encircles eye and bare red skin at base of bill. Bill long, drooping, silvery; neck and legs long. Flies with neck out; alternates flaps and glides; often in lines. Nests in colonies. **VOICE** Low grunts. **HABITAT** Marshes. **RANGE** May–Sept.: se OR.

Waterfowl

The waterfowl family (Anatidae) contains the huge white swans, the medium-size geese, and a wide variety of smaller ducks. All have webbed feet and thick bills designed for filtering small organisms in the water or for grasping underwater vegetation and invertebrates, often mollusks. Most waterfowl undergo lengthy migrations between northern or inland breeding areas and southern and/or coastal wintering waters. Their nests, made of grasses and lined with feathers, are usually on the ground, hidden in tall grass or reeds, and contain many eggs. Ducks may be split into two main groups. Dabbling ducks upend on the surface of fresh and brackish waters, and can jump up and take flight straight out of the water. Diving ducks dive well under the surface of fresh and salt waters; in taking flight, they run and flap horizontally over the water's surface before gain-

Mallard dabbling

Mallard taking off, straight up, from surface of water

Canada Goose taking off by running across water

ing altitude. Swans and geese upend like dabbling ducks, rather than dive for food; most patter across the water to get airborne. Waterfowl males are in breeding plumage from fall through early summer, but in late summer develop a drab nonbreeding plumage similar to that of females.

TRUMPETER SWAN
Cygnus buccinator
WATERFOWL FAMILY

L 6'; WS to 8'. Adult all white; bill and legs black; black facial skin envelops front of eye. Neck very long. Imm. grayish white; bill reddish on sides. Flies with neck outstretched. **VOICE** Loud deep *coo-hoo.* **HABITAT** Marshes, lakes. Winter: also farms. **RANGE** Oct.–Apr.: w WA, nw OR. Resident at Malheur N.W.R., se OR. **Tundra Swan** *(C. columbianus)* smaller (4'5"); adult usu. has yellow spot in front of eye; winters in w WA, w and sc OR.

GREATER WHITE-FRONTED GOOSE
Anser albifrons
WATERFOWL FAMILY

29". Adult body brown; wings solid gray-brown; head and neck dark brown; bill pink; ring of white on face at base of bill; irreg. black bands on brown belly; legs and feet orange; vent white. **VOICE** Barking *kla-hah.* **HABITAT** Migration and winter: coastal and inland wetlands, fallow grainfields. **RANGE** Apr., Sept.–Oct.: west and east of Cascades. Sept.– Apr.: sc and se OR; coast (rare).

SNOW GOOSE
Chen caerulescens
WATERFOWL FAMILY

28". Adult pure white, with black primaries; bill pink, with black "lips"; face often stained rusty; legs pink. Imm. pale brown above, white below; bill, legs, and primaries black. Flight reveals black wingtips. Flies in V formation high overhead. **VOICE** High nasal honks. **HABITAT** Coastal and inland wetlands, fallow fields. **RANGE** Apr., Oct.–Dec.: east and west of Cascades. Oct.–Apr.: nw WA, nw and sc OR.

BRANT
"Black Brant"
Branta bernicla
WATERFOWL FAMILY

26". Head, neck, chest, and mid-belly black; thin white patch on sides; patch of white lines on upper neck (absent in imm.); back and wings dark brown; vent and large rump patch white. **VOICE** Throaty *cur-onk.* **HABITAT** Nov.–May: coastal marshes, beaches. **RANGE** Coastal NW.

CANADA GOOSE
Branta canadensis
WATERFOWL FAMILY

L 3'7"; WS 4–6'. Adult back and wings dark brown; head and long neck black, large white chinstrap; breast pale to dark brown; vent and rump white; tail short, black. Often flies in V formation. **VOICE** Honking *car-uunk*. **HABITAT** Marshes, mudflats, ponds, wide lawns, fallow fields. **RANGE** Resident in NW. Oct.–Apr.: several small races from Alaska.

WOOD DUCK
Aix sponsa
WATERFOWL FAMILY

19". Dabbler. Male iridescent; back dark purple; chest purple with white spots; sides buffy; head green with laid-back crest; throat and 2-pronged chinstrap white; eye ring and base of bill red. Female brown, with elongated white eye ring. Holds head high in flight, which reveals longish tail, white belly. **VOICE** Male usu. quiet; high whistle when courting. Female: *oo-eek.* **HABITAT** Swamps, marshes, slow rivers. **RANGE** Apr.–Sept.: all NW. Sept.–Apr.: west of Cascades.

MALLARD
Anas platyrhynchos
WATERFOWL FAMILY

male (left), female (right)

24". Dabbler. Male body and wings gray; head and neck green; white ring above purplish chest; rump black; tail yellow; bill yellow. Female buffy, heavily mottled with brown; bill pale orange with dark saddle. Legs orange. Flight reveals blue wing patch, bordered with white. NW's most widespread inland duck. **VOICE** Male: quiet; gives *reeb* call when fighting. Female: quack. **HABITAT** Ponds, rivers, marshes, parks. **RANGE** Resident in NW.

GREEN-WINGED TEAL
Anas crecca
WATERFOWL FAMILY

14". Dabbler. Male body gray, with vertical white stripe behind chest; head chestnut; green eye patch extends to fluffy nape; vent patch yellow; bill small, black. Female brown. Flight reveals green wing patch. NW's smallest duck. **VOICE** Male: whistled *crick-et.* **HABITAT** Marshes, ponds. **RANGE** Resident in NW; in winter, east of Cascades (local).

NORTHERN PINTAIL
Anas acuta
WATERFOWL FAMILY

Male 28"; female 21". Dabbler. Male back, wings, and sides gray; head and hindneck brown; foreneck and belly white; tail very long, black. Female smaller, pale brown, with bronzy-brown wing patch. Neck thin; tail sharp, pointed. **VOICE** Male: wheezy *prip prip*. Female: quack. **HABITAT** Marshes, ponds. **RANGE** Resident east of Cascades. Aug.–Apr.: west of Cascades.

BLUE-WINGED TEAL
Anas discors
WATERFOWL FAMILY

15". Dabbler. Male body brown with black dots; head dull blue-gray with white crescent before eye; crown black. Female mottled brown. Bill heavier, longer than Green-winged Teal's. Flight reveals pale cerulean blue forewing patches and green wing patch. **VOICE** Male: *peep*. **HABITAT** Marshes, weedy ponds. **RANGE** Apr.–Sept.: mainly east of Cascades. Apr.–May, Aug.–Sept.: all NW.

CINNAMON TEAL
Anas cyanoptera
WATERFOWL FAMILY

15". Dabbler. Male head, neck, sides, and belly reddish chestnut; crown black; back scalloped brown; cerulean blue forewing patch visible in flight. Female mottled brown; in flight, like Blue-winged Teal. Bill heavy, black. **VOICE** Male: soft *chuck*. Female: soft quack. **HABITAT** Marshes, shallow lakes. **RANGE** Apr.–Oct.: all NW.

NORTHERN SHOVELER
Anas clypeata
WATERFOWL FAMILY

18". Dabbler. Male head green; chest white; sides rusty; eyes yellow; bill black. Female brown, speckled. Neck short; bill long, wide, held close to water. Flight reveals blue forewing patch. **VOICE** Male: low *took*. Female: quack. **HABITAT** Marshes, ponds. **RANGE** Apr.–Oct.: all NW. Sept.–Apr.: west of Cascades (local east).

GADWALL
Anas strepera
WATERFOWL FAMILY

20". Dabbler. Male body and head gray; bill black; rear end black. Female brown; bill black, with orange edge. Flight reveals square white wing patch bordered in black, white belly. **VOICE** Male: croaks, whistles. Female: subdued quack. **HABITAT** Lakes, marshes. **RANGE** Resident in NW.

AMERICAN WIGEON
Anas americana
WATERFOWL FAMILY

21″. Dabbler. Both sexes brownish with dull rusty-orange sides and speckled head. Male has green patch behind eye; forehead white; vent black and white. Flight reveals white forewing patch. **VOICE** Whistled *whee whee whew*. **HABITAT** Shallow lakes, ponds, fields, park lawns. **RANGE** Apr.–Oct.: east of Cascades. Aug.–Apr.: west and east of Cascades.

CANVASBACK
Aythya valisineria
WATERFOWL FAMILY

21″. Diver. Male back and sides white; chest and tail black; head reddish brown; eyes red. Female back, wings, sides gray; chest dark brown; head light brown, with white eye ring, dark eyes; tail blackish. Sloping forehead forms straight line with long black bill. Flight reveals plain gray wings. **VOICE** Male: *coo*. Female: quack. **HABITAT** Lakes, estuaries. **RANGE** Apr.–Apr., Oct.–Nov.: all NW. Oct.–Mar.: west of Cascades.

REDHEAD
Aythya americana
WATERFOWL FAMILY

20″. Diver. Male body gray; head rufous; chest and rear end black; eyes yellow. Female all plain brown; whitish eye ring. Forehead steep, rounded; bill blue-gray, with black tip. **VOICE** Male: cat-like *meeow* in courtship. Female: soft quack. **HABITAT** Summer: ponds, lakes. Migration and winter: lakes. **RANGE** Apr.–Sept.: east of Cascades. Mar.–Apr., Sept.–Nov.: all NW. Oct.–Mar.: west of Cascades (local).

RING-NECKED DUCK
Aythya collaris
WATERFOWL FAMILY

17″. Diver. Male head, chest, back, and tail black; sides gray; white slash behind black breast; head has purple gloss; crown peaked. Female brown, with pale buffy wash on face, pale eye ring. Bill has white base. Flight reveals gray wing stripe, black forewing. **VOICE** Male: loud whistles. Female: soft purring. **HABITAT** Summer: lakes. Migration and winter: lakes, rivers. **RANGE** Apr.–Oct.: all WA, c and e OR. Oct.–Apr.: all NW.

LESSER SCAUP
Aythya affinis
WATERFOWL FAMILY

17". Diver. Male back gray; head black (dark purple gloss); sides pale gray; chest and tail area black. Female dark brown, with distinct white face. Bill blue-gray; eyes yellow. Flight reveals white stripe on base of gray wings. **VOICE** Usu. silent. **HABITAT** Summer: lakes, marshes. Migration and winter: lakes, estuaries, bays. **RANGE** Apr.–Oct.: east of Cascades. Oct.–Apr.: west and east of Cascades. **Greater Scaup** (*A. marila*) has longer white wing stripe; male has green gloss on head; large flocks in winter.

HARLEQUIN DUCK
Histrionicus histrionicus
WATERFOWL FAMILY

17". Diver. Male slaty blue above and below, boldly marked with large white stripes and spots; sides rusty. Female dark brown; 3 white spots on head. Bill short, black. Flight reveals dark wings; white line on edge of male's back. **VOICE** Squeaks and whistles. **HABITAT** Summer: mtn. rivers. Winter: salt water, rocky coasts. **RANGE** May–Sept.: mtns., nw and ne OR, w and ne WA. Aug.–May: entire coast.

OLDSQUAW
Clangula hyemalis
WATERFOWL FAMILY

Male 22"; female 17". Diver. Winter male mainly white; chest, wings, and long tail black; bill pink and black. Winter female chest and upperparts brown; head and sides buffy white. Usu. in flocks of its own species. **VOICE** Male yodels *ow-owdle-ow*. **HABITAT** Deep coastal waters. **RANGE** Oct.–Apr.: coastal NW.

BLACK SCOTER
Melanitta nigra
WATERFOWL FAMILY

18". Male all black; bill black with swollen orange knob on top. Female body brown; crown dark brown; cheeks silvery; bill thinner, black. Flight reveals silvery flight feathers. **VOICE** Silent in NW. **HABITAT** Coastal waters. **RANGE** Nov.–Apr.: entire coast.

SURF SCOTER
Melanitta perspicillata
WATERFOWL FAMILY

20″. Male black; white patches on forehead and nape; eyes white; bill swollen, orange and white, with black spot on side. Female dark brown above; midbelly white; 2 white spots on cheek. Flight reveals all dark wings. **VOICE** Silent in NW. **HABITAT** Winter: coastal waters. Migration: also lakes. **RANGE** Aug.–May: entire coast.

WHITE-WINGED SCOTER
Melanitta fusca
WATERFOWL FAMILY

22″. Diver. Male black; white teardrop around eye; bill orange with black knob. Female dark brown. Flight reveals white patch on secondaries. **VOICE** Silent in NW. **HABITAT** Winter: coastal waters. Migration: also lakes. **RANGE** Aug.–May: entire coast. Sept.–Oct.: also east of Cascades.

BARROW'S GOLDENEYE
Bucephala islandica
WATERFOWL FAMILY

female (left), male (right)

19″. Diver. Male black above with rectangular white spots; black extends to sides of chest; neck and underparts white; head black (dark purple gloss), fluffed out at rear; large white crescent on face; bill black. Female body pale brown; head dark brown; bill yellow-orange in winter and spring. Eyes golden. **VOICE** Male: grunts and clicks in courtship. **HABITAT** Summer: lakes. Winter: ocean, lakes. **RANGE** Apr.–Nov.: Cascades, e highlands. Nov.–Apr.: entire coast, open inland waters.

COMMON GOLDENEYE
Bucephala clangula
WATERFOWL FAMILY

18″. Diver. Male striped black and white above; white below; head black (dark green gloss), fluffed out at rear, with large, round, white spot near bill. Female head all dark brown, with white neck ring; body paler brown. Eyes golden. **VOICE** Male: high *jee-up*. Female: low quack. **HABITAT** Summer: lakes. Migration and winter: lakes, rivers, ocean. **RANGE** Apr.–Oct.: far ne WA. Nov.–Apr.: all NW.

BUFFLEHEAD
Bucephala albeola
WATERFOWL FAMILY

14″. Diver. Male back black; chest and underparts white; white wedge on rear half of head, which has greenish-purple gloss. Female brown, with large white spot behind eye. Bill short. Flight reveals white base of wings (male), white secondaries (female). **VOICE** Male: squeaky whistle. Female: hoarse quack. **HABITAT** Summer: lakes. Migration and winter: coast, inland open waters. **RANGE** Apr.–Nov.: Cascades, ne WA. Nov.–Apr.: all NW.

RED-BREASTED MERGANSER
Mergus serrator
WATERFOWL FAMILY

23″. Diver. Male back black; chest buffy; sides gray; neck and belly white; head dark green. Female gray; head rusty; throat and foreneck white. Bill long, slender, red; nape crest shaggy. **VOICE** Usu. silent. **HABITAT** Winter: coastal waters. Migration: also inland waters. **RANGE** Oct.–Apr.: entire coast. Oct.–Nov., Apr.–May: inland waters.

HOODED MERGANSER
Lophodytes (Mergus) cucullatus
WATERFOWL FAMILY

18″. Diver. Adult male back, head, and neck black; sides rufous; head patch and chest white; eyes yellow. Female gray-brown, with fluffy brown crest. Crest expandable, fan-like; bill black. **VOICE** Low grunts; usu. silent. **HABITAT** Tree-fringed ponds, rivers. **RANGE** Resident in NW.

COMMON MERGANSER
Mergus merganser
WATERFOWL FAMILY

25″. Diver. Male back black; chest and underparts white; head black (green gloss), rounded. Female body gray; head and neck rusty; chin distinctly white. Bill red, slender but with thick base. **VOICE** Usu. silent. **HABITAT** Rivers; lakes and coastal bays in winter. **RANGE** Resident in NW.

RUDDY DUCK
Oxyura jamaicensis
WATERFOWL FAMILY

16″. Diver. Breeding male: body bright ruddy; top half of head black, lower half white; bill thick, bright blue. Winter male: head as above; body slaty brown; bill gray. Female body and cap brown; dark line on pale buff cheeks. Tail black, stiff, fan-shaped, often raised. Usu. in parties of several dozen when not breeding. **VOICE** Usu. silent. **HABITAT** Summer: reedy lakes. Migration and winter: saltwater bays, lakes. **RANGE** Apr.–Oct.: east of Cascades. Apr., Sept.–Oct.: all NW. Sept.–May: west of Cascades, s OR.

Raptors

The word "raptor" is usually used for birds of prey that are active in the daytime (it is also sometimes used for the nocturnal owls, described on page 293). Families found in the Pacific Northwest include the American vultures (Carthartidae), the hawks and eagles (Accipitridae), and the falcons (Falconidae). The bills of raptors are strong for tearing flesh, while the feet (usually yellow) are generally powerful (except in vultures), with curved talons for grasping prey. The carrion-feeding vultures are black, with broad wings and bare heads. Members of the hawk and eagle family are the very large eagles, with feathered legs; the eagle-size Osprey; harriers, which fly low over open areas and use their superb hearing as an aid in hunting; and the hawks. There are two types of hawks: the accipiters, whose shorter wings allow them to achieve rapid twisting flight, and the broad-winged, soaring buteos. The pointed-winged falcons are fast fliers. Immature raptors, often striped below, take a year or more to reach adulthood. Females are 10 to 20 percent larger than males in most species. Some raptors migrate to warmer climes in winter (flying during the day unlike most songbirds). When feeding and during migration, they save energy by riding rising columns of air (thermals) and updrafts of wind created at the tops of ridges. Acute vision allows raptors to spot unsuspecting prey from great heights.

Flight silhouettes of raptors *(illustrations not to relative scale)*

Turkey Vulture

Osprey

Bald Eagle

Northern Harrier

Sharp-shinned Hawk (Accipiter)

Red-tailed Hawk (Buteo)

American Kestrel (Falcon)

TURKEY VULTURE
Cathartes aura
AMERICAN VULTURE FAMILY

L 28″; WS 6′. Adult all black, brown-tinged above; head small, naked, red; bill yellow. Imm. head naked, gray. Soars with wings held at 20° above horizontal; seldom flaps wings. Long rounded tail and pale silver flight feathers can be seen from below. Gathers at nightly communal roosts in tall trees or towers. **VOICE** Grunts and hisses; usu. silent. **HABITAT** Lowland forests, grasslands. **RANGE** Mar.–Oct.: all NW.

OSPREY
Pandion haliaetus
HAWK AND EAGLE FAMILY

L 23″; WS 5′6″. Brown above with white crown; dark line through eye; white below. Feet gray; eyes yellow. Seen from below, flies with wings bent at "wrist" like flattened M; flight feathers and tail finely banded. Hovers frequently; often flies grasping fish in talons. Nest is mass of sticks topping dead tree or platform on Osprey pole. **VOICE** Emphatic repeated *kee-uk*. **HABITAT** Coastal estuaries, rivers, lakes. **RANGE** Apr.–Sept.: all NW.

BALD EAGLE
Haliaeetus leucocephalus
HAWK AND EAGLE FAMILY

immature and adult (left), immature (right)

L 32″; WS 7′. Adult body, wings, and thighs dark chocolate brown (may appear black); massive head white; bill yellow, strongly hooked; eyes, feet, and massive legs yellow; tail white, somewhat rounded. Imm. all dark brown when perched; flight reveals diffuse whitish wing linings and base of tail. Flies with slow deliberate wingbeats, wings held flat, straight out, primaries spread. Perches on tall trees. Numbers increasing, with DDT ban and protection. NW has influx of Alaskan and Canadian birds spending the winter. **VOICE** Piercing scream. **HABITAT** Coastal bays, estuaries, rivers, lakes. **RANGE** Apr.–Oct.: west of Cascades, Columbia R., sc OR. Oct.–Mar.: all NW; large roosts along many rivers.

NORTHERN HARRIER
Circus cyaneus
HAWK AND EAGLE FAMILY

L 22″; WS 4′. Wings and tail long, narrow; rump white; head and bill small, with owl-like facial disks. Male pearly gray; whiter below. Female brown above, dirty white with brown stripes below. Flies low over open areas, wings raised at an angle, listening and watching for rodents, frogs, and baby birds; often hovers and drops. Generally perches on ground, not in trees. **VOICE** Weak *pee*. **HABITAT** Marshes, fields. **RANGE** Resident in NW.

SHARP-SHINNED HAWK
Accipiter striatus
HAWK AND EAGLE FAMILY

L 12″; WS 21″. Adult slate gray above; rusty, barred below. Tail long, narrow, square with notch in middle. Feet small, yellow. Imm. (pictured) brown above, striped below. Flies with fast wingbeats followed by glides. Expert at capturing small birds. Soars during migration. **VOICE** High *kek* notes. **HABITAT** Forests, esp. coniferous; in winter, all areas. **RANGE** Apr.–Oct.: all wooded NW. Sept.–Apr.: all NW.

adult (left), immature (right)

COOPER'S HAWK
Accipiter cooperii
HAWK AND EAGLE FAMILY

L 17″; WS 28″. Plumages nearly identical to Sharp-shinned Hawk, but head and feet larger and tail longer, distinctly rounded; adult has black cap. Imm. belly whiter, with fewer streaks than Sharp-shin. **VOICE** High *kek* notes. **HABITAT** Forests, esp. broadleaf. **RANGE** Resident in NW.

NORTHERN GOSHAWK
Accipiter gentilis
HAWK AND EAGLE FAMILY

L 23″; WS 3′7″. Adult dark gray above, fine gray barring below; black crown and stripe behind eye; wide white eyebrow. Imm. has heavy stripes below; wide white eyebrow. Flight reveals long rounded tail; fluffy white undertail feathers in adult. **VOICE** Harsh *kek* notes. **HABITAT** Mixed forests, esp. coniferous; in winter, all areas. **RANGE** Apr.–Oct.: all wooded NW. Oct.–Apr.: all NW.

SWAINSON'S HAWK
Buteo swainsoni
HAWK AND EAGLE FAMILY

L 20″; WS 4′. Adult plain brown above; throat white; upper chest rufous; rest of underparts whitish. Flight reveals white underwing linings and blackish flight feathers; wingtips pointed for a Buteo; tail gray with fine black bands. Dark-morph adult solid brown, with rufous underwing linings. Imm. streaked below. Winters in Argentina. **VOICE** Whistled *kreee*. **HABITAT** Prairies, farms. **RANGE** Apr.–Sept.: east of Cascades.

immature (left), adult (right)

RED-TAILED HAWK
Buteo jamaicensis
HAWK AND EAGLE FAMILY

L 22″; WS 4′2″. Adult head, back, and wings dark brown; lower chest has band of heavy brown streaks; varies from whitish to dark rufous or blackish below; tail pale orange below, rufous above. Imm. similar, but tail pale brown with many indistinct bands; underparts usu. white. Seen from below, underwings mainly white, with dark leading edge and black crescent beyond wrist. Most frequently seen large hawk in NW year-round. **VOICE** Down-slurred squeal: *keee-rrr*. **HABITAT** Woodland edges, isolated trees in fields. **RANGE** All NW; withdraws from mtns. in winter.

FERRUGINOUS HAWK
Buteo regalis
HAWK AND EAGLE FAMILY

L 24″; WS 4′8″. Adult rufous above, white below; thighs rufous; head streaked brown. Flight reveals white breast, flight feathers, and tail; rusty wing linings; dark thighs that form a V. Dark-morph adult body and wing linings brown; tail and flight feathers white. Imm. brownish above, all white below. **VOICE** Descending *kree-ahh*. **HABITAT** Arid grasslands, farms, canyons. **RANGE** Apr.–Oct.: east of Cascades.

ROUGH-LEGGED HAWK
Buteo lagopus
HAWK AND EAGLE FAMILY

L 22″; WS 4′8″. Adult head and upper chest striped black and white; back and wings dark brown; black patch across lower belly; tail white, with broad black terminal band. Dark-morph adult black, with paler flight feathers. Flight reveals, from above, white patch at base of primaries; from below, black patch at bend of wing. Often hovers. **VOICE** Usu. silent. **HABITAT** Open country. **RANGE** Nov.–Apr.: all NW.

GOLDEN EAGLE
Aquila chrysaetos
HAWK AND EAGLE FAMILY

L 3'; WS 6'6". Adult dark brown with golden nape; base of tail banded gray. Bill heavy; legs heavily feathered; feet yellow. Imm. dark brown; wide band of white at base of tail. Flight reveals white window at base of primaries, esp. in imm. Flies on wings slightly angled up. **VOICE** High *kee-kee-kee*; screams. **HABITAT** Mtns., forests, grasslands. **RANGE** Resident in Cascades and east; nw WA (local).

adult (left), immature (right)

AMERICAN KESTREL
Falco sparverius
FALCON FAMILY

L 11"; WS 23". Male back rufous; wings blue-gray; chest pale buffy with black spots; tail rufous with black terminal band. Female rufous above, with fine black bars. 2 thin black sideburns on white face. In flight, pointed wings obvious; often hovers. **VOICE** Shrill *killy killy*. **HABITAT** Fields, farms, open woodlands, towns. **RANGE** Resident in NW; withdraws from mtns. in winter.

MERLIN
Falco columbarius
FALCON FAMILY

L 12"; WS 25". Adult male medium to dark gray above; pale buffy below, with heavy brown streaks; tail has wide black band near tip. Female and imm. dark brown above, heavily striped below; tail finely banded. 1 thin black sideburn. Flies fast and low when chasing small birds. **VOICE** High *ki ki ki ki*. **HABITAT** Forests, grasslands, marshes. **RANGE** Apr.–Oct.: WA Cascades, ne WA. Sept.–Apr.: all NW.

PEREGRINE FALCON
Falco peregrinus
FALCON FAMILY

L 18"; WS 3'4". Adult upperparts and tail dark slaty gray; underparts and underwing finely gray-barred; head black above, white below, with 1 thick black sideburn. Feet heavy, powerful. Imm. brown above, streaked below. Flight reveals pointed wings, broad at base; tail tapers to squared end. Flies low and high, often surveying bird flocks to spot slow-flying, injured individuals. Nests on ledges of cliffs, tall buildings. Numbers plummeted with DDT; now in assisted recovery. **VOICE** Harsh *kak kak* at nest. **HABITAT** Coasts, marshes, cities. **RANGE** Apr.–Sept.: all NW (very local). Apr.–May, Sept.–Oct.: all NW. Oct.–May: mainly west of Cascades.

PRAIRIE FALCON
Falco mexicanus
FALCON FAMILY

L 18"; WS 3'6". Adult pale brown above, whitish with brown speckles below; crown brown; eyebrow pale; throat white; 1 narrow sideburn below eye. Imm. streaked below. Flight reveals pointed wings, longish tail, black patch at base of wing linings. **VOICE** Loud *ki-ki-ki-ki.* **HABITAT** Grasslands, sagebrush, canyons. **RANGE** Resident east of Cascades.

RING-NECKED PHEASANT
Phasianus colchicus
PARTRIDGE FAMILY

female (left), male (right)

Male 34"; female 22". Male head and neck iridescent dark green, with white necklace, red bare skin around eye. Rest of body rufous and bronze, with 1" black and white chevrons above. Female warm buffy, with black spots above. Tail feathers long, pointed. Flies with rapid wingbeats followed by glides. **VOICE** Male: loud *kaw kawk.* **HABITAT** Farms, meadows, brush. **RANGE** Resident west and east of Cascades.

CHUKAR
Alectoris chukar
PARTRIDGE FAMILY

14". Plain gray above and on chest; belly white; sides barred chestnut and black; wings brown. Thick black line through eye and down foreneck frames white throat. Bill and legs red. Tail short, outer tail feathers rufous. **VOICE** Loud *chuk-chuk-chukar.* **HABITAT** Arid rocky hills, canyons. **RANGE** East of Cascades. **Gray Partridge** *(Perdix perdix)* of grasslands and farms east of Cascades is gray-brown; eyebrow, throat, patch on belly, and outer tail feathers rufous.

BLUE GROUSE
Dendragapus obscurus
PARTRIDGE FAMILY

18". Male mainly blue-gray; wings brown; tail fairly long, black; with pale gray band at end in most of region; in courtship display has fried-egg-like patch on neck. Female brown, finely barred with black. **VOICE** Male: 5–7 deep *whoop* notes. **HABITAT** Coniferous and mixed forests, brush. **RANGE** Resident in Cascades and forested regions west and east. **Spruce Grouse** *(D. canadensis)* occurs in WA Cascades, ne WA, ne OR; male has black throat and tail, white spots on sides and rump.

summer (left), winter (right)

WHITE-TAILED PTARMIGAN
Lagopus leucurus
PARTRIDGE FAMILY

13". Summer: back, chest, and head gray-brown; belly, wings, and outer tail white; male has red wattle over eye. Winter: all white, ex. for black eye and bill. White feathers cover feet. When molting: irreg. gray-brown feathers on white. **VOICE** High cackles; low clucks. **HABITAT** Alpine tundra, above tree line. **RANGE** Resident in High Cascades of WA.

RUFFED GROUSE
Bonasa umbellus
PARTRIDGE FAMILY

18". Grayish to reddish brown, speckled white and black; neck patch and terminal tail band black. Head small, slightly crested; tail fairly long, gray. Hard to see until it flies up on rapid noisy wingbeats. Male "drums" on low perch in spring by thumping wings against chest—slow at first, then faster. **VOICE** Alarm call: *quit quit.* **HABITAT** Broadleaf and riverine woodlands. **RANGE** Resident in Cascades and west, forested e highlands.

female, male

SAGE GROUSE
Centrocercus urophasianus
PARTRIDGE FAMILY

Male 28"; female 22". Mottled gray-brown above; belly black. Male chest white; yellow wattle over eye; throat black; black V on white foreneck; tail long, with pointed feathers. Female smaller; head and chest scaled brown. In early spring male fans tail, inflates 2 naked, yellowish-orange air sacs on chest. **VOICE** When flushed, *kuk-kuk-kuk.* Courting male: weak *wom-poo;* popping sound of air sacs. **HABITAT** Sagebrush. **RANGE** Resident in se OR, c WA east of Cascades.

CALIFORNIA QUAIL
Callipepla californica
PARTRIDGE FAMILY

10". Male pale brown above; chest gray; crown chestnut; rounded black plume on forehead; eyebrow and necklace white; throat black. Female head and chest plain pale brown; plume smaller. White stripes on rusty sides; black scaling on white belly. **VOICE** *Chi-CAH-go.* **HABITAT** Pine and broadleaf woodlands, scrub, towns. **RANGE** Resident west and east of Cascades.

MOUNTAIN QUAIL
Oreortyx pictus
PARTRIDGE FAMILY

11″. Sexes similar, with tall, thin, erect black plume on head. Back and tail gray or brown; wings brown; belly rusty with wide black and white bars; crown and chest gray; white line from eye to foreneck frames rusty throat. **VOICE** Male: loud *quark;* long series of mellow *took* notes. **HABITAT** Dry pine and mixed woodlands, mtn. scrub. **RANGE** Resident in OR west and east of Cascades; sw and se WA (local).

VIRGINIA RAIL
Rallus limicola
RAIL FAMILY

10″. Adult brown above; chest and wings rufous; sides barred black and white; cheeks gray; eyes red; bill long, thin, drooping, red with black tip. Legs dull red; toes long; tail short. Imm. has black chest. Usu. secretive. **VOICE** Repeated *kid ick;* grunting *oink* notes. **HABITAT** Freshwater marshes. **RANGE** Apr.–Sept.: all NW. Oct.–Apr.: west of Cascades.

AMERICAN COOT
Fulica americana
RAIL FAMILY

15″. Body duck-shaped; feet not webbed, but toes lobed. Sooty gray; head and neck black; bill thick, white, black near tip; sides of undertail white. Dives and skitters over surface to become airborne like a diving duck, swims like a duck—but not a duck. Flocks often graze on lawns near water. **VOICE** Grating *kuk* notes. **HABITAT** Marshes, ponds, lakes, shallow coastal waters. **RANGE** Resident in NW.

SANDHILL CRANE
Grus canadensis
CRANE FAMILY

L 3′4″; WS 6′. Mostly gray, often stained rusty; forecrown red; cheeks white. Neck long, thin; bill shortish, thin, straight, black; legs long, black. Flies with neck outstretched. **VOICE** Loud rattling *kar-r-r-r-o-o-o,* often given in flight. **HABITAT** Marshes, shallow lakes, fallow fields. **RANGE** Apr.–Sept.: local in e OR and sc WA. Mar.–Apr., Sept.–Oct.: west and east of Cascades. Sept.–Apr.: lower Columbia R.

Shorebirds

The term "shorebird" is used for certain members of the order Charadriiformes: plovers, oystercatchers, avocets, stilts, and sandpipers, including godwits, dowitchers, yellowlegs, curlews, and small sandpipers informally known as "peeps." Most shorebirds frequent open muddy, sandy, or rocky shores on the coast and around open inland wetlands. On the coast they tend to roost in moderate-size to enormous mixed-species flocks at high tide; at low tide they spread out to feed on small invertebrates. Most American shorebirds have a distinct breeding plumage in late spring and early summer. Most seen in the Northwest travel thousands of miles yearly between their breeding and wintering grounds. Shorebirds are most numerous in the region in May and from July through September. Some nonbreeding individuals pass the entire summer in the Northwest. In the identification of shorebirds, proportion and shape, as well as behavior and voice, are frequently more important than plumage color.

SNOWY PLOVER
Charadrius alexandrinus
PLOVER FAMILY

6″. Pale brown above, white below; bill short, thin, black; legs dark gray. Breeding male forecrown, patch behind eye, and partial neck ring black. Female eye patch and partial neck ring dark brown. Declining due to overuse of beaches by people, ORVs, unleashed dogs. **VOICE** Musical *chu wee.* **HABITAT** Coastal beaches; alkaline lake edges in summer. **RANGE** Resident in coastal sw WA and w OR. Apr.–Aug.: se OR.

BLACK-BELLIED PLOVER
Pluvialis squatarola
PLOVER FAMILY

12″. Breeding: back and wings speckled black and white; crown, hindneck, and sides of chest white; face, foreneck, and chest black. Nonbreeding: grayish above, white below; back speckled; flight reveals black patch at base of underwing. Bill short, straight; eyes large, black; legs black. Usu. in flocks. **VOICE** Whistled *pee-a-wee.* **HABITAT** Coastal beaches, mudflats. **RANGE** Apr.–May, July–Oct.: east and west of Cascades. July–May: entire coast.

SEMIPALMATED PLOVER
Charadrius semipalmatus
PLOVER FAMILY

7″. Upperparts dark brown; white below. Breeding: base of bill and legs yellow; black breast band. Nonbreeding and imm.: bill black; breast band brown. Appears neck-less; bill short. **VOICE** Whistled *tu-wheet.* **HABITAT** Mudflats, beaches. **RANGE** Apr.–May, July–Sept.: coast and inland. Oct.–Mar.: coast (uncommon).

KILLDEER
Charadrius vociferus
PLOVER FAMILY

10″. Brown above, white below; 2 black chest bands; pied face with red eye ring; legs pinkish. Flight reveals wing stripe, unique orange rump. Common inland plover in open habitats. Parent feigns broken wing to attract intruders away from nest or chicks. **VOICE** Strident *dee dee dee;* also *kill-dee.* **HABITAT** Farms, fields, playgrounds, golf courses, mudflats. **RANGE** Resident west of Cascades. Mar.–Oct.: interior.

BLACK OYSTERCATCHER
Haematopus bachmani
OYSTERCATCHER FAMILY

18″. Adult all black; bill long, chisel-shaped, red; eye yellow, with red eye ring; legs sturdy, pinkish. Imm. browner; bill orange with black tip. Feeds on clinging mollusks such as limpets. **VOICE** Piercing *kleep,* often repeated. **HABITAT** Rocky shorelines. **RANGE** Resident on coast.

BLACK-NECKED STILT
Himantopus mexicanus
AVOCET AND STILT FAMILY

14″. Dark above (male black, female dark brown), white below; rump and tail white. Head mainly black, with large white spot over eye; bill long, thin, black. Legs very long, red. Flight reveals wings uniformly blackish above and below. Wades up to its belly, eating aquatic insects, small fish. **VOICE** Sharp *yip yip yip.* **HABITAT** Shallow freshwater marshes. **RANGE** May–Sept.: mainly se OR; sc WA.

AMERICAN AVOCET
Recurvirostra americana
AVOCET AND STILT FAMILY

18″. Back and wings pied black and white; white below; rump and tail white. Neck long; bill long, slender, up-turned, black. Legs long, light blue. Nonbreeding head and neck gray. Breeding head and neck pale rusty orange. Feeds in flocks; sweeps bill from side to side in water when feeding. Nests in colonies. **VOICE** Loud *wheep.* **HABITAT** Shallow lakeshores, mudflats. **RANGE** Apr.–Oct.: mainly se OR; sc WA.

GREATER YELLOWLEGS
Tringa melanoleuca
SANDPIPER FAMILY

14″. Breeding: back brown-black with white dots; head, neck, and sides speckled dark brown. Nonbreeding: paler. Belly and rump white. Neck long; legs long, bright yellow; bill 1½ times longer than head, with relatively thick gray base and thin, black, slightly up-curved tip. VOICE Excited *tew tew tew.* HABITAT Coastal and inland mudflats, marshes. RANGE Mar.–May, July–Oct.: west and east of Cascades. Oct.–Mar.: coast (uncommon).

LESSER YELLOWLEGS
Tringa flavipes
SANDPIPER FAMILY

11″. Smaller version of Greater Yellowlegs (see previous species): plumages similar; legs also bright yellow; bill shorter (equal to length of head), straight, all black. VOICE 1–2 mellow *tu* notes. HABITAT Coastal mudflats, marshes. RANGE Apr.–May, July–Oct.: west and east of Cascades.

WILLET
Catoptrophorus semipalmatus
SANDPIPER FAMILY

nonbreeding in flight (left), on land (right)

15″. Breeding: speckled brownish gray. Nonbreeding: plain gray. Bill thick-based, fairly long, straight; legs blue-gray; tail gray. Flight reveals startling black wings with broad white central stripe. VOICE Song: *pill-will-willet.* Call: *kip, kip, kip.* HABITAT Summer: shallow inland lakeshores. Migration and winter: coastal beaches, marshes. RANGE Apr.–Sept.: se OR. July–May: coastal OR; WA (uncommon).

WANDERING TATTLER
Heteroscelus incanus
SANDPIPER FAMILY

11″. Breeding: plain gray above; white eyebrow; cheeks striped; wavy blackish bars on white underparts. Nonbreeding: head, breast, and upperparts gray; midbelly white. Bill straight, medium-length, black; legs shortish, yellow. VOICE High ringing notes. HABITAT Rocky ocean shores. RANGE Apr.–May, July–Oct.: entire coast.

SPOTTED SANDPIPER
Actitis macularia
SANDPIPER FAMILY

8″. Breeding: brown above; large black spots on white underparts. Nonbreeding: unspotted; smudge on sides of chest. Often teeters rear end. Flies on stiff bowed wings. **VOICE** *Peet-weet-weet.* **HABITAT** Riversides, ponds. **RANGE** May–Sept.: all NW. Winter: coastal shores and rivers (rare).

WHIMBREL
Numenius phaeopus
SANDPIPER FAMILY

18″. Adult and imm. neck, chest, and back speckled brown; belly dirty white; head has 4 dark brown stripes through eye and bordering pale midcrown stripe; legs bluish. Neck thin; bill very long, thin, downcurved. In flight, appears uniformly brown. **VOICE** 5–7 whistled *whi* notes. **HABITAT** Beaches, coastal and inland mudflats, fields. **RANGE** Apr.–May, July–Oct.: west and east of Cascades.

LONG-BILLED CURLEW
Numenius americanus
SANDPIPER FAMILY

23″. Head, neck, and upperparts brown with buffy spots; buffy below. Neck long; legs long, gray. Bill very long, down-curved, lower mandible red at base. In flight, appears uniformly buffy, with rufous wing linings. **VOICE** Loud *cur-leee;* rapid *kli-li-li-li.* **HABITAT** Summer: open grasslands. Migration and winter: mudflats. **RANGE** Apr.–Aug.: east of Cascades. Aug.–Apr.: entire coast (local).

MARBLED GODWIT
Limosa fedoa
SANDPIPER FAMILY

18″. Breeding: head, neck, and upperparts brown with buffy spots; buffy below, with streaks on neck, bars on breast. Nonbreeding: clear unbarred buff below. Neck long; legs long, blackish. Bill very long, slightly up-curved, red with black tip. In flight, appears uniformly buffy, with rufous wing linings. **VOICE** Loud *god-WIT.* **HABITAT** Mudflats, beaches. **RANGE** Apr.–May, Aug.–Sept.: east of Cascades. Aug.–May: coast.

RUDDY TURNSTONE
Arenaria interpres
SANDPIPER FAMILY

9″. Breeding: back orange and black; head and chest pied black and white. Nonbreeding: more somber, with solid brown chest patch. Bill short, wedge-shaped; legs orange. Flight reveals harlequin wing and back pattern. **VOICE** Rattling *tuk-e-tuk.* **HABITAT** Beaches, mudflats. **RANGE** July–May: entire coast.

BLACK TURNSTONE
Arenaria melanocephala
SANDPIPER FAMILY

9″. Breeding: head, chest, and upperparts black, with white dots on chest; belly white; large white spot on face; thin white eyebrow. Nonbreeding: head, back, and chest sooty black, without white spots. Bill short, wedge-shaped; legs short, blackish. Flight reveals pied harlequin pattern on back, wings, tail. **VOICE** Rattled *skeeer;* higher than Ruddy. **HABITAT** Rocks; less often sand beaches, mudflats. **RANGE** July–May: entire coast.

SURFBIRD
Aphriza virgata
SANDPIPER FAMILY

10″. Breeding: back and chest gray-brown with black speckling; rusty spots on back; belly white with small black Vs. Nonbreeding: back and chest plain gray-brown; belly white with few dark spots. Bill short, thick, black, lower mandible with yellow base; legs short, yellow. Flight reveals white wing stripe, black band near tip of white tail. **VOICE** Sharp *kee-a-weet.* **HABITAT** Rocky shores. **RANGE** July–May: entire coast.

RED KNOT
Calidris canutus
SANDPIPER FAMILY

11″. Breeding: back scaled with black; face and underparts orange. Nonbreeding: uniformly gray above; belly white. Legs short; bill straight, with thick base. Flight reveals thin white wing stripe, barred rump. Congregates in large flocks at a few sites. **VOICE** Soft *knut.* **HABITAT** Coastal beaches, mudflats. **RANGE** Apr.–May, Aug.–Oct.: coast (local).

SANDERLING
Calidris alba
SANDPIPER FAMILY
8". Breeding: head and upperparts rusty; belly white. Nonbreeding: gray above, white below; bend of wing often black. Bill short; legs black. Imm. crown and back heavily black-spotted. Runs ahead of incoming waves. Usu. in flocks. VOICE Sharp *plic.* HABITAT Sand beaches. RANGE July–May: entire coast.

WESTERN SANDPIPER
Calidris mauri
SANDPIPER FAMILY
6½". Breeding: rusty above; fine black dots on foreparts. Nonbreeding: gray above, white below. Bill fairly long, black, droops at tip; legs black. Fall imm. rusty on sides of back. VOICE High *cheep.* HABITAT Coastal and inland mudflats. RANGE Apr.–May, July–Sept.: coast and inland. Nov.–Mar.: coast.

LEAST SANDPIPER
Calidris minutilla
SANDPIPER FAMILY
6". Reddish brown above; chest buffy brown, lightly spotted. Bill short, thin, slightly drooping, black; legs greenish yellow. VOICE High *kreet.* HABITAT Coastal and inland mudflats. RANGE July–May: coast. Apr.–May, July–Oct.: inland.

BAIRD'S SANDPIPER
Calidris bairdii
SANDPIPER FAMILY
7½". Breeding: back brown with heavy black spots; head and chest pale brown with fine black dots. Bill straight, medium length; legs black; wingtips extend beyond tail. Juv. (seen in fall migration): buffy, with paler scalloping on back. VOICE Low raspy *kreep.* HABITAT Marshy pools, mudflats. RANGE Apr.–May (rare), July–Sept.: coast and inland.

ROCK SANDPIPER
Calidris ptilocnemis
SANDPIPER FAMILY
8½". Breeding: back rufous, black-spotted; whitish below, with fine spots; may show black patch on chest. Nonbreeding: head, chest, and back slaty; belly white; slaty spots on flanks. Bill thick, drooping, shorter than Dunlin's; legs greenish black. Flight reveals white wing stripe, black stripe on white rump. VOICE Low *du-du-du.* HABITAT Rocky coasts. RANGE Oct.–May: entire coast.

DUNLIN
Calidris alpina
SANDPIPER FAMILY
8". Breeding: bright reddish brown above; white below, with fine black dots; black midbelly patch. Nonbreeding: gray-brown; belly white. Bill long, drooping. **VOICE** Soft *cheerp.* **HABITAT** Mudflats. **RANGE** Oct.–May: entire coast. Apr.–May, Oct.: also east of Cascades.

SHORT-BILLED DOWITCHER
Limnodromus griseus
SANDPIPER FAMILY
12". Breeding: speckled brown above; neck and breast buffy orange. Nonbreeding: gray-brown above, whitish below. Bill very long, straight; legs greenish, short. Flight reveals white V on lower back. Feeds with rapid motion. **VOICE** Musical *tu tu tu.* **HABITAT** Mudflats, pond shores. **RANGE** Apr.–May, July–Oct.: mainly coastal. **Long-billed Dowitcher** *(L. scolopaceus)* mainly an inland migrant; call is high sharp *keek.*

COMMON SNIPE
Gallinago gallinago
SANDPIPER FAMILY
11". Dark brown above, with a few white stripes, head with 4 bold blackish stripes; sides barred; midbelly white; tail rusty. Legs short; bill very long, straight. Flies in erratic zigzag. In aerial courtship display, vibrating tail feathers hum. **VOICE** Hoarse *skaip.* **HABITAT** Wet meadows, marshes. **RANGE** Resident west of Cascades. Apr.–Oct.: east of Cascades.

WILSON'S PHALAROPE
Phalaropus tricolor
SANDPIPER FAMILY
9". Breeding female (pictured): back gray with reddish stripes; white below; crown and hindneck silvery; line through eye and on sides of neck black, becoming reddish; foreneck buffy orange. Breeding male: duller; crown and sides of neck brown. Bill needle-like. Swims in circles; runs erratically on mud. **VOICE** Soft *chek-chek-chek;* nasal *wurk.* **HABITAT** Marshy ponds. **RANGE** Apr.–Aug.: east of Cascades. May: also coastal NW.

RED-NECKED PHALAROPE
Phalaropus lobatus
SANDPIPER FAMILY
8". Breeding: back black with rusty stripes; head blackish; throat and underparts white; neck rusty; chest slaty; male duller than female (pictured). Nonbreeding: gray above with white stripes; white below; crown and line behind eye black. Bill thin, black. Swims in circles. **VOICE** Low *whit.* **HABITAT** Ocean, shallow lakes. **RANGE** Apr.–May, July–Oct.: mainly offshore; inland (uncommon).

Gulls and Terns

All members of the gull family (Laridae)—gulls, jaegers, terns, and skimmers—have webbed feet and breed in the open, in colonies, on islands free of land predators; their nests are usually mere depressions on the ground. Although gulls are common near the sea (and are often called "seagulls"), few are found far at sea; in fact, many breed far inland near fresh water. Superb fliers, most gulls have wings with white trailing edges, and fairly long, strong bills that are slightly hooked at the tip. These generalist feeders and scavengers eat living and dead animal life, and many have adapted to feed on human refuse. Gulls go through a confusing array of plumages and molts until they reach adulthood in two years (small species), three years (medium), or four years (large). For many gull species, this guide describes selected life-stage categories, including juvenile (the bird's birth summer), first winter, first summer (bird is one year old), second winter, summer adult, and winter adult. Jaegers are quite large, dark brown seabirds that attack other seabirds and steal their fish. The small to medium-size terns, sleek and slender-billed, fly in a buoyant or hovering manner, diving headfirst for small fish; most have black caps (in summer) and elegant, forked tails. Skimmers (none present in the Northwest) are large and have extra-long lower bills that they use to skim fish from the water.

PARASITIC JAEGER
Stercorarius parasiticus
GULL AND TERN FAMILY

L 18"; WS 3'6". 2 color morphs, both with whitish patch at base of primaries. Typical adult dark brown above; white or light dusky sides and belly; yellowish-white collar; thin brown chest band; tail has 2 longer, pointed central tail feathers. Dark adult all brown. Bill strongly hooked at tip. Chases other seabirds; forces them to drop food. **VOICE** Silent at sea. **HABITAT** Open ocean; beaches (uncommon). **RANGE** May, Aug.–Oct.: ocean, coast.

BONAPARTE'S GULL
Larus philadelphia
GULL AND TERN FAMILY

13". Summer adult: back and wings silvery; neck, underparts, and tail white; head black; white leading edge of wing, black tips on primaries; legs red; bill short, black. Winter adult: head white; black spot behind eye. 1st winter: head white, tail black-tipped. Often hovers. **VOICE** Nasal *cher*. **HABITAT** Estuaries, bays. **RANGE** July–May: ocean, coast. Apr.–May, Aug.–Oct.: also inland (local).

HEERMANN'S GULL
Larus heermanni
GULL AND TERN FAMILY

20″. Summer adult: dark gray above, gray below; head white. Winter adult: head streaked gray. Bill red, black-tipped; legs black. Flight reveals blackish wings and tail, pale gray rump. 1st winter: uniformly unspotted dark brown; base of bill pink. Breeds on nw Mexico islets in spring. VOICE Loud *cah-wok;* high *whee-ee.* HABITAT Ocean, rocky and sandy shores, protected waters. RANGE July–Oct.: entire coast.

MEW GULL
Larus canus
GULL AND TERN FAMILY

17″. Summer adult: gray above; head, tail, and underparts white; eyes dark; legs yellow. Winter adult: brownish streaks on head. Flight reveals black wingtips, long white spot on first 2 primaries, gray upperwing, white tail. Bill short, unmarked yellow. 1st winter: gray-brown; bill pink, black-tipped; legs pink. VOICE High *KEE-yer;* low *MEE-yew.* HABITAT Coasts, mudflats, ports. RANGE Aug.–May: coasts, major valleys west of Cascades.

summer adult (left), 1st winter (right)

RING-BILLED GULL
Larus delawarensis
GULL AND TERN FAMILY

L 19″; WS 4′. Summer adult: head and underparts white; back and wings silvery; wingtips black with white spots; bill yellow with black ring near tip; legs greenish yellow. Winter adult: head flecked brown. 1st winter: back gray; wing coverts speckled brown; tail whitish with black terminal band; bill pink with black tip; legs pink. Juv.: pale brown, speckled; bill black; legs pink. Nests in colonies on lakes. VOICE High-pitched mewing. HABITAT Estuaries, lakes, urban parks, parking lots. RANGE Resident in NW.

CALIFORNIA GULL
Larus californicus
GULL AND TERN FAMILY

21″. Summer adult: dark gray above; head, tail, and underparts white; eyes dark; legs pale yellow-green. Winter adult: brownish streaks on head and shoulders. Bill yellow, with red and black spot near tip. Flight reveals black wingtips, long white spot on first primary, dark gray upperwing, white tail. 1st winter: gray-brown with barring above; bill pink, black-tipped; legs pink. Nests in colonies on islets in lakes. **VOICE** High *kee-yah;* low *cow-cow-cow.* **HABITAT** Summer: inland lakes. Winter: coasts, fallow fields. **RANGE** Apr.–Oct.: east of Cascades. Apr., July–Oct.: all NW. Aug.–Apr.: coast, Columbia R., sc OR.

WESTERN GULL
Larus occidentalis
GULL AND TERN FAMILY

26″. Adult: dark slaty gray above; head, tail, and underparts white; eyes yellowish; legs pink; bill large, yellow, with red spot near tip. Flight reveals slaty upperwing; black outer primaries, with large white spot on first; white tail. 1st winter: mottled gray-brown; rump pale; tail blackish; bill black; legs pink. Nests in colonies. **VOICE** High *whee-whee-whee;* low *kuk-kuk-kuk.* **HABITAT** Ocean, coasts, estuaries, towns. **RANGE** Resident on coast.

GLAUCOUS-WINGED GULL
Larus glaucescens
GULL AND TERN FAMILY

26″. Summer adult: gray above; head, tail, and underparts white; eyes dark; legs pink. Winter adult: brownish spots on head. Bill large, yellow, with red spot near tip. Flight reveals gray upperwing and outer primaries, darker near tips; white tail. 1st winter: white, mottled with gray-brown; bill black; legs pink. Nests in colonies. **VOICE** Raucous *kow-kow-kow;* soft *ga-ga.* **HABITAT** Ocean, coasts, mudflats, farms, towns. **RANGE** Resident west of Cascades, ex. does not breed on sw OR coast; wanders inland.

CASPIAN TERN
Sterna caspia
GULL AND TERN FAMILY

21″. Pale silvery above, white below; flight reveals black underside of primaries. Bill thick for a tern; legs short, black; tail notched, short. Summer adult: cap black; bill bright red. Winter adult: cap blackish, streaked white; bill red with black tip. Imm. like winter adult, but with dark scalloping on back; bill orange. **VOICE** Harsh *kra-haa.* **HABITAT** Mainly inner coastal waters; inland lakes, rivers. **RANGE** May–Aug.: coastal c and s WA, sc and se OR (local).

COMMON TERN
Sterna hirundo
GULL AND TERN FAMILY

15″. Summer adult: back and wings silvery, with blackish primaries; white below; cap and hindneck black; bill reddish orange with black tip; legs short, reddish orange; tail deeply forked, outer streamers dusky. Winter adult: forehead white; nape black. Juv. has scaly brown edges to gray back feathers. Flight shows primaries blackish above, with wide black trailing edge below. **VOICE** Short *kip;* drawn-out *kee-arr.* **HABITAT** Beaches, coastal waters. **RANGE** May, Aug.–Oct.: entire coast.

FORSTER'S TERN
Sterna forsteri
GULL AND TERN FAMILY

15″. Pale silvery above, white below; primaries white; bill slender; tail forked, long. Summer adult: cap black; bill red-orange with black tip; legs red. Winter adult: crown white; long black eyemask; bill black. Imm.: back brownish; bill and eyemask black. Nests in colonies. **VOICE** Grating *kay-r-r-r;* a repeated *kip.* **HABITAT** Marshes, lakes, beaches. **RANGE** Apr.–Oct.: east of Cascades. Rare migrant on coast.

BLACK TERN
Chlidonias niger
GULL AND TERN FAMILY

10″. Summer: back, wings, and tail all gray; head and underparts black; bill and legs black; vent white. Winter: dark gray above; face and underparts white; nape and ear spot black. Tail short, notched. Nests in small colonies. **VOICE** Sharp *kreek.* **HABITAT** Summer: inland reedy lakes, wet meadows. Migration: ocean, ponds. **RANGE** May–Sept.: east of Cascades. May, Aug.–Sept.: coast (local).

Puffins and Murres

Members of this family, also known as alcids from their scientific family name, Alcidae, are chunky, penguin-like seabirds. Most are either black above and white below, or grayish. Their webbed feet are placed far back, making it difficult for them to walk on land. Their short pointed wings whir in the air, and they fly in long arcs, as the very short tail is useless in making sharp turns. Members of this family dive for fish and squid from the surface of the sea and spend their nonbreeding months offshore. Their colonial nest sites vary from burrows to seaside ledges; most are on steep-sided offshore islets. Most members of this family have distinct summer and winter plumages.

COMMON MURRE
Uria aalge
PUFFIN AND MURRE FAMILY

17". Summer: black above, white below; head and neck black, with grayish-brown wash on crown. Winter: throat, cheeks, and foreneck white; black line down cheeks. Bill fairly long, slender, black; feet blackish; trailing edge of secondaries white. Nests in colonies. **VOICE** Purring *murrr;* low croak; high bleat. **HABITAT** Ocean, seaside cliffs. **RANGE** Resident on coast.

PIGEON GUILLEMOT
Cepphus columba
PUFFIN AND MURRE FAMILY

13". Summer: black; large, oval, white patch on wing partly crossed by black bar. Winter: wing patch similar; body grayish above, whitish below; black line through eye. Bill slender, black, with bright red lining; feet red. **VOICE** Wheezy *peeee.* **HABITAT** Ocean, seaside rocks. **RANGE** Resident on coast.

MARBLED MURRELET
Brachyramphus marmoratus
PUFFIN AND MURRE FAMILY

9". Summer: crown and back dark brown; brown below, with fine white scaling. Winter: crown and back black; white stripe on either side of back; throat, cheeks, and underparts white. Neck and tail short; bill short, thin, black. Requires old-growth forest for nesting; flies to and from nest only at night. **VOICE** High *keer-keer.* **HABITAT** Feeds in ocean; nests inland. **RANGE** Resident on coast.

CASSIN'S AUKLET
Ptychoramphus aleuticus
PUFFIN AND MURRE FAMILY

7½". Head, neck, back, and sides slaty gray; belly white; eye and incomplete eye ring white. Tail very short; bill stubby, base of lower mandible pale. Flies to and from seaside burrow only at night. Nests in colonies. **VOICE** Croaks and whistles, in colony, at night. **HABITAT** Ocean. **RANGE** Resident on coast.

RHINOCEROS AUKLET
Cerorhinca monocerata
PUFFIN AND MURRE FAMILY
14". Summer: slaty gray; 2 rows of white plumes on head; bill reddish with yellow, upward-slanting "horn." Winter: bill yellow; lacks horn and head plumes. Tail short; bill swollen and pointed; eyes yellow. **VOICE** High groans, low growls, in colony at night. **HABITAT** Ocean. **RANGE** Resident on coast.

TUFTED PUFFIN
Fratercula cirrhata
PUFFIN AND MURRE FAMILY
14". Summer: body, neck, and crown black; face mostly white; long, yellow, down-curled plumes extend from eyebrow to rear of neck; bill reddish orange, yellow at base; short legs and wide webbed feet bright orange. Winter: all slaty, with dull reddish bill. Bill massive, vertically flattened; eyes yellow with red eye ring. Nests in colonies. **VOICE** Growls and purrs at nest. **HABITAT** Ocean, seaside cliffs. **RANGE** May–Aug.: coast. Sept.–Apr.: well offshore.

ROCK DOVE
Columba livia
PIGEON AND DOVE FAMILY
13". Typical head dark gray; coppery iridescence on neck; body and tail pale gray; white on upper rump; 2 black bars on secondaries. Bill short, black; legs short, red; tail tipped black. Colors range from black to pale brown and white. Common city pigeon. Flight reveals pointed wings. **VOICE** Gurgling *coo-cuk-crooo*. **HABITAT** Towns, farms, cliffs. **RANGE** Settled areas west and east of Cascades.

BAND-TAILED PIGEON
Columba fasciata
PIGEON AND DOVE FAMILY
15". Back, wings, and tail slaty; head and underparts soft purplish gray; white crescent on nape; eyes red; bill and feet yellow. Flight reveals blackish base of tail, pale gray tip of tail and rump. In courtship, flying male circles with stiff wings and fanned tail. Largest pigeon in NW. **VOICE** Low, owl-like *hoo-hooo*. **HABITAT** Forests, urban parks. **RANGE** Resident west of Cascades; many roam higher into mtns. in fall, fewer in winter.

MOURNING DOVE
Zenaida macroura
PIGEON AND DOVE FAMILY
12". Back, wings, and tail dull brown; head and underparts pale buffy; bill short, black; black spot below eye; legs short, red; black and white edges on wedge-shaped, pointed tail. Male cap and nape blue-gray. Head small; tail long. Wings whistle when taking flight. **VOICE** Mournful *coo WHO-o coo, coo, coo.* **HABITAT** Fields, open woodlands, gardens, sandy scrub. **RANGE** Resident in NW (local in w WA).

Owls

Owls are nocturnal birds of prey that range in size in the Pacific Northwest from about 6 to 24 inches long. They have large heads, with large, forward-facing, yellow or brown eyes. Their eyesight and hearing are both acute. Distinct facial disks conceal large ear openings that provide them with keen hearing, which can pinpoint a squeak or a rustle in the grass in total darkness. The ears are asymmetrically placed on either side of the head, providing greater range of sound and better triangulation for pinpointing sources of sounds. Some owls have ornamental tufts of feathers at the corners of the head that look like ears or horns and are called ear tufts. The fluffy-looking bodies of owls are cryptically colored and patterned to blend with the background of their daytime nest or roost. Owls are most readily seen in winter in open areas and leafless woodlands. Their bills are short but strongly hooked. The legs are typically short, and the feet have sharp curved talons. Owls fly silently; their feathers are very soft and delicately fringed. Imitations and tapes of their distinctive voices, given or played at night, bring a response from an owl, which may call or fly in close to the source of the call, or both; in daytime, the same sound may bring crows, jays, and other birds, which usually mob roosting owls they discover.

Parts of an Owl

ear tuft

facial disk

BARN OWL
Tyto alba
BARN OWL FAMILY

18″. Pale orange washed with gray above; white or buff flecked with black dots below. Head large, round, without ear tufts; white, heart-shaped facial disk; eyes dark. Legs long, feathered; feet gray. Superb "mouser" with acute hearing. Strictly nocturnal; perches on poles at night. **VOICE** Variety of harsh screams, hisses, clicks. **HABITAT** Farms with old buildings, riversides, deserts, towns. **RANGE** Resident west and east of Cascades at lower elevs.

WESTERN SCREECH-OWL
Otus kennicottii
OWL FAMILY

9″. Dark brown west of Cascades, grayish to east. Facial disks ringed in black; row of white spots on either side of back; blackish streaks on finely barred breast. Fluffy ear tufts (can be laid flat); eyes yellow; bill black; tail short. **VOICE** Low short whistles that speed up like a bouncing ball; series of quick, evenly spaced hoots. **HABITAT** Broadleaf and riverine woodlands, towns. **RANGE** Resident west and east of Cascades.

GREAT HORNED OWL
Bubo virginianus
OWL FAMILY

L 23″; WS 4′7″. Dark brown with black spots above; underparts pale brown with heavy, dark brown bars; dark streaks on upper chest; facial disks rich rusty brown, ringed in black. Head large; eyes yellow; fluffy ear tufts. **VOICE** 5–8 deep hoots, 2nd and 3rd rapid and doubled. **HABITAT** Forests, riverine woodlands, cliffs in sagebrush deserts, towns. **RANGE** Resident in NW.

NORTHERN PYGMY-OWL
Glaucidium gnoma
OWL FAMILY

7″. Crown, upperparts, and chest brown or gray with fine whitish dots; breast white, striped brown or gray. Lacks ear tufts; eyes yellow; false black eyes with white eyebrows on back of head; tail long, banded dark and light brown. Feeds by day on small birds; often mobbed by them. **VOICE** Long series of even *toot* notes. **HABITAT** Coniferous forests. **RANGE** Resident in NW.

BURROWING OWL
Speotyto cunicularia
OWL FAMILY

9″. Brown above, spotted with white; white below, scaled brown. Head rounded, lacks ear tufts; facial disks light brown; eyes yellow. Legs long, grayish; tail short. Digs burrow in open field; sentinel may stand on earthen mound by burrow in daytime. **VOICE** Mellow *coo-coo* at night; *quick* notes if alarmed. **HABITAT** Dry grasslands, sagebrush deserts. **RANGE** Mar.–Aug.: east of Cascades in se WA, e OR; valleys of w OR (local).

SPOTTED OWL
Strix occidentalis
OWL FAMILY

18″. Dark brown with white spots above; underparts barred brown on white; facial disks edged in black; crown brown with white dots. Eyes brown; lacks ear tufts. Restricted to larger old-growth forest tracts; in small patches, loses out to Barred Owl and Great Horned Owl. Northern subspecies endangered. **VOICE** Dog-like, barking *hoo-hoo-hoo-hoooah.* **HABITAT** Wet coniferous forests. **RANGE** Resident west of Cascades.

BARRED OWL
Strix varia
OWL FAMILY

L 20″; WS 3′8″. Gray-brown with black spots above; heavily striped underparts; dark bars on upper chest; facial disks gray, ringed in black. Eyes brown; lacks ear tufts. Feeds at night; some sit conspicuously on horizontal limbs by day. Invading fragmented forest west of Cascades, displacing Spotted Owl. **VOICE** 2 sets of *hoo* notes: *Who cooks for you? Who cooks for you all?* Caterwauling mating calls in spring. **HABITAT** Swamps, woodlands. **RANGE** Resident in Cascades and west, e highlands.

LONG-EARED OWL
Asio otus
OWL FAMILY

15″. Ear tufts long, placed close together on smallish head; eyes yellow; eye disks rufous-orange, edged in black. Speckled dark brown and blackish above; striped blackish below, over finer brown banding. Much thinner than Great Horned Owl. **VOICE** Varied; 1 or 2 long *hoooos;* wails and screams. **HABITAT** Riverine woodlands near fields; in winter, also planted conifer groves. **RANGE** Apr.–Oct.: mostly east of Cascades. Oct.–Mar.: all NW, ex. higher mtns.

SHORT-EARED OWL
Asio flammeus
OWL FAMILY

16″. Brown above, with darker and paler brown spots; buffy below, with brown stripes; facial disks buffy with blackish "eye shadow" around yellow eyes. Head has tiny inconspicuous ear tufts. Flight reveals brown wings above, with buffy patch near bend of wing. **VOICE** Barking *wow* near nest. **HABITAT** Marshes, meadows, farms. **RANGE** All NW; local in summer, more widespread in winter.

COMMON NIGHTHAWK
Chordeiles minor
NIGHTJAR FAMILY

10″. Dark brown, heavily gray-spotted; throat white (buff in female); legs very short. Flight reveals long, pointed, black primaries with prominent white bar; long notched tail. Flies high and erratically. Hunts at night for insects. **VOICE** Nasal *peeent*. **HABITAT** Open woodlands, sagebrush. **RANGE** June–Sept.: all NW.

VAUX'S SWIFT
Chaetura vauxi
SWIFT FAMILY

4½″. Sooty gray with diffuse whitish throat; bill and feet tiny; wings extend beyond short spiny tail. Flight reveals long pointed wings, bowed in crescent when gliding. Does not perch; clings upright, though rarely seen at rest. In migration, roosts communally in hollow trees and chimneys. **VOICE** High *chit-ter* and *chip* notes. **HABITAT** Forests, lakes, towns. **RANGE** Cascades and west; forested mtns. to east (local).

WHITE-THROATED SWIFT
Aeronautes saxatilis
SWIFT FAMILY

6½″. Mainly black; white throat narrows down to midbelly; flanks and trailing edge of secondaries white; bill tiny; tail deeply notched. Flight reveals long pointed wings. Very fast flier. Does not perch; clings upright. Nests in small colonies. **VOICE** Shrill descending *ji-ji-ji-ji-ji*. **HABITAT** Cliffs, canyons, deserts. **RANGE** Apr.–Aug.: east of Cascades.

BLACK-CHINNED HUMMINGBIRD
Archilochus alexandri
HUMMINGBIRD FAMILY

3½″. Male green above and on sides; chest crescent and midbelly stripe white; throat patch black above, violet below; tail black, notched. Female green above; throat and underparts white; tail green, with white corners. Bill long, needle-like, black. **VOICE** Loud *teeuw*. **HABITAT** Riverine woodlands, canyons, towns. **RANGE** May–Aug.: east of Cascades.

CALLIOPE HUMMINGBIRD
Stellula calliope
HUMMINGBIRD FAMILY

female (left), male (right)

3". Male crown and upperparts green; white below, with throat patch of red stripes; tail very short, black. Female green above, white below; washed buffy on sides; tail has white corners. Bill short, needle-like, black. Smallest bird in N. Amer. **VOICE** High *tsik*. **HABITAT** Dry coniferous forests, wooded canyons. **RANGE** Apr.–Aug.: Cascades, e highlands.

RUFOUS HUMMINGBIRD
Selasphorus rufus
HUMMINGBIRD FAMILY

3½". Male crown, upperparts, and sides rufous; chest crescent and midbelly stripe white; throat patch red; tail rufous, feathers pointed; in display flight, wings make loud staccato sounds. Female green above, white below; sides buffy; outer tail feathers rufous, black, and white. Bill needle-like, black. **VOICE** Short single notes. **HABITAT** Coniferous, broadleaf, and riverine forests, parks. **RANGE** Mar.–Sept.: all NW.

BELTED KINGFISHER
Ceryle alcyon
KINGFISHER FAMILY

13". Male blue above, with tiny white spots; throat, neck, and belly white; blue belt on chest. Female (pictured) similar; belly has 2nd (rufous) belt extending onto sides. Front-heavy; head large, with ragged fore and rear crests; bill very long, thick, pointed, black; white spot before eye. Active, calls often; dives headfirst to seize small fish. For nest, excavates tunnel 1–2' into earthen bank, sometimes far from water. **VOICE** Loud woody rattle. **HABITAT** Rivers, lakes, coast. **RANGE** Resident in NW.

Woodpeckers

Woodpeckers, which range in size from small to midsize birds, cling to the trunks and large branches of trees with their sharp claws (on short legs) and stiff, spine-tipped tails that help support them in the vertical position. Their long pointed bills are like chisels, able to bore into wood. Curled inside the woodpecker head is a narrow tongue twice the length of the bill, tipped with spear-like barbs that impale wood-boring insects. Members of this family laboriously dig out nest holes in living or dead tree trunks and limbs. The sexes are very much alike, but the red (or yellow) patches on the heads of the males are reduced or lacking in females of many species. In spring, males rapidly bang their bills against resonant wood on trees and buildings in a territorial drumming that is louder and more rapid than the tapping made while feeding.

LEWIS'S WOODPECKER
Melanerpes lewis
WOODPECKER FAMILY

11". Sexes alike. Crown, back, and wings black (glossed dark green); face and cheeks dark red; chest and complete collar silvery; belly pink. In flight, all dark above. Flight is crow-like, with steady wingbeats. Takes large insects in trees, high in air. **VOICE** Harsh *churr;* soft drum. **HABITAT** Open areas with pine, oak, cottonwood trees; farms, orchards. **RANGE** Resident in sw OR; sc WA (local). Apr.–Aug.: e Cascades.

ACORN WOODPECKER
Melanerpes formicivorus
WOODPECKER FAMILY

9". Male black above; white forehead joined to white throat in front of eye; belly white, streaked black on sides; crown red. Female similar; crown black over eye; hindcrown red. Eyes white. Flight reveals white rump and base of primaries. Caches acorns in trees, poles. Nests communally: 4–6 breeding adults and young of previous year raise new generation. **VOICE** Loud repeated *wake-up.* **HABITAT** Open oak and pine-oak woodlands towns. **RANGE** Resident in sw OR, most of Willamette Valley.

RED-NAPED SAPSUCKER
Sphyrapicus nuchalis
WOODPECKER FAMILY

8". Adult male back and wings black, weakly barred white; long white patch on wing; pale yellow below, with dark speckles; head boldly pied; red forecrown and nape split by black line; throat red. Adult female similar, but upper throat white. Drills holes in bark; returns for sap, insects. **VOICE** Slurred mewing note; irreg. drum. **HABITAT** Pine, fir, aspen forests; orchards. **RANGE** Apr.–Sept.: east of Cascades.

RED-BREASTED SAPSUCKER
Sphyrapicus ruber
WOODPECKER FAMILY

8″. Sexes alike. Adult back and wings black with irreg. white markings; long white patch on wing; belly pale yellow with dark speckles; head and chest red. Drills holes in bark; returns for sap, insects. **VOICE** Slurred nasal *cheer*; irreg. drum. **HABITAT** Moist broadleaf and mixed forests. **RANGE** Resident in Cascades and west.

WILLIAMSON'S SAPSUCKER
Sphyrapicus thyroideus
WOODPECKER FAMILY

9″. Sexes very different. Adult male mainly black; shoulder and rump white; 2 thin white head stripes; throat red; midbelly yellowish. Adult female mainly barred black and buff; head plain dull brown; belly pale yellow; rump white. **VOICE** Slurred nasal *cheer*; irreg. drum. **HABITAT** Coniferous forests. **RANGE** Apr.–Sept.: Cascades, e highlands.

DOWNY WOODPECKER
Picoides pubescens
WOODPECKER FAMILY

6½″. Like Hairy Woodpecker, head boldly pied; back white; wings black, white-spotted; underparts pale gray (whiter east of Cascades); male has red nape patch. Downy is smaller than Hairy, with much shorter bill and black spots on white outer tail feathers. **VOICE** Rapid descending whinny; flat *pick*; long drum. **HABITAT** Lowland broadleaf and riverine woodlands, thickets, parks. **RANGE** Resident in NW.

HAIRY WOODPECKER
Picoides villosus
WOODPECKER FAMILY

9″. Like Downy Woodpecker, head boldly pied; back pale brown; wings black, white-spotted; underparts pale brown (whiter east of Cascades); male has red nape patch. Hairy is larger than Downy, has much longer bill, and clear, white, unspotted outer tail feathers. **VOICE** Loud rattle; sharp *peek*; long drum. **HABITAT** Coniferous forests. **RANGE** Resident in NW.

WHITE-HEADED WOODPECKER
Picoides albolarvatus
WOODPECKER FAMILY

9″. All black, ex. for white crown, cheeks, and throat; male has small red patch on nape. Flight reveals white patch at base of primaries. **VOICE** Sharp *pi-pick*; rapid drum, lasts 1–2 seconds. **HABITAT** Pine forests, esp. Ponderosa; at 4,000–9,000′ in summer, somewhat lower in winter. **RANGE** Resident in Cascades, forested e highlands.

BLACK-BACKED WOODPECKER
Picoides arcticus
WOODPECKER FAMILY

9″. Black above, white below; sides gray-barred. Head black, with white and black "mustache" lines; male has yellow crown patch. In flight, all black above, ex. for white outer tail feathers. **VOICE** Soft *pick;* long drum. **HABITAT** Coniferous forests, esp. after fires. **RANGE** Resident in Cascades, e highlands. **Three-toed Woodpecker** *(P. tridactylus)* has white line behind eye; back white-barred; similar range, but slightly higher in mtns.

NORTHERN FLICKER
Colaptes auratus
WOODPECKER FAMILY

12″. Highly patterned. Red-shafted race: male back brown with blackish bars; belly pale buff with heavy black spots; tail black, wedge-shaped; crown and hindneck brown; cheeks and throat gray, with thick red "mustache"; wide black crescent on chest. Female similar, but lacks red "mustache." Bill long; legs short. Flight reveals white rump, reddish pink underwing and undertail. Often feeds on ground. **VOICE** Rapid series of *wic* and *woika* (or *flicker*) notes; loud *klee-err;* soft drum. **HABITAT** Woodlands, farms, towns. **RANGE** Resident in NW.

PILEATED WOODPECKER
Dryocopus pileatus
WOODPECKER FAMILY

16″. Black; crest pointed, red; white and black stripes on face and down sides of neck. Male forehead and "mustache" red; female forehead and "mustache" black. Neck thin; bill heavy, silver. Flight reveals white underwing linings contrasting with black flight feathers. **VOICE** Rapid irreg. series of *cuk* and *wucka* notes. **HABITAT** Coniferous forests. **RANGE** Resident in Cascades and west, e mtns.

Songbirds (Passerines)

The birds described from here to the end of the birds section belong to a single order called Passeriformes. Known as passerines or, more commonly, perching birds or songbirds, they are the most recently evolved of the 25 bird orders. Members of this order comprise more than half the world's birds. Their sizes range from 3½-inch kinglets to 24-inch ravens, but they are generally small land birds with pleasing songs; among the finest songsters are the wrens and thrushes. Songbirds use call notes year-round, while most give their songs only during the breeding season (spring and early summer). In some species, the male has a particularly colorful summer breeding plumage that changes in winter to drabber, female-like coloration. In the spring, migrant males generally arrive in the Northwest seven to ten days before the females and stake out breeding territories, which they defend against neighboring males. After a male shows a female around his territory, she may be satisfied (especially if the vegetation and insect life are plentiful) and stay with him, or search for another singing male whose territory is more to her liking. Most songbirds build open-topped, rounded nests of grasses, sticks, vegetable fibers, and rootlets in a tree fork, in a shrub, or tucked under tall grass. Some eat insects year-round, while others focus on seeds, grains, or fruit; all feed insects to their hatchlings. In the fall, the sexes may migrate south together, the adults often several weeks or more before the young born that year.

OLIVE-SIDED FLYCATCHER
Contopus borealis
TYRANT FLYCATCHER FAMILY

7½". Upperparts and crown dark olive-brown; sides olive-brown, form a vest; throat and mid-belly stripe white. Bill thick; tail medium length. Perches on highest twigs of trees. **VOICE** Song: whistled *hic . . . three-beers;* Call: rapid *pip-pip-pip.* **HABITAT** Summer: coniferous forests. Migration: also broadleaf woodlands, parks. **RANGE** May–Sept.: all NW.

WESTERN WOOD-PEWEE
Contopus sordidulus
TYRANT FLYCATCHER FAMILY

6½". Adult pale grayish brown above; 1 or 2 pale whitish wing bars; dingy whitish below; sides grayish; bill often orangy beneath. Head peaked at rear; bill thin; tail fairly long. Imm. wing bars buffy; bill black. **VOICE** Song: harsh nasal *peee-err.* **HABITAT** Broadleaf, pine, and riparian woodlands. **RANGE** May–Sept.: all NW.

HAMMOND'S FLYCATCHER
Empidonax hammondii
TYRANT FLYCATCHER FAMILY

5½". Pale olive-brown above; gray below, with trace of yellow on belly; 2 whitish wing bars; bold white eye ring; throat gray. Bill tiny, dark. **VOICE** Song: *hiccup-syrup-seek.* Call: high *peak.* **HABITAT** Summer: wet coniferous and mixed forests. Migration: all forests, thickets. **RANGE** Apr.–Sept.: all NW.

PACIFIC-SLOPE FLYCATCHER
"Western Flycatcher"
Empidonax difficilis
TYRANT FLYCATCHER FAMILY

5½". Olive above; chest greenish; belly yellow, olive on sides; 2 whitish wing bars; white eye ring pointed at rear; throat yellow. Bill tiny, dark. **VOICE** Song: high *seet-sick-seet.* Male call: rising *sweeet.* **HABITAT** Wet coniferous forests. **RANGE** Apr.–Sept.: west of Cascades, east in WA.

SAY'S PHOEBE
Sayornis saya
TYRANT FLYCATCHER FAMILY

7½". Crown and upperparts dull brown; throat and chest gray; belly and vent dull cinnamon; 2 faint wing bars; tail fairly long, black, wagged often. Bill thin, black. Hovers above grass and flies sorties from perch. **VOICE** Song: *pit-cedar*. Call: falling *peeurr*. **HABITAT** Shrubby grasslands, cliffs, farms. **RANGE** Mar.–Sept.: east of Cascades, sw OR.

ASH-THROATED FLYCATCHER
Myiarchus cinerascens
TYRANT FLYCATCHER FAMILY

8". Crown, cheeks, and upperparts dull brown; throat and chest pale gray; belly pale yellow; 1 whitish wing bar; primaries and longish tail rusty. Head fluffy to rear; bill thin, black. **VOICE** Soft *pur-weer* and *pwit;* harsher *ka-brick*. **HABITAT** Open woodlands, brush. **RANGE** Apr.–Sept.: east of Cascades in sc WA, e OR; sw OR.

WESTERN KINGBIRD
Tyrannus verticalis
TYRANT FLYCATCHER FAMILY

9". Crown and back gray; thin dark line through eye; throat, chest pale gray; belly yellow; tail black, with white outer feathers. Bill short, wide. Aggressive toward larger birds near nest. Sits on wires, other exposed perches. **VOICE** Shrill *kit* and *kit-kit-kiddledit*. **HABITAT** Riverine woodlands, grasslands, farms. **RANGE** Apr.–Sept.: valleys of w OR, east of Cascades.

HORNED LARK
Eremophila alpestris
LARK FAMILY

7½". Brown above, with light streaks; belly white; black crown stripe ends in 2 tiny "horns"; black, yellow, and white patches on head and foreneck. Bill slender, pointed, black. Flight reveals black tail, white outer tail feathers. **VOICE** Song: high tinkling. Call: *tsee-titi*. **HABITAT** Grasslands, farms, deserts; also alpine meadows in summer, coastal beaches in winter. **RANGE** Resident in NW.

TREE SWALLOW
Tachycineta bicolor
SWALLOW FAMILY

6". Adult dark iridescent green-blue above, entirely snowy white below. 1st year female and imm. brown above. Tail notched. Slow flier; short flapping circles and a climb. **VOICE** Song: *weet-trit-weet*. Call: *cheat cheat*. **HABITAT** Wetlands, towns. **RANGE** Mar.–Sept.: all NW. **Purple Martin** *(Progne subis)* larger (8"); male all purple, tail forked; female breast dusky; summers west of Cascades (local).

VIOLET-GREEN SWALLOW
Tachycineta thalassina
SWALLOW FAMILY

5″. Crown, back, and forewing green; back of neck, flight feathers, midrump stripe, and tail dark violet; white underparts continue up behind eye; sides of rump white. Tail short, notched. Flight very fluttery. **VOICE** Thin *chip;* rapid *chit-chit-chit-weet-weet.* **HABITAT** Forest edges, towns. **RANGE** Mar.–Sept.: all NW.

NORTHERN ROUGH-WINGED SWALLOW
Stelgidopteryx serripennis
SWALLOW FAMILY

5½″. Dull brown above; throat and chest pale brown; breast and vent dull white. Tail notched. Tree swallow imm. brown above, all snowy white below. Flies with slow deep wingbeats. Often in solitary pairs. **VOICE** Raspy *brit.* **HABITAT** Wetlands with earth banks. **RANGE** Apr.–Aug.: all NW.

BANK SWALLOW
Riparia riparia
SWALLOW FAMILY

5″. Dull brown above; white below, crossed by distinct brown neck band. Northern Rough-winged Swallow has pale brown throat; lacks neck band. Tree Swallow imm. brown above, all snowy white below. Flies with rapid wingbeats. Often in flocks, very social. **VOICE** Low flat *chert chert;* buzzy chatter. **HABITAT** Rivers and lakes with sandbanks. **RANGE** May–Sept.: east of Cascades. May, Aug.–Sept.: all NW.

CLIFF SWALLOW
Hirundo pyrrhonota
SWALLOW FAMILY

6″. Adult crown, back, and wings dark blue; rump buffy; throat dark chestnut; breast grayish white; forehead cream; hindneck gray; tail black, short, square. Glides in circles high in air. Nests in colonies. **VOICE** Song: harsh creaking. Call: grating *syrup.* **HABITAT** Farms, waterways with cliffs. **RANGE** Apr.–Sept.: all NW.

BARN SWALLOW
Hirundo rustica
SWALLOW FAMILY

7″. Adult glossy blue above; forehead chestnut; throat dark orange, with thin blue necklace; rest of underparts buffy orange; outer tail streamers very long. Imm. pale buff below, with dark necklace. Fast flier. **VOICE** Song: long twittering. Calls: soft *vit vit* and *zee-zay*. **HABITAT** Fields, farms, waterways, towns. **RANGE** Apr.–Sept.: all NW.

GRAY JAY
Perisoreus canadensis
CROW AND JAY FAMILY

12″. Northwest race: adult back, wings, and tail dull, dark gray; forehead, cheeks, and underparts white; rear crown black. Bill black; tail long, rounded. Juv. all slaty with white mustache. Bold food robber at human campsites. **VOICE** Low *chuck*. **HABITAT** Wet coniferous forests mostly in mtns. **RANGE** Resident in NW.

STELLER'S JAY
Cyanocitta stelleri
CROW AND JAY FAMILY

12″. All dark; bill heavy. Long shaggy crest black; thin blue stripes on forehead; head, back, and upper breast blackish; belly and rump plain blue; wings and tail blue with fine black barring. Brash and nearly omnivorous; visits campsites for scraps. **VOICE** Loud *shaq-shaq-shaq*. **HABITAT** Coniferous forests, parks. **RANGE** Resident in Cascades and west, forested mtns. east of Cascades.

WESTERN SCRUB JAY
Aphelocoma californica
CROW AND JAY FAMILY

13″. Back gray-brown; belly gray; crown, hindneck, partial necklace, wings, rump, and tail blue; throat white with faint blue streaks. No crest; bill heavy; tail long, rounded. Shy at nest, but bold rest of year at picnic sites and parks. Caches acorns in ground for winter. **VOICE** Loud series of *kwesh* or *check* notes. **HABITAT** Oak woodlands, towns. **RANGE** Resident in sw WA along Columbia R., Willamette Valley, sc OR.

CLARK'S NUTCRACKER
Nucifraga columbiana
CROW AND JAY FAMILY

13". Head, back, and underparts plain silvery gray; vent white; wings black, trailing edge of secondaries white; tail fairly short, black in center, with white outer tail feathers. Bill long, pointed, black. Walks like crow on ground (jays hop). Caches pine seeds. **VOICE** Guttural *kraaah.* **HABITAT** Open coniferous forests in mtns. **RANGE** Resident in Cascades, wooded mtns. east of Cascades.

BLACK-BILLED MAGPIE
Pica pica
CROW AND JAY FAMILY

20". Head, chest, back, rump, and vent black; belly and long shoulder patch white; wings and tail iridescent purple and green. Bill stout, black; tail very long, with wedge-shaped tip. Flight reveals mainly white primaries. Feeds on insects, fruit, baby birds, roadkills. Mobs hawks, larger birds. Uses communal roosts. **VOICE** Rapid series of *jack* notes; rising *maayg?* **HABITAT** Riverine woodlands, sagebrush deserts, farms. **RANGE** Resident east of Cascades.

AMERICAN CROW
Corvus brachyrhynchos
CROW AND JAY FAMILY

18". All glossy black; bill heavy, black. Flight reveals rounded wings, "fingered" wingtips, squarish tail with rounded corners. Bold, noisy, conspicuous. Huge night roosts in winter outside breeding season. Smaller (16") birds on w WA beaches. **VOICE** Loud falling *caaw* or *klaah* (west of Cascades). **HABITAT** Shores, towns, farms, woodlands fields. **RANGE** Resident in NW.

COMMON RAVEN
Corvus corax
CROW AND JAY FAMILY

24". All glossy black; bill black, very heavy; throat has long shaggy feathers. Flight reveals pointed wings, "fingered" wingtips; long, wedge-shaped tail. Soars frequently. Shy, but conspicuous. **VOICE** Very low *croonk.* **HABITAT** Mtns., forests, fields, farms, deserts. **RANGE** Resident in NW.

BLACK-CAPPED CHICKADEE
Parus atricapillus
CHICKADEE FAMILY

5½". Back, wings, and long narrow tail gray; white below, with light buffy sides; wings edged white; cap and throat black; face white. Friendly, inquisitive; often in family groups. Acrobatic when feeding. **VOICE** Song: clear *fee-bee*. Call: *chick-a-dee-dee-dee-dee*. **HABITAT** Broadleaf and riverine woodlands, thickets, towns. **RANGE** Resident in NW.

MOUNTAIN CHICKADEE
Parus gambeli
CHICKADEE FAMILY

5½". Back, wings, belly, and tail gray; crown and throat black; cheek and sides of neck white; white line over eye. Tail long, narrow. Often in flocks; acrobatic when feeding. **VOICE** Song: high whistled *fee-bee-bee*. Call: raspy *chick-a dee-dee-dee*. **HABITAT** Coniferous forests. **RANGE** Resident in Cascades and east. **Plain Titmouse** (*P. inornatus*) of sw OR all gray, with crest.

Attracting Birds to Your Yard

Many people enjoy attracting birds into their yards, and supplemental feeding helps birds in winter, when naturally occurring seeds are covered by snow. Once started, winter feeding should be continued into spring. Throughout the birds section, species that will come into a yard to feed are indicated by the icon 🐦.

Birdfeeders come in many designs. Hanging, clear seed feeders with short perch sticks are popular with goldfinches, siskins, and other finches. Window boxes and platforms on a pole are best for such medium-size birds as Evening Grosbeaks and Steller's Jays, while Mourning Doves, Dark-eyed Juncos, and many sparrows prefer to feed on the ground. Mounting a birdfeeder inevitably means an ongoing struggle with squirrels, who are endlessly resourceful at defeating devices intended to keep them out of the feeders.

Grains and seeds are the best all-purpose fare for feeders. Many species like sunflower seeds, but your local birds may have particular preferences. Thistle seed is popular with goldfinches, white millet seed is a good choice for small species, and cracked corn is appreciated by large, ground-feeding birds. Many seed mixes are available at supermarkets and garden supply stores.

Birds also like nuts and fruit. Suet, in a mesh holder hung from a branch or mounted on a tree trunk, attracts birds such as nuthatches and woodpeckers that feed on insects in tree bark and bushes; it should be discontinued in summer, when it spoils quickly

CHESTNUT-BACKED CHICKADEE
Parus rufescens
CHICKADEE FAMILY

5". Back, rump, and sides chestnut; rest of underparts white; crown and throat dark brown; cheeks and sides of neck white; wings and tail gray. Tail long, narrow. Often in flocks; feeds high in trees. **VOICE** Call: high *zitta-zitta-zee.* **HABITAT** Wet coniferous forests, parks, towns. **RANGE** Resident in Cascades and west, mtns. of e WA, ne OR.

BUSHTIT
Psaltriparus minimus
BUSHTIT FAMILY

4". Coastal birds brownish gray, interior birds lead gray. Head small; bill tiny; tail long, narrow. Eyes dark in male, yellow in female. Acrobatic feeder; gathers in flocks of up to 30 birds when not nesting. **VOICE** Song: high trill. Call: frequently given, weak *pit.* **HABITAT** Broadleaf woodlands, thickets, parks. **RANGE** Resident west of Cascades, east of Cascades in sc WA, ec OR, ex. ne.

and mats feathers. Hummingbirds will come to specially designed red plastic dispensers of sugar water.

Water is important, especially during periods when natural water sources dry up or freeze over. Many species are attracted to a bird bath, which should be regularly scrubbed with a brush to rid it of algae and prevent diseases from spreading.

You might want to make or purchase a nestbox to attract breeding birds. The most popular—inviting to woodpeckers, chickadees, nuthatches, wrens, bluebirds, and even some owls—is an enclosed box with a square floor area 4 to 7 inches wide and deep, and about twice as high as it is wide (8 to 12 inches). Specifications for such a box vary depending on the species and include floor area, the size of the entrance hole, the height from the base of the box to the hole, and proper siting of the box. Other birds will nest in open-fronted shelves or martin houses. Information on building and siting nestboxes and feeders is available at your local Audubon Society or nature center. In the birds section, the icon ⬛ denotes species that have used nestboxes in the right habitat.

Some people argue against feeding birds at any time of year because it can help spread diseases among birds that otherwise would not come into contact with each other. Also, the abundance of plant and animal food in the warmer months makes it unnecessary to feed birds in the Northwest from May to October.

RED-BREASTED NUTHATCH
Sitta canadensis
NUTHATCH FAMILY

4½". Male back steel blue; underparts rufous; cap black; black line through eye and white line over it. Female similar, but crown gray; buffy below. Tail short. **VOICE** High nasal *enk* series. **HABITAT** Summer: coniferous forests. Winter: also broadleaf woodlands. **RANGE** Resident in Cascades and west, e mtns. Aug.–Apr.: all NW.

WHITE-BREASTED NUTHATCH
Sitta carolinensis
NUTHATCH FAMILY

6". Male back gray-blue; wings edged white; face and underparts white; narrow black crown; vent and sides washed rusty. Female crown gray. Creeps headfirst in all directions on tree trunks. **VOICE** Song: rapid *wer* notes. Call: loud *yank.* **HABITAT** Dry woodlands. **RANGE** Resident in w OR, sw WA, Cascades and east, ex. se OR.

PYGMY NUTHATCH
Sitta pygmaea
NUTHATCH FAMILY

4". Blue-gray above, pale buffy below; crown brown; dark brown line through eye; whitish spot at back of nape; throat white. Tail short. Climbs over branches and needles, often upside down. Often in small flocks. **VOICE** High series of *peep* notes. **HABITAT** Ponderosa Pine forests. **RANGE** Resident on e slope of Cascades, forested mtns. of east.

BROWN CREEPER
Certhia americana
CREEPER FAMILY

5½". Brown with buff stripes above; white below; wing stripe buffy; rump rufous; eye line white; tail tips spiny. Looks like a wren; sings like a warbler; climbs trees like a woodpecker: starts at bottom of trunk, probes bark with slender bill. **VOICE** Song: high *see see see tu wee.* Call: 1–2 high *tsee* notes. **HABITAT** Summer: coniferous forests. Winter: all wooded areas. **RANGE** Resident in most of NW.

ROCK WREN
Salpinctes obsoletus
WREN FAMILY

6″. Gray-brown above, speckled with buff and white; whitish below; pale buffy on sides; buffy eyebrow. Bill slender; tail fairly long. Often bobs body. **VOICE** Song: loud repeated *cha-wee.* Call: sharp *tee-keer.* **HABITAT** Canyons, rocky areas in deserts. **RANGE** Apr.–Oct.: mainly east of Cascades. **Canyon Wren** *(Catherpes mexicanus)* body and tail rufous; throat clear white; song: falling series of *tew* notes; resident east of Cascades.

BEWICK'S WREN
Thryomanes bewickii
WREN FAMILY

5½″. Crown and upperparts brown; pale gray below; white eyebrow; faintly striped cheeks; throat white; black dots on white outer tail feathers. Bill slender; tail fairly long, rounded. Tail often raised or flicked sideways. **VOICE** Song: melodious, complex. **HABITAT** Broadleaf and riverine woodlands, thickets, towns. **RANGE** Resident west of Cascades; east of Cascades (local).

HOUSE WREN
Troglodytes aedon
WREN FAMILY

5″. Head and back plain dull brown; wings and tail lightly dotted or barred black; light brown below; sides finely barred. Tail cocked. Aggressive to other nearby hole-nesters; destroys their eggs. **VOICE** Song: long, pleasing, descending gurgle. Call: *chuurr.* **HABITAT** Riverine and oak woodlands. **RANGE** May–Sept.: all NW.

WINTER WREN
Troglodytes troglodytes
WREN FAMILY
4″. Dark brown above and below; sides, wings, and tail finely black-barred; indistinct eyebrow and throat buffy. Often cocks very short tail over back. N. Amer.'s smallest wren. **VOICE** Song: beautiful long series of warbles and trills. Call: hard *kip kip.* **HABITAT** Coniferous forest ravines, brush piles. **RANGE** Resident in Cascades and west, forested e mtns.

MARSH WREN
Cistothorus palustris
WREN FAMILY
5″. Back brown, with narrow white stripes; white below; wings, rump, and tail chestnut; sides buffy; white eyebrow under dark brownish crown. Tail often cocked. **VOICE** Song: gurgling rattle. Call: loud *check.* **HABITAT** Cattail and bulrush marshes. **RANGE** Resident in NW.

AMERICAN DIPPER
Cinclus mexicanus
DIPPER FAMILY
8″. Adult uniformly gray. Bill black, narrow; eyelid white; legs pale pink; tail short, often cocked like a wren's. Juv. slaty above, pale gray below; bill pinkish. Bobs on rocks in streams; flies low over water. Walks underwater to feed on large insect larvae; scales cover nostrils; eyelids transpar-

ent; oil glands waterproof dense plumage. **VOICE** Song: loud, musical, varied; repeats phrases. Call: piercing *zeet.* **HABITAT** Rocky mtn. streams. **RANGE** Resident in Cascades and west, mtns. east of Cascades.

GOLDEN-CROWNED KINGLET
Regulus satrapa
OLD WORLD WARBLER SUBFAMILY
3½″. Back olive; dingy olive below; wings have yellowish edging and wing bars; crown black, with center orange and yellow (male) or yellow (female); eyebrow white; black line through eye. Tail short, notched. **VOICE** Call: 3 high *tsee* notes. Song: same, then chatter. **HABITAT** Wet coniferous forests; in winter, all woodlands, parks. **RANGE** Resident in Cascades and west, mtns. east of Cascades. Oct.–Apr.: also lowlands east of Cascades.

RUBY-CROWNED KINGLET
Regulus calendula
OLD WORLD WARBLER SUBFAMILY

4". Drab olive all over, but paler below; 2 white wing bars; large white eye ring. Tail has short notch. Male raises red midcrown patch when displaying; often flicks wings. **VOICE** Song: high warbles ending with 3 *look-at-me*'s. Call: scolding *je-dit*. **HABITAT** Dry coniferous forests; in winter, all woodlands, parks. **RANGE** May–Sept.: Cascades, mtns. to east. Sept.–May: west of Cascades.

WESTERN BLUEBIRD
Sialia mexicana
THRUSH SUBFAMILY

7". Male back rusty; head, throat, wings, rump, and tail intense blue; chest and sides rusty orange; belly grayish white. Female head and back gray; wings and tail pale blue; orange wash on chest; white eye ring. Bill short, thin. Hovers over grassy areas; drops to ground from low perches. **VOICE** Song (varied): musical *cheer cheer-lee churr.* Call: soft *pheew.* **HABITAT** Open pines, oak woodlands, farms. **RANGE** Resident west (local) and east of Cascades. Apr.–Oct.: all NW.

MOUNTAIN BLUEBIRD
Sialia currucoides
THRUSH SUBFAMILY

7". Male all blue, darkest on wings, slightly paler below. Female head, back, and chest gray; wings and tail pale blue; narrow white eye ring. Wings and tail longer than Western Bluebird's; bill short, thin. Hovers over grassy areas; drops to ground from low perches; often in large flocks when not nesting. **VOICE** Song: short weak warbling. Call: low *churr.* **HABITAT** Open pines, sagebrush deserts, alpine meadows, farms. **RANGE** Apr.–Oct.: Cascades and east. Oct.–Apr.: e OR.

TOWNSEND'S SOLITAIRE
Myadestes townsendi
THRUSH SUBFAMILY

9". Head and body uniformly gray or brownish gray; white eye ring; wings dusky with small buffy patches; tail black with white outer tail feathers. Flight reveals buffy stripe at base of flight feathers. Bill short; tail fairly long. Feeds on berries, esp. juniper, in cool months, flying insects in summer. **VOICE** Song: rising and falling fluty whistles. Call: high *eeek.* **HABITAT** Summer: coniferous and mixed forests. Winter: open woodlands, incl. pinyon-juniper. **RANGE** Apr.–Oct.: all higher mtns. Oct.–Apr.: lower elevs. in all NW.

SWAINSON'S THRUSH
Catharus ustulatus
THRUSH SUBFAMILY

7″. Back, head, wings, and tail brown; dark brown spots on buffy throat and chest; belly white; lores and wide eye ring buffy. **VOICE** Song: beautiful, breezy, up-slurred whistles. Calls: *whit* and *heep*. **HABITAT** Wet coniferous and broadleaf forests, riverine thickets. **RANGE** May–Sept.: all NW. **Veery** (*C. fuscescens*) summers in riverine woodlands east of Cascades; reddish brown above; fine spots on grayish upper chest.

HERMIT THRUSH
Catharus guttatus
THRUSH SUBFAMILY

7″. Head, back, and wings brown; sides grayish; dark brown spots on throat and upper chest; belly whitish; rump and tail rufous brown; very thin, pale eye ring. **VOICE** Song: clear, flute-like; similar phrases repeated at different pitches. Call: low *chuck*. **HABITAT** Summer: wet coniferous forests. Winter: forest edges, parks. **RANGE** May–Sept.: Cascades, forested e mtns. Apr.–May, Sept.–Oct.: all NW. Sept.–May: west of Cascades.

AMERICAN ROBIN
Turdus migratorius
THRUSH SUBFAMILY

10″. Male breast and sides rufous-orange; back and wings gray-brown; head blackish, with broken white eye ring; throat striped; bill yellow; tail black, with tiny white corners; vent white. Female head and back duller brown. Tail fairly long. In spring and summer, an earthworm specialist; in fall and winter, roams in berry-searching flocks, forms large communal roosts. **VOICE** Song: prolonged, rising and falling *cheery-up cheery-me*. Calls: *tut tut tut* and *tseep*. **HABITAT** Woodlands, shrubs, lawns. **RANGE** Resident in NW.

VARIED THRUSH
Ixoreus naevius
THRUSH SUBFAMILY

9″. Male back, crown, rump, and tail blue-gray; cheeks and wide breast band black; line behind eye, throat, underparts, 2 wing bars, and patches on wing orange. Female similar, but slaty and black areas replaced by brown; breast band thin. Feeds mainly on ground; shier than American Robin. **VOICE** Song: long quavering trills at varied pitches. Call: soft *took*. **HABITAT** Wet coniferous forests, parks. **RANGE** Resident in NW.

WRENTIT
Chamaea fasciata
BABBLER SUBFAMILY

6″. Dark brown above; buffy below, with faint brown stripes. Head large; bill thin, short; eyes yellow; tail long, thin, rounded at tip. Skulks around in bushes with tail cocked; sings all year. **VOICE** Song: rising, accelerating *pee-pee-pee-pe-pe-pe-pe-pipipipi.* Call: dry *churr.* **HABITAT** Chaparral, dense shrubs. **RANGE** Resident in coastal and sw OR.

GRAY CATBIRD
Dumetella carolinensis
MOCKINGBIRD FAMILY

9″. Entirely slaty gray, ex. for black crown, rusty vent, and long, rounded, black tail. A skulker; often cocks or swings tail. **VOICE** Song: mimics other birds; doesn't repeat songs. Calls: cat-like *meeah;* sharp *check.* **HABITAT** Thickets in broadleaf and riverine woodlands. **RANGE** May–Sept.: east of Cascades in e WA, ne OR.

SAGE THRASHER
Oreoscoptes montanus
MOCKINGBIRD FAMILY

8″. Dull brownish gray above; whitish below, with dark brownish stripes; pale brownish-gray wash on chest and sides; white corners on tail. Bill thin, slightly curved; eyes yellow; tail fairly long. Runs on ground for insects and spiders in summer; feeds in fruiting bushes in winter. **VOICE** Song: clear, sweet, continuous warbling. Call: harsh *chuck.* **HABITAT** Sagebrush deserts. **RANGE** Apr.–Aug.: east of Cascades.

AMERICAN PIPIT
Anthus rubescens
WAGTAIL AND PIPIT FAMILY

6". Summer: gray-brown above, with faint streaking on back; buffy below; weak brown streaks on chest. Winter: dark brown above; whitish below, with brown streaks. Bill thin; white outer tail feathers. **VOICE** Flight song: series of *chwee* notes. Call: *pi-pit.* **HABITAT** Summer: alpine meadows. Winter: plains, fields, shorelines. **RANGE** May–Aug.: Cascades, highest e mtns. Apr.–May, Sept.–Nov.: all NW. Sept.–Apr.: west of Cascades.

BOHEMIAN WAXWING
Bombycilla garrulus
WAXWING FAMILY

7". Adult back, rump, and underparts gray; head brown; throat and line through eye black; white and yellow lines on black primaries; red-tipped secondaries. Bill thin; pointed crest; tail slaty with yellow tip; vent rusty. **VOICE** High buzzy *zeeee.* **HABITAT** Summer: coniferous forests. Winter: fruiting trees in all habitats. **RANGE** Apr.–Oct.: rare in n (WA) Cascades and ne WA. Oct–Mar.: all NW (erratic).

CEDAR WAXWING
Bombycilla cedrorum
WAXWING FAMILY

7". Adult back and laid-back crest brown; soft brown chest grades to yellow belly; wings gray, with waxy red tips to secondaries; black eyemask, edged in white. Yellow band at tip of gray tail. Imm. striped brown, with white eye line. Often seen in flocks. **VOICE** Call: high thin *seee.* **HABITAT** Forests, mainly broadleaf; parks. **RANGE** Resident in NW (irreg. movements).

NORTHERN SHRIKE
Lanius excubitor
SHRIKE FAMILY

10". Adult back and crown gray; white below, with fine gray bars; wings black with large white spot; black eyemask; long, rounded, white-edged black tail. Imm. barred brown below; brown eyemask. Head large; bill heavy, hooked. Preys on small birds and rodents; impales surplus on thorns. **VOICE** Call: loud *chek-chek.* **HABITAT** Trees and shrubs in open country. **RANGE** Oct.–Mar.: all NW.

summer adult (left), winter adult (right)

EUROPEAN STARLING
Sturnus vulgaris
STARLING FAMILY

8". Summer adult: glossy green-purple; bill yellow. Winter adult: blackish, heavily speckled with white; bill dark. Wings short, pointed, rusty-edged; bill sturdy, pointed; legs dull red; tail short, square. Introduced from Europe; detrimental to native birds; boldly takes over most nest holes and birdhouses, occupied or not; depletes wild fruit stock, feeder suet. **VOICE** Song: mix of whistles, squeals, and chuckles; mimics other birds. Calls: rising, then falling, *hoooeee;* harsh *jeer.* **HABITAT** Towns, farms, fields. **RANGE** Resident in NW.

SOLITARY VIREO
"Cassin's Vireo"
Vireo solitarius (cassini)
VIREO FAMILY

5½". Vireos have thicker hooked bills and move more slowly than warblers (see below). This species: stocky; head gray; upperparts dull greenish olive; 2 white wing bars; sides pale olive; spectacles, throat, and midbelly white. **VOICE** Song: low burry phrases with long pauses. Call: husky *churr.* **HABITAT** Coniferous and broadleaf forests. **RANGE** Apr.–Sept.: all NW.

HUTTON'S VIREO
Vireo huttoni
VIREO FAMILY

4½". Crown and upperparts dark olive-gray; pale, dingy olive-gray below; 2 white wing bars; white eye ring incomplete at top. Head large. Similar Ruby-crowned Kinglet has thinner bill, flicks wings constantly. **VOICE** Song: oft-repeated *zu-weep.* Call: hoarse *day-dee-dee.* **HABITAT** Wet coniferous and broadleaf forests. **RANGE** Resident west of Cascades.

WARBLING VIREO
Vireo gilvus
VIREO FAMILY

5″. Drab-looking. Pale gray above, with slight olive cast; dusky white below; no wing bars; eyebrow white, not outlined. Imm. sides washed yellow-green. **VOICE** Song: melodious warbling; like that of Purple Finch, but burry. Call: wheezy *twee*. **HABITAT** Broadleaf and riverine forests. **RANGE** May–Sept.: all NW.

RED-EYED VIREO
Vireo olivaceus
VIREO FAMILY

6″. Olive green above; white below, yellow wash on belly in fall; no wing bars; crown gray, bordered by black; black line through eye; white eyebrow; eyes red. **VOICE** Song: monotonous *cher-eep cher-oop*, repeated up to 40 times a minute, all day long. Call: scolding *meew*. **HABITAT** Broadleaf and riparian woodlands. **RANGE** May–Aug.: mainly east of Cascades.

Wood Warblers

As there is a bird subfamily called Old World warblers, those in the New World are often called wood warblers or just warblers; they are the subfamily Parulinae, part of the warbler, grosbeak, and sparrow (Emberizidae) family. Many adult males have the same plumage year-round, but some have breeding (summer) and nonbreeding (winter) plumages. Females, fall males, and immature birds often have a trace of the summer male pattern. Each species has a distinct song, while the warbler call tends to be a simple *chip*. During the summer, these birds breed in a variety of woodland and scrub habitats. Most nests are cups on small forks of branches or hidden under bushes. Warblers glean insects from leaves with their thin, unhooked bills. In early autumn, most return to more southerly regions.

ORANGE-CROWNED WARBLER
Vermivora celata
WOOD WARBLER SUBFAMILY

5″. Very plain. Adult olive green above; yellow below; orange crown patch rarely seen. Usu. forages low. **VOICE** Song: high trill, drops and tapers at end. Call: sharp *chit*. **HABITAT** Broadleaf forests, thickets, brushy fields, parks. **RANGE** Apr.–Oct.: all NW. Oct.–Apr.: coastal NW (uncommon).

NASHVILLE WARBLER
Vermivora ruficapilla
WOOD WARBLER SUBFAMILY

4¾". Back, wings, and tail olive green; no wing bars; throat and underparts clear, unstriped yellow; gray head with white eye ring. **VOICE** Song: 2-part *see-it see-it see-it tititi-titi*. **HABITAT** Open broadleaf and pine woodlands. **RANGE** May–Sept.: Cascades, sw and ne OR, ne WA. May, Aug.–Sept.: all NW.

YELLOW WARBLER
Dendroica petechia
WOOD WARBLER SUBFAMILY

5". Male olive-yellow above; head, underparts, and wing and tail edging bright yellow; chestnut stripes on chest and sides. Female lacks stripes. **VOICE** Song: cheerful rapid *sweet sweet sweet I'm so sweet*. **HABITAT** Shrubby areas, woodlands near water. **RANGE** May–Sept.: all NW.

YELLOW-RUMPED WARBLER
Dendroica coronata
WOOD WARBLER SUBFAMILY

Audubon's race summer male (left), immature (right)

5½". Audubon's race: rump and throat yellow; dark cheek patch. Summer male: gray above, with black streaks; chest black; belly white; yellow tuft on sides; large white wing patch; head gray with yellow crown patch, broken white eye ring. Summer female: gray-brown above; whitish below, streaked brown. Winter adults: brown, heavily striped. Myrtle race: darker cheeks, white throat; winters in lowlands. Imm. (both races) duller, variable. **VOICE** Song: warbling *seet-seet-seet-seet-turrrr*. Call: soft *check*. **HABITAT** Summer: coniferous forests. Winter: woodlands, thickets. **RANGE** Mar.–Oct.: all NW.

BLACK-THROATED GRAY WARBLER
Dendroica nigrescens
WOOD WARBLER SUBFAMILY

5″. Male back and rump gray; white below, with black streaks; 2 white wing bars; head black with wide white "mustache" and line behind eye; yellow lore spot. Adult female similar, but has black necklace below white throat. **VOICE** Song: buzzy *weze-weze-weze-weze-weet*. Call: dull *tup*. **HABITAT** Mixed woodlands. **RANGE** Apr.–Sept.: west of Cascades; east of Cascades in sc WA, c OR.

TOWNSEND'S WARBLER
Dendroica townsendi
WOOD WARBLER SUBFAMILY

5″. Male greenish above, with black streaks; upper breast yellow with black streaks; belly white; 2 white wing bars; crown, throat, and ear patch black; yellow eyebrow and "mustache." Female throat yellow. **VOICE** Song: buzzy *zir-zir-zir-zir-see-see*. Call: soft *chip*. **HABITAT** Wet coniferous forests; parks in winter. **RANGE** May–Sept.: Cascades, high e mtns. Apr.–May, Sept.–Oct.: all NW. Oct.–Apr.: coast (uncommon).

HERMIT WARBLER
Dendroica occidentalis
WOOD WARBLER SUBFAMILY

5″. Male gray above, lightly streaked black; clear white below; 2 white wing bars; forehead and face yellow; rear crown and throat black. Female similar; little or no black on throat. Feeds high in trees. **VOICE** Song: 3 high and 2 low *sweety-sweety-sweety-chup-chup*. **HABITAT** Coniferous forests, esp. fir and spruce. **RANGE** May–Sept.: Cascades west from c WA south.

MACGILLIVRAY'S WARBLER
Oporornis tolmiei
WOOD WARBLER SUBFAMILY

5″. Male green above, clear yellow below; head and throat slaty gray, throat scaled black. Female similar; no black scales on throat. Incomplete white eye ring; legs pink. Hops in undergrowth. **VOICE** Song: loud *chitle-chitle-chitle-cheer-cheer*. Call: loud *check*. **HABITAT** Thickets in broadleaf and riverine woodlands. **RANGE** May–Sept.: all NW.

COMMON YELLOWTHROAT
Geothlypis trichas
WOOD WARBLER SUBFAMILY

female (left), male (right)

5″. Male upperparts and sides uniformly brownish olive; throat and chest yellow; midbelly white; black mask over forehead and cheeks; broad white line above mask. Female olive-brown above; pale eye ring; throat yellow. Feeds low; often raises tail at angle. **VOICE** Song: rollicking *witchity-witchity-witchity-witch.* Call: flat *chep.* **HABITAT** Wooded swamps, marshes, shrubs. **RANGE** Apr.–Sept.: all NW.

WILSON'S WARBLER
Wilsonia pusilla
WOOD WARBLER SUBFAMILY

4¾″. Male olive green above; underparts, forehead, and eyebrow yellow; round black cap. Imm. and many females have trace only of black cap. **VOICE** Song: rapid thin *chi chi chi chi jet jet.* **HABITAT** Thickets in coniferous forests. **RANGE** May–Sept.: all NW.

YELLOW-BREASTED CHAT
Icteria virens
WOOD WARBLER SUBFAMILY

7″. Olive green above; throat and breast yellow; belly and vent grayish white; "spectacles" white; lores black in male, gray in female. Sings in low fluttering flight, day or night. Tail long. **VOICE** Song: long series of scolds, whistles, and soft, crow-like *caw* notes. Call: loud *chack.* **HABITAT** Dense thickets, riverine scrub. **RANGE** May–Aug.: east of Cascades, valleys of w OR.

WESTERN TANAGER
Piranga ludoviciana
TANAGER SUBFAMILY

female (left), male (right)

7". Summer male back and tail black; collar, rump, and underparts yellow; wings black, with yellow shoulder, 1 white wing bar; head and throat red. Female and imm. back gray; head, rump, and underparts yellow; 2 whitish wing bars. Lives in treetops. **VOICE** Song: 3 slurred hoarse phrases. Call: *per-dick.* **HABITAT** Coniferous forest. **RANGE** May–Sept.: all NW, ex. se OR.

BLACK-HEADED GROSBEAK
Pheucticus melanocephalus
GROSBEAK SUBFAMILY

7½". Male back black; collar, chest, sides, and rump rusty orange; mid-belly striped rusty and white; white patches on wing; head black. Female striped brown above; 2 white wing bars; buffy orange below; cheeks and crown dark brown; eyebrow and midcrown stripe white or buffy. Bill thick, upper mandible dark, lower pale. **VOICE** Song: sweet fast warble. Call: high *eek.* **HABITAT** Broadleaf and riverine woodlands, thickets. **RANGE** May–Aug.: entire NW.

LAZULI BUNTING
Passerina amoena
GROSBEAK SUBFAMILY

5½". Male head and upperparts pale powdery blue; 2 white wing bars; chest pale orange; belly white. Female head and back brown; 2 buffy wing bars; buffy below; rump bluish. Forages in weeds. **VOICE** Song: series of rising and falling warbles. Call: short *pit.* **HABITAT** Riverine woodlands, thickets. **RANGE** May–Aug.: all NW, ex. nw WA.

GREEN-TAILED TOWHEE
Pipilo chlorurus
AMERICAN SPARROW SUBFAMILY

7". Adult back, wings, and tail olive green; face, neck, and sides gray; mid-belly white; crown rufous; chin and short "mustache" white. Scratches on ground under brush. **VOICE** Song: slurred *weet-weet-churrr*. Call: cat-like *meeow*. **HABITAT** Thickets, shrubby areas. **RANGE** May–Sept.: e OR; se WA (rare).

SPOTTED TOWHEE
"Rufous-sided Towhee"
Pipilo maculatus
AMERICAN SPARROW SUBFAMILY

8". Male head, chest, rump, and tail black; back and wings black with white spots; sides rufous; midbelly white. Female: brown replaces black of male. Eyes red; tail corners white. Scratches on ground under brush. **VOICE** Song: long buzzy *cheweee*. Call: cat-like *meee*. **HABITAT** Thickets, forest underbrush (west). **RANGE** Resident west of Cascades. Apr.– Sept.: east of Cascades (few in winter).

CHIPPING SPARROW
Spizella passerina
AMERICAN SPARROW SUBFAMILY

5½". Summer: brown above, with black streaks; clear pale gray below; white wing bars; rufous cap; white eyebrow; black eye line; narrow notched tail. **VOICE** Song: long, run-together series of about 20 dry *chip* notes. **HABITAT** Dry open coniferous and broadleaf woodlands. **RANGE** Apr.–Sept.: all NW, ex. Puget Sound.

BREWER'S SPARROW
Spizella breweri
AMERICAN SPARROW SUBFAMILY

5½". Back and crown buffy brown, finely streaked with black; faint buffy wing bars; clear grayish below; indistinct brown cheek patch and "mustache." Tail notched. **VOICE** Song: complex series of musical trills lasting up to 10 seconds. Call: soft *seep*, given in flight. **HABITAT** Sagebrush deserts. **RANGE** May–Sept.: east of Cascades.

VESPER SPARROW
Pooecetes gramineus
AMERICAN SPARROW SUBFAMILY

6″. Pale brown with fine black stripes above and below; small rusty shoulder patch; 2 buffy wing bars; white eye ring; bill and legs pink. Tail notched at tip, blackish, with white outer feathers. Feeds on ground. **VOICE** Song: melodious *slurr-slurr-slee-slee-teuw-teuw-teuw.* **HABITAT** Grasslands, sagebrush deserts. **RANGE** Apr.–Sept.: all NW.

LARK SPARROW
Chondestes grammacus
AMERICAN SPARROW SUBFAMILY

6″. Brown above, with black streaks and buffy wing bars; white below, with black spot on chest. Bold head pattern, with black-edged chestnut cheek and crown patches; mid-crown, eyebrow, and throat white; black "mustache." Tail rounded, white with black wedge in middle. **VOICE** Song: complicated broken trills, buzzes, and clear notes. Call: sharp *tsip.* **HABITAT** Sagebrush deserts, open pine woodlands. **RANGE** Apr.–Oct.: east of Cascades, sw OR.

SAGE SPARROW
Ampispiza belli
AMERICAN SPARROW SUBFAMILY

6″. Back pale sandy brown with few streaks; whitish below, with black breast spot; sides finely streaked; head gray; throat, short eyebrow, and eye ring white; thin gray "mustache." Tail long, narrow, notched. **VOICE** Song: musical *sit-sit-soo-see-say-soo-see.* Call: soft tinkle. **HABITAT** Sagebrush deserts. **RANGE** Apr.–Aug.: east of Cascades from c WA south.

SAVANNAH SPARROW
Passerculus sandwichensis
AMERICAN SPARROW SUBFAMILY

5½″. Brown and white striped above and below; front of and often entire eyebrow yellow; bill and legs pink. Tail short, notched. **VOICE** Song: high buzzy *zit zit zit zeeee zaaay.* Call: light *tzip.* **HABITAT** Moist grasslands, farms. **RANGE** Apr.–Sept.: all NW. Sept.–Apr.: coast.

FOX SPARROW
Passerella iliaca
AMERICAN SPARROW SUBFAMILY

7". Head, back, and rump dark slaty brown; wings and tail tinged rufous brown; buffy white below, heavily spotted with slaty brown; bill dark above, yellowish below. Tail long. Birds east of Cascades somewhat paler gray-brown above. **VOICE** Song: musical series of clear whistles. Call: sharp *chink*. **HABITAT** Shrubby hillsides, thickets. **RANGE** Apr.–Sept.: tip of Olympic Peninsula, Cascades, mtns. east of Cascades. Oct.–Apr.: west of Cascades.

SONG SPARROW
Melospiza melodia
AMERICAN SPARROW SUBFAMILY

6¼". Dark brown stripes on warm brown back and on pale gray underparts; grayish-brown eyebrow; large, central, dark brown spot on chest. Tail fairly long, unpatterned, rounded. **VOICE** Song: *sweet zeet zeet zeee diddle diddle dee.* **HABITAT** Shrubs, marshes, parks, watersides. **RANGE** Resident in NW.

LINCOLN'S SPARROW
Melospiza lincolnii
AMERICAN SPARROW SUBFAMILY

5½". Brown above, with black stripes on back; chest and sides buffy, with fine black streaks, sharply demarcated from clear white belly; broad gray eyebrow; crown rusty, with gray midcrown stripe; buffy eye ring. **VOICE** Song: musical gurgling. Calls: flat *chup;* buzzy *zeee.* **HABITAT** Summer: bogs, wet meadows. Winter: shrubby thickets. **RANGE** Apr.–Sept.: Cascades, wetter e mtns. Apr.–May, Sept.: all NW. Oct.–Apr.: coast.

GOLDEN-CROWNED SPARROW
Zonotrichia atricapilla
AMERICAN SPARROW SUBFAMILY

7". Summer: brown above, with black stripes; wings rusty, with 2 white wing bars; cheeks, throat, and chest gray; crown black with yellow midcrown. Winter: pale buff below; crown dark brown with trace of yellow. **VOICE** Song: down-slurred *ohh-dear-mee.* Call: sharp *chink.* **HABITAT** Thickets, shrubby fields, parks. **RANGE** Sept.–May: all NW.

WHITE-CROWNED SPARROW
Zonotrichia leucophrys
AMERICAN SPARROW SUBFAMILY

7″. Adult back and nape brown with heavy black streaks; gray below; 2 thin white wing bars; crown striped black and white; bill yellow-orange. Imm. crown striped brown and buff. **VOICE** Song: 1–3 clear notes, then a trill. Call: sharp *pink*. **HABITAT** Forests, thickets, parks. **RANGE** Apr.–Oct.: Cascades and west; e highlands (local). Oct.–Apr.: all NW.

DARK-EYED JUNCO
Junco hyemalis
AMERICAN SPARROW SUBFAMILY

6″. Oregon race: adult head and chest black (female gray); back rufous brown (female dull brown); rump gray; sides rusty; midbelly white; bill pale pink, conical. Outer tail feathers white. Travels in flocks. **VOICE** Song: loose musical trill. Call: light *tsik*. **HABITAT** Forests, thickets; in winter, all areas. **RANGE** Apr.–Oct.: all forested NW. Oct.–Apr.: all NW.

RED-WINGED BLACKBIRD
male (left), female (right)
Agelaius phoeniceus
BLACKBIRD SUBFAMILY

9″. Male all glossy black, with red shoulder bordered by yellow. Female heavily streaked brown; crown and eye line dark brown; eyebrow buffy. Bill fairly long, pointed; eyes black; tail rounded. In flocks outside breeding season; forms enormous roosts at night in marshes. **VOICE** Song: gurgling *conk-a-ree*. Calls: harsh *check;* high *tee-eek*. Calls from trees, shrubs, tall reeds. **HABITAT** Marshes, ditches; fields and farms in winter. **RANGE** Resident in NW.

WESTERN MEADOWLARK
Sturnella neglecta
BLACKBIRD SUBFAMILY

10″. Speckled brown above; throat and breast yellow; belly and sides white, sides striped black; black V on chest; crown brown and white striped. Bill long, pointed, gray; tail short. Flight reveals white outer tail feathers. Flies with flutters and glides. **VOICE** Song: 4–5 loud, flute-like whistles: *too tee too tiddleyou.* Call: low *chupp.* **HABITAT** Grasslands, sagebrush deserts, farms. **RANGE** Resident in NW.

YELLOW-HEADED BLACKBIRD
Xanthocephalus xanthocephalus
BLACKBIRD SUBFAMILY

10″. Male head and chest yellow-orange; rest of body and lores black; white patch near bend of wing. Female mainly dark brown above; throat, chest, and eyebrow pale yellow; belly striped black and white. Bill heavy, silvery; tail fairly long, rounded. Nests in colonies. **VOICE** Song: gurgling *gunk-eeeeeee,* like a rusty hinge. Call: low *kruck.* **HABITAT** Marshes; fields in winter. **RANGE** May–Sept.: east of Cascades (local to west); a few in winter.

BREWER'S BLACKBIRD
Euphagus cyanocephalus
BLACKBIRD SUBFAMILY

9″. Male entirely black with iridescent purple on head, green on body; eyes yellow. Female (pictured) entirely grayish brown; eyes dark. Bill thin. Walks on ground. In flocks outside breeding season; nests in small colonies. **VOICE** Song: creaky *squeak.* Call: sharp *chek.* **HABITAT** Farms, sagebrush deserts, towns. **RANGE** Resident in NW.

BROWN-HEADED COWBIRD
female (left), male (right)
Molothrus ater
BLACKBIRD SUBFAMILY

7″. Male dark, shiny, greenish black with brown head. Female uniformly dull brown. Bill medium long, black, conical. Spread west from Great Plains; causes great losses in numbers of native songbirds; female lays single eggs in several nests of natives; baby cowbird pushes out other eggs and babies, is raised by foster parents. **VOICE** Song: bubbly creaking *bubble-lee come seee*. Flight call: high *weee teetee*. **HABITAT** Most open and partially wooded lowland habitats; farms in winter. **RANGE** Apr.–Oct.: all NW. Sept.–Apr.: west of Cascades.

BULLOCK'S ORIOLE
Icterus bullockii
BLACKBIRD SUBFAMILY

8″. Male crown, eye line, throat stripe, back, wings, and central tail black; large white wing patch; much of head, eyebrow, underparts, and outer tail feathers orange. Female olive above; 2 white wing bars; chest pale orange; belly white. Bill slender, pointed; tail rounded. **VOICE** Song: 4–8 doubled whistles. Call: rapid chatter. **HABITAT** Broadleaf and riverine woodlands, parks, towns. **RANGE** May–Sept.: west and east of Cascades.

GRAY-CROWNED ROSY-FINCH
Leucosticte tephrocotis
FINCH FAMILY

6″. Male back, cheeks, and underparts dark brown; rump, shoulder, and vent rosy; forecrown black; hindcrown gray. Female forecrown brown. Bill thick, brown; tail notched. Forms large flocks in winter. **VOICE** Song: harsh descending *chew-chew-chew-chew*. Call: high *cheep*. **HABITAT** Summer: rocky alpine areas. Winter: lower grasslands with cliffs. **RANGE** May–Sept.: Cascades, high e mtns. Oct.–Apr.: east of Cascades.

PINE GROSBEAK
Pinicola enucleator
FINCH FAMILY

9″. Male back black-striped; underparts, head, and rump pink; sides and belly gray; wings black, with white wing bars; tail black, long, notched. Female body gray; head rusty. Bill rather small, stubby. **VOICE** Song: musical warble. Call: whistled *tee wee tee.* **HABITAT** Summer: coniferous forests. Winter: broadleaf trees with remaining fruit. **RANGE** Resident in Cascades and mtns. to east; much rarer in OR.

female (left), male (right)

PURPLE FINCH
Carpodacus purpureus
FINCH FAMILY

6″. Male back and wings mixed brown and rose; head, throat, chest sides, and rump red; dull brownish-red cheek and "mustache." Female has white eyebrow, dark brown cheek patch, and wide brown "mustache." Tail notched. **VOICE** Song: lively complex warbling. Calls: musical *pur-lee;* sharp *chink.* **HABITAT** Coniferous and mixed forests, forest edges, yards. **RANGE** Resident from Cascades west.

female (left), male (right)

CASSIN'S FINCH
Carpodacus cassinii
FINCH FAMILY

6″. Male back and wings pale gray-brown with dark brown stripes; throat and chest rosy; belly whitish; sides lightly streaked; crown red; cheeks striped brown. Female head and body heavily brown-striped; lacks solid brown cheek and "mustache" of female Purple Finch. Tail notched. **VOICE** Song: lively fluty warbling. Call: high *pwee-de-lip.* **HABITAT** Coniferous forests. **RANGE** Apr.–Oct.: Cascades, high e mtns.

HOUSE FINCH
Carpodacus mexicanus
FINCH FAMILY

5½". Male back, midcrown, wings, and tail brown; sides and belly whitish, streaked brown; 2 pale wing bars; wide eyebrow, throat, chest, and rump rosy red. Female upperparts and head plain dull brown; dusky below, with brown streaks. **VOICE** Song: musical warbling ending with a down-slurred *jeer.* Call: musical *chirp.* **HABITAT** Towns, farms, riverine woodlands. **RANGE** Resident in NW.

RED CROSSBILL
Loxia curvirostra
FINCH FAMILY

6". Adult male head and body brick red; wings and tail blackish. Adult female head and body yellow-olive; wings and tail blackish. Tips of bill cross; tail notched. Juv. head and body olive, with brown stripes; wings and tail blackish. **VOICE** Song: *chipa-chipa-chipa-che-chee-chee.* Call: sharp repeated *kip.* **HABITAT** Coniferous forests. **RANGE** Resident in Cascades and west, forested e mtns.

PINE SISKIN
Carduelis pinus
FINCH FAMILY

5". Sexes and plumages alike all year. Very heavily striped brown above and below; yellow stripe on wing; yellow on basal sides of notched tail. Bill thin, pointed. **VOICE** Song: wheezy trills and warbles mixed with calls. Calls: loud *clee-up;* rising *shreee.* **HABITAT** Coniferous and mixed forests, yards. **RANGE** Resident in NW.

AMERICAN GOLDFINCH
Carduelis tristis
FINCH FAMILY

5". Summer male: brilliant yellow; cap, wings, and notched tail black; rump white. Summer female: olive green above; throat and chest yellow. Winter male: brown above; face and shoulder yellow. Winter female: grayish with or without trace of yellow on throat. White wing bars on black wings. **VOICE** Song: canary-like; long, pleasing, rising and falling twittering. Call: rising *sweee-eat*. Flight call: *per chicory*. **HABITAT** Lowland fields, forest edges, farms, yards. **RANGE** Resident in NW.

EVENING GROSBEAK
Coccothraustes vespertinus
FINCH FAMILY

8". Male back and breast brown; rump and belly yellow; head dark brown with yellow eyebrow and forehead; wings black with white secondaries. Female plain gray-brown; wings black with large white spots. Bill massive, ivory; head large; tail black, fairly short. **VOICE** Song: short warble. Call: ringing *cleeer*. **HABITAT** Coniferous and mixed forests. **RANGE** Resident in NW.

HOUSE SPARROW
Passer domesticus
OLD WORLD SPARROW FAMILY

female (left), male (right)

6". Male back and wings rufous, streaked with black; underparts, crown, cheeks, and rump gray; 1 white wing bar; throat and upper chest black (only chin black in winter); wide chestnut stripe behind eye. Female plain brown above, ex. for blackish back streaks, buffy stripe above eye; pale dusky below. Abundant European import; takes bulk of seed at most feeders; kills nestlings, removes eggs of other birds from birdhouses. **VOICE** Song: often-given *chireep* and *chereep* notes. Call: *chir-rup*. **HABITAT** Towns, parks, farms. **RANGE** Resident in NW.

Mammals

All members of the vertebrate class Mammalia are warm-blooded and able to maintain a near-constant body temperature. Males generally have an external penis for direct internal fertilization of the female's eggs. Almost all mammals are born live rather than hatching from eggs (exceptions are the platypus and the echidnas of Australia). Mammary glands, unique to mammals, produce milk that is high in nutrients and fat and promotes rapid growth in the young. Mammals have abundant skin glands, used for temperature regulation (sweating), coat maintenance, territory marking, sex and species recognition, breeding cycle signals, and even defense, as in skunks and others that can repel predators with powerful secretions.

Nine mammalian orders are represented in the Pacific Northwest, including humans (members of the primates order). Opossums (order Didelphimorphia) give birth to young in an embryonic state; they then develop in a separate fur-lined pouch on the mother's belly. The tiny energetic shrews and moles (Insectivora), which eat insects and other invertebrates, have long snouts, short dense fur, and five toes on each foot. Bats (Chiroptera), with their enlarged, membrane-covered forelimbs, are the only mammals that truly fly.

Hares, rabbits, and pikas (Lagomorpha) resemble large rodents but have four upper incisor teeth—a large front pair and a small pair directly behind them—that grow continuously, and five toes on their front feet and five in back; digits on all feet are very small. Rodents (Rodentia—including chipmunks, marmots, squirrels, mice, rats, muskrats, voles, porcupines, and beavers) have two upper incisor teeth that grow continuously, and most have four toes on their front feet and five in back.

Carnivores (Carnivora)—bears, the Coyote, wolves, foxes, raccoons, weasels, cats, and seals—have long canine teeth and sharp cheek teeth for killing and eating prey. The even-toed hoofed mammals (Artiodactyla), in the Northwest represented by deer, goats, sheep, and the Pronghorn, have two or four toes that form a cloven hoof. The whales, dolphins, and porpoises (Cetacea) are hairless; in both seals and cetaceans, the legs have evolved into flippers.

Most mammals have an insulating layer of fur that allows them to maintain a fairly constant body temperature independent of their surroundings, thus making them successful in cold climates. Many molt twice a year and have a noticeably thicker coat in winter. Some, such as certain weasels and hares, change colors, developing a concealing white coat in winter. In whales, porpoises, and dolphins, thick layers of insulating blubber, rather than hair, retain body heat. The ability to maintain a high body temperature allows many mammals to prosper in below-freezing temperatures.

The body parts and appendages of mammals exhibit a wide and adaptive variety of sizes, shapes, and functions. Most mammals have well-developed eyes, ears, and noses that provide good night vision, hearing, and sense of smell. Mammalian teeth range from fine points for capturing insects (bats and insectivores) to chisel-like gnawing teeth (rabbits, rodents, and hoofed mammals), wide plant-crushers (rodents and hoofed mammals), and heavy pointed instruments for flesh-ripping (carnivores). The whales' huge brushes, called baleen, for straining plankton, are not actually teeth but composed of fingernail-like keratin.

Mammals generally have four limbs. In many rodents, in some carnivores, and in primates, the ends of the forelimbs are modified into complex, manipulative hands. Solid hooves support the heavy weight of deer and the Pronghorn.

In the species accounts that follow, the typical adult length given is from the tip of the nose to the end of the tail, followed by the tail length; for larger mammals shoulder height is also given. Wingspan is given for bats.

Mammal Signs and Tracks

The evidence that a particular animal is or has been in a certain area is called its "sign." The sign can be scat (fecal matter), burrow openings, nutshells, tracks, or other evidence. Tracks are a useful aid in confirming the presence of mammal species. Impressions vary depending on the substrate and whether the animal was walking or running. Animals can leave clear tracks in mud, dirt, snow, and sand, usually larger ones in wet mud and snow. Because animals come to ponds or streams to drink or feed, tracks are likely to be found on their shores; damp mud often records tracks in fine detail, sometimes showing claws or webbing. Prints in snow may leave a less clear impression but can often be followed for a long distance, and may show the pattern of the animal's stride. The track drawings below, of selected mammals that live in the Pacific Northwest, are not to relative scale.

Virginia Opossum

Snowshoe Hare

Eastern Gray Squirrel

American Beaver

Common Muskrat

Common Porcupine

Coyote

Red Fox

Common Gray Fox

Black Bear

Common Raccoon

Long-tailed Weasel

Mink

Striped Skunk

Northern River Otter

Mountain Lion

Bobcat

Elk

White-tailed Deer

Mountain Goat

Bighorn Sheep

VIRGINIA OPOSSUM
Didelphis virginiana
OPOSSUM FAMILY

L 30"; T 12". Grizzled gray, with mix of black underfur and longer white guard hairs. Head pointed; nose long; face white, with long whiskers; ears small, round, black with white tip. Legs short, black; feet have 5 digits; hind-feet have opposable, grasping inner thumbs. Tail long, tapered, naked, pink with black base. Eats fruit, nuts, bird eggs, large insects, carrion. Hangs from branches using wraparound, prehensile tail. If surprised at close range, may "play possum" (play dead). Introduced from e U.S. **BREEDING** 1–14 (avg. 8) pea-size young attach themselves to nipples in mother's pouch for 2 months; 1–2 litters per year. **SIGN** Tracks: 2" hindprint, 3 middle toes close, outer toes well spread; foreprint slightly smaller, star-like. **HABITAT** Broadleaf woods, watersides, farms, residential areas. **ACTIVITY** Nocturnal; much less active in winter. **RANGE** West of Cascades.

WATER SHREW
Sorex palustris
SHREW FAMILY

L 6"; T 3". Dark gray above, white below. Tail as long as body. Nose long, conical; eyes tiny; ears hidden on sides of head. Comb of stiff hairs on hindfeet. Swims well; can run over water surfaces; fur water-resistant. Eats aquatic insects, small fish. **BREEDING** 2–3 litters of 6 young Feb.–Aug. **HABITAT** Mtn. streams, sphagnum bogs. **ACTIVITY** Very active day and night, year-round. **RANGE** Olympics, Cascades, forested inland ranges.

TROWBRIDGE'S SHREW
Sorex trowbridgii
SHREW FAMILY

L 4½"; T 2". Gray-brown above and below. Tail dark above, white below. Nose long, conical; eyes tiny; ears hidden on sides of head. Legs and feet short. Eats invertebrates and Douglas fir seeds. **BREEDING** 1 litter of 3–6 young Apr.–July. **HABITAT** Mature forest floors. **ACTIVITY** Very active day and night, year-round. **RANGE** w WA, w OR.

VAGRANT SHREW
Sorex vagrans
SHREW FAMILY

L 4"; T 2". Reddish brown in summer, black in winter. Tail gray. Nose long, conical; eyes tiny; ears hidden on sides of head. Legs and feet short. Feeds on invertebrates and fungi in vole runways. **BREEDING** 2 litters of 2–9 young Feb.–May, Oct.–Nov. **HABITAT** Mixed forests, meadows, bogs. **ACTIVITY** Very active day and night, year-round.

TOWNSEND'S MOLE
Scapanus townsendii
MOLE FAMILY

L 8½"; T 1½". Body blackish brown. Nose long, conical, naked, pink; eyes not visible; ears hidden on sides of head. Feet broadly flattened, pink, with long white claws. Tail short, pink, nearly naked. Tunnels just under soil surface and deeper, seeking earthworms, other invertebrates. **BREEDING** 2–6 young Mar.–Apr. **SIGN** Prominent mounds of soil up to 12" high. **HABITAT** Soft moist soils in forests, lawns, meadows. **ACTIVITY** Mostly nocturnal; uses deeper tunnels in cold periods. **RANGE** w WA, w OR.

SHREW-MOLE
Neurotrichus gibbsii
MOLE FAMILY

L 5"; T 1½". Body black. Forefeet grasping (shrew-like); hindfeet flattened, with short claws (mole-like). Tail hairy, black, about ½ body length. Nose long, conical, naked, pink; eyes tiny; ears hidden. Only mole that forages aboveground; even climbs in shrubs; eats worms, sowbugs, insects. **BREEDING** 1–2 litters of 1–4 young Feb.–Sept. **SIGN** Tunnels just under leaf litter. **HABITAT** Forested and weedy ravines. **ACTIVITY** Day and night, year-round. **RANGE** w WA, w OR.

Bats

Bats are the only mammals that truly fly (flying squirrels glide). The bones and muscles in the forelimbs of bats are elongated; thin, usually black wing membranes are attached to four extremely long fingers. When bats are at rest, the wings are folded along the forearm; they use their short, claw-like thumbs for crawling about. Small insectivorous bats beat their wings six to eight times a second.

Bats are mainly nocturnal, though some species are occasionally active in the early morning and late afternoon. Their slender, mouse-like bodies are well-furred, and their eyesight, while not excellent, is quite adequate to detect predators and general landscape features. Most use echolocation (sonar) to locate flying insects and avoid obstacles. In flight, they emit 30 to 60 high-frequency calls per second that rebound off objects. Their large ears receive these reflected sounds, and the bats interpret them as they close in on prey or evade an obstacle. Echolocation sounds are mainly inaudible to humans, but bats also give shrill squeaks most humans can hear. By day, most bats hang upside-down from the ceilings of caves, tree hollows, and attics, using one or both feet. Members of solitary species may roost alone under a branch or amid the foliage of a tall tree. In other species, large colonies gather in caves and under natural and man-made overhangs.

All bats of the Pacific Northwest are insect-eaters. By night they pursue larger individual insects through the air or glean them from foliage. Some skim open-mouthed through swarms of mosquitoes or midges. A bat will trap a large flying insect in the membrane between its hindlegs, then seize it with its teeth. Because of the lack of insects in winter, Northwest bats either hibernate here or migrate south to hibernate or feed in winter. Sheltered hibernation roosts provide protection from extreme cold.

Watch for bats overhead on warm summer evenings, especially around water, where insects are abundant and where bats may skim the water surface to drink.

Parts of a Bat

Echolocation

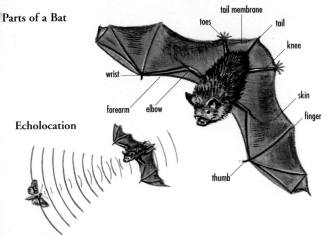

LITTLE BROWN MYOTIS
"Little Brown Bat"
Myotis lucifugus
VESPERTILIONID BAT FAMILY

L 3½"; WS 9". Rich glossy brown above, buffy below. Face broad, black; ears short, rounded, black. Often flies before dusk; flight erratic. Squeaks audible. One of 8 similar myotises in NW. **BREEDING** 1 young in June in attics, barns, caves. **HABITAT** Roosts in trees, caves, mines, attics; forages widely, esp. over water. **ACTIVITY** Summer: active. Winter: hibernates in caves.

HOARY BAT
Lasiurus cinereus
VESPERTILIONID BAT FAMILY

L 5"; WS 15". Mahogany brown above, heavily frosted with white hairs; throat buffy yellow. Ears short, rounded, with naked black rims. Nose blunt. Tail membrane heavily furred, brown. Most highly migratory bat in NW; many winter in Chile and Argentina. **BREEDING** 2 young in June. **HABITAT** Wooded areas; roosts in foliage. **ACTIVITY** Emerges late in evening to feed on moths. **RANGE** Summer: all NW.

SILVER-HAIRED BAT
Lasionycteris noctivagans
VESPERTILIONID BAT FAMILY

L 4"; WS 11". Black, frosted with silvery hairs on back. Face blunt; ears fairly short, rounded, naked, black. Flies high, straight; feeds in treetops and at water surface. **BREEDING** 2 young in June in tree cavity. **HABITAT** Wooded areas; roosts under bark, in tree cavities, rarely in buildings. **ACTIVITY** Nocturnal. **RANGE** Summer: all NW. Winter: most or all migrate south.

BIG BROWN BAT
Eptesicus fuscus
VESPERTILIONID BAT FAMILY

L 4½"; WS 13". Dark brown above, pale brown below. Wing and tail membranes furless. Face and ears broad, black. Flight straight, fast. Flies later in autumn, earlier in spring than others. Occ. seen in daytime in autumn, searching for hibernation site. **BREEDING** 2 young in June. **HABITAT** Roosts and breeds in attics, barns, tree hollows, behind shutters, under bridges. **ACTIVITY** Spring–fall: active. Winter: hibernates.

TOWNSEND'S BIG-EARED BAT
"Western Big-eared Bat"
Plecotus townsendii
VESPERTILIONID BAT FAMILY
L 4″; WS 13″. Pale gray or brown above, buffy below. Enormous ears (to 1½″) with rounded tip; joined in middle of crown; extend to middle of body when laid back. 2 large lumps on nose. **BREEDING** Females form nursery colonies in caves and buildings; 1 young May–June. **HABITAT** Open or forested areas with crevices for roosting, caves for hibernation. **ACTIVITY** Emerges in late evening to feed on moths. **RANGE** All NW; most common east of Cascades.

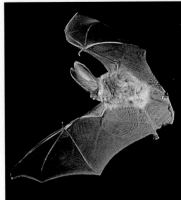

PALLID BAT
Antrozous pallidus
VESPERTILIONID BAT FAMILY
L 5″; WS 15″. Pale creamy buff above, paler below. Ears large (to 1¼″) with rounded tip; not joined in middle of crown. Flies low; often lands on ground to feed on large insects. **BREEDING** 1–2 young May–June in small nursery colonies in rock crevices or buildings. **HABITAT** Deserts, canyons. **ACTIVITY** Flies late at night; hibernates locally in winter. **RANGE** e WA, e OR.

AMERICAN PIKA
Ochotona princeps
PIKA FAMILY
L 8″. Fur gray-brown to buff. Eyes small; ears round, black with white edges. Legs short; no visible tail. Sits on rock pile, proclaiming territory with series of high-pitched calls (*peeks*). **BREEDING** 2–6 young May–June; sometimes 2nd litter in Aug. **SIGN** Piles of fresh hay in rock slides or spread out to dry in sun. Scat: small, round, black pellets; white urine stains on rocks. **HABITAT** Boulder-covered hillsides in mtns. **ACTIVITY** Mainly by day; feeds on stored hay under snow in winter. **RANGE** Cascades and higher ranges to east; as low as 2,000′.

PYGMY RABBIT
Brachylagus idahoensis
HARE AND RABBIT FAMILY

L 11"; T 1". Slate gray with pinkish tinge. Ears fairly short for a rabbit (1½"), pale. White spot at side of nostril. Tail short, gray below. Digs own burrow system, unlike other rabbits. Scampers rather than leaps. Feeds on sagebrush leaves and grasses. Smallest rabbit in NW. **BREEDING** 4–8 young June–July. **SIGN** Burrows have 2–5 entrances, each entrance 3". **HABITAT** Clumps of tall sagebrush in deserts. **ACTIVITY** Appears by day, but mainly nocturnal. **RANGE** sc WA, e OR (rare and local).

BRUSH RABBIT
Sylvilagus bachmani
HARE AND RABBIT FAMILY

L 14"; T 1". Dark reddish brown, mottled with black hairs; paler in winter. Ears medium length (2½"), dark. Legs medium length. Tail short, white below. May climb into thick brush to escape predators. **BREEDING** Up to 5 litters of 1–7 young Mar.–Sept. Mother covers young with grass when leaving nest site. **SIGN** Maze of runways connecting close-cropped feeding areas. **HABITAT** Thick brushy areas in and near forests. **ACTIVITY** Mainly nocturnal. **RANGE** w OR.

MOUNTAIN COTTONTAIL
Sylvilagus nuttallii
HARE AND RABBIT FAMILY

L 15"; T 2". Pale grayish brown above, white below. Ears medium-length (2½"), black-tipped. Legs medium-length. Tail short, white below. Spends most of day resting in tall grass or rocky crevice. **BREEDING** 3–8 young Mar.–July; several litters each year. **SIGN** Tracks: foreprint round, 1"; hindprint oblong, 3½". **HABITAT** Open woodlands, shrubby areas, sagebrush. **ACTIVITY** Mainly nocturnal. **RANGE** East of Cascades.

SNOWSHOE HARE
"Varying Hare"
Lepus americanus
HARE AND RABBIT FAMILY

L 19"; T 1½". Summer: brown, grizzled with blackish; short tail dusky white below; feet sometimes white. Winter: thickly furred hindfeet serve as snowshoes; pure white ex. for black ear tips (in and east of Cascades) or pale brown (west of Cascades). Larger than a cottontail, with longer (4") black-tipped ears, larger hindfeet. Usu. shy; if surprised, may thump hindfeet, then run off at up to 30 mph; if frightened, grunts, chirps, or screams. **BREEDING** 3 litters of 3 young Apr.–Aug; alert, furred, able to hop in hours. **SIGN** Packed-down trails in snow. Scat: piles of brown, lima-bean-size pellets. Tracks: hindprint 5"; toes widely spaced. **HABITAT** Coniferous and mixed forests. **ACTIVITY** Nocturnal; rests by day in nest-like "form" or a hollow log.

BLACK-TAILED JACKRABBIT
Lepus californicus
HARE AND RABBIT FAMILY

L 24"; T 4". Hare. Buffy brown above, peppered with black; white below. Neck longer than rabbits'. Ears very long (5"), brownish with black tip. Legs long, thin, with large hindfeet (5"). Tail black above (black extends onto rump), white below. Stands up high when alert. Usu. hops rather than walks; can run to 35 mph; every 5th leap higher to check for predators. Gives squeals, thumps feet when distressed. **BREEDING** 2–4 litters of 2–4 young Mar.–Oct. **SIGN** Trails in grass. Tracks: foreprint round, 1½"; hindprint oval, 2½"; 5–20' apart, depending on speed. **HABITAT** Prairies, scrubby deserts, cultivated fields. **ACTIVITY** Day or night; avoids midday summer heat. **RANGE** s and e OR, se WA.

summer coat (left), winter coat (right)

WHITE-TAILED JACKRABBIT
Lepus townsendii
HARE AND RABBIT FAMILY

L 26"; T 3½". Hare. Summer: gray-brown above, peppered with black, paler below; ears tipped black. Winter: all white. Ears to 4⅜" long. Legs long, thin; hindfeet to 6¾" long. Tail white. Runs to 45 mph. Numbers diminished. **BREEDING** 1–3 litters of 1–6 young Apr.–Sept. **SIGN** Makes tunnels in snow. Tracks: foreprint round, 1½"; hindprint oval, 2½"; tracks 5–20' apart. **HABITAT** Open grassy and sagebrush plains. **ACTIVITY** Mainly nocturnal. **RANGE** East of Cascades.

Rodents

Rodentia is the world's largest mammalian order; more than half of all mammal species and many more than half of all mammal individuals on earth are rodents. In addition to the mice and rats (a family that also includes the mouse-like but chubbier voles and the muskrats), other rodent families in the Northwest are the squirrels (including chipmunks and marmots), jumping mice, pocket mice, pocket gophers, porcupines, beavers, and the Mountain Beaver. Species in the Pacific Northwest range from mice weighing roughly an ounce to the American Beaver, which may weigh up to 66 pounds, but most rodents are relatively small. They are distinguished by having only two pairs of incisors—one upper and one lower—and no canines, leaving a wide gap between incisors and molars. Rodent incisors are enameled on the front only; the working of the upper teeth against the lower ones wears away the softer inner surfaces, producing a short, chisel-like, beveled edge ideal for gnawing. The incisors grow throughout an animal's life (if they did not, they shortly would be worn away), and rodents must gnaw enough to keep the incisors from growing too long. The eyes are bulbous and placed high on the sides of the head, enabling the animals to detect danger over a wide arc.

MOUNTAIN BEAVER
Aplodontia rufa
MOUNTAIN BEAVER FAMILY

L 14″; T 1″. Dark brown above, paler brown below. Long whiskers. Eyes small, white spot just below. Ears small, rounded, on sides of head. Legs short; 5 toes per foot; claws long, strong. Tail tiny. Makes extensive burrows that may also be used by other animals. Feeds on soft vegetation, incl. ferns; gnaws bark; climbs trees to gnaw off lower branches to length of about 12″, leaving useful stepladder. **VOICE** Vocal: shrill whistles and squeals when cornered; otherwise silent. **BREEDING** 2–3 young in Apr.; not weaned until autumn. **SIGN** Piles of grass and ferns up to 24″ tall. Burrow entrances to 6–8″ wide, sometimes protected by tent of sticks covered with ferns and leaves. Tracks: 2″; 5 digits, hand-like. **HABITAT** Moist forests near streams. **ACTIVITY** Day and night, year-round. **RANGE** Cascades and west.

YELLOW-PINE CHIPMUNK
Tamias amoenus
SQUIRREL FAMILY
L 9″; T 4″. Brightly patterned: 5 black stripes on back (middle 3 reach tail) enclose 2 interior gray stripes and 2 flanking white stripes; sides yellowish orange; belly whitish. White stripes above and below eye, flanked by 3 black stripes. Small ears blackish in front, white behind. Tail bushy, mainly tawny. Common at high elevs. in Olympic N.P. and Mt. Rainier N.P. Bold; steals campground food. **BREEDING** 4–7 young in May. **HABITAT** Clearings and shrubs at edges of mtn. coniferous forests. **ACTIVITY** By day; hibernates in winter. **RANGE** Olympics, Cascades, e WA, e OR.

LEAST CHIPMUNK
Tamias minimus
SQUIRREL FAMILY
L 8″; T 4″. 5 brown and 4 whitish stripes on back (reaching tail); sides yellow-gray; belly pale. 3 brown, 2 whitish stripes each side of face. Tail light brown. **BREEDING** 4–7 young in May, in tunnel or tree hole. **HABITAT** Juniper woodlands, sagebrush deserts. **ACTIVITY** By day; hibernates in winter. **RANGE** sc WA, e OR.

TOWNSEND'S CHIPMUNK
Tamias townsendii
SQUIRREL FAMILY
L 10″; T 4½″. Dark. 5 dark brown and 4 gray stripes on back (not reaching tail); sides rusty brown; belly pale. Dark and light brown stripes on head. Tail very bushy, dark brown. **BREEDING** 3–6 young in May. **HABITAT** Coniferous forests. **ACTIVITY** By day; hibernates part of winter. **RANGE** Cascades and west.

HOARY MARMOT
Marmota caligata
SQUIRREL FAMILY
L 30″; T 9″. Silver gray above; rump brownish; belly pale. Black V on shoulders. Feet black, strong claws. Tail bushy, reddish brown. **BREEDING** 4–5 young May–June. **SIGN** 12″ burrow entrance, often under rock. **VOICE** Shrill whistle. **HABITAT** Meadows and rockslides near timberline. **ACTIVITY** By day; hibernates Oct.–Apr. **RANGE** Cascades of WA.

YELLOW-BELLIED MARMOT
Marmota flaviventris
SQUIRREL FAMILY
L 24″; T 7″. Coat reddish brown; belly yellow; sides of neck buffy. Head dark brown; pale brown patches on muzzle. Feet buffy or brown, short, strongly clawed. Tail large, bushy, bright reddish brown. Often sits on boulder above burrow. May engage in wrestling matches over territory. **VOICE** Vocal: high soft chirps and whistles. **BREEDING** 4–5 young in May. **SIGN** Den near large boulder. **HABITAT** Rocky areas in valleys, foothills, mtns. to 7,000′. **ACTIVITY** Mainly by day; hibernates Aug.–Mar. **RANGE** Cascades and east.

OLYMPIC MARMOT
Marmota olympus
SQUIRREL FAMILY
L 26″; T 9″. Brownish above in spring, bleaches to yellow in summer; frosted white; brown below. Head brown; muzzle silvery. Feet dark brown, heavily clawed. Related individuals live together. **BREEDING** 4 young in May. **SIGN** 10″ burrow opening. **HABITAT** Mtn. meadows, rocky slopes. **ACTIVITY** By day; hibernates Sept.–Mar. **RANGE** Upper slopes of Olympics of w WA.

WHITE-TAILED ANTELOPE SQUIRREL
Ammospermophilus leucurus
SQUIRREL FAMILY
L 9″; T 2¾″. Back gray; sides and thighs orangish; 1 white stripe on each side; white below. Head tan; whitish eye ring. Tail gray above, white below. Runs with tail arched over back. **BREEDING** 5–14 young in Apr. **SIGN** Burrows with pathways radiating outward. **HABITAT** Rocky desert scrub. **ACTIVITY** By day; hibernates in winter. **RANGE** se OR.

CALIFORNIA GROUND SQUIRREL
Spermophilus beecheyi
SQUIRREL FAMILY

L 18"; T 8". Back and rump dark brown, with paler brownish-buffy spots or bars, wide silvery patch extending from neck to sides. Head plain gray-brown; white eye ring. Tail rather bushy, fairly long, brown edged with white. **BREEDING** 5–8 young in May. **SIGN** Burrows with pathways radiating from entrance mound. **HABITAT** Primarily oak woodlands. **ACTIVITY** By day; hibernates Nov.–Feb. **RANGE** w OR, sc WA (expanding northward).

BELDING'S GROUND SQUIRREL
Spermophilus beldingi
SQUIRREL FAMILY

L 11"; T 2¾". Plain rusty brown above, with darker brown stripe on midback; buffy or gray below. Head plain gray with pink wash, white eye ring. Ears relatively small. Tail a mix of gray, pink, and rust; tip black. **VOICE** 1 chirp note and a trill. **BREEDING** 3–8 young June–July; somewhat colonial. **SIGN** Burrows with 2 openings. **HABITAT** Meadows, pastures. **ACTIVITY** By day; hibernates Sept.–May. **RANGE** e OR.

COLUMBIAN GROUND SQUIRREL
Spermophilus columbianus
SQUIRREL FAMILY

L 14"; T 4". Grayish, spotted with black and buff above, belly, legs, and face rusty orange. Tail bushy, rusty orange, edged in white. **VOICE** Most vocal ground squirrel in NW; high-pitched calls. **BREEDING** 2–7 young May–June; often colonial. **SIGN** Holes in ground without mounds. **HABITAT** Grasslands, clearings in conifer forests. **ACTIVITY** By day; hibernates Sept.–Apr. **RANGE** e WA, ne OR.

GOLDEN-MANTLED GROUND SQUIRREL
Spermophilus lateralis
SQUIRREL FAMILY

L 11"; T 4". Resembles oversize chipmunk without facial stripes. Back gray-brown or buff; 1 white stripe on each side bordered by heavy black stripe; belly whitish. Head and shoulders plain golden orange. Tail grizzled grayish on black. **VOICE** Variety of *chips* and squeals. **BREEDING** 4–6 young in June. **HABITAT** Mainly mtn. forests; sparse in open sagebrush and meadows. **ACTIVITY** By day; hibernates Oct.–Apr. **RANGE** Most of OR; extreme se and ne WA.

CASCADE GOLDEN-MANTLED GROUND SQUIRREL
Spermophilus saturatus
SQUIRREL FAMILY

L 12″; T 4″. Resembles oversize chipmunk without facial stripes. Back dark gray-brown; 1 white stripe on each side bordered by faint black stripe. Head and shoulders plain golden orange. Tail grizzled grayish on black. **BREEDING** 1–5 young in late May. **HABITAT** Coniferous forests up to rocky slopes above tree line. **ACTIVITY** By day; hibernates Sept.–Apr. **RANGE** Cascades of WA.

TOWNSEND'S GROUND SQUIRREL
Spermophilus townsendii
SQUIRREL FAMILY

L 9″; T 2″. Smoky gray above, washed with pinkish buff; belly paler gray or pale buff. Head plain gray-brown; eye ring white. Tail tawny with white edge. **BREEDING** 4–10 young in Mar. **SIGN** Burrow openings rimmed with dirt piles. **HABITAT** Sagebrush deserts. **ACTIVITY** By day; hibernates July–Feb. **RANGE** sc WA, e OR.

EASTERN GRAY SQUIRREL
Sciurus carolinensis
SQUIRREL FAMILY

L 19″; T 9″. Tail bushy; black, gray and white. Summer: gray above; legs and haunches washed buffy; white below; buffy eye ring; back of ears reddish brown; feet buffy. Winter: lacks buffy tones ex. for eye ring; back of ears white; feet pale gray. Feeds on nuts, buds, inner bark, fruit. Introduced from e U.S.; widespread around cities. **VOICE** Vocal: variety of harsh calls. **BREEDING** 2 litters of 2–3 young Apr.– May, Aug.–Sept.; born in nest in tree cavity. **SIGN** Summer: leaf and twig nests high in broadleaf trees. Tracks: foreprint round, 1″; hindprint triangular, 2¼″. **HABITAT** Forest, parks, suburbs. **ACTIVITY** By day, year-round. **RANGE** w WA.

RED SQUIRREL
Tamiasciurus hudsonicus
SQUIRREL FAMILY

L 13"; T 5". Underparts white; tail long, bushy, reddish. Summer: dark reddish gray above, with black side stripe; ears rounded. Winter: pale reddish gray above; no side stripe; ears tufted. Mainly arboreal. Diet includes seeds, nuts, mushrooms, bird eggs, and sap; caches food for winter. **VOICE** Bird-like, chattering territorial call; emphatic *tchick, tchick, tchick* alarm call. **BREEDING** Usu. 4–5 young Apr.–May and Aug.–Sept. in tree cavity or exposed leaf-and-stick nest in treetop. **SIGN** Piles of stripped cones; nuts with ragged hole at one end. Tracks: hindprint 1½"; 5 toes print. **HABITAT** Mixed forests, esp. conifers. **ACTIVITY** Mainly by day, year-round. **RANGE** East of Cascades in n WA; far e WA; ne OR.

DOUGLAS' SQUIRREL
"Chickaree" "Pine Squirrel"
Tamiasciurus douglasii
SQUIRREL FAMILY

L 13"; T 5". Much like Red Squirrel, but darker overall and browner above; narrower white eye ring and blackish tail. Summer: dark reddish olive above; blackish stripe on side; orange below; ears rounded; lower legs and feet tawny. Winter: back brown; sides, lower legs, and feet gray; pale yellowish-gray below; ears tufted. **VOICE** Call: chattering *chick-r-r-r-r.* **BREEDING** 1–2 litters of 4–6 young May–June, Aug.–Sept. **SIGN** Summer: ball-shaped nests in trees; piles of stripped cones on logs and stumps. **HABITAT** Coniferous forests. **ACTIVITY** By day; very active year-round. **RANGE** Cascades and west, e OR mtns.

WESTERN GRAY SQUIRREL
Sciurus griseus
SQUIRREL FAMILY

L 22"; T 11". Gray above, with many white-tipped hairs; white below. White eye ring. Toes often blackish. Tail very bushy; black, mixed with gray and white hairs. Eats pinenuts, acorns, fungi. **VOICE** Gives hoarse barking call, mainly in late summer. **BREEDING** 3–5 young Mar.–June. **SIGN** Summer: nests of leaves and twigs, 20' or higher in trees (winters in tree hollows). Tracks: foreprints to 1½", paired, usually behind hindprints (to 3"). **HABITAT** Open oak and oak-pine woodlands. **ACTIVITY** By day, year-round. **RANGE** sw and sc WA (rare), w OR.

NORTHERN FLYING SQUIRREL
Glaucomys sabrinus
SQUIRREL FAMILY

L 13″; T 6″. Body and tail rich brown above, white below. Fur soft. Loose folds of furred skin connect both legs on each side out to hand. Face blunt, rounded; eyes large. Tail long, flattened; base narrow. Glides up to 200′. Eats lichens, subterranean fungi, nuts, seeds, insects; visits birdfeeders at night. Dens in tree cavities, abandoned buildings; summer nest of barks and twigs. **BREEDING** 2–5 young Apr.–May. **SIGN** Piles of cone remnants and nutshells under dead trees with many woodpecker holes. **HABITAT** Coniferous and mixed forests. **ACTIVITY** Strictly nocturnal.

WESTERN POCKET GOPHER
Thomomys mazama
POCKET GOPHER FAMILY

L 8″; T 2½″. Reddish brown, gray, or black, matching local soil color; black ear patch. Orange, chisel-like pair of upper and lower incisors. Ears small, pointed. Excavates burrows near surface for food-gathering, deeper ones for shelter and food storage. Eats mostly roots in winter, stems and leaves in summer; pulls small plants underground. Common, but not easy to see. **BREEDING** 2 or more litters of 5–6 young in summer. **SIGN** Fan-shaped mounds with earth plug (mole mounds lack plug). **HABITAT** Meadows. **ACTIVITY** Mainly nocturnal. **RANGE** West of Cascades.

GREAT BASIN POCKET MOUSE
Perognathus parvus
POCKET MOUSE AND KANGAROO RAT FAMILY

L 7″; T 3½″. Gray-brown above, white below. Ears small; fur-lined cheek pouch. Tail long, bicolored. Makes extensive burrows with chambers for sleeping, nesting, food storage. Eats seeds. **BREEDING** 2 litters of 2–8 young May–Aug. **SIGN** Mounds of soil at burrow entrance. **HABITAT** Sagebrush, juniper woodlands. **ACTIVITY** Nocturnal; hibernates in winter. **RANGE** East of Cascades.

ORD'S KANGAROO RAT
Dipodomys ordii
POCKET MOUSE AND KANGAROO RAT FAMILY

L 10″; T 5″. Tan above, white below. White spot above eye, below ear. Hindfeet 2″ long. Tail striped brown and white with dark tip. Jumps to 8′. **BREEDING** 3–5 young. **SIGN** 3″ burrow openings on slopes; scooped-out dusting areas nearby. Narrow, 1½″ hindprints. **HABITAT** Open deserts with hard or sandy soils. **ACTIVITY** Nocturnal; winters in burrows. **RANGE** East of Cascades in sc WA, e OR.

gnawed tree (center), lodge (right)

AMERICAN BEAVER
Castor canadensis
BEAVER FAMILY

L 3′4″; T 16″. Rich dark brown. Back high, rounded. Eyes and ears small. Legs short; feet webbed, black; claws small. Paddle-shaped tail black, scaly, rounded, flattened horizontally. Eats bark and twigs of broadleaf trees; stashes branches underwater for winter use. Swims with only head above water. Slaps tail on water loudly to warn family of danger. Fells trees by gnawing trunk down to a "waist" that finally cannot support the tree. Dams small streams with sticks, reeds, and saplings caulked with mud. In middle of new pond, builds dome-like lodge up to 6′ high and 20′ wide; underwater tunnels reach up to dry chambers, hidden from view, above water level. Dens in banks of canals and streams in treeless areas. Ponds formed by dams promote growth of habitat (broadleaf trees) favored by beavers; dams also help form marshes for other wildlife. N. Amer.'s largest rodent. **BREEDING** Usu. 3–5 young May–June inside lodge. **SIGN** Dams, lodges, cone-shaped tree stumps; 12″ territorial scent mounds of mud and grass. Tracks: 5″, 5-toed hindprint covers smaller foreprint. **HABITAT** Ponds, rivers, adjacent woodlands. **ACTIVITY** Mainly at dusk and night, year-round.

WESTERN HARVEST MOUSE
Reithrodontomys megalotis
MOUSE AND RAT FAMILY

L 5½"; T 3". Brown above; sides buffy; pale below. Ears medium-size, round. Tail dusky above, pale below. Travels in vole runways. Nimble climber. Eats insects and new growth in summer, seeds in fall and winter. **BREEDING** Several litters of 2–6 young. **SIGN** Builds 4" globular woven nest near ground; entrance at bottom. **HABITAT** Cultivated and weedy fields, grasslands. **ACTIVITY** Nocturnal, year-round. **RANGE** e WA, e and s OR.

DEER MOUSE
Peromyscus maniculatus
MOUSE AND RAT FAMILY

L 7"; T 3". Brown (adult) or gray (juv.) above (darker west of Cascades), white below. Ears round, medium-size. Feet white. Tail dark above, white below. In most habitats, outnumbers all other rodents combined. Agile climber; feeds on seeds, insects, fungi. **BREEDING** 2–4 litters of 3–5 young Mar.–Oct. **HABITAT** All habitats, ex. wet or swampy areas. **ACTIVITY** Nocturnal, year-round.

NORTHERN GRASSHOPPER MOUSE
Onychomys leucogaster
MOUSE AND RAT FAMILY

L 7"; T 2". Pale cinnamon brown (adult) or pale gray (juv.) above, white below. Head large; ears medium-size. Feet white. Tail short, mainly white. Eats large insects, occ. other mice, few plants. Uses burrows of other rodents. **VOICE** Vocal: sharp barks; long shrill whistles. **BREEDING** 2 litters of 1–6 young Apr.–Aug. **HABITAT** Desert valleys. **ACTIVITY** Nocturnal, year-round. **RANGE** se WA, e OR.

BUSHY-TAILED WOODRAT
Neotoma cinerea
MOUSE AND RAT FAMILY

L 17"; T 8". Tan above, peppered with black; white below. Ears large. Feet white. Tail bushy, brown. Brings shiny, metal objects to nest. Makes tapping sound with hindfeet. Eats foliage, seeds, fruit. **BREEDING** 1–2 litters of 2–6 young May–Sept. **SIGN** Large nest of sticks under log or in crevice; piles of leaves in autumn (pikas store grasses, herbs). **HABITAT** Rocky areas in all habitats, up to alpine zone. **ACTIVITY** Nocturnal, year-round.

DUSKY-FOOTED WOODRAT
Neotoma fuscipes
MOUSE AND RAT FAMILY

L 17"; T 8". Grayish brown above, gray below. Face grayish; ears medium-size, rounded. Feet dusky; toes white. Tail long, dusky above, slightly paler below, lightly furred. Brown and Black Rats have naked tails. Caches greenery, fruit, nuts, and fungi in nest chambers. **BREEDING** 1–4 young Apr.–Aug. **SIGN** Conical piles of plant cuttings below bluff; large stick houses up to 8' leaning against tree trunk or up in tree. **HABITAT** Forests; chaparral. **ACTIVITY** Nocturnal, year-round. **RANGE** Willamette Valley, sw OR.

BROWN RAT
"Norway Rat"
Rattus norvegicus
MOUSE AND RAT FAMILY

L 15"; T 7". Grayish brown above; belly gray. Ears partly hidden in fur. Tail long and scaly, a bit shorter than body. Excavates network of 3" tunnels in ground near buildings, dumps, water. Eats insects, stored grain, garbage. Introduced from Eurasia. **BREEDING** Usu. 5–6 litters of 6–10 young a year. **SIGN** Dirty holes in walls; droppings in houses; pathways to steady food supplies. Tracks: long, 5-toed hindprint forward of rounder foreprint. **HABITAT** Cities, buildings, farms. **ACTIVITY** Mostly nocturnal, year-round.

BLACK RAT
"Roof Rat"
Rattus rattus
MOUSE AND RAT FAMILY

L 16"; T 8½". All blackish (Black Rat), or brown above, light gray below (Roof Rat). Face narrow; ears large. Tail black, scaly, longer than body and head. Excellent climber. Introduced from s Asia. **BREEDING** 3–5 litters of 2–8 young a year. **SIGN** Similar to Brown Rat's. **HABITAT** Seaports, buildings, rooftops, fields, urban areas (local). **ACTIVITY** Mainly nocturnal, year-round. **RANGE** w WA, w OR.

HOUSE MOUSE
Mus musculus
MOUSE AND RAT FAMILY

L 7"; T 3". Gray or brownish tan above; gray or buffy below. Tail long, naked, with ring-like scales. **BREEDING** 2–5 litters of 3–11 young Mar.–Oct.; year-round indoors. **SIGN** Small dark droppings; musky odor; damaged materials. **HABITAT** Homes, farms, fields. **ACTIVITY** Mainly nocturnal, year-round.

SOUTHERN RED-BACKED VOLE
Clethrionomys gapperi
MOUSE AND RAT FAMILY
L 5″; T 1½″. Bright chestnut stripe above, from nose to tail; sides buffy; belly gray. Ears small; tail short. Uses runways of other voles. Varied diet of plants and fungi. **BREEDING** Several litters of 2–8 young Mar.–Oct. **HABITAT** Moist coniferous forests, bogs. **ACTIVITY** Day and night, year-round. **RANGE** Cascades, e WA, ne OR.

CREEPING VOLE
Microtus oregoni
MOUSE AND RAT FAMILY
L 5″; T 1″. Brown above, gray below; short-haired. Ears protrude from fur. Tail short, indistinctly bicolored. Seldom above ground; usu. in shallow burrows or under roots, leaves. Often uses mole runways. **BREEDING** 4–5 litters of 3–4 young Mar.–Nov. **HABITAT** Grassy, brushy edges of upland coniferous forests. **ACTIVITY** Day and night, year-round. **RANGE** Cascades and west.

TOWNSEND'S VOLE
Microtus townsendii
MOUSE AND RAT FAMILY
L 8″; T 2½″. Upperparts dark brown, sprinkled with black hairs; grayish below. Fairly large ears project above coarse fur. Feet dusky. Tail fairly long, blackish, bicolored. Good swimmer; burrow entrances often below water. **BREEDING** Several litters of 5–8 young Mar.–Oct. **SIGN** Runways in grass to 2″ deep with piles of cuttings. **HABITAT** Fields, moist meadows, marshy areas. **ACTIVITY** Day and night, year-round. **RANGE** Cascades and west.

SAGEBRUSH VOLE
Lemmiscus curtatus
MOUSE AND RAT FAMILY
L 5″; T ¾″. Ashy gray above, silvery below. Nose and small ears buff. Feet silvery. Tail very short. Feeds on grasses in summer; bark, twigs, and roots in winter. **BREEDING** Several litters of 2–11 young Apr.–Nov. **SIGN** Colonial burrow entrances under bush clumps. **HABITAT** Sagebrush and bunchgrass flats. **ACTIVITY** Day and night, year-round. **RANGE** East of Cascades.

COMMON MUSKRAT
Ondatra zibethicus
MOUSE AND RAT FAMILY

L 23″; T 10″. Fur rich brown, dense, glossy; belly silver. Eyes and ears small. Hindfeet partially webbed, larger than forefeet. Tail long, scaly, blackish, vertically flattened, tapering to a point. Excellent steady swimmer, with head, back, and sculling tail visible. Mainly eats aquatic vegetation. **BREEDING** 2–3 litters of usu. 6–7 young Apr.–Sept. **SIGN** Conspicuous "lodge" of cattails, roots, and mud floats in marsh or other body of water; rises up to 3′ above water surface; burrows in stream banks. Tracks: 2–3″ narrow hindprint (5 toes print); smaller round foreprint; often with tail drag mark. **HABITAT** Freshwater marshes, ponds, lakes, canals. **ACTIVITY** Day and night; lodge-bound on coldest days.

PACIFIC JUMPING MOUSE
Zapus trinotatus
JUMPING MOUSE FAMILY

L 9½″; T 5½″. Wide, olive-brown stripe on back; sides yellowish brown; white below. Ears fairly large. Very large hindfeet. Tail very long, dark above, white below. Agile jumper to 4′; uses tail for balance. When flushed in daytime, may be mistaken for frog. **BREEDING** 1–2 litters of 3–7 young May–Sept. **HABITAT** Wet meadows, marshes, forests. **ACTIVITY** Mainly nocturnal; hibernates Oct.–Apr. **RANGE** Cascades and west.

COMMON PORCUPINE
Erethizon dorsatum
NEW WORLD PORCUPINE FAMILY

L 33″; T 8″. Blackish. Long wiry guard hairs on front half of body; thousands of shorter, heavier quills (hairs modified into sharp, mostly hollow spines) on front of body but mainly on rump and longish rounded tail; underfur long, soft, wooly. Back high-arching; legs short. Soles of feet knobbed; claws long, curved; walks pigeon-toed on ground. Eats green plants, and twigs, buds, and bark of trees; sometimes damages wooden buildings and poles. **VOICE** Squeals and grunts. **BREEDING** 1 young Apr.–June. **SIGN** Tooth marks on bark; irreg. patches of bark stripped from tree trunks and limbs. Tracks: inward-facing, up to 3″; claw tips well forward. Scat: piles of variably shaped pellets near crevice or base of feeding tree. **HABITAT** Forests, esp. coniferous, and open areas. **ACTIVITY** Mainly nocturnal, year-round.

Carnivores

Members of the order Carnivora eat meat, although many also eat fruit, berries, and vegetation. They have long canine teeth for stabbing prey, and most have sharp cheek teeth for slicing meat. None truly hibernate, but several retire to well-insulated logs and burrows to sleep soundly during colder parts of the winter. Most live on land, although otters spend most of their time in water, and seals and sea lions (covered with other marine mammals, page 362) haul out on land mainly for mating and giving birth. Most carnivores have a single yearly litter of offspring, which are born blind and receive many months to a year or more of parental care. The Northwest's carnivore families include bears, dogs (foxes and the Coyote), weasels (skunks, otters, badgers, martens, and the Mink), raccoons, cats, eared seals (fur seals, sea lions), and hair seals.

COYOTE
Canis latrans
DOG FAMILY

H 25″; L 4′; T 13″. Coat long, coarse; grizzled gray, buffy, and black. Muzzle long, narrow, brownish; ears rufous. Legs long; tail long, bushy, black-tipped. Runs up to 40 mph. Eats small mammals, birds, frogs, snakes. Only large carnivore to persist in heavily settled areas. **VOICE** Bark; flat howl; series of *yip* notes followed by wavering howl. **BREEDING** 4–8 pups in spring. **SIGN** 24″ den mouths on slopes. Tracks: dog-like, but in nearly straight line; foreprint larger, 2⅜″. Scat: dog-like, but usu. full of hair. **HABITAT** Open plains, scrub deserts, farms, urban areas, forests (rare). **ACTIVITY** Day and night, year-round.

RED FOX
Vulpes vulpes
DOG FAMILY

H 15″; L 3′2″; T 14″. 3 color morphs: rusty orange with white underparts, black legs and feet; mostly blackish; gray-brown with black markings above. Muzzle narrow; ears pointed, blackish. Tail long, bushy, white-tipped. Eats rodents, rabbits, birds, insects, berries, fruit. Has strong scent. **VOICE** Gives short *yap* and long howls. **BREEDING** 1–10 young Mar.–Apr. **SIGN** Den often a rodent burrow on a rise, with entrance enlarged to 3′. Tracks: foreprint slightly larger, 2⅛″; 4 toe pads print. **HABITAT** Brushy and open areas in forested regions. **ACTIVITY** Mainly nocturnal, year-round. **RANGE** West of Cascades, ne OR.

COMMON GRAY FOX
Urocyon cinereoargenteus
DOG FAMILY

H 15″; L 3′2″; T 13″. Grizzled silvery gray above; throat and mid-belly white; collar, lower sides, legs, sides of tail rusty; top and tip of tail black. Eats rabbits, rodents, birds, grasshoppers, fruit, berries. Often climbs trees, unlike Red Fox and Coyote. **BREEDING** 2–7 young in summer. **SIGN** Den hidden in natural crevice in woods; often has snagged hair and bone scraps near entrance. Tracks: foreprint 1½″; hindprint slightly narrower. **HABITAT** Wooded and brushy areas. **ACTIVITY** Mainly nocturnal, year-round. **RANGE** w half of OR.

BLACK BEAR
Ursus americanus
BEAR FAMILY

H 3′4″; L 5′; T 4″; female much smaller. Heavy, bulky. Head round; muzzle long, brownish; ears short, rounded. Legs long. Tail tiny. Black, long-haired, often with white patch on chest. Some individuals cinnamon brown. More vegetarian than most carnivores; eats inner layer of tree bark, berries, fruit, plants, honeycombs, insects in rotten logs, and vertebrates, incl. fish and small mammals. Powerful swimmer and climber; can run up to 30 mph. **CAUTION** Do not feed, approach, or get between one and its food or cubs; will usu. flee, but can cause serious injury. Campers must firmly seal up food. **BREEDING** Usu. 2 cubs, about ½ lb at birth, born in den Jan.–Feb. **SIGN** Torn-apart stumps; turned-over boulders; torn-up burrows; hair on shaggy-barked trees. Tracks: foreprints 5″ wide; hindprints up to 9″ long. Scat: dog-like. **HABITAT** Forests, swamps, brushy hillsides. **ACTIVITY** Mainly nocturnal, but often out in daytime; does not hibernate. **Grizzly Bear** *(U. arctos),* of ne WA mtns. (very rare), larger, with humped shoulders; dark brown, with frosted hairs.

COMMON RACCOON
Procyon lotor
RACCOON FAMILY

L 32"; T 9". Coat long and thick, grizzled grayish brown. Black mask below white eyebrow; white sides on narrow muzzle. Legs medium-length; paws buffy; flexible toes used for climbing trees and washing food. Tail ⅓ body length, thick, banded yellow-brown and black. Swims well; can run up to 15 mph. Omnivorous; feeds in upland and aquatic habitats; raids trash bins. **BREEDING** Usu. 4 young Apr.–May. **SIGN** Den in hollow tree or crevice. Tracks: flat-footed; hindprint much longer than wide, 4"; foreprint rounded, 3"; claws show on all 5 toes. **HABITAT** Forests and scrub near water; towns, cities. **ACTIVITY** Mainly nocturnal, but sometimes seen in daytime; dens up in winter; active in milder periods.

AMERICAN MARTEN
Martes americana
WEASEL FAMILY

L 24"; T 9"; female smaller. Fur soft, dense; entirely brown; throat and chest buffy orange. Snout pointed; ears small, rounded. Legs medium-length; feet heavily clawed. Tail bushy, fairly long, dark brown. Feeds on voles, squirrels, birds, berries. Active on ground and in trees. **VOICE** Vocal: variety of growls, screams, whines. **BREEDING** 2–5 young Mar.–Apr. in hollow tree or usurped burrow. **SIGN** Prints round, 1¾". **HABITAT** Spruce, fir, and hemlock forests. **ACTIVITY** Late afternoon to early morning, year-round. **RANGE** Cascades and west; e mtns.

SHORT-TAILED WEASEL
"Ermine"
Mustela erminea
WEASEL FAMILY

L 11"; T 2"; female smaller. Summer: brown above; underparts, inside of legs, and feet white; tail has brown base, black tip. Winter: white, with black tail tip. Neck long; legs short; tail thin, furred. Expert mouser; also takes rabbits, birds, frogs, insects. Tireless, active hunter; hunts by smell and sight. **BREEDING** 4–9 young in Apr. **SIGN** Spiral scat along trails. Tracks: similar to Long-tailed Weasel's, but usu. slightly smaller. **HABITAT** Brush, fields, wetlands. **ACTIVITY** Day and night, year-round.

LONG-TAILED WEASEL
Mustela frenata
WEASEL FAMILY

L 16"; T 5"; female smaller. Summer: brown above, white below; feet and outside of legs brown; tail thin, furred, with brown base, black tip. Winter: inland individuals white, with black tail tip. Neck long; legs short. Wraps sinewy body around prey as it kills by biting base of skull. Good swimmer and climber. **BREEDING** 6–8 young Apr.–May. **SIGN** Cache of dead rodents under log; drag marks in snow. Tracks: hindprint ¾" wide, 1" long; foreprint a bit wider, half as long. **HABITAT** Woodlands, brush, fields. **ACTIVITY** Day and night, year-round. **RANGE** w WA, w OR, mtns. of e WA and ne OR.

MINK
Mustela vison
WEASEL FAMILY

L 21"; T 7"; female smaller. Lustrous blackish brown above and below; chin white. Muzzle pointed; ears tiny; legs short; tail fairly long, bushy. (Weasels are white below; have thinner tails.) Swims often; feeds mainly on fish, some birds, rodents, frogs; often travels far in search of food. **BREEDING** 3–4 young Apr.–May. **SIGN** Holes in snow (where Mink has pounced on vole). 4" burrow entrances in stream bank. Tracks: round, 2", in snow. **HABITAT** Freshwater shores. **ACTIVITY** Late afternoon to early morning, year-round; dens up in coldest, stormiest periods.

AMERICAN BADGER
Taxidea taxus
WEASEL FAMILY
L 28"; T 5". Body wide, flattish. Shaggy, gray-brown above; white below. Snout upturned, black; white stripe from nose to midback. Legs short, black; strong claws. Tail bushy, yellowish. Moves clumsily. Digs up burrowing snakes, rodents. **BREEDING** 1–5 young in Apr. **SIGN** Burrow entrance 12" wide; nearby mound of bones, fur, dung. Tracks: toes point inward; prints round, 2". **HABITAT** Grasslands, sagebrush, open juniper and pine woodlands. **ACTIVITY** Day and night, year-round. **RANGE** East of Cascades.

WESTERN SPOTTED SKUNK
Spilogale gracilis
WEASEL FAMILY
L 16"; T 6". Body black, with several long, wavy, white stripes. Head small, black with small white spots; ears tiny, at sides of head. Feet short, black. Tail short for a skunk, bushy, black with white tip. If threatened, stands on forepaws; can spray foul-smelling liquid to 13'. **BREEDING** 4–7 young in June. **SIGN** Lingering stench. Tracks: like Striped Skunk's, but smaller. **HABITAT** Woodlands, scrub, farms. **ACTIVITY** Nocturnal; dens up during winter. **RANGE** West of Cascades, se WA, e OR.

STRIPED SKUNK
Mephitis mephitis
WEASEL FAMILY
L 24"; T 9". Coat thick, fluffy, mainly black; large white nape patch continues as 2 stripes along sides of back, usu. reaching long bushy tail; narrow white forehead stripe. Head pointed; ears and eyes small. In some individuals, most of upper back and tail white. If threatened, raises tail, backs up, may stomp ground; may emit foul-smelling, sulphurous spray that travels to 15', stings eyes of predators, pets, humans. Eats insects, rodents, bird and turtle eggs, fruit, roadkills, garbage. **CAUTION** Can turn and spray in an instant. **BREEDING** 6–7 young in May. **SIGN** Foul odor if one has sprayed or been run over recently. Scratched-up lawns and garbage bags. Tracks: round foreprint 1"; hindprint broader at front, flat-footed, 1½". **HABITAT** Woodlands, fields, towns. **ACTIVITY** Dusk to dawn; dens up and sleeps much of winter.

NORTHERN RIVER OTTER
Lutra canadensis
WEASEL FAMILY

L 3'7"; T 16". Fur dense, dark brown, often silvery on chin and chest. Ears and eyes small. Legs short; feet webbed. Tail long, thick-based, tapering to a point. Swims rapidly, stops with head raised out of water. Eats fish, frogs, turtles, muskrats. Runs well on land; loves to exercise and play; wanders widely. **BREEDING** Mates in water; 2–3 young born blind

but furred in Apr. **SIGN** 12" wide slides on sloping muddy riverbanks in flat areas; vegetation flattened in large patch for rolling, feeding, defecating; trails between bodies of water. Tracks: 3", toes fanned. **HABITAT** Clean rivers, wood-edged ponds and lakes. **ACTIVITY** Day and night, year-round.

MOUNTAIN LION
"Cougar" "Puma"
Felis concolor
CAT FAMILY

H 30"; L 8'; T 30"; female smaller. Tawny reddish or grayish above, whitish below. Head fairly small; dark spot at base of whiskers; ears erect, blackish on back; neck fairly long. Legs long; paws wide; claws long, sharp, retractile. Tail long, blackish at end. Young longer-tailed than Bobcat; dark-spotted for 1st 6 months. Feeds on deer, rabbits, large rodents and birds. Solitary terri-torial hunter, ex. for mother with older cubs and during 2-week breeding period; good climber. **VOICE** Screams, hisses, growls. **CAUTION** Shy of humans, but fatal attacks have occurred. **BREEDING** 2–4 young in July every other year. **SIGN** Scratch marks left 6–10' up on tree; piles of dirt and leaves urinated on by male. Tracks: round; 4 toe prints show no claws. **HABITAT** Semiarid canyons and mtns.; forests. **ACTIVITY** Mainly nocturnal, year-round.

LYNX
Lynx lynx
CAT FAMILY

H 23″; L 3′; T 4″. Coat buffy grayish with few black hairs. Facial ruff whitish with black streaks; ears have pointed black tufts. Legs long, buffy; feet very large, well-furred to serve as snowshoes. Tail short, outer third black. Climbs trees to rest; pounces down on prey. Feeds mainly on Snowshoe Hare. **BREEDING** 2–3 young May–June. **SIGN** Tracks: prints 3½″; shows 4 toes, no claws. **HABITAT** Deep coniferous forests with thickets. **ACTIVITY** Nocturnal, year-round. **RANGE** ne WA; Cascades (rare).

BOBCAT
Lynx rufus
CAT FAMILY

H 20″; L 33″; T 4″. Orange-brown in summer, paler grayish in winter; black spots and bars on long legs and rear; underparts and inside of legs white. Face wide and flat; black lines radiate onto facial ruff; ears slightly tufted, backside black. Tail bobbed. Stalks and ambushes birds and small mammals. **VOICE** Yowls and screams (though mostly silent). **BREEDING** 2–3 young in May. **SIGN** Tracks in snow at scent posts and scratching trees. Tracks: like domestic cat's, but 2″ vs. 1″. **HABITAT** All terrestrial habitats. **ACTIVITY** Mainly nocturnal, year-round.

Hoofed Mammals

Most hoofed mammals worldwide are in the order Artiodactyla, the even-toed ungulates. (Ungulates are mammals that have hooves, an adaptation for running. The order Perissodactyla—the odd-toed ungulates: horses, zebras, rhinos, and tapirs—has no extant native species in North America.) Even-toed ungulates have a split, two-part hoof (actually two modified toes) and two small dewclaws (vestigial toes) above the hoof on the rear of the leg. Their lower incisors are adapted for nipping or tearing vegetation, their molars for grinding it. Most hastily swallow their food, which is stored temporarily in the first compartment of their four-chambered stomachs before passing to the second stomach, where it is shaped into small pellets of partly digested plant fiber (the cud). While the animal is at rest, the cud is returned to the mouth, slowly chewed to pulp, and swallowed; it then passes through all four chambers of the stomach. This process allows an animal to feed quickly, reducing its exposure to predators, and afterward chew its cud in a concealed spot.

Members of the deer family (Cervidae) have paired bony antlers that grow, usually only on males, in summer, at which time they are soft and tender, and covered with a fine-haired skin ("velvet") containing a network of blood vessels that nourishes the growing bone beneath. By late summer the antlers reach full size, and the velvety skin dries up and peels off. The bare antlers then serve as sexual ornaments; rival males may use them as weapons in courtship battles in fall. As winter nears the antlers fall off. As long as an individual has an adequate diet, its antlers become larger and have more points each year. The Pronghorn, the sole species in its family (Antilocapridae), has permanent short horns, each with one broad, short prong jutting forward; the horns develop keratin sheaths that are shed each year. Cattle, goats, and sheep (family Bovidae) have permanent horns that grow continuously.

ELK
"Wapiti"
Cervus elaphus
DEER FAMILY

H 5'; L 9'; T 6". Pale gray, brown, or tan. Neck thick, chestnut brown; shaggy on buck. Head and muzzle brown; nose black. Summer buck develops large antlers: 2 rear-projecting beams up to 5' long, with 6 upward-projecting points along each beam; sheds antlers in early winter. Legs long, brown; hooves black. Rump and very short tail white. Juv. spotted for 1st 3 months. Roosevelt race, which lives west of Cascades, darker, with heavy crowning antlers, longer skull. Rocky Mountain race, of Cascades and interior, lighter in color, with lighter spreading antlers, broader skull. Moves silently in woods; can run up to 35 mph. Very social; bull herds on fringes of cow/calf herds; combined herd can contain up to 400 animals. "Wapiti" is Shawnee word for "white (or pale) deer," alluding to light sides of Rocky Mountain race. **VOICE** Vocal: bull in fall gives low bellow followed by far-carrying whistle; cow whistles in spring. **BREEDING** Mates Sept.–Nov.; 1–2 young June–July. **SIGN** Buck thrashes saplings and polishes antlers on small tree trunks during rut. Muddy wallows that smell of urine. Tracks: 4½" "split hearts," larger than those of deer; dewclaws behind hooves often print. **HABITAT** Summer: high mtn. pastures. Rest of year: deep forests at lower elevs. **ACTIVITY** Day and night, year-round. **RANGE** West of Cascades; e WA, e OR (local).

MULE DEER
"Black-tailed Deer"
Odocoileus hemionus
DEER FAMILY

H 3′4″; L 7′; T 8″. Reddish brown in summer, light gray-brown in winter. White muzzle and eye ring contrast with black nose and eyes; ears large, mule-like. Legs slender, buffy. In summer, buck develops antlers: 2 upward-angled beams fork twice into total of 4 points per beam. Rocky Mountain race, of Cascades and interior, has white rump extending above white, black-tipped tail. Coastal race ("Black-tailed Deer,"pictured), chiefly west of Cascades, is smaller, darker; top of blackish tail merges with dark back. Juv. of both races spotted. Runs with stiff-legged, bounding gait. In winter, forms small herds of both sexes. **BREEDING** Mates Oct.–Jan.; 1–2 young June–Aug. **SIGN** Browse marks; buck rubs. Tracks: narrow "split hearts," male's 3¼″; female's 2⅝″. **HABITAT** Forests; sagebrush meadows. **ACTIVITY** Day and night (mostly nocturnal where hunted), year-round.

WHITE-TAILED DEER
Odocoileus virginianus
DEER FAMILY

H 3′3″; L 6′; T 12″. Rich reddish brown in summer, gray-brown in winter. Neck long; ears large; legs long; tail fairly long. Nose and hooves black. Ring around nose, eye ring, throat, midbelly, and underside of tail white. Summer male develops antlers with main beam curving out and up, points issuing from it. Fawn reddish orange, with many white spots. Flees with tail erect, white underfur exposed. **BREEDING** Mates Oct.–Nov.; 1–2 fawns in late spring; nibble greens at 2–3 weeks; weaned at 4 months. **SIGN** Raggedly browsed vegetation along well-worn trails; buck rubs, where male rubs bark off with antlers; flattened beds in grass or snow. Tracks: 2–3″ "split hearts," with narrow, pointed end forward, dots of dewclaws behind. Scat: ¾″ cylindrical dark pellets. **HABITAT** Broadleaf and mixed woodlands and edges, shrubs, fields, watersides. **ACTIVITY** Day and night, year-round. **RANGE** e WA, lower Columbia R.; OR (local).

PRONGHORN
"Antelope"
Antilocapra americana
PRONGHORN FAMILY

H 3′4″; L 4′6″; T 4″. Pale reddish tan above, white below. Neck tan with 2 partial white collars; buck has short black mane. Head tan and white; eyes large; ears pointed. Horns black, straight; doe's 3″, male's 6″. Each summer and fall, adult male grows a hard sheath another 9″ high that tapers to a point and has a separate forward prong; it is shed in winter. Legs long, tan on outside. Rump white; tail short. Can run at 30 mph for 15 miles, with spurts to 70 mph. **BREEDING** Mates Sept.–Oct.; 1–2 young May–June. **SIGN** Tracks: "split hearts," about 3″. **HABITAT** Dry open grasslands with sagebrush and bunchgrass. **ACTIVITY** Day and night, year-round. **RANGE** se OR.

MOUNTAIN GOAT
Oreamnos americanus
CATTLE, GOAT, AND SHEEP FAMILY

H 3'6"; L 5'; T 6". Coat entirely white or yellowish white; long and shaggy in winter, shorter in summer. Raised hump at shoulders. Head rectangular; nose wide, black; beard below muzzle; ears pointed. Horns black, thin, dagger-like, with slight backward curl; male's to 12", female's to 8". Legs thick; hooves black, sharp on edges, with rubbery soles for traction. Tail short. Amazingly agile in navigating narrowest cliff ledges. **BREEDING** Mates Nov.–Dec.; 1–2 young May–June. **SIGN** White hair snagged on plants and rocks. Tracks: widely splayed in front; 2½–3½". **HABITAT** Steep rocky mountainsides; often above timberline, but moves lower in winter. **ACTIVITY** Day and night, year-round. **RANGE** WA Cascades; ne WA, ne OR (local); introduced to Olympics (where it is overgrazing rare alpine plants).

BIGHORN SHEEP
"Mountain Sheep"
Ovis canadensis
CATTLE, GOAT, AND SHEEP FAMILY

H 3'4"; L 5'6"; T 5". Coat brown; belly whitish. Muzzle whitish; ears small, rounded. Horns brown; male's extremely thick, ridged, curved backward, encircle ear; female's shorter, more slender, form half circle. Neck very thick. Legs sturdy, leading edges black; hooves black, sharp on edges, with rubbery soles for traction on rocks. Rump white; tail dark brown, short. Summer: small segregated herds of 3–5 rams, 5–15 ewes; winter: sexes join in herds of hundreds. Rams have autumn head-butting contests that last up to 20 hours, are audible for miles. **BREEDING** Mates Oct.–Dec.; 1 young May–June. **SIGN** Snagged long brown hair along steep trails. Tracks: splayed 3–3½" hoofprints, less pointed than deer's. **HABITAT** Lightly wooded canyons. **ACTIVITY** By day, year-round. **RANGE** e WA, e OR (local).

Marine Mammals

Marine mammals—seals, sea lions, and Walrus (order Carnivora), and whales and dolphins (order Cetacea)—mainly live in ocean waters. Seals are covered with fine dense fur and insulating layers of fat; their legs have been modified into front and rear flippers. Fast swimmers when waterborne and chasing fish, seals spend weeks or months at sea but will haul out when near shore or when tending their young, which are born on beaches and seaside rocks. Seals and sea lions of the eared seal family (Otariidae) have external ear flaps and lack nails on their forelimbs; they can move fairly fast on land, walking on all four limbs. Seals of the hair (or earless) seal family (Phocidae) lack ear flaps, have shorter necks and limbs, and have claws on all flippers; they move slowly on land, humping their bodies and dragging their rear flippers. Cetaceans (dolphins, porpoises, and whales) have thick hairless skin and insulating layers of blubber. Their front legs have been modified into flippers. The tail ends in wide, horizontally flattened flukes used for propulsion. They breathe through one or two nostrils, called blowholes, on the top of the head; the cloud of vapor exhaled is called a spout or a blow. Cetaceans can dive deep and swim fast; larger species can remain submerged for lengthy periods. Most smaller species prey on large fish, while many of the larger whales are equipped with broom-like structures called baleen through which they strain water for schools of tiny fish and krill. The baleen whales have throat grooves (pleats) that can expand when the animal takes in a vast amount of water and prey, and contract as water strains out. Cetaceans never haul out on land; their young are born live in the water.

Lengths given in the following accounts are from the tip of the snout to the end of the tail (or flukes).

NORTHERN SEA LION
"Steller Sea Lion"
Eumetopias jubatus
EARED SEAL FAMILY

Male 10′; female 7′. Heavy, larger than California Sea Lion. Ears visible, small; tail tiny. Male buff above, reddish brown below; flippers blackish; neck and forequarters massive; forehead sloping. Female uniformly brown; body cylindrical. Young blackish. Fairly quiet at colonies; shier, more easily disturbed than California Sea Lion. Major population drop in recent years; only a few scattered colonies in NW. **BREEDING** Mates May–Aug.; 1 young late May–June in colony. **HABITAT** Deep and shallow ocean waters; enters major rivers. **ACTIVITY** Hauls out on rocks by day; feeds mainly at night. **RANGE** Summer: NW coast. Winter: moves into protected waters, such as San Juan Is.

NORTHERN FUR SEAL
"Alaska Fur Seal"
Callorhinus ursinus
EARED SEAL FAMILY

Male 7′; female 4′. Heavy; flippers large; tail tiny. Face blunter than sea lions'; ears small, visible. Male blackish above, reddish below; shoulders and front of neck gray-washed; neck greatly swollen; forehead high. Female gray above, reddish below. Sleeps on ocean surface on its back with black front and rear flippers touching in cup-handle shape; often swims with 1 flipper waving in air. **BREEDING** Breeds on Pribilof Islands of Bering Sea and in w Alaska. **HABITAT** Deep ocean waters; rarely on shore in NW. **ACTIVITY** Feeds mainly at night. **RANGE** Winter (Nov.–Apr.): off NW (almost all females).

CALIFORNIA SEA LION
Zalophus californianus
EARED SEAL FAMILY

Male 7′; female 6′. Heavy, smaller than Northern Sea Lion. Ears small, pointed; tail tiny. Male dark brown, with blackish flippers; neck and forequarters enlarged; forehead high. Female yellow-brown, with brownish flippers; body cylindrical; forehead sloping. Young blackish. Playful. Numbers increasing in recent years; becoming a nuisance at salmon runs at river mouths. **VOICE** Vocal: noisy, honking barks. **BREEDING** In CA. **HABITAT** Shallow ocean waters, sea caves, rocks, beaches; often hauls out on floating buoys, platforms. **ACTIVITY** Day and night, year-round. **RANGE** Winter (Nov.–Apr.): nonbreeders along NW coast, mostly in protected waters.

HARBOR SEAL
Phoca vitulina
HAIR SEAL FAMILY

5′. Appears neckless. Color varies: pale or dark brown or gray; may have dark spots and whitish rings. Wide face has short, dog-like muzzle; nostrils V-shaped; eyes large, round, black. Playful, shy, curious in water. Feeds on incoming and high tides; hauls out at low tide. May follow fish runs up rivers. **VOICE** Can be noisy: snorts, growls, barks, grunts. **BREEDING** 1 pup Apr.–May, in small colonies. **HABITAT** Shallow ocean waters; hauls out on rocks, spits, islands. **ACTIVITY** Day and night. **RANGE** NW coast.

GRAY WHALE
Eschrichtius robustus
GRAY WHALE FAMILY

40′. Tapered at both ends; mottled shades of gray. Back lacks fin, has series of 6 bumps. Head narrow, triangular; slopes steeply from 2 blowholes; 2–4 throat grooves. Mouth curves slightly upward; baleen plates yellowish white. Clouds water as it scours sea bottoms for invertebrates. Numbers rebounding. **BREEDING** 1 young, usu. in Baja CA lagoons in winter. **SIGN** Spout quick, low, about 10′ high. **HABITAT** Inshore ocean waters. **RANGE** Nov.–Jan.: migrates southbound offshore. Feb.–June: migrates northbound nearshore.

MINKE WHALE
Balaenoptera acutorostrata
RORQUAL FAMILY

25′. Fairly slender; head smallish; snout pointed. Dark blue-gray above, white below. Baleen plates yellowish white; about 50 throat grooves. Flippers pointed, smallish; white band above; white below. Dorsal fin two-thirds of way back on body; swept-back, with pointed, curved tip. Tail dark above, white below. Swims under boats and ships. **BREEDING** 9′ young born in winter. **SIGN** Spout single, short, with rounded vapor cloud. **HABITAT** Inshore waters. **RANGE** Resident on NW coast and in Puget Sound.

HUMPBACK WHALE
Megaptera novaeangliae
RORQUAL FAMILY

45′. Blackish above, white below. Head adorned with fleshy bumps and barnacles; throat has about 25 massive grooves. Small hump just in front of leading edge of rounded dorsal fin; when diving, back angles down sharply after dorsal fin. Extremely long, white flippers: 15′, with fleshy knobs along leading edge. Tail variously patterned, with white below; variations help researchers identify individuals (hundreds have been catalogued). Sometimes playful and active. Only large whale that regularly breaches (jumps clear out of the water), rolls, and then comes crashing down. Also rolls on surface from side to side, slapping long flippers, and performs head-down "lobtail," slapping flukes down. Creates cylindrical "net" of rising air bubbles deep down that confuses and walls in schools of small fish; whale then rises up with mouth open inside the "net." **BREEDING** Gestation 1 year; 1 young, 16′ at birth, born in tropics; stays with mother 1 year. **SIGN** Spout is expanding column up to 20′ high. **HABITAT** Ocean. **RANGE** Sept.–Nov.: migrates off NW coast; visits Puget Sound.

KILLER WHALE
"Orca"
Orcinus orca
OCEAN DOLPHIN FAMILY

Male 28′; female 20′. Male more robust than female. Head rounded, broad, without beak; teeth large, pointed. Male dorsal fin huge, tall, erect, appears to lean forward; female's smaller, swept-back. Both sexes shiny black, with large white oval spot above and behind eye; white throat; white patch on belly and rear side. Flukes black above, usu. white below. At top of oceanic food chain. Feeds on seals and sea lions, large fish, birds, occ. young and even adult whales. 3 resident pods in Puget Sound collectively number 60–90 individuals. **CAUTION** Unpredictable; do not harass; leave water when they are nearby. **BREEDING** 1 young born every 3–10 years. **HABITAT** Surface ocean waters, deep sounds. **RANGE** NW coast, Puget Sound.

NORTHERN RIGHT-WHALE DOLPHIN
Lissodelphis borealis
OCEAN DOLPHIN FAMILY

To 10′. Elongated, slender, tapers to very narrow base of tail. No bulge on forehead or chin; upper beak shorter than lower. All black ex. for white lower beak and variably-sized white patch below black flipper. Lacks dorsal fin. Occurs in pods of up to 100. Rides bow waves of ships. **BREEDING** 1 young probably born in spring. **HABITAT** Deep ocean waters. **RANGE** Off NW coast.

PACIFIC WHITE-SIDED DOLPHIN
Lagenorhynchus obliquidens
OCEAN DOLPHIN FAMILY

7'. Elongated. Head rounded down to short black beak. Back black; belly white; sides have blurry-edged grayish-white areas above flippers and before tail. Dorsal fin at midback; swept-back; black forward edge, gray trailing edge. Flukes black. Black stripe from jaw past black flippers to anus. Occurs in herds of up to 2,000. **BREEDING** 1 young born in summer. **HABITAT** Deeper offshore waters. **RANGE** Off NW coast.

DALL'S PORPOISE
Phocoenoides dalli
PORPOISE FAMILY

6'. Forehead slopes steeply to short beak with small mouth. All shiny black, ex. for large, white, oval patch on side. Dorsal fin triangular with wide base; often pale-tipped. Tail keeled, vertically flattened with wavy top edge. Flukes small, black. Occurs in herds of up to 20. Very fast swimmer; sends up large, hydroplane-like "rooster tails" of spray when surfacing. Commonly seen from ferries off WA. **BREEDING** 1 young born in summer. **HABITAT** Offshore waters, sounds, deep straits. **RANGE** NW coast; enters n Puget Sound.

Parks and Preserves

Introduction

The Pacific Northwest states of Washington and Oregon contain considerable natural beauty within their 165,173 square miles: rocky headlands along the Pacific, moss-strewn rain forests, snow-crowned and forested mountains, explosive volcanoes, broad inland waterways, glacial lakes, and other assorted geological and biological wonders. Whether your interests are in geology, glaciers, fossil formations, rain forests, tidepools, wildflowers, butterflies, reptiles, birds, or mammals, this region offers wonderful opportunities of nearly endless variety.

Mount Spokane State Park

The 50 featured parks and reserves and the supplementary listings selected for Washington and Oregon have been grouped into three subregions in each state. Both states' subregions are defined in terms of the Cascade Range, the Pacific Northwest's cardinal topographic feature. We begin with the area of Washington west of the Cascades, then cover the Cascades of Washington, and then dry eastern Washington. We cover the subregions of Oregon in the same sequence: the western side, then the Cascades, and lastly the area east of the Cascades.

Selecting just 50 sites to detail in a region with such a wealth and variety of natural areas is no small challenge. Regional importance, wildlife and habitat uniqueness and variety, natural beauty, accessibility, and other factors all played a role. The annotated listings might be thought of as alternatives rather than lesser sites.

Mailing addresses and phone numbers are given for all sites (most will send brochures or other information), and driving directions are given for the 50 featured sites. We give locations of visitor centers (V.C.) for those areas that have them. Since fees and exact hours of operation change frequently, they are not included in the listings, although seasonal access is noted. Planning ahead for visits to more remote sites, or to those where weather or hunting seasons may affect access, or to popular sites with limited facilities, is highly recommended.

This guide highlights some of the predominant plants and animals you may see as you visit the parks and preserves, but always ask if local lists of flora and fauna are available, as these can help pin down identifications.

Western Washington

This area occupies the northwestern corner of the Pacific Northwest, from the outer coast to the Cascade foothills, and from the Strait of Juan de Fuca to the Columbia River. We include here Washington's Pacific coastline, the Olympic Peninsula, and the Puget Sound area. This region occupies the wetter side of the Cascade Range in terms of rainfall, and claims the only temperate rain forest in the lower 48 states. It is defined by water, bordering the Pacific in the west and the Strait of Juan de Fuca in the north, with Puget Sound running down its midsection and a host of river drainages flowing into it from the Cascades and the Olympics.

The Olympic Mountains rise up in the heart of the Olympic Peninsula as a craggy realm of forested and glaciated peaks. Near the northern end sits the Hurricane Ridge area of Olympic National Park. Over 5,000 feet high, this vertical wall of mountains stops moisture coming off the ocean, causing up to 14 feet of rain to fall each year on the lush Hoh Rain Forest on the wet seaward slopes of the range. These same mountains create a rain shadow to the east, where the long, narrow spit at Dungeness National Wildlife Refuge on the Strait of Juan de Fuca and the bluffs of San Juan Island National Historical Park are lucky to get 18 inches of moisture per year. At the northern end of Puget Sound, the upland woods and rocky shorelines of Deception Pass State Park also sit in the rain shadow, while the western and southern edges of Puget Sound feature low-elevation tidelands, marshes, and varied upland habitats.

Farther south along the coast, Grays Harbor National Wildlife Refuge sits on tidal flats at the inner recesses of the estuary of the same name, while Oyhut Wildlife Area hugs the mouth of Grays Harbor near the tip of Ocean Shores Peninsula. Still farther south is Willapa National Wildlife Refuge, which protects outer coast, marsh, and tidal flat habitats.

OLYMPIC NATIONAL PARK   **Port Angeles**

Bigleaf Maples covered with moss, Hoh Rain Forest

The largest national park in the Pacific Northwest region, Olympic National Park has a long list of attractions. Occupying about half of the Olympic Peninsula, the main part of the park encompasses 835,000 acres; a narrow strip along the coast extends 57 miles. Olympic National Forest surrounds much of the park. While the jagged, snow-capped peaks of the Olympic Mountains are the centerpiece, the park sustains three distinct ecosystems: an undeveloped marine coast, a temperate rain forest, and a complex series of mountain life zones, some at over 6,000 feet elevation.

The Olympic coastal strip, which extends southward from Cape Alava (the westernmost point of the U.S. mainland), is principally a hiker's milieu, except for the southernmost 10 miles, which border Highway 101. The coastal scenery is adorned with sea stacks, cliffs, rocky shorelines, sand and cobble beaches, and masses of driftwood. Wildflowers bloom in the wet meadows, albino Mule Deer are often seen along the boardwalk trails from Ozette Ranger Station, and a few Sea Otters may be spotted feeding in the kelp beds along the coast. Tidepools can be explored near Rialto and Kalaloch Beaches, Gray Whales migrate along the coast in spring, and Bald Eagles are common residents. Hikers along the coast must keep track of tide schedules to avoid being trapped by incoming tides.

Hoh Rain Forest offers an utterly different natural world. The immense vertical barrier of the Olympic Range stops enough precipitation coming off the ocean to drop about 12 to 14 feet of rain per year on the forest. Dense stands of enormous conifers, particularly Sitka Spruce and Western Red Cedar, surround the Hoh Visitor Center and part of the entrance road. Look among the intense greenness of lush ferns and mosses for nurse logs, fallen trees that serve as nursery beds for future trees. The short Hall of Mosses Trail features enormous Bigleaf Maples overhung with Licorice Ferns and Oregon Spikemoss, resembling giant columns in a cathedral. Fauna here includes Roughskin Newts and other salamanders, Winter Wrens, Northern Pygmy-Owls, endangered Northern Spotted Owls, Pileated Woodpeckers, Townsend's Chipmunks, and the Roosevelt race of Elk. An interpretive hike along the Spruce Nature Trail illustrates the birth of a forest. The 18½-mile Hoh River Trail leads to Blue Glacier on Mount Olympus.

The main visitor center near park headquarters is an ideal start-

Cape Alava

ing point for the 17-mile drive up to Hurricane Ridge, near the northern edge of the Olympic Mountains. The sights get better as you climb through montane and then subalpine habitats, and in clear weather the pull-offs offer views of steep conifer-filled valleys with Dungeness Spit and Victoria, British Columbia, in the distance. The higher elevations also supply the best evidence of the region's long geographic isolation: endemic plant and animal species, including Flett's Violet, Piper's Bellflower, Olympic Mountain Daisy, and Olympic Marmot. Mid-July is the peak of the extraordinary wildflower display along the roadside, where pale Slender Bog Orchids, nodding Chocolate Lilies, and pink Elephant's Heads bloom.

A short walk up the Switchback Trail brings you to a tiny creek crossing the trail. Look on the wet boulders here for Butterworts, carnivorous plants that dissolve tiny insects in their basal leaves. Subalpine Firs dominate the parkland at the point where the Hurricane Ridge Visitor Center comes into view. Several trails that depart from the visitor's center meander along mountain meadows where Blue Grouse forage and butterflies flourish on sunny days. Don't miss the viewing platform behind the visitor center, which has interpretive maps to help you name the mountain peaks and glaciers in view.

CONTACT Olympic N.P., 600 E. Park Ave., Port Angeles, WA 98362; 360-452-4501. **HOW TO GET THERE** U.S. 101 encircles the park: The road to Hurricane Ridge leaves U.S. 101 in Port Angeles; the road to the Hoh Rain Forest leaves U.S. 101 south of Forks; the roads to the coast leave U.S. 101 north of Forks. **SEASONAL ACCESS** Year-round. **VISITOR CENTERS** The main V.C. and park hdqtrs. are at the park's northern end in Port Angeles. Hurricane Ridge V.C. is located south of Port Angeles. Hoh Rain Forest V.C. is at the park's western end.

■ Information
••• Hoh River Trail

GRAYS HARBOR
NATIONAL WILDLIFE REFUGE   Hoquiam

One of the greatest shorebird spectacles anywhere unfolds each spring at the Grays Harbor National Wildlife Refuge, located a short distance from Washington's outer coast. The refuge protects Bowerman Basin, a key estuary for about 1 million northbound shorebirds that feed and rest here before flying to their tundra nesting areas. In late April, as many as 500,000 sandpipers may be on hand at one time; the sight of their huge aerobatic flocks is astounding. Of the five most common spring species, Western Sandpipers are the most abundant by far, making up 85 percent of the shorebirds, followed by Dunlins, Short-billed Dowitchers, and Semipalmated Plovers. Brilliant Red Knots turn up reliably, as do swift Peregrine Falcons and Merlins, whose presence may be signaled by thousands of shorebirds simultaneously taking flight.

Western Sandpipers in Bowerman Basin mudflats during spring migration stopover

Shorebird flocks are present from mid-April to early May; the best viewing times are two hours either side of high tide. The trail through this undeveloped refuge to the viewing areas is predictably wet and muddy, so rubber boots are a necessity unless you plan to watch from the parking area, which is much farther away. During peak weekends, shuttle buses run continuously between nearby Hoquiam High School and the trailhead.

The refuge's 1,500 acres of mudflats, salt marshes, and uplands also host Coyotes, Mule Deer, salmon, crabs, shrimp, clams, and oysters; thousands of Dunlins and smaller numbers of Black-billed Plovers winter here. En route to the refuge, visitors will pass directly alongside an expansive pond, which attracts a diversity of ducks, gulls, and swallows. In spring and summer, adjacent open areas host Common Yellowthroats and Savannah Sparrows.

CONTACT Grays Harbor N.W.R., c/o Nisqually N.W.R. Complex, 100 Brown Farm Rd., Olympia, WA 98506; 360-753-9467. HOW TO GET THERE From Olympia, follow Hwy. 8 and U.S. 12 west to Hoquiam. Turn left on Paulson Rd. to the refuge parking area. SEASONAL ACCESS Year-round.

WILLAPA NATIONAL WILDLIFE REFUGE   Ilwaco

Situated in the southwestern corner of the state along one of the largest and richest estuarine bays on the Pacific coast, Willapa National Wildlife Refuge encompasses several units totaling 11,000 acres. Extensive expanses of American Glasswort and Eelgrass make it a favorite stopping point for migrating shorebirds and a key wintering area for Brant, Canada Geese, and other waterfowl. For hiking, beachcombing, all-around bird-watching, and

exploring coastal dune and saltmarsh habitats, the Leadbetter Point Unit at the northern tip of Long Beach Peninsula is the top choice. A trail up the Willapa Bay side of the spit offers views of the tidelands, and visitors can follow the trend of the trail northward around tidal channels for more

View of Willapa Bay from Leadbetter Point

than 2 miles. Shorebirding can be excellent in late summer, when Pacific Golden-Plovers are regulars among many other species, including such Asian rarities as Sharp-tailed Sandpipers. Sandy trails flanked by Hooker's Willows and dunes carpeted with Kinnikinnick and Salal lead to the ocean side of the spit, where in late summer you will find Brown Pelicans and Sooty Shearwaters along the shore (avoid the areas seasonally closed for Snowy Plover nesting).

The Lewis Unit, at the mouth of the Bear River, encompasses extensive marshes with hiking trails. Watch for Northern River Otters on the river where it parallels the entrance road. Garter snakes abound in summer, and rails feed in the marshes. Across Long Island Slough from the refuge headquarters is the Long Island Unit, accessible only by boat. Its main attraction is a 274-acre coastal old-growth forest, now known as Cedar Grove, that miraculously has escaped the axe. This remnant of a pre-logging landscape is a rare find in the region.

CONTACT Willapa N.W.R., HC 01 Box 910, Ilwaco, WA 98624-9707; 360-484-3482. **HOW TO GET THERE** From Ilwaco: take Hwy. 103 north to the Leadbetter Pt. Unit (about 20 miles); take U.S. 101 northeast to the Lewis Unit (about 10 miles) and refuge hdqtrs. (about 13 miles). **SEASONAL ACCESS** Year-round. **VISITOR CENTER** Refuge hdqtrs.

DUNGENESS NATIONAL WILDLIFE REFUGE
Port Angeles

The preeminent feature of this refuge is Dungeness Spit, a narrow, driftwood-strewn spit of land that arcs 5½ miles out into the Strait of Juan de Fuca, and is likely the longest natural sandspit in the United States. Dungeness Spit frames and protects Dungeness Bay to the south, while its unprotected northern shore takes the brunt of the strait's weather and waves, evidenced by its mixture of sand and gravel beaches. The spit's flora is exceptional, still rich in American Dunegrass, while European Beachgrass has taken over many

similar Pacific coast habitats. A hike from the spit's base to the lighthouse near the tip is a full-day commitment, but a variety of wildlife can be seen by walking even a short distance. Red Foxes den in the massive driftwood piles, and Harbor Seals patrol the waters along the strait side of the spit (areas beyond the lighthouse are closed to hikers during pupping season). Dungeness Bay has extensive tidal flats and Eelgrass beds that draw waterfowl and shorebirds. Spring and fall migrations bring the

Dungeness Spit

greatest diversity of shorebirds, including Whimbrels, dowitchers, turnstones, plovers, and smaller "peeps." Winter bird concentrations are truly impressive: thousands of Dunlins and Brant are attracted by the Eelgrass beds, and diving birds including scoters, goldeneyes, Harlequin Ducks, loons, grebes, and cormorants are numerous. Rhinoceros Auklets are abundant in summer, and Marbled Murrelets and Pigeon Guillemots forage near the spit year-round. Bald Eagles often perch on pilings, and Merlins and Peregrine Falcons prey on the wealth of wintering birds.

The trail from the parking lot to the base of the spit passes through a second-growth forest, which hosts Townsend's Chipmunks and chattering Douglas' Squirrels. Watch on the trail for yellow Banana Slugs and overhead for Hutton's Vireos, Chestnut-backed Chickadees, and Red Crossbills. Additional trails, including horse trails, weave through wooded and brushy habitats of the contiguous Dungeness Recreation Area, and clear days offer epic views from cliffsides on the strait.

CONTACT Dungeness N.W.R., 33 S. Barr Rd., Port Angeles, WA 98362; 360-457-8451. **HOW TO GET THERE** From Sequim, drive west on U.S. 101 for about 5 miles, then turn right (north) on Kitchen-Dick Rd.; drive 3 miles to refuge entrance road, which passes first through Dungeness Rec. Area, then ends at refuge parking lot. **SEASONAL ACCESS** Year-round. Some areas on spit may be off-limits; check at refuge.

SAN JUAN ISLAND
NATIONAL HISTORICAL PARK Friday Harbor

Among the most intriguing wildlife-viewing areas in the San Juan Islands is San Juan Island National Historical Park. The park, on San Juan Island, comprises two discrete units—American Camp and English Camp—and there is also a visitor center in downtown Friday Harbor. The camps' names reflect the disputed ownership of the island in the mid-19th century.

American Camp, at the southern end of the island, comprises a mix of woodlands and tundra-like meadows created by grazing introduced European Hares. Eurasian Sky-larks, colonizing from Vancouver Island, sing over the meadow adjacent to Pickett's Lane. Nearby a pair or two of Golden Eagles nest. The eagles and a local population of Red Foxes take advantage of the abundant rabbits.

Beach near Cattle Point, San Juan Island

At the southeastern end of the island is Cattle Point, an excellent spot for viewing marine and rocky-shore wildlife, including Harbor Seals, Northern River Otters, Northwestern Crows, and Black Oystercatchers. You can see San Juan Channel from here, loaded with Rhinoceros Auklets in the summer and Pacific Loons, Harlequin Ducks, and other divers in winter. Watch for the short, triangular, black and white dorsal fins of Dall's Porpoises.

English Camp sits at the far northwestern tip of the island. With its madrones, mixed conifers, and venerable Bigleaf Maples, it has great songbird habitat for migrants and residents such as Red-breasted Sapsuckers and Hutton's Vireos; it also hosts a thriving population of introduced Wild Turkeys. In spring, the meadows between the two camps (especially along Westside Road) display a flourish of wildflowers, including the rare Great Camas. Western Tiger Swallowtails flutter about the meadows.

CONTACT San Juan Is. N.H.P., P.O. Box 429, Friday Harbor, WA 98250; 360-378-2240. **HOW TO GET THERE** Ferry from Anacortes, WA, or Sidney, B.C., to Friday Harbor on San Juan Is. Call Wash. State Ferries at 206-464-6400 or 1-800-84-FERRY within Washington. **SEASONAL ACCESS** Year-round. **VISITOR CENTERS** In Friday Harbor at 125 Spring St., and at American Camp at the southeastern end of the island.

DECEPTION PASS STATE PARK   Whidbey Island

This park preserves a narrow channel between Fidalgo and Whidbey Islands. The whole of the park—with sections both north and south of Deception Pass—is strikingly scenic. Its 3,600 acres, many miles of saltwater shoreline and other trails, and wonderfully diverse habitats of ancient Douglas Fir forest, rocky islets and headlands, sandy beaches, tidepools, marine bays, and freshwater lakes make for a fascinating composite with enough elbow room to enjoy it all.

Rosario Strait

The park has great natural history interest in any season, but October through April is the best time to see waterbirds. Near West Point, hundreds of Red-throated Loons may be seen flying back and forth over the fast-moving waters. Black Oystercatchers, whose brilliant red bills and giddy calls betray their presence on the dark rocks, as well as numerous cormorants, scoters, and mergansers, are often close by.

Watch anywhere in the park along the rocky marine habitat—along Bowman Bay, for instance—for Harlequin Ducks, Harbor Seals, and Northern River Otters; even Killer Whales occasionally are seen offshore. Rosario Bay, popular with scuba divers, has plentiful tidepools full of anemones, limpets, chitons, and sculpins. Trails on Goose Rock are known for mosses, saxifrages, succulents, and stunning wildflowers. Trails up Hoypus Hill pass among monstrous Douglas Firs to overlook Similk Bay. From the pull-off where the bridge crosses Pass Island, walk the paths among wind-shaped madrones and pines and watch the pass below, as all of Skagit Bay somehow rushes in and out to Rosario Strait in the daily tidal exchange. Bird's-eye views from near the bridge are stunning.

CONTACT Deception Pass S.P., 5175 N. Hwy. 20, Oak Harbor, WA 98277; 360-675-2417. **HOW TO GET THERE** Along Hwy. 20 at the northern end of Whidbey Is. Hwy. 20 can be reached from I-5 (exit 230), or by ferry from Mukilteo (just south of Everett) to Clinton at the southern end of Whidbey Is. Park entrances are just north and just south of Deception Pass Bridge. For ferry information call Wash. State Ferries at 206-464-6400 or 1-800-84-FERRY within Washington. **SEASONAL ACCESS** Year-round. **VISITOR CENTER** Park hdqtrs. is on Hwy. 20.

PADILLA BAY NATIONAL ESTUARINE RESEARCH RESERVE

Bay View

Padilla Bay Reserve's 11,000 acres incorporate much of Padilla Bay, including more than 7,000 acres of Eelgrass beds, the essential food resource for migrating and wintering Brant. Numbers of Brant may reach into the tens of thousands here during April. A good starting point is the Breazeale Interpretive Center, which has habitat and wildlife exhibits, aquariums, and a knowledgeable staff to point you toward trails and overlooks. The adjacent Shore Trail follows the bayfront for a couple of miles, and you can also survey the bay from an observation deck. A mile-long upland trail traverses some of the reserve's 64 acres of woods and brushy fields. A few miles north on Bayview-Edison Road are fields called the Samish Flats—a premier area in winter for Gyrfalcons and other raptors.

CONTACT Padilla Bay N.E.R.R., 1043 Bayview-Edison Rd., Mount Vernon, WA 98273; 360-428-1558. **HOW TO GET THERE** From Seattle, head north on I-5 for 60 miles to exit 230, then drive west on Hwy. 20 to Bayview-Edison Rd. Drive north on Bayview-Edison about 5 miles to V.C. **SEASONAL ACCESS** Year-round **VISITOR CENTER** Breazeale Interpretive Ctr., open Wed.–Sun.

SKAGIT WILDLIFE AREA

Milltown

Snow Geese in flight

Just an hour north of Seattle, the Skagit Wildlife Area consists of 12,000 acres bordering Skagit Bay and the Skagit River. Best known for its tens of thousands of wintering Snow Geese, the area is popular with birders. Wintering swans and birds of prey are also plentiful, with lots of Bald Eagles and Red-tailed Hawks. In certain years when Arctic-dwelling Snowy Owls are pushed southward in numbers, the driftwood along Skagit Bay can be liberally sprinkled with them. The North Fork Access is a reliable winter spot for Short-eared Owls, and scores of Bald Eagles fly by here at sunset. The headquarters area features a 2-mile loop trail that sidles along slough, river, and salt marsh, through Sitka Spruce and willows. Mule Deer, beavers, and Northern River Otters figure among the mammals here, and dragonflies can be abundant in summer.

CONTACT Skagit W.A., Wash. Dept. of Fish and Wildlife, 16018 Mill Creek Blvd., Mill Creek, WA 98012; 206-775-1311. **HOW TO GET THERE** From Seattle, head north on I-5 to the Conway exit, then turn west on Fir Is. Rd. Turn left on Mann Rd. to area hdqtrs. **SEASONAL ACCESS** Year-round.

DISCOVERY PARK   **Seattle**

A superb example of an urban
wildlife preserve, 535-acre Discovery Park contains a surprising array
of habitats, including second-
growth forest, meadows, brushy
thickets, tiny ponds, and extensive
marine shoreline and bluffs along
Puget Sound. The 2¾-mile Loop

Trail provides a sampling of habitats; keep an eye out for Anna's
Hummingbirds. The ½-mile Wolf Tree Nature Trail follows a lush,
shady ravine. Judging by the number of burrows, Mountain Beavers
are prevalent in the park, although hard to see—for all but the resident Barred Owls. The Beach Trails (North and South) meet at
West Point, an excellent place for spotting seasonal seals, sea lions,
and diving birds. Parasitic Jaegers are seen in September, and Ancient Murrelets from November to December.

CONTACT Discovery Park, 3801 W. Government Way, Seattle, WA 98199;
206-386-4236. **HOW TO GET THERE** From Elliott Way/15th Ave. in Seattle,
take the Fisherman's Terminal/Emerson exit, then drive west on Emerson to
Gilman; turn right on Gilman to Government Way. **SEASONAL ACCESS** Year-
round. **VISITOR CENTER** Just past entrance.

NISQUALLY NATIONAL
WILDLIFE REFUGE   **Olympia**

Winding its way down from a
glacier on the south side of
Mount Rainier, the Nisqually
River joins Salmon and McAllis-
ter Creeks to form the last remaining undisturbed estuarine
delta on southern Puget Sound.
Habitats include tidal flats, fresh-
and saltwater marshes, grassy

meadows, and riparian woodlands. Three loop trails traverse the
multiple habitats. The 5½-mile Brown Farm Dike Trail leads
through marshes and grasslands and along the river and sloughs.
Northern River Otters, Minks, and Common Muskrats frequent
this route, Marsh Wrens and Pacific Chorus Frogs supply background music, thousands of wigeons graze in winter, and raptors
soar above the open country. Rufous Hummingbirds dart through
the Salmonberry thickets under the cottonwoods of the Nisqually
River Trail, where Great Horned Owls reside and Swainson's
Thrushes sing all summer long.

CONTACT Nisqually N.W.R. Complex, 100 Brown Farm Rd., Olympia, WA
98506; 360-753-9467. **HOW TO GET THERE** The refuge is located between
Tacoma and Olympia. From I-5, take exit 114 to the adjacent refuge entrance road on the north side of the interstate. **SEASONAL ACCESS** Year-round.
VISITOR CENTER Kiosk and refuge office at entrance.

OYHUT WILDLIFE AREA   Ocean Shores

While Grays Harbor National Wildlife Refuge hosts the big shorebird spectacle, Oyhut Wildlife Area attracts birders from August through September seeking diverse and rare species. Situated near the mouth of Grays Harbor and separating North Bay to the east and the Pacific Ocean to the west, Oyhut combines sandspits, tidal flats, rocks, and large beds of American Glasswort. Not just for birders, the bay here receives regular visits from Gray Whales (try Damon Point or the base of Point Brown Jetty). Harbor Seals are common, and pelicans, terns, and gulls abound in season. Both Pacific and American Golden-Plovers are also commonly seen. Take a short hike on Ocean Shores Boulevard on the western end of Oyhut and check the bushes and ponds for migrants. Damon Point, at the eastern end of the wildlife area, has the coast's northernmost nesting sites of Snowy Plovers.

CONTACT Oyhut W.A., Wash. Dept. of Fish and Wildlife, Region 6, 48 A/B Devonshire Rd., Montesano, WA 98563; 360-249-4628. HOW TO GET THERE From downtown Ocean Shores, take Ocean Shores Blvd. south to Pt. Brown and then east to the sewage treatment plant at the west end of Oyhut. SEASONAL ACCESS Year-round; some areas restricted during breeding season.

PROTECTION ISLAND
NATIONAL WILDLIFE REFUGE   Sequim

A commercial boat tour can take visitors within 200 yards of this jam-packed seabird rookery, summer home to thousands of Rhinoceros Auklets, a few Tufted Puffins, and pupping Harbor Seals. Call Sequim Bay Tours at 360-681-7408. CONTACT Protection Is. N.W.R., c/o Nisqually N.W.R. Complex, 100 Brown Farm Rd., Olympia, WA 98506; 360-753-9467.

Salt Creek Recreation Area

SALT CREEK RECREATION AREA   Port Angeles

Walk down to the rocky shoreline of this 196-acre marine sanctuary for a look at tidepools, Black Oystercatchers, Harlequin Ducks, and a seasonally variable array of seabirds. CONTACT Salt Creek R.A., Clallam County Parks, 223 E. 4th St., Port Angeles, WA 98362; 360-452-7831.

EDIZ HOOK   Port Angeles
Drive, bike, or walk along this marine spit and watch for Harbor Seals, Harlequin Ducks, Peregrine Falcons, and a wide assortment of seabirds. Shorebirds prefer the cobble beach and the log rafts, where gulls and herons roost in impressive numbers. **CONTACT** Ediz Hook, Clallam County Parks, 223 E. 4th St., Port Angeles, WA 98362; 360-452-7831.

CAPE FLATTERY   Neah Bay
This area on Makah Nation offers visitors a short hike to the northwesternmost tip of the state, where Tufted Puffins nest, Gray Whales pass by, and raptors migrate in spring. **CONTACT** Makah Indian Nation, P.O. Box 115, Makah Tribal Center, Neah Bay, WA 98357; 360-645-2201.

Columbian White-tailed Deer at Julia Butler Hansen National Wildlife Refuge

JULIA BUTLER HANSEN NATIONAL WILDLIFE REFUGE
FOR THE COLUMBIAN WHITE-TAILED DEER   Cathlamet
Roads and trails lead through this preserve dedicated to saving an endemic subspecies of deer. It is also a good place to see Elk, swans, Bald Eagles, and Ospreys. **CONTACT** Julia Butler Hansen N.W.R., P.O. Box 566, Cathlamet, WA 98612; 360-795-3915.

BOGACHIEL STATE PARK   Forks
A nature trail, massive Western Hemlocks, remnant old-growth wet forest and a top Steelhead fishing spot along the Bogachiel River are all reasons to visit this park. **CONTACT** Bogachiel S.P., State Hwy. 101, P.O. Box 500, Forks, WA 98331; 360-374-6356.

THE NATURE CENTER AT SNAKE LAKE   Tacoma
Trails through forests, meadows, and wetlands offer easy access to viewing area wildlife, including Wood Ducks, Red Foxes, and Common Raccoons. **CONTACT** The Nature Ctr. at Snake Lake, 1919 S. Tyler St., Tacoma, WA 98405; 253-591-6439.

POINT DEFIANCE PARK   Tacoma
This forested 700-acre park along Puget Sound includes the excellent 29-acre Port Defiance Zoo and Aquarium. Exhibits of Polar Bears and Belugas are among the highlights. **CONTACT** Point Defiance Park, Metropolitan Park District of Tacoma, 5400 N. Pearl, Tacoma, WA 98407; 253-591-5337.

WOODLAND PARK ZOO   Seattle
This first-rate zoological park offers a series of habitat exhibits, ranging from the African savanna to a lovely rose garden. **CONTACT** Woodland Park Zoo, 5500 Phinney Ave. North, Seattle, WA 98103; 206-684-4800.

SEATTLE AQUARIUM   Seattle
Located near downtown along Puget Sound, this aquarium offers visitors the chance to see a superb series of exhibits, including diving puffins, Sea Otters, and Northern Fur Seals. **CONTACT** Seattle Aquarium, 1483 Alaskan Way, Seattle, WA 98101; 206-386-4320.

KEYSTONE AND PORT TOWNSEND
FERRY CROSSING
Port Townsend

This state ferry crossing from Port Townsend to Whidbey Island traverses waters favored by large numbers of seabirds. For a small fare you can experience the best birding of any Puget Sound area ferry crossing. Pacific Loons, Oldsquaws, and Marbled Murrelets can be seen in winter, many other birds at any season. **CONTACT** Keystone and Port Townsend Ferry Crossing, Wash. State Ferries, Colman Dock/Pier 52, 801 Alaskan Way, Seattle, WA 98104-1487; 206-464-6400 or 1-800-84-FERRY within Washington.

SAN JUAN ISLANDS FERRY
Anacortes

These state ferries depart from Anacortes and offer an excellent means for traveling among the San Juan Islands and across the Strait of Juan de Fuca to observe seabirds, porpoises, whales, and other marine wildlife. Be sure to check the ferry schedule for the many island stops on this trip. Walk on or take your vehicle. **CONTACT** San Juan Is. Ferry, Wash. State Ferries, Colman Dock/Pier 52, 801 Alaskan Way, Seattle, WA 98104-1487; 206-464-6400 or 1-800-84-FERRY within Washington.

FORT FLAGLER STATE PARK
Port Townsend

The sandspit on Admiralty Inlet is a reliable place to see Harbor Seals, beautiful Harlequin Ducks, and a diversity of shorebirds in season. **CONTACT** Fort Flagler S.P., 10541 Flagler Rd., Nordland, WA 98358; 360-385-1259.

SPENCER ISLAND COUNTY PARK
Everett

Miles of level hiking trails along lowland riparian and marsh environs make this a popular birding spot. American Bitterns and Marsh Wrens peer out from the Reed Canary Grass, and raptors can be plentiful. **CONTACT** Spencer Is. C.P., Snohomish C.P.'s, M/S 303, 3000 Rockefeller Ave., Everett, WA 98201-4046; 425-339-1208.

Lake O'Neil at Fort Canby State Park

FORT CANBY STATE PARK
Westport

Birders can watch from the jetty for a host of wintering and some nesting seabirds. The Lewis and Clark Interpretive Center intoduces visitors to these legendary travelers. **CONTACT** Fort Canby S.P., P.O. Box 488, Ilwaco, WA 98624; 360-642-3078.

PACIFIC OFFSHORE WILDLIFE TRIPS
Ilwaco

There is a whole world of marine wildlife off Washington's Pacific coast. The pelagic birding tours leaving from Westport and organized by ornithologist Terry Wahl have been the premier offshore trips in the region for years. Most are from July through October; they feature Black-footed Albatrosses and other birds seen only on the open ocean. **CONTACT** Westport Seabirds, 3041 Eldridge, Bellingham, WA 98225; 360-733-8255.

Central Washington

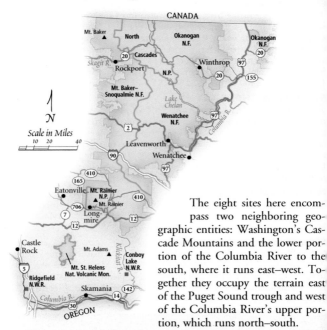

The eight sites here encompass two neighboring geographic entities: Washington's Cascade Mountains and the lower portion of the Columbia River to the south, where it runs east–west. Together they occupy the terrain east of the Puget Sound trough and west of the Columbia River's upper portion, which runs north–south.

Not only do the Cascades catch the eye for hundreds of miles, they catch much of the eastbound precipitation on their western slopes and prevent much of it from reaching the eastern slope, especially the arid Columbia Plateau. The Cascades include two of the best known landmarks in the Northwest: the iconic Mount Rainier and the freshly volcanic Mount St. Helens.

Mount Rainier National Park allows visitors to experience the mountain's grandeur up close and gives access to a range of subalpine and alpine realms. Mount St. Helens National Volcanic Monument offers a living study in volcanism and a grand experiment in the natural restoration of ecosystems. Mount Baker–Snoqualmie National Forest traces the northwestern segment of the Washington Cascades, where statuesque Mount Baker stands the tallest. North Cascades National Park, just to the east, is largely untrammeled wilderness. Still farther east, Wenatchee and Okanogan National Forests offer over 3½ million acres of montane habitat, both with ample wilderness areas.

Conboy Lake National Wildlife Refuge, which sits about 20 miles north of the lower Columbia River, looks up at the south face of Mount Adams and has perhaps the region's best wildflower show on Bird Creek Meadows. Located farther west and on the Columbia River floodplain, Ridgefield National Wildlife Refuge preserves extensive wetland and Garry Oak habitats.

MOUNT ST. HELENS
NATIONAL VOLCANIC MONUMENT   Swift

Mount St. Helens was perhaps the prettiest of the High Cascades—at least until the morning of May 18, 1980, when it suddenly and startlingly became the most famous modern volcano in North America. The well-documented cataclysmic explosion leveled 230 square miles of forest and left behind a scene of destruction, filling the Toutle River and Spirit Lake with debris and sending 15 miles into the air clouds of ash that was deposited over the eastern part of the state, with some of it circling the earth in two weeks' time. The 110,000-acre volcanic monument was created in 1982, and although it's 1,300 feet shorter now, Mount St. Helens attracts more attention than ever.

Mount St. Helens and log-covered Spirit Lake, 1982

Visitors have the unique opportunity not only to marvel at an active volcano and the extraordinary results of its explosive force, but also to observe the rebirth of plant and animal life in the blast zone. The visitor center at Silver Lake offers videos and exhibits that document the eruption and subsequent recovery of Mount St. Helens.

Perhaps the most fascinating areas are those within the blast zone where trees downed by the blast have been left in place, and natural revegetation and re-establishment of animal life is occurring. In only five years Elk and deer herds were restored to pre-eruption levels and 90 percent of plant species were again present, although in very different proportions and locations. Visitors can explore and compare this with the south side of the monument, which was barely affected by the eruption—it features ancient lava tubes and tree casts as well as a nature trail through a lowland forest.

CONTACT Mount St. Helens N.V.M., 42218 NE Yale Bridge Rd., Amboy, WA 98601; 360-247-3900. **HOW TO GET THERE** From Olympia, drive south on I-5 to monument entrance roads at Castle Rock and Woodland. **SEASONAL ACCESS** Year-round. **VISITOR CENTERS** Mount St. Helens V.C. at Silver Lake is 5 miles east of Castle Rock; Coldwater Ridge V.C. is on Hwy. 504 about 43 miles east of Castle Rock; Johnston Ridge Observatory is at the terminus of Hwy. 504 about 51 miles east of Castle Rock.

MOUNT RAINIER NATIONAL PARK   Longmire

View of Mount Rainier from Paradise area

Visible from just about anywhere in the western half of the state as it rises in regal solitude, Mount Rainier, established in 1899 as the country's fifth national park, stands as a symbol for the entire region. The mountain itself—at 14,410 feet, the highest of the Cascade volcanoes—and the natural world it holds on its slopes are the principal attractions here. It is a popular summer destination, although some winter visitors come with skis and snowshoes (parts of the area average about 50 feet of snowfall per year).

Wildflowers cover the park's subalpine and alpine slopes in mid- to late summer, spreading upslope as they follow the receding melting snow. Butterflies (and flies) can be abundant up here, with some species seeking out mates in these heights. Mountain Goat herds reside in several areas: Panhandle Gap, Emerald Ridge, and Indian Henry's Hunting Ground. Elk, Mountain Lions, Black Bears, and many Mule Deer inhabit the park. Hoary Marmots dwell along the lower alpine edge, pikas' *peent*s can be heard from most talus slopes, and Golden-mantled Ground Squirrels and Townsend's Chipmunks greet visitors at picnic spots, competing with Clark's Nutcrackers for illegal handouts. Birds of the summer alpine zone include White-tailed Ptarmigans, Gray-crowned Rosy-Finches, and American Pipits. Seemingly oblivious Blue Grouse inhabit the subalpine area, sometimes dust-bathing on the main hiking trails. Migrating raptors follow the mountain ridges, and it is an awesome sight to see Prairie and Peregrine Falcons gliding across the blue-white glacial landscape.

There are four main entrances to the park, more or less at each of its four corners. The Nisqually Entrance at the park's southwestern corner brings visitors through tall montane forest filled with the entrancing songs of Varied and Hermit Thrushes. Take a side trip up Westside Road to see the results of a massive lahar, or mudflow, from the glaciers above. Farther up the main park road are the Longmire Museum and the Longmire Visi-

Wildflowers, Paradise area

tor Center; continue along the road to Narada Falls to check for American Dippers, small wren-like birds that feed in fast-moving streams. Drive up to 5,400 feet and you will come to the Paradise area, which has several excellent trails for hiking up into the subalpine and alpine realms. The wonderfully varied expanses of wildflowers above Paradise peak in July and August include the brilliant and assorted colors of lupines, paintbrushes, monkeyflowers, bistorts, heathers, and fragrant Sitka Valerian. Subalpine Firs and Mountain Hemlocks dominate the small, isolated groves of subalpine conifers here, and provide cover for Blue Grouse and smaller birds and mammals.

As you continue counterclockwise around the mountain from Paradise, one dramatic natural feature unfolds after another. Reflection Lakes, home to nesting Barrow's Goldeneyes, best hold the mirror image of the mountain in the morning. Stevens Canyon's steep walls create a breathtaking effect, and the subalpine forest here shows the full range of snow-shedding trees. A stop at Box Canyon to view the narrow gap in the rock walls may also produce a view of Black Swifts, which nest behind waterfalls in the park. The Grove of the Patriarchs has an easy trail through some stupendous old-growth Western Red Cedars, Douglas Firs, and Western Hemlocks; these patriarchs are 500 to 1,000 years old. The White River Entrance near the park's northeastern corner takes visitors on a road into the Sour-

Stevens Canyon

dough Mountains to Sunrise Ridge and leads to a view of five volcanic mountains in the High Cascades and finally to Sunrise Visitor Center. The subalpine region here lies on the drier side of the mountain and has a more porous, pumice-based soil. Here Whitebark Pines are more prevalent, and grasses and sedges mix with the wildflowers on the meadows. Sunrise gets fewer visitors than Paradise, and offers an easier route into truly alpine surroundings and ptarmigan habitat.

CONTACT Mount Rainier N.P., Ashford, WA 98304; 360-569-2211. **HOW TO GET THERE** From Seattle, drive south on I-5, then follow one of several routes: Hwy. 410 leads to White River and Sunrise; Hwy. 706 leads to Paradise; and Hwy. 165 leads to Carbon River. **SEASONAL ACCESS** Only the Nisqually Entrance is open year-round; the others are closed in winter. **VISITOR CENTERS** Five: one at Longmire, about 5 miles past the Nisqually Entrance on Hwy. 706; two at Paradise, about 5 miles past Longmire; one at Ohanapecosh, on Hwy. 123 at the southeastern end of the park; and one at Sunrise, about 10 miles past the White River Entrance on Hwy. 706.

MOUNT BAKER–SNOQUALMIE NATIONAL FOREST

Skykomish

The more than 1½-million-acre Mount Baker–Snoqualmie National Forest stretches along the western slopes of the Cascades from the Canadian border to the northern edge of Mount Rainier National Park, covering a distance of more than 140 miles. This vast area has hundreds of streams, rivers, and lakes, and offers many recreational and wildlife opportunities, with eight wilderness areas, more than 50 campgrounds, 1,400 miles of trails, and seven downhill ski areas.

Alpine meadow with Mount Baker in background

Mount Baker is the predominant peak here: a lovely glacier-capped sight at 10,778 feet tall. Visitors can drive up Highway 542 along the Nooksack River through the montane and subalpine forests to the Heather Meadows area on the northeastern side of the mountain. From here, hike out from Artist's Point (about 5,000 feet) along Ptarmigan Ridge for a firsthand view of an alpine ecosystem. Hoary Marmots and pikas call from the talus slopes, Mountain Goats feed in small meadows dotted with Beargrass, American Pipits flit from boulder to boulder, and White-tailed Ptarmigans blend in perfectly with the lichen-covered terrain. Snow is slow to melt at these altitudes, so mid- to late summer is the best time to insure a visible hiking trail. The Heliotrope Ridge Trail on the western side of Mount Baker begins at 3,700 feet and climbs upward for more than 3 miles into the alpine zone.

Drive the Mountain Loop Highway for an exceptional view of the interior of the Cascade Range. The road follows the courses of three different rivers, crosses Barlow Pass before looping northward, and offers many potential side trips and additional hiking trails. Quite a bit farther south but still in the national forest and near Snoqualmie Pass (an hour east of Seattle), you can hike in high montane forest, including some old growth, and explore an excellent wildflower area along Asahel Curtis Nature Trail. Interpretive panels and plant checklists are available from the forest office.

CONTACT Mt. Baker–Snoqualmie N.F., 21905 64th Ave. West, Mountlake Terrace, WA 98043; 206-775-9702 or 1-800-627-0062. **HOW TO GET THERE** I-90, U.S. 2, and Hwy. 20 pass through the forest. **SEASONAL ACCESS** Year-round; snow closes some access roads. **VISITOR CENTERS** There are information and ranger stations throughout the forest. Glacier Public Service Ctr. is on Hwy. 542; Snoqualmie Pass is on I-90; and Heather Meadows, open July and August only, is at the terminus of Hwy. 542.

OKANOGAN NATIONAL FOREST   Okanogan

Located in the north-central part of the state, the 1½-million-acre Okanogan National Forest abuts North Cascades National Park on the west and the Okanogan River valley on the east. The forest incorporates the huge Pasayten Wilderness, a high-elevation backpacker's wonderland, and the North Cascades Scenic Highway, which is widely acclaimed as the most captivating drive in the state (especially for viewing late September's foliage colors). The scenic highway, which is part of Highway 20, is open in the warmer

Liberty Bell Mountain

months and offers epic views of the North Cascades, including Liberty Bell Mountain and Ross Lake, and crosses two of the state's high mountain passes—Rainy Pass at 4,860 feet and Washington Pass at 5,700 feet.

There are many spots in Okanogan and the adjacent lands where visitors can gain insight into local flora and fauna. A favorite route is the road to Hart's Pass and Slate Peak above the town of Mazama, a superb run through true subalpine habitats that affords quick access to alpine reaches. Subalpine Larches, endemic to this region,

Larches at Hart's Pass

grow along the road. Slate Peak is a good spot for hawk-watching during migration periods. Late summer wildflowers here can be astounding, from patchy carpets of phlox to acres of lupines and paintbrushes. Hike into the Pasayten Wilderness from here (the trails typically have the least snow in August) and see Hoary Marmots and Golden-mantled Ground Squirrels. Hikers on the West Fork Pasayten Trail often spot White-tailed Ptarmigans, Spruce Grouse, Three-toed Woodpeckers, Boreal Chickadees, and other northern species.

Loup Loup Campground sits in the southeastern portion of the forest; its mountains and wet meadows harbor Snowshoe Hares, Black Bears, Barred Owls, and Williamson's Sapsuckers. The Sinlahekin Wildlife Area just east of the forest follows riparian and forest habitats north to Palmer and Chopaka Lakes.

CONTACT Okanogan N.F., 1240 S. 2nd Ave., Okanogan, WA 98840; 509-826-3275. HOW TO GET THERE Hwy. 20 passes directly through the forest. SEASONAL ACCESS Year-round; snow closes some access roads. VISITOR CENTERS Methow Valley V.C. is on Hwy. 20 in Winthrop, and Twisp Ranger Station is on Hwy. 20 about 10 miles south of Winthrop.

WENATCHEE NATIONAL FOREST   Wenatchee

The more than 2-million-acre Wenatchee National Forest, the largest of the state's forests, fills much of the area just east of the Cascade crest and eastward to the Columbia River, encompassing the Wenatchee, Entiat, and Chelan Mountains, as well as much of lengthy Lake Chelan. This vast area of montane and lower-elevation habitats on the drier eastern side of the Cascades is bounded on the north by the Okanogan National Forest and North Cascades National Park and on the south by I-90.

Wenatchee River flowing through Tumwater Canyon

Among the many areas to visit here is Red Top Mountain, one of the state's most acclaimed hawk-watching spots in September and October and home to Elk, Mule Deer, and a wide range of other mammals and butterflies. To reach this spot from U.S. 97 between Ellensburg and Wenatchee, turn west on Forest Road 9738 just north of the Mineral Springs Resort and drive about 9 miles along the well-marked route to Red Top Mountain. From here it's a short hike to the viewing area, which also offers an eye-popping view of Mount Rainier, the Stuart Range, and the Alpine Lakes Wilderness. Among the migrating raptors that pass through are all three accipiters, eagles, falcons, and Turkey Vultures.

Other noteworthy areas include Icicle and Tumwater Canyons. Follow U.S. 2 northwest from Leavenworth along Tumwater Canyon and stop at the pull-offs for good views of spawning Chinook Salmon along the stream from mid-September to mid-October. Icicle Canyon starts just south of the town of Leaven-

Calliope Hummingbird

worth. Both canyons offer great butterfly-watching on sunny summer days and golden larches in the fall. Bird species are many, including the Calliope Hummingbird, the tiniest North American hummingbird.

CONTACT Wenatchee N.F., 215 Melody La., Wenatchee, WA 98801; 509-662-4335. HOW TO GET THERE I-90 and U.S. 2 are the major routes to this huge area. SEASONAL ACCESS Year-round; some access roads may be closed because of snow. VISITOR CENTERS The Chelan Ranger Station is off Alt. 97 on S. Woodin Ave. in Chelan; the Leavenworth Ranger Station is on U.S. 2 in Leavenworth; and the Lake Wenatchee Ranger Station is just north of the lake off Hwy. 207.

RIDGEFIELD NATIONAL WILDLIFE REFUGE

Ridgefield

Ridgefield National Wildlife Refuge, like nearby Conboy National Wildlife Refuge, is an example of watery lowland terrain at the southern edge of the Washington Cascades. Two distinct sections of Ridgefield (the Carty Unit is located north of Ridgefield, and the River "S" Unit is located south of Ridgefield) offer a contrast in habitats along the lower Columbia River floodplain. The refuge's habitats include lakes, marshes, woods, and grasslands; some areas flood annually. Although the more than 5,000-acre refuge is worth visiting any time of year, winter is an especially busy time for wildlife, often with more than 50,000 waterfowl on hand, including migratory Canada Geese, Mallards, and American Wigeons. As

Slough and bottomland forest

you drive through the River "S" Unit, watch for migrating Sandhill Cranes and wintering Bald Eagles. A walk along Bower Slough in summer may turn up Long-tailed Weasels, Red Foxes, and Northern River Otters, but the most conspicuous mammals are Nutrias, large brown aquatic rodents.

The Carty Unit features the 2-mile Oaks-to-Wetlands Wildlife Trail, which meanders through meadows and along the sloughs and ponds that are home to Pacific Chorus Frogs and Northern Harriers. Keep an eye out for Painted Turtles basking on logs in the sun. Garry Oaks provide acorns for Western Gray Squirrels and noisy families of Western Scrub Jays, and wooded knolls along the trail light up with blue-violet Common Camas and other wildflowers in the spring.

CONTACT Ridgefield N.W.R., 301 N. 3rd St., P.O. Box 457, Ridgefield, WA 98642; 360-887-4106. **HOW TO GET THERE** From I-5 about 15 miles north of Vancouver, WA, take the Ridgefield exit. Once in Ridgefield, follow Pioneer St. (Hwy. 501) and turn south on S. 9th St. to reach the River "S" Unit entrance; turn north on N. Main St. to reach the Carty Unit entrance. **SEASONAL ACCESS** Year-round. Check with refuge about hunting closures in River "S" Unit. **VISITOR CENTER** Refuge office in Ridgefield has maps and brochures.

NORTH CASCADES NATIONAL PARK

Newhalem

Huckleberries and Subalpine Firs

One of the least visited of the national parks, North Cascades is almost unimaginably scenic, with steep evergreen-covered slopes, jagged rocky summits, alpine meadows, waterfalls, glaciers (half of all the glaciers in the lower 48 states are here), and gorgeous mountain lakes. Ninety-two percent of the area covered by the park is designated wilderness; Ross Lake National Recreational Area runs through its midsection. Highway 20 is the only driving road through the forest. A paradise for backcountry hikers, remote corners of the park are reported to sustain such scarce mammals as Gray Wolves, Grizzly Bears, and Fishers. More than 1,700 plant species have been identified in the North Cascades, the highest number of any national park. Along Highway 20 are a short loop walk (Happy Creek Forest Walk) through an old-growth forest, and superb views at Diablo Lake Overlook.

CONTACT North Cascades N.P., 2105 Hwy. 20, Sedro Woolley, WA 98284; 360-856-5700. **HOW TO GET THERE** Follow Hwy. 20 east from Burlington or west from Twisp to various access roads. **SEASONAL ACCESS** Snow closes highway access from approximately November to April. **VISITOR CENTERS** North Cascades V.C. is just west of Newhalem on Hwy. 20; Golden West V.C. is located in the town of Stehekin.

CONBOY LAKE NATIONAL WILDLIFE REFUGE

Glenwood

Conboy Lake National Wildlife Refuge's seasonal marshes and pine- and fir-forested uplands are nestled at the base of lovely snow-capped Mount Adams. This 5,500-acre refuge hosts large concentrations of migrating and wintering swans, geese, and ducks, as well as the only known nesting

Quaking Aspens

pairs of Sandhill Cranes in the state. Deer and Elk are residents, as are many smaller mammals. Beginning near the refuge headquarters, the 2-mile Willard Springs Trail follows the lake edge and leads into pine forests. In late July to early August, one of the most renowned wildflower spectacles in the Northwest can be seen at Bird Creek Meadows near the southeastern edge of Mount Adams.

CONTACT Conboy Lake N.W.R., 100 Wildlife Refuge Rd., Box 5, Glenwood, WA 98619; 509-364-3410. **HOW TO GET THERE** From the town of White Salmon, drive 10 miles north on Hwy. 141, then drive 9 miles northeast on BZ Corners-Glenwood Rd. to entrance. **SEASONAL ACCESS** Year-round. **VISITOR CENTER** Refuge office in Glenwood.

METHOW WILDLIFE AREA Winthrop

Washington's largest herd of Mule Deer winters here. Visitors may also see Black Bears, Elk, and Lewis's Woodpeckers. Lower-elevation Bitterbrush gives way to higher-elevation Ponderosa pinelands. **CONTACT** Methow W.A., Wash. Dept. of Fish and Wildlife, Region 2, 1550 Alder St. NW, Ephrata, WA 98823; 509-754-4624.

PEARRYGIN LAKE STATE PARK Winthrop

This lake was carved out by retreating glaciers, and the surrounding hillsides of glacial till gleam with wildflowers in the spring. Look for Yellow-bellied Marmots and fauna of the sage steppe. **CONTACT** Pearrygin Lake S.P., Rte. 1, Box 300, Winthrop, WA 98862; 509-996-2370.

SKAGIT RIVER BALD EAGLE NATURAL AREA Rockport

One of the largest concentrations of wintering Bald Eagles can be found at this 6,000-acre preserve. The birds are attracted by the Skagit River wild salmon runs, with the greatest numbers in mid-January. **CONTACT** Skagit River Bald Eagle Natural Area, c/o Nature Conservancy of Wash., Skagit River Pres., P.O. Box 100, Rockport, WA 98283; 360-853-7263.

Roosevelt Elk at Northwest Trek Wildlife Park

NORTHWEST TREK WILDLIFE PARK Eatonville

This 600-acre wildlife park features a tram tour, hiking trails, indoor and outdoor displays, and hands-on activities for children. Visitors can also observe and learn about mammals such as Grizzly Bears, Gray Wolves, Mountain Lions, American Bison, Moose, and Mountain Goats, as well as birds of prey. **CONTACT** Northwest Trek W.P., 11610 Trek Dr. East, Eatonville, WA 98328; 360-832-6117.

SWAKANE WILDLIFE AREA Wenatchee

A drive up Swakane Canyon passes through a series of habitats from sage steppe to mixed coniferous forest. A herd of Bighorn Sheep ranges here, and birding is very good. **CONTACT** Swakane W.A., Wash. Dept. of Fish and Wildlife, 3860 Chelan Hwy., Wenatchee, WA 98801; 509-784-1511.

BEACON ROCK STATE PARK Skamania

Beacon Rock, the world's second-largest monolith after Gibraltar, is itself worth seeing, and this 4,500-acre area can be good for viewing waterfowl and for recreational rock-climbing. The view from the top of the rock—handrails line most of the ascent—features rugged basalt cliffs and stunning waterfalls. **CONTACT** Beacon Rock S.P., 34841 State Rd. 14, Skamania, WA 98648; 509-427-8265.

Eastern Washington

The rain shadow cast by the Cascade Mountains shows its most dramatic effects from the lower eastern Cascade slopes eastward to the north–south stretch of the Columbia River. The subregion covered here includes this rain-shadow area and the dry remainder of the state east to the Idaho border. Columbia National Wildlife Refuge, in the central part of eastern Washington, receives a scant 11 inches of rain per year. Although its lakes are filled with water channeled from the Grand Coulee Dam irrigation project into former canyons and low spots, the native habitats beyond the water's edge are primarily sagebrush and grassland. The rugged Channeled Scablands terrain of the Columbia refuge and the Turnbull National Wildlife Refuge farther east, as well as the coulees and massive Dry Falls at Sun Lakes State Park to the north, are all evidence of the extraordinary Pleistocene floods from Glacial Lake Missoula, the greatest land-sculpting force the region has ever witnessed. In even drier areas to the south, both the Yakima River canyon and the Klickitat Wildlife Area offer routes into wonderfully scenic, basalt-faced canyons. Along the Yakima River, towering basalt edifices reach hundreds of feet high, creating a grand realm for nesting raptors and other cliff dwellers. The Klickitat River canyon leads into extensive oak habitat, the best example of its kind in the state. Little Pend Oreille National Wildlife Refuge and Sullivan Lake, in the northeastern corner of the state in the Selkirk Range, are home to a surprising variety of Rocky Mountain wildlife, including Spruce Grouse, Northern Waterthrushes, Boreal Owls, and a few Moose. A wildlife recovery plan for Caribou and Grizzly Bears is in the works near Sullivan Lake.

TURNBULL NATIONAL WILDLIFE REFUGE   Cheney

Located only 20 miles west of the Idaho border, Turnbull National Wildlife Refuge is the only place in the state to find nesting Trumpeter Swans, and is also a reliable area for spotting diminutive, elegant Black Terns (both birds can be found on Winslow Pool near refuge headquarters). The area is well supplied with good hiking trails, and no hunting is permitted at any time. Intensive restoration and conservation efforts beginning with the refuge's creation in 1937 have revived this important wetland, which was nearly drained by settlers in the 1920s.

The refuge's nearly 15,500 acres incorporate a good deal of Ponderosa Pine forest together with aspen groves, shrubby thickets, and numerous lakes and marshes. Today's refuge area was once used by the Spokane Indians as a place to collect foods like Common Camas and Bitterroot, as well as wild onion, Kinnikinnick, and waterfowl eggs. Pygmy Nuthatches, Elk, White-tailed Deer, Common Porcupines, American Beavers, American Badgers, Columbian Ground Squirrels, and Yellow-pine Chipmunks can all be found here. During spring and fall migrations, large numbers of waterfowl (including Tundra Swans) and songbirds stop to feed and rest. In May and early June, a splendid display of wildflowers appears among the pines, and colorful male Ruddy Ducks perform their comical courtship displays on the lakes and ponds. The Pine Creek Auto Tour traverses a 6-mile cross section of habitats, and a drive around the circumference of the refuge passes through grasslands (watch for Grasshopper Sparrows and Gray Partridges). The short loop trail around Middle Pine Lake provides a good sampling of the refuge and intersects with longer trails.

CONTACT Turnbull N.W.R., 26010 S. Smith Rd., Cheney, WA 99004; 509-235-4723. HOW TO GET THERE From Cheney, drive south on Cheney-Plaza County Rd. (Badger Lake Rd.) to refuge entrance sign, then drive 2 miles east on Smith Rd. SEASONAL ACCESS Year-round, but snow closes some roads in season. VISITOR CENTER Information is available at refuge hdqtrs.

COLUMBIA NATIONAL WILDLIFE REFUGE   Othello

Comprising more than 23,000 acres, Columbia is the largest national wildlife refuge in Washington. It sits in the most arid region of the state—a ruggedly scenic area of basalt cliffs, canyons, buttes, sagebrush grasslands, and small to medium-size lakes whose riparian edges harbor willows and Russian Olives. Its location in the rain shadow of the Cascade Mountains prevents much precipitation from reaching the refuge: annual averages are less than 8 inches.

This fascinating geological area is set in the Columbia River Basin's Channeled Scablands, which got a topographic facelift when Glacial Lake Missoula, located on what is now the Idaho–Montana border, burst its glacial dam between 18,000 and 12,000 years ago. The strangely jumbled terrain of the refuge's northern half, the Drumheller Channels, best shows this topographic scarring, and was named a National Natural Landmark in 1986. The eruption of

Northwest Balsamroot

Mount St. Helens in 1980 dropped up to 4 inches of ash on the refuge area, some of which is still in evidence today as a white powder on the ground. Tracks of common yet secretive Coyotes, as well as Mule Deer, are frequently found in the volcanic ash.

The most productive seasons for wildlife-viewing are spring and early summer, when almost the entire refuge is open to the public. The sage habitat is at its peak early in this period, with specially adapted bird life and lots of blooming wildflowers, but it grows rather dry as the heat of summer increases. Look for lovely Sage Mariposa Lilies and pink Long-leaved Phlox. Brewer's Sparrows and Sage Thrashers are sage specialists, and both sing elaborate songs. There are Bobcats and American Badgers here, too, if you are lucky enough to see them, and Muskrats abound in the lakes. The many "pothole" lakes, which owe their water to the Grand Coulee Dam irrigation project, are amazingly busy with wildlife in summer. Raucous Yellow-headed Blackbirds, Caspian and Forster's Terns, Blue-winged and Cinnamon Teals, and bright Ruddy Ducks compete in sound and

Butte and sagebrush steppe

color. The increasingly scarce Burrowing Owl maintains a foothold here, and Gopher Snakes are ubiquitous. Be aware that a good number of Western Rattlesnakes also reside here, especially around rocky areas and wet edges; they are most active during the cooler hours, especially in the evening. The ledges and holes in the basalt cliffs provide nesting grounds for Red-tailed Hawks and American Kestrels. The numbers of migrating Sandhill Cranes that visit the refuge are increasing. Thousands of waterfowl winter here, with the largest concentration of these birds flocking to undisturbed areas of the refuge that are closed to the public during fall and winter migration seasons. The waterfowl can be viewed, however, from the overlook onto Royal Lake at the southern end of Byers Road.

Similar habitats, as well as an area with rolling sand dunes between Potholes Reservoir and Moses Lake, can be explored just north of the refuge in several units of the state-managed South Columbia Basin Wildlife Area. Burrowing Owls, Swainson's Hawks, and Caspian Terns can all be found at Moses Lake, where hundreds of thousands of waterfowl reside in the fall. Flocks of White Pelicans sometimes visit the area, and Great Egrets are regulars in the summer—this is one of the

Great Egret

few places in Washington to see these majestic birds. Forster's Terns are often plunge-diving here for small fish, American Avocets feed in the shallows, and many species of shorebirds stop over during migration. There is a heron and cormorant rookery at the northwestern corner of Potholes Reservoir.

CONTACT Columbia N.W.R., 735 E. Main St., P.O. Drawer F, Othello, WA 99344; 509-488-2668. **HOW TO GET THERE** From I-90 west of Moses Lake, turn south on Dodson Rd. then east on O'Sullivan Dam Rd. to the refuge. There are many access roads to the refuge. **SEASONAL ACCESS** Year-round.

SULLIVAN LAKE AND
SALMO-PRIEST WILDERNESS   **Metaline Falls**

Tucked up in the far northeastern corner of the state, Sullivan Lake and the adjoining Salmo-Priest Wilderness—both within the more than 1-million-acre Colville National Forest—present unique wildlife-viewing possibilities and a lot of truly wild country to explore. This site lies in the Selkirk Range, a foothill range of the Rockies, and its array of boreal mammal and bird species includes Moose, American Martens, Northern Bog Lemmings, Spruce Grouse, Pine Grosbeaks, Boreal Chickadees, White-winged Crossbills, Boreal Owls, and an occasional Northern Hawk Owl. Lynx and Wolverine can be sighted, if rarely, and there is a winter feed-

Sullivan Lake in Colville National Forest

ing station for Bighorn Sheep at the southern end of Sullivan Lake. Many of the riparian bird species found here are typical eastern species, such as American Redstarts and Northern Waterthrushes, both regulars. This is also one of the few places in the country where you can see four species of chickadees—Boreal, Chestnut-backed, Mountain, and Black-capped—in one day. The area is also rich in more widespread regional fauna, from pikas, American Beavers, and Red Squirrels to White-tailed and Mule Deer.

Visitors can explore the many hiking trails around Sullivan Lake; Sullivan Lake Trail number 504 is a relatively easy hike and can be very good for wildlife-viewing. A drive up Sullivan Creek Road to more boreal habitats is another option. Harlequin Ducks nest at Sullivan Creek; watch for them sitting on rocks in the stream. A

visit to the 500-acre Salmo Research Natural Area near a trailhead into the Salmo-Priest Wilderness reveals a fascinating array of plant communities, from Western White Pines and Western Larches to Western Red Cedars and Devil's Clubs. For a more challenging foray into nature, try the many miles of trails within the Salmo-Priest Wilderness.

Harlequin Ducks

CONTACT Colville N.F., Sullivan Lake Ranger District, 12641 Sullivan Lake Rd., Metaline Falls, WA 99153; 509-446-2681. **HOW TO GET THERE** From Colville, drive northeast on Hwy. 20 for about 30 miles, then drive north on Hwy. 31 for about 2 miles, then drive northeast on Sullivan Lake Rd. to the lake. **SEASONAL ACCESS** Year-round. Snow limits access in winter. **VISITOR CENTER** Maps and brochures are available at the Sullivan Lake Ranger Station on Sullivan Lake Rd.

L. T. MURRAY AND OAK CREEK WILDLIFE AREAS

Yakima

These two adjacent wildlife areas —together covering 200,000 acres—lie along the transition zone between Ponderosa Pine forests to the north and shrub steppe to the south; they are separated by the Wenas Valley. These habitats create a rich and exciting area of bird and other wildlife diversity. The pine forest suits such

Umtanum Canyon, L. T. Murray Wildlife Area

species as Blue Grouse and Mountain Chickadee, the lowland riparian plant communities of cottonwoods, willows, and aspens along Wenas and Umtanum Creeks support nesting populations of lovely Lewis's Woodpeckers and noisy Bullock's Orioles, and the oaks harbor Ash-throated Flycatchers and Lark Sparrows. Hillsides of Bitterbrush and other shrubs intergrade with the pines and host brilliant Lazuli Buntings in the summer.

The L. T. Murray Wildlife Area can be reached via unpaved roads south of I-90 from Cle Elum to Ellensburg. Its sage habitat is readily accessible along Umtanum Road near Ellensburg. This soft green landscape is alive in spring with the songs of Sage Thrashers, Brewer's and Vesper Sparrows, and Western Meadowlarks. Short-

horned Lizards and Townsend's Ground Squirrels scuttle among Bitterroot and Linear-leaf Daisies in spring, and Arrowleaf Balsamroot carpets the higher slopes up to the edge of the pines. The oak woodlands of Oak Creek Wildlife Area are home to the localized and declining Western Gray Squirrel. Hundreds of Elk appear at feeding stations in winter.

Bitterroot

At the southern terminus of Umtanum Road is Wenas Creek, which flows through a narrow canyon between the L. T. Murray and Oak Creek areas. Creekside cottonwoods and aspens resound with the marvelous low tones of Veeries and the complex songs of Townsend's Solitaires in summer. Yellow-pine Chipmunks scramble up and down the handsome orange trunks of Ponderosa Pines, which also provide food and nesting sites for three species of nuthatches. The strikingly patterned White-headed Woodpecker is an uncommon but regular denizen of the pines.

CONTACT L. T. Murray and Oak Creek W.A.'s, c/o Wash. Dept. of Fish and Wildlife, Region 3, 1701 S. 24th Ave., Yakima, WA 98902; 509-575-2740. **HOW TO GET THERE** For L. T. Murray, follow Umtanum Rd. south from Ellensburg for 6 miles. For Oak Creek, follow U.S. 12 northwest from Yakima to 2 miles past the Hwy. 410 junction. **SEASONAL ACCESS** Year-round.

LITTLE PEND OREILLE
NATIONAL WILDLIFE REFUGE
Colville

Old-growth Ponderosa Pines

This 40,000-acre refuge supports some of the richest habitats and most diverse wildlife of the entire Northwest. Elevations range from 1,800 to 5,600 feet, from lowland Ponderosa Pine forests to upper montane firs, spruces, hemlocks, and cedars. The Little Pend Oreille River, a branch of a complex watershed of streams, lakes, and marshes within the refuge, tracks through the northern section. Open meadows and former farmlands add further habitats. This refuge helps preserve a once-threatened regional White-tailed Deer population, and it is one of the few places in the state where Moose occur. At least 186 bird species, including a great variety of woodpeckers, a have been observed here. A detailed map of back roads is essential in this area.

CONTACT Little Pend Oreille N.W.R., 1310 Bear Creek Rd., Colville, WA 99114; 509-684-8384. **HOW TO GET THERE** From Spokane, drive north on Hwy. 395, then east on Hwy. 20 to refuge signs. **SEASONAL ACCESS** Year-round. **VISITOR CENTER** Refuge hdqtrs. on Bear Creek Rd.

YAKIMA RIVER CANYON
Yakima

Canyon Road (Highway 821) runs along the 20-mile-long Yakima River Canyon, offering terrific scenery and superb wildlife. The southern end is framed by epic basalt faces that tower hundreds of feet above the river. The cliffs provide nesting sites for Golden Eagles, Prairie Falcons, Canyon Wrens, White-throated Swifts, and Cliff Swallows. A herd of Bighorn Sheep resides in the hills along the western side of the river, and is most often seen between mileposts 18 and 19. A Nature Conservancy holding protects cliffs, grasslands, and the state-threatened Basalt Daisy. For an excellent nature hike, pull off at the Umtanum Recreation Site about 10 miles south of Ellensburg, walk west across the footbridge, and follow the trail up Umtanum Canyon.

CONTACT Wenatchee Resource Area Office of B.L.M., 915 Walla Walla, Wenatchee, WA 98801; 509-665-2100. **HOW TO GET THERE** To enter the canyon from its northern end and head south: From I-90 near the southern end of Ellensburg, take the exit for Canyon Rd. (Hwy. 821). To enter the canyon from its southern end and head north: From I-82 in Yakima, take the exit for the Yakima Training Center and turn left (west) to Hwy. 821. **SEASONAL ACCESS** Year-round.

KLICKITAT WILDLIFE AREA   Goldendale

Not only is the drive along the Klickitat River canyon one of the scenic highlights of the entire region, but the oak- and pine-covered slopes here are the state's best example of this habitat. The deep, narrow-walled canyon cut by the river is ablaze with wildflowers in spring and sumac in early autumn. The open habitats are home to reptile species such as Southern Alligator Lizards and Western Skinks, mammals such as California Ground Squirrels and Bobcats, and birds such as lovely Lewis's Woodpeckers, Wild Turkeys, Lark Sparrows, and Ash-throated Flycatchers.

CONTACT Klickitat W.A., Wash. Dept. of Fish and Wildlife, Region 5, 5405 NE Hazeldale Ave., Vancouver, WA 98663; 350-696-6211. **HOW TO GET THERE** From Goldendale, drive west on Hwy. 142 for about 9 miles, then drive north on Glenwood Rd. Watch for several unpaved wildlife area access roads, the first after about 3 miles. **SEASONAL ACCESS** Year-round. Snow may close some roads in winter.

SUN LAKES STATE PARK   Coulee City

The crowning geological feature of this 4,000-acre park is the massive, 400-foot-high Dry Falls, which, like the huge coulees nearby, stands as a stone testimonial to the cataclysmic forces that shaped the landscape of the Columbia Basin. Like the Channeled Scablands farther south, these features were formed during the

Dry Falls on Columbia River

gargantuan floods from Glacial Lake Missoula. A stop at the Dry Falls Interpretive Center near the northeastern corner of the park will provide insight into the events of these great floods. The tall rocky features suit nesting raptors, Rock Wrens, and White-throated Swifts, and the lakes host nesting Wilson's Phalaropes and waterfowl. Gray-crowned Rosy-Finches sometimes roost in the cliffs above the lakes and along nearby Banks Lake in winter.

CONTACT Sun Lakes S.P., HCR 1, Box 136, Coulee City, WA 99115; 509-632-5583. **HOW TO GET THERE** Take U.S. 2 east from Wenatchee (or west from Spokane) to the Hwy. 17 junction. Head south on Hwy. 17 to the park. **SEASONAL ACCESS** Year-round. **VISITOR CENTER** Dry Falls Interpretive Ctr.

CURLEW LAKE STATE PARK Republic

Located in remote northeastern Washington, this lake hosts Ospreys and riparian bird species. Bobolinks—a local species in the region—nest near the lake's northern end. **CONTACT** Curlew Lake S.P., 974 Curlew State Park Rd., Republic, WA 99166; 509-775-3592.

RIVERSIDE STATE PARK Spokane

Hike, canoe, or kayak along the Spokane River and explore adjacent riparian and pine forests. Wildlife in this 7,655-acre area includes wintering Bald Eagles, roosting herons, American Beavers, Common Porcupines, and Coyotes. The Little Spokane River Natural Area has Indian petroglyphs at a downstream trailhead. **CONTACT** Riverside S.P., 4427 N. Aubrey Lane White Pkwy., Spokane, WA 99205; 509-456-3964.

View from Mount Spokane

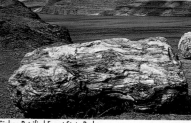

Ginkgo Petrified Forest State Park

MOUNT SPOKANE STATE PARK Spokane

A popular spot for winter activities, this park also features miles of trails for hikers, mountain bikers, and equestrians. Glorious views, and plenty of mammal and bird species, can be seen from atop Mount Spokane. **CONTACT** Mount Spokane S.P., North 26107 Mount Spokane Park Dr., Mead, WA 99021; 509-238-4258.

FLUME CREEK MOUNTAIN GOAT VIEWING AREA Metaline

Mountain Goats can be seen from late March through June from this 1-acre area located in the Colville National Forest near Sullivan Lake. **CONTACT** Colville N.F., Sullivan Lake Ranger District, 12641 Sullivan Lake Rd., Metaline Falls, WA 99153; 509-446-2681.

SHERMAN CREEK Republic

This 35-mile creek in Colville National Forest offers a sampling of montane habitats. Deer, American Beavers, grouse, owls, and other wildlife can all be found here. **CONTACT** Colville N.F., Kettle Falls Ranger Sta., 225 W. 11th St., Kettle Falls, WA 99141; 509-738-6111.

CHIEF JOSEPH WILDLIFE AREA Asotin

This wildlife area along the immensely scenic Grande Ronde River is a great place to watch for Mountain Quail, Golden Eagles, Prairie Falcons, Elk, deer, marmots, reptiles, and wildflowers. **CONTACT** Chief Joseph W.A., Wash. Dept. of Fish and Wildlife, Region 1, 8702 N. Division St., Spokane, WA 99218; 509-456-4082.

WILLIAM T. WOOTEN WILDLIFE AREA Dayton

Located in the Blue Mountains, this area offers bunchgrasses and coniferous forests that harbor Bighorn Sheep, Black Bears, Bobcats, grouse, and other wildlife. **CONTACT** William T. Wooten W.A., Wash. Dept. of Fish and Wildlife, Region 1, 8702 N. Division St., Spokane, WA 99218; 509-456-4082.

GINKGO PETRIFIED FOREST STATE PARK Vantage

Look among the fossil trees for lizards, snakes, Say's Phoebes, and Loggerhead Shrikes. An interpretive center offers a view of the Triassic Era. **CONTACT** Ginkgo Petrified Forest S.P., P.O. Box 1203, Vantage, WA 98950; 509-856-2700.

Palouse River and Canyon, Palouse Falls State Park

TOPPENISH NATIONAL WILDLIFE REFUGE — Toppenish

This 1,700-acre refuge is among the few spots in the state where Bobolinks nest. Waterfowl, raptors, waders, and songbirds also use the area. Watch for Burrowing Owls in the sage steppe. **CONTACT** Toppenish N.W.R., 21 Pumphouse Rd., U.S. 97 South, Toppenish, WA 98948; 509-865-2405.

CRAB CREEK WILDLIFE AREA — Beverly

There is plenty to see along this 18,000-acre creek drainage area, including sage, rocky bluffs, and riparian habitats. Golden Eagles and Chukar live along the canyon walls, and phalaropes and avocets can be seen on alkaline ponds. **CONTACT** Crab Creek W.A., Wash. Dept. of Fish and Wildlife, Region 2, 1550 Alder St. NW, Ephrata, WA 98823; 509-754-4624.

PALOUSE FALLS STATE PARK — Starbuck

Massive basalt walls and a 198-foot-high waterfall make this a visually spectacular site. Listen for Canyon Wrens and explore adjoining arid habitats. **CONTACT** Palouse Falls S.P., P.O. Box 157, Starbuck, WA 99359; 509-646-3252.

FIELDS SPRING STATE PARK — Anatone

With two environmental learning centers, ample trails for walking or cross-country skiing, a remarkable array of woodpecker species (including White-headed) in its woods, and great wild-flowers, this 850-acre park is a "can't miss" spot. **CONTACT** Fields Spring S.P., P.O. Box 37, Anatone, WA 99401; 509-256-3332.

Fields Spring State Park

McNARY NATIONAL WILDLIFE REFUGE — Pasco

Located southeast of Pasco, this 3,600-acre refuge hosts many thousands of migratory waterfowl. In addition, this is one of the most reliable places in the state to see wintering American White Pelicans. Long-billed Curlews nest in the grasslands. **CONTACT** McNary N.W.R., P.O. Box 544, Burbank, WA 99323; 509-547-4942.

COULEE DAM NATIONAL RECREATION AREA — Coulee Dam

The dominant feature of this area, Lake Roosevelt, is ideal for water sports and wildlife observation. Stretching 130 miles along the lake, Coulee Dam Recreation Area is home to Bald Eagles, Black Bears, and Bobcats. More than 30 species of game fish, including Walleye, Rainbow Trout, and White Sturgeon, inhabit the lake and its tributaries. **CONTACT** Coulee Dam N.R.A., 1008 Crest Dr., Coulee Dam, WA; 509-633-9441.

Western Oregon

This westernmost slice of Oregon encompasses the area from the state's varied Pacific coast eastward across the Willamette Valley to the western slopes of the Cascades. The Coast Ranges, which rise from the southern Oregon shoreline and run parallel to the coast up through Washington, and the more easterly Cascades have wet habitats on their western flanks and dry ones to the east. The valleys that lie between the ranges, like the Willamette, receive sufficient rainfall for woodlands and grasslands, while the western slopes of the Cascades receive even more precipitation.

In the northwestern corner of Oregon, extending from the mouth of the Columbia River eastward along the river's southern bank, Fort Stevens State Park is comprised of coastline habitats as well as salt marshes, lakes, and wet forests. Birders won't want to miss the South Jetty, where rare birds frequently turn up. As you travel south along the outer coast, it becomes evident that although it lacks Washington's wilderness beaches, Oregon's coastline is punctuated with dramatic headlands, sea stacks, sand dunes, and huge offshore rocks. Stop at Cape Lookout State Park, Yaquina Head, and Cape Perpetua Scenic Area to explore tidepools, view whales and nesting seabirds, and hike coastal forest trails.

About 145 miles south of the Washington–Oregon border are the shifting sand hills called the Oregon Dunes, a 40-mile stretch of wind-sculpted coast that is by far the most extensive dune habitat in the Pacific Northwest. Farther south along the coast near Coos Bay, the wetlands of the South Slough National Estuarine Research Reserve offer a departure from the rocky shoreline cliffs to the north. Farther inland, in Siuslaw National Forest, is Marys Peak, the highest mountain in Oregon's Coast Ranges. In addition to sweeping views, Marys Peak features a pure stand of Noble Firs and a colorful spring alpine meadow. Where the Willamette River meets the Columbia, Sauvie Island Wildlife Area is a migration stopover for Sandhill Cranes and vast numbers of geese. For wildlife-viewing close to the Willamette Valley's cultural centers, try the Portland Audubon Wildlife Sanctuary or Fern Ridge Wildlife Area, five miles west of Eugene.

FORT STEVENS STATE PARK

Hammond

Fort Stevens State Park is located at the mouth of the Columbia River, a strategic site fortified during the Civil War and World War II. An expansive park, the overall flatness of its 3,763 acres belies the diversity of its habitats: beaches and dunes, rocky jetties, salt marshes, mudflats, shallow lakes, freshwater swamps, brushy thickets, and wet

Wreck of the *Peter Iredale*

forests. Along Coffenbury Lake at the southern end of the park, Sitka Spruce and Western Red Cedar mix with Red Alder and luxuriant Salal and ferns. Douglas' Squirrels can be heard chattering in the surrounding woods, and Wrentits offer their peculiar, bouncing notes. The woods and lake edges are busy year-round with a seasonally variable array of birds. Wood Ducks, Northern River Otters, and other animals also frequent the lake.

At the southern end of the beach near the campground entrance, the rusting shipwreck remains of the *Peter Iredale* underscore the park's living history. Drive north toward South Jetty and witness the habitat change as woodland is replaced by stabilized dunes covered with Shore Pine, Pacific Wax Myrtle, and Scotch Broom, home to deer and Elk. Trestle Bay is loaded with waterfowl in the winter, and Peregrine Falcons sometimes sit on the pilings that remain from the old trestle. From the jetty itself you can see Gray Whales during migration, as well as seals, sea lions, and many species of waterbirds, from loons and alcids to kittiwakes and pelicans. Winters on Clatsop Spit bring an occasional Snowy Owl and an even more occasional Gyrfalcon. The tiny tidal flat of sand and glassworts at the base of the jetty is the last resort for shorebirds at high tide; keen birders can compile an impressive list of rarities from this area and from the jetty itself. A short trail from the jetty's base takes you to the mouth of the Columbia, where gulls and terns loaf on the sand, and seals and scoters bob in the surf. The viewing blind at parking lot "D" is good for waterfowl and assorted diving birds.

CONTACT Fort Stevens S.P., Ridge Rd., Hammond, OR 97121; 503-861-3170. **HOW TO GET THERE** From Seaside, take U.S. 101 north for about 12 miles and follow signs to the park. **SEASONAL ACCESS** Year-round.

OREGON DUNES NATIONAL RECREATION AREA

Reedsport

The 31,566-acre Oregon Dunes National Recreation Area extends 40 miles along the coast from Florence south to Coos Bay; multiple access points from coastal U.S. 101 lead visitors to 14 trails and many lakes and overlooks. The Oregon coastal dune habitat is at its showiest in spring, when its wealth of pink-blossomed rhododendrons is in full color. The area includes an array of coastal habitats, from coastal forests to estuaries and salt marshes. The real draw here, though, is the dunes themselves: a shifting sea of sand and waving grass whose contours change with the elements—here moving east to impound islets of trees, and there leaving a crater that becomes a miniature marshy wetland called a deflation plain. European Beachgrass, planted along the coast to stabilize the dunes, has largely taken over, supplanting native grasses like American Dunegrass.

Hiking is a great way to explore the dunes. One good spot to hike is the 1½-mile Waxmyrtle Trail, which follows the Siltcoos River Estuary (watch here for American Beavers, Ospreys, and herons) to the beach. You'll need to skirt the areas posted for nesting endangered Snowy Plovers, whose exquisitely camouflaged nests above the tideline are easily disturbed. About a ½ mile farther down the coast are trailheads for the Carter and Taylor Dune Trails; the former is a 1½-mile walk that crosses the dunes to the beach, and the latter is a ½-mile trail that ends at a viewing platform overlooking the dunes and ocean. A comprehensive hiking guide prepared by Siuslaw National Forest (see page 410) and available from Oregon Dunes National Recreation Area is indispensible. Black Bears, Common Raccoons, Minks, Northern River Otters, and alligator lizards might be encountered in the dunes or along the waterways through them. When near the beach, keep an eye out for migrating Gray Whales, seals, sea lions, shorebirds, and seabirds.

CONTACT Oregon Dunes N.R.A., 855 Highway Ave., Reedsport, OR 97467; 541-271-3611. **HOW TO GET THERE** Along U.S. 101 from just north of Florence to Coos Bay. **SEASONAL ACCESS** Year-round. **VISITOR CENTER** Hdqtrs. is on U.S. 101 at Reedsport.

FERN RIDGE WILDLIFE AREA   Eugene

Just five miles west of Eugene, Fern Ridge Wildlife Area offers a sampling of typical habitats of the Willamette Valley: varied freshwater marshes, alder and willow thickets, Oregon White Oak and Douglas Fir stands, and farmlands. The three units of the wildlife area occupy 5,103 acres of the 12,716-acre Fern Ridge Reservoir. The reservoir, which is a tributary of the Willamette River, is a key flood-control area that also supports wildlife by maintaining extensive wetland habitats. Visitors can explore the wildlife area via paths, dikes, and roadways, or by kayak or canoe.

Coyote Creek Nature Trail, near the southeastern corner, winds through riparian, marsh, and field habitats, and has benches and interpretive markers. A walk here might turn up American Beavers, Nutria, Brush Rabbits, Wood Ducks, or Northwestern Salamanders, among many possibilities. The dam on the northern edge of

Aerial view of Long Tom River winding through Fern Ridge Wildlife Area

the area is a good spot for scoping waterfowl. Thousands of swans, geese, and ducks winter on the reservoir, under the watchful eye of Coyotes. Both Red and Gray Foxes occur, as do Minks and Long-tailed Weasels. When the waters are drawn down to low levels to catch floodwater overflow, extensive mudflats make this a terrific shorebirding spot. Birds of prey, such as Bald Eagles and handsome White-tailed Kites and Rough-legged Hawks, can be plentiful in winter. Other winter visitors include Western Screech-, Northern Pygmy-, and Northern Saw-whet Owls, while noisy colonies of Yellow-headed Blackbirds, sweet-singing Black-headed Grosbeaks, and Lazuli Buntings spend the summer here. Visitors will greatly benefit from having a map of the area in hand.

CONTACT Fern Ridge W.A., 26969 Cantrell Rd., Eugene, OR 97402; 541-935-2591. **HOW TO GET THERE** Hwy. 126 (W. 11th Ave.) heading west from Eugene runs through the southern part of the reservoir and wildlife area. **SEASONAL ACCESS** Year-round. **VISITOR CENTER** Information is available at area hdqtrs., located at the southern end of the area on Cantrell Rd.

CAPE LOOKOUT STATE PARK   Tillamook

This 1,974-acre park, which is staffed by whale-spotting volunteers in November, December, and March, may well be the premier whale-watching spot in Oregon. A bit of exercise is involved in getting to the viewing area at the tip of Cape Lookout, but the sight of a Gray Whale breaching with a tremendous splash or just rolling on its finless back and showing its massive flukes will not be forgotten. The 2½-mile Cape Trail passes through an old-growth forest and offers sparkling views of Cape Meares and Three Arch Rocks along the way. More than 150 species of birds have been recorded here.

CONTACT Cape Lookout S.P., 13000 Whiskey Creek Rd. West, Tillamook, OR 97141; 503-842-4981. **HOW TO GET THERE** From Tillamook, take U.S. 101 south for about 12 miles. **SEASONAL ACCESS** Year-round.

YAQUINA HEAD OUTSTANDING NATURAL AREA   Newport

This is one of the best wildlife observation areas on the coast, and it is all packed into about 100 acres. From the lighthouse area, watch for Gray Whales in migration and summer-nesting seabirds on nearby rock faces, among them Brandt's Cormorants, Pigeon Guillemots, Tufted Puffins, and Western Gulls; Rhinoceros Auklets may be seen in the surrounding waters. Take the stairs down the south side of the headland to some excellent tidepools, home to Giant Green Anemones, Mossy Chitons, and hermit crabs. At very low tides rangers are on hand to offer an interpretive view of the natural history of the tidepools. Keep in mind that tidepool life is fragile and that the rocky surfaces can be extremely slippery underfoot.

CONTACT Yaquina Head Outstanding Natural Area, P.O. Box 936, Newport, OR 97365; 541-574-3100. **HOW TO GET THERE** From Newport, take U.S. 101 north for 3.4 miles, then turn west onto Lighthouse Dr. and follow signs to the headland. **SEASONAL ACCESS** Year-round. **VISITOR CENTER** An interpretive center is at 750 Lighthouse Dr.

CAPE PERPETUA SCENIC AREA   Yachats

The headland that forms Cape Perpetua is a 50-million-year-old
chunk of ancient lava; it
rises more than 800 feet
above the ocean and still
holds forth against the destructive power of the waves.
Much of the 2,700 acres of
this scenic area is forested
and is large enough to sustain Black Bears and Bob-
cats. Several trails depart
from the visitor center; stop
in for trail maps and other
information. One trail leads to marine tidepools and spouting rocks

along the coastline, another tracks up the south face of the cape
through a coastal forest to the Whispering Spruce Loop Trail. Listen for the long musical trills and chatters of Winter Wrens and
watch for Gray Whales and Marbled Murrelets in the waves.

CONTACT Cape Perpetua S.A. Visitor Ctr., P.O. Box 274, Yachats, OR
97498; 541-547-3289. **HOW TO GET THERE** From Yachats, take U.S. 101
south for 2–3 miles and follow signs to the V.C. **SEASONAL ACCESS** Year-
round. **VISITOR CENTER** Adjacent to the parking area.

SOUTH SLOUGH NATIONAL
ESTUARINE RESEARCH RESERVE   Charleston

Situated on the southern
arm of Coos Bay estuary,
South Slough Reserve
preserves about 4,400
acres of freshwater and
saltwater tidal wetlands,
including Eelgrass mead-
ows, as well as upland
habitats supporting stands
of Port Orford Cedars.
This is a great place to
learn firsthand about the nature of wetlands; the reserve's interpretive center runs interesting and informative tours and workshops.
Canoeing is an ideal way to see the reserve; alternatively a series of
trails has been carefully laid out through varied habitats, and
brochures for self-guided interpretive walks are available. Many wetland bird species, Elk, deer, Common Raccoons, and local Brush
Rabbits can be seen.

CONTACT South Slough N.E.R.R., P.O. Box 5417, Charleston, OR 97420;
541-888-5558. **HOW TO GET THERE** From Charleston (near the mouth of
South Slough), drive south on Seven Devils Rd. to the interpretive center.
SEASONAL ACCESS Year-round. **VISITOR CENTER** An interpretive center is located on Seven Devils Rd., ¼ mile past the reserve's entrance.

SIUSLAW NATIONAL FOREST   Corvallis

The more than 630,000-acre Siuslaw National Forest stretches 135 miles north to south along Oregon's coast and extends eastward through the Coast Ranges. One area of interest here—located 15 miles southwest of Corvallis—is Marys Peak, which at 4,097 feet is the highest mountain in Oregon's Coast Ranges. Marys Peak Meadow features an unusual mix of flora, including species more characteristic of dry eastern Oregon, the High Cascades, and the Willamette Valley floor, as well as an equally out-of-place stand of Noble Firs. Birds of the peak area include Mountain Quail, Gray-crowned Rosy-Finches, and a long list of other songbirds and woodpeckers. The view of the Cascades from the top is dramatic.

CONTACT Siuslaw N.F., P.O. Box 1148, Corvallis, OR 97339; 541-750-7000. **HOW TO GET THERE** From Corvallis, drive west on U.S. 20, then drive south on Hwy. 34 (Alsea Hwy.) to the forest turnoff. **SEASONAL ACCESS** Year-round. **VISITOR CENTERS** Information is available at four ranger stations: Alsea is on Hwy. 34; Hebo is on Hwy. 22; Mapleton is on Hwy. 126; and Waldport is just off U.S. 101.

WESTERN OREGON NATIONAL WILDLIFE REFUGE COMPLEX   Corvallis

This complex of three sister refuges—Ankeny, Baskett Slough, and William L. Finley—encompasses more than 10,000 acres that provide crucial wintering habitat for thousands of Dusky Canada Geese, a smaller, dark-breasted subspecies of the Canada Goose.

These birds breed in southern Alaska, return to the Willamette Valley each fall, and stay until spring. Dusky Canada Geese as well as other subspecies, such as Lesser, Aleutian, and Cackling Canada Geese, congregate in open fields in winter. Foot trails are closed from mid-fall to mid-spring when the geese are present,

Canada Geese at William L. Finley Refuge

but visitors can view the birds from refuge roads. The 1-mile Woodpecker Loop, an excellent birding trail through grasslands, Douglas Fir, and old-growth maples, is open year-round at the William L. Finley Refuge.

CONTACT Western Oregon N.W.R. Complex, 26208 Finley Refuge Rd., Corvallis, OR 97333; 541-757-7236. **HOW TO GET THERE** Ankeny: From I-5 about 10 miles south of Salem, take the Ankeny Hill exit and drive west on Wintel Rd. for 2 miles. Baskett Slough: From Rickreall, drive west on Hwy. 22 for 2 miles. Wm. L. Finley: From Corvallis, drive south on Hwy. 99W for 10 miles. **SEASONAL ACCESS** Year-round. **VISITOR CENTERS** Individual refuge offices have information.

SAUVIE ISLAND WILDLIFE AREA — Portland

Leafless cottonwoods and dry grasses

Sauvie Island lies nestled in the Columbia River just north of where the Willamette River empties into it. This 13,000-acre area is a key migration spot, and thousands of Sandhill Cranes, swans, geese, and ducks rest and feed here before flying on. It is an excellent place to canoe or kayak. Bald Eagles and other raptors, including a few Short-eared Owls, preside in winter. One of the best viewing areas for cranes and waterfowl is Coon Point at Sturgeon Lake, although the cranes also frequent the open fields nearby. Migrating shorebirds also gather at Coon Point, and at Racetrack Lake to the north. At the end of Oak Island Road, Oregon White Oak groves with brushy edges provide habitat for Western Scrub Jays, White-breasted Nuthatches, and mixed flocks of wintering sparrows. Day-use permits are available at the convenience store at the foot of the Sauvie Island Bridge.

CONTACT Sauvie Is. W.A., Oreg. Dept. of Fish and Wildlife, 18330 NW Sauvie Is. Rd., Portland, OR 97231; 503-621-3488. **HOW TO GET THERE** From Portland, take Hwy. 30 west for about 10 miles, then turn right across the Sauvie Is. Bridge. **SEASONAL ACCESS** Year-round; some areas closed October–March. **VISITOR CENTER** Information available at area hdqtrs.

PORTLAND AUDUBON WILDLIFE SANCTUARY — Portland

Formerly known as Pittock Bird Sanctuary, this 160-acre wildlife preserve is also home to Portland Audubon's nature center, wildlife rehabilitation center, bookstore, and offices. Several miles of walking trails circle a small pond and ramble through a second-growth forest where woodland wildflowers abound in the spring, and where Northwestern Garter Snakes and Roughskinned Newts reside. Birders will find a good seasonal sample of species typical of this habitat, including Wood Ducks, Band-tailed Pigeons, Pileated Woodpeckers, Chestnut-backed Chickadees, Varied Thrushes, Spotted Towhees, and Black-headed and Evening Grosbeaks. Interpretive materials and a schedule of guided walks and classes are available.

CONTACT Audubon Soc. of Portland, 5151 NW Cornell Rd., Portland, OR 97210; 503-292-6855. **HOW TO GET THERE** In Portland, drive west on NW Lovejoy past NW 25th, where the road curves right and is renamed NW Cornell. Continue on NW Cornell and watch for entrance on right. **SEASONAL ACCESS** Year-round. **VISITOR CENTER** Information available at nature center.

JEWELL MEADOWS WILDLIFE AREA   Birkenfeld

In the early morning and evening, the meadows in this 1,123-acre refuge offer views of the Roosevelt race of Elk. The assorted lowland habitats are also good for scoping raptors and Coyotes. **CONTACT** Jewell Meadows W.A., Elsie Route, Box 1565 (Hwy. 202), Seaside, OR 97138; 503-755-2264.

Sea Lion Caves

SEA LION CAVES   Florence

The largest sea cave in the country hosts the largest permanent colony of Northern Sea Lions, which are now endangered in more northerly parts of their range; California Sea Lions can also be seen at this private facility. **CONTACT** Sea Lion Caves, 91560 Hwy. 101, Florence, OR 97439; 541-547-3111.

DEVIL'S ELBOW STATE PARK   Florence

Together with the adjoining Oregon Islands N.W.R., this 645-acre park is an important nesting area for Cormorants, Tufted Puffins, gulls, and other seabirds. **CONTACT** Devil's Elbow S.P., c/o Oregon S.P.'s, Area 3, 84505 Hwy. 101 South, Florence, OR 97439; 541-997-5755.

OREGON COAST AQUARIUM   Newport

Come here to see the resident Killer Whale, as well as Sea Otters, sea lions, and octopus. **CONTACT** Oregon Coast Aquarium, 2820 SE Ferry Slip Rd., Newport, OR 97365; 541-867-3474.

MARK O. HATFIELD MARINE SCIENCE CENTER   Newport

This university-run center features aquariums, whale-watching programs, a nature trail along dunes, and an estuary. **CONTACT** Mark O. Hatfield Marine Science Ctr., 2030 S. Marine Science Dr., Newport, OR 97365; 541-867-0100.

ECOLA STATE PARK   Cannon Beach

Adjacent to photogenic Haystack Rock with its nesting Tufted Puffins, this 1,303-acre coastal park has rugged headlands and tidepools and is a good spot for watching whales, seals, and sea lions. **CONTACT** Ecola S.P., P.O. Box 681, Cannon Beach, OR, 97110; 503-436-2844.

Ecola State Park

CAPE BLANCO STATE PARK
Sixes

Known as a prime whale-watching spot, the park's nearly 1,900 acres include beach, headlands, conifer forest, marsh, and an estuary. A lighthouse marks the state's most westerly point. **CONTACT** Cape Blanco S.P., 91814 Cape Blanco Rd., P.O. Box 1345, Port Orford, OR 97465; 541-332-6774.

Sea stack, Cape Blanco State Park

JACKSON BOTTOM
WETLANDS PRESERVE   Hillsboro

This 650-acre wetlands preserve has an interpretive trail that offers visitors the chance to see Northern River Otters, Minks, and Common Raccoons, as well as waterfowl. **CONTACT** Jackson Bottom Wetlands Coordinator, City of Hillsboro, 123 W. Main St., Hillsboro, OR 97123; 503-681-6206.

BANDON MARSH NATIONAL WILDLIFE REFUGE   Bandon

The estuary at the mouth of the Coquille River boasts a remarkable list of rare shorebirds, as well as lots of the regulars, with the best viewing available from Riverside Road. **CONTACT** Bandon Marsh N.W.R., 2127 SE O.S.U. Dr., Newport, OR 97365; 541-867-4550.

Low tide at Bandon Marsh National Wildlife Refuge

SADDLE MOUNTAIN STATE PARK   Seaside

A hike part of the way up Saddle Mountain in this 2,922-acre park brings you to an area renowned for its wildflowers, including an abundance of scarce and local specialties. **CONTACT** Saddle Mountain S.P., c/o Newhalem S.P., 9500 Sandpiper La., Newhalem, OR 97131; 503-368-5154.

LEWIS AND CLARK
NATIONAL WILDLIFE REFUGE   Brownsmead

Best visited by boat, this 8,313-acre refuge consists of marshes, tidal flats, and islets in the Columbia River estuary, and is known for its wintering swans and other waterfowl. **CONTACT** Lewis and Clark N.W.R., c/o Julia Butler Hansen N.W.R., P.O. Box 566, Cathlamet, WA 98612; 360-795-3915.

Central Oregon

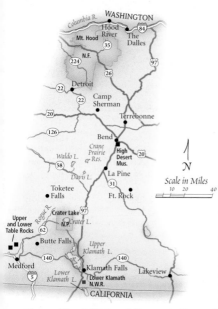

The five sites featured in this subregion lie within or near the Cascade Range, in the lower Klamath Mountains southwest of the Cascades, and in the Klamath Basin just to the east. Washington's Mount St. Helens may be the volcanic wonder of the contemporary Cascades, but Crater Lake in Oregon surely stands out in its own right. Mount Mazama erupted with three times the explosive force of Mount St. Helens, creating Crater Lake, the country's deepest, in the process. Mount Hood, north of Crater Lake in the Mount Hood National Forest, is Oregon's tallest peak.

Both Crater Lake and Mount Hood provide ample subalpine and alpine wildlife-viewing opportunities—from strolling through mountain meadows full of summer wildflowers to observing Elk, marmots, Varied Thrushes, or, with a little luck, such scarce or reclusive species as American Martens and Short-tailed Weasels.

Oregon's span of the Cascades, like Washington's, forms a barrier to the flow of moist, westerly air across the region, and creates profound differences between the wet, west-facing expanses and the much drier areas to the east, which lie in the rain shadow created by the high peaks. These vastly different moisture levels in combination with changes in elevation up and down the slopes have given rise to a considerable variety of forest types in this region. Similarly, the ancient Klamath Mountains rise from the southern shore of Oregon, blocking the onshore flow of marine air and creating a warm, dry ecosystem in the valley to the east. The Lower Klamath National Wildlife Refuge, in the Klamath Basin of south-central Oregon, features wetlands and drier, open-country habitats. Like a microcosm of the dry California habitats well to the south, the Upper and Lower Table Rocks area along the Rogue River Valley supports chaparral plant species and associated fauna, like Ringtails and California Mountain Kingsnakes. On the eastern slopes of the Cascades near Bend, the High Desert Museum presents a close-up view of the flora, fauna, and cultural heritage of the high desert realm between the Cascades and the Rockies to the east.

MOUNT HOOD NATIONAL FOREST   Welches

Oregon's signature volcanic peak, Mount Hood is both a regional symbol and a popular recreation destination, in addition to being the state's loftiest summit, at 11,245 feet. While this Cascade peak is famed for its skiing, the mountain and the 1-million-acre forest that encircles it offer many opportunities to observe wildlife. Even a short midsummer walk along the 40-mile Timberline Trail, which runs the circumference of the mountain, takes you through meadows full of wildflowers, including tall spikes of scented Beargrass that sometimes cover entire slopes. You can reach the trail by driving to Cloud Cap Campground on the northeastern face of the mountain.

Another splendid feature of Mount Hood National Forest is Little Crater Lake, a miniature spring-fed lake in the midst of an expansive wet mountain meadow of the same name, where nighthawks

boom at dusk. Walk a few hundred yards south and you'll find the northern tip of the more widely known Timothy Lake, among the foremost birding spots on the mountain. An astonishing variety of migrating waterbirds—including all four loon species and many sea ducks—have been recorded from viewpoints on the lake's south shore. Hike around the lake and check the trees for Rufous Hummingbirds, Varied Thrushes, and Hermit Warblers.

Some old-growth forest remains here and can be explored via many miles of hiking trails. About 15 miles west of Mount Hood and just south of Zigzag is the 6-mile Salmon River Trail, which follows a canyon rim, giving you a bird's-eye view (and a view of birds) of some venerable, moss-laden Bigleaf Maples. The trail then descends into a stand of beautiful old-growth conifers. Visitors can continue south and venture into the Salmon-Huckleberry Wilderness, one of four wilderness areas in the forest.

CONTACT Mount Hood Info. Ctr., 65000 E. Hwy. 26, Welches, OR 97067; 503-622-7674. Mount Hood N.F., 16400 Champion Way, Sandy, OR 97845; 503-668-1400. **HOW TO GET THERE** From Portland, many access roads to Mount Hood lead from U.S. 26 and Hwy. 35. **SEASONAL ACCESS** Year-round. **VISITOR CENTER** Mount Hood Info. Ctr. is on U.S. 26 in Welches.

CRATER LAKE NATIONAL PARK   Crater Lake

When Mount Mazama erupted with cataclysmic force some 7,700 years ago, it left behind a caldera, or broad basin, that eventually filled with water and formed 1,932-foot-deep Crater Lake. The snow-free visiting season is from June through September, when narrated boat tours circle the inside of the caldera and take visitors to Wizard Island at the western end of the lake; skiing is popular the rest of the year.

There are many trails to explore, too, if you can take your eyes off this marvel of rock and water. Those wishing to reach the lakeshore can take Cleetwood Trail at the northern rim of the lake. The 2½-mile Mount Scott Trail, off the eastern edge of the lake, climbs to the highest point in the park, 8,926-foot Mount Scott, where there is an isolated sphagnum bog with insect-eating plants like bladderworts and sundews. A clear day brings views of California's Mount

Wizard Island

Shasta and the headwaters of the Rogue River. The ½-mile Castle Crest Wildflower Trail near the visitor center lives up to its name. South of the visitor center, 1-mile Godfrey Glen Trail leads to a high-elevation forest of Shasta Red Fir, Mountain Hemlock, and some Subalpine Fir and Lodgepole Pine.

The fauna of the montane, forested realms includes such scarce and elusive mammals as American Martens, Fishers, and Short-tailed Weasels, but you are more likely to encounter Snowshoe Hares, pikas, Yellow-bellied Marmots, Common Porcupines, Elk, deer, and a host of squirrels and chipmunks. The endangered native Bull Trout hangs on in nearby Sun Creek. Birds such as Gray-crowned Rosy-Finches and Black-backed and Three-toed Woodpeckers live up here, as do Mountain Bluebirds, Gray Jays, and Clark's Nutcrackers.

CONTACT Crater Lake N.P., P.O. Box 7, Crater Lake, OR 97604; 541-594-2211. **HOW TO GET THERE** From Klamath Falls, take U.S. 97 north, then Hwy. 62 northwest. **SEASONAL ACCESS** Hwy. 62 entrance open year-round; other access roads closed Oct.–May. **VISITOR CENTER** Steel Info. Ctr. off Rim Dr. on southern end of lake.

THE HIGH DESERT MUSEUM **Bend**

Rubber Boa

This privately operated facility on 150 acres has indoor and outdoor exhibits on the natural and cultural history of the rugged landscape between the Cascades and the Rockies, stretching south from British Columbia over parts of eight states. The caged wildlife afford visitors a close look at secretive regional specialties such as Common Porcupines, Pallid Bats, Ord's Kangaroo Rats, Rubber Boas, Mojave Black-collared Lizards, and Longnose Leopard Lizards. Birds of prey are also shown at close range by staff. Wild, uncaged animals frequent the outdoor pine forest and wetland habitats. Watch for Belding's and Golden-mantled Ground Squirrels, Pygmy Nuthatches, and Red Crossbills. The cultural heritage of Native Americans and of later pioneers and settlers is portrayed in the Earle A. Chiles Center on the Spirit of the West.

CONTACT High Desert Museum, 59800 S. Hwy. 97, Bend, OR 97702; 541-382-4754. **HOW TO GET THERE** On Hwy. 97, about 6 miles south of Bend. **SEASONAL ACCESS** Year-round. **VISITOR CENTER** Information available in the museum.

UPPER AND LOWER TABLE ROCKS **Medford**

Upper Table Rock and farmland

These two mesas along the Rogue River Valley level off at 800 feet above the valley floor. Here in the rain shadow of the Klamath Mountains, the habitats are drier and warmer than those just to the north and, together with the wildlife, are more typical of southern California. Oregon tree species coexist here with typical California species like Tan Oak, Sugar Pine, and Incense Cedar, as well as shrubby species such as manzanita and *Ceanothus*. Follow the trails at either rock (keep a careful eye out to avoid the ever-present Poison Oak) and look for secretive California Mountain Kingsnakes, Ringtails, California Kangaroo Rats, Plain Titmice, California Towhees, and a wide range of other dry-habitat species. In spring, the vernal pools atop the mesas host an explosion of wildflowers.

CONTACT Upper and Lower Table Rocks, c/o Medford B.L.M., Medford, OR 97504; 541-770-2200. **HOW TO GET THERE** From downtown Medford, drive north on Table Rock Rd.: To get to Upper Table Rock, drive 5 miles and turn right onto Modoc Rd.; to get to Lower Table Rock, drive 7½ miles and turn left onto Wheeler Rd. **SEASONAL ACCESS** Year-round. **VISITOR CENTER** Information is available at the Medford B.L.M. office.

LOWER KLAMATH NATIONAL
WILDLIFE REFUGE   Tulelake, CA

The close proximity of five national wildlife refuges in the Klamath Basin in south-central Oregon and north-central California creates one of the premier waterfowl migration stopovers and Bald Eagle wintering areas in the country. Of the five, the 53,600-acre Lower Klamath National Wildlife Refuge, which extends into California, is by far the best designed for visitor access. Highway 161 (Stateline Road) runs east to west through the refuge traversing a mixture of marshes, alkaline ponds, sage, and grassland—breeding milieu for avocets and stilts, teals, American Bitterns, curlews, American White Pelicans, and Wilson's Phalaropes in spring and early summer. In winter, look for lots of Tundra Swans and other waterfowl. Those who visit in the winter can also watch the sunrise flyout of scores of Bald Eagles as they leave from their night roost in the more

Canada Geese in marshes with Mount Shasta in background

westerly Bear Valley National Wildlife Refuge, just south of the town of Worden. Ask the refuge staff for specific directions.

CONTACT Lower Klamath N.W.R., c/o Klamath Basin N.W.R. Complex, Rte. 1 Box 74, Tulelake, CA 96134; 916-667-2231. **HOW TO GET THERE** From I-97 south of Klamath Falls, drive east on Hwy. 161 (Stateline Rd.). **SEASONAL ACCESS** Year-round. **VISITOR CENTER** At Tule Lake N.W.R. in California.

EAGLE RIDGE PARK   Klamath Falls
This 40-acre county park sits on a forested finger of land that juts into Upper Klamath Lake. A trail from Kovich Grove leads to grand views of the Cascades. **CONTACT** Klamath Co. Public Works, Parks Division, 3735 Shasta Way, Klamath Falls, OR 97603; 541-883-4696.

FREMONT NATIONAL FOREST   Lakeview
This 1-million-acre forest features lakes, marshes, juniper and mountain mahogany, and an array of wildlife. **CONTACT** Fremont N.F., Lakeview Ranger District, HC 64 Box 60, Lakeview, OR 97630; 541-947-3334.

FORT ROCK STATE PARK   Fort Rock
Fort Rock, known locally as "the Rock," towers 325 feet above the surrounding sagebrush fields; look for nesting Prairie Falcons, White-throated Swifts, and swallows. **CONTACT** Fort Rock S.P., c/o Oregon S.P.s, 62976 O.B. Riley Rd., Bend, OR 97701; 541-388-6055.

COLUMBIA RIVER GORGE
NATIONAL SCENIC AREA   Hood River
This 300,000-acre area stretches about 80 miles along both the Oregon and Washington sides of the lower Columbia River, offering spectacular scenery and many recreational opportunities. **CONTACT** Columbia River Gorge N.S.A., 902 Wasco Ave., Ste. 2000, Hood River, OR 97031; 503-386-2333.

METOLIUS FISH OVERLOOK   Camp Sherman
The observation platform at Camp Sherman sits above the spring-fed Metolius River, where hefty Rainbow Trout range year-round and Kokanee Salmon (lake populations of Sockeye Salmon) spawn in early fall. **CONTACT** Deschutes N.F., 1645 Hwy. 20 East, Bend, OR 97701; 541-388-2715.

NEWBERRY NATIONAL VOLCANIC MONUMENT   La Pine
Explore a volcanic landscape of cinder, spatter, and pumice cones, calderas, and massive obsidian flows at this 55,500-acre site. **CONTACT** Deschutes N.F., Bend-Fort Rock Ranger District, 1230 NE 3rd St., Bend, OR 97701; 541-388-5664.

SMITH ROCK STATE PARK   Terrebonne

This 641-acre park is a premier rock-climbing spot in the dramatic Crooked River Canyon. Birds of prey nest on ledges and in crevices, White-throated Swifts buzz by, and mammals forage along the river. **CONTACT** Smith Rock S.P., 9241 NE Crooked River Dr., Terrebonne, OR 97760; 541-548-7501.

DETROIT LAKE STATE PARK
Detroit
This 104-acre park is a popular recreation spot where birders can find loons, grebes, and other divers. **CONTACT** Detroit Lake S.P., P.O. Box 549, Detroit, OR 97342; 541-854-3346.

Crooked River rock formations, Smith Rock State Park

CRANE PRAIRIE RESERVOIR   Bend
Ospreys and Bald Eagles nest near this 4,167-acre reservoir surrounded by wetlands, meadows, and conifer forests that are also home to Elk, deer, and the increasingly scarce Spotted Frog. **CONTACT** Deschutes N.F., 1645 Hwy. 20 East, Bend, OR 97701; 541-388-2715.

DAVIS LAKE   Crescent Lake
This 3,900-acre lake offers a beautiful mountain setting featuring a wide range of Cascades species, from Coyotes, Elk, and squirrels to nesting Sandhill Cranes and Bald Eagles. **CONTACT** Deschutes N.F., Crescent Ranger District, P.O. Box 208, Crescent, OR 97701; 541-433-2234.

WALDO LAKE   Oakridge
The forested rim of Waldo Lake in the 39,200-acre Waldo Lake Wilderness Area is known for its resident Hermit Warblers and Northern Goshawks. **CONTACT** Willamette N.F., Rigdon Ranger District, P.O. Box 1410, Oakridge, OR 97463; 541-782-2283.

MARSTER'S BRIDGE AND SODA SPRINGS
FISH OVERLOOKS   Toketee Falls
These are two adjacent and fascinating areas along the wild and scenic North Umpqua River, where Chinook Salmon spawn and Steelhead and Rainbow and Brown Trout swim. **CONTACT** Umpqua N.F., Diamond Lake Ranger District, Idleyld Park, OR 97447; 541-498-2531.

Eastern Oregon

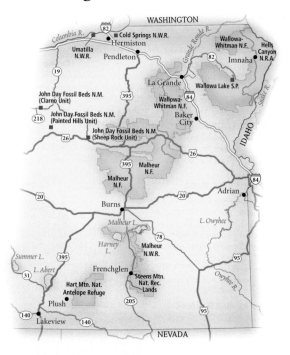

The northern part of eastern Oregon includes both the Blue and Wallowa Mountains as well as the deepest river gorge in North America, Hells Canyon, which cradles the winding Snake River. In the northeastern corner are forested mountains, most notably the Wallowa Mountains. These snowy peaks (some reach 10,000 feet) occupy an area of rich habitat diversity and beautiful natural surroundings. Wallowa Lake State Park provides access to this scenic area. Farther west along the Columbia River are the Umatilla and Cold Springs National Wildlife Refuges, critical migration stops for thousands of waterfowl. The sedimentary rock of the John Day Basin, in the center of this region, preserves records of plant and animal life some 40 million years old. The dry southern section of eastern Oregon is rich in beautifully colored rock walls and rock formations. Malheur National Wildlife Refuge, in Oregon's southeastern corner, is an expansive freshwater marsh surrounded by high desert. Southeast of Malheur, Steens Mountain rises to nearly 10,000 feet. The Alvord Desert, a large alkaline basin, spreads out over 60 miles to the east in the shadow of Steens Mountain. In the far southwestern corner of this region is Summer Lake Wildlife Area, a large alkaline lake surrounded by sage habitat. The adjacent Hart Mountain National Antelope Refuge is home to bands of Pronghorn from spring through fall.

WALLOWA LAKE STATE PARK   Joseph

Routinely cited as one of the outstanding state parks in the West because of its stunning natural setting, this 166-acre park and the adjacent area rate highly for their wildlife-viewing potential. Wallowa is a Nez Perce word for "fish trap," and Chief Joseph and the Nez Perce people favored this region for its rich resources. The Wallowa Mountains are the Alps of Oregon—snow-crowned peaks rising up to 10,000 feet along the southern end of Wallowa Lake. Wallowa Lake itself, at an elevation of 4,400 feet, is framed by huge glacial moraines, and dense forests of larch, pine, and fir blanket its southern end. Also at the southern end, where the Wallowa River meets the lake, is dense riparian growth, while the lake's northern end, in contrast, is brushy and dry with small groves of conifers.

Wallowa Lake with snow-capped Chief Joseph Mountain in background

The park's spectrum of montane habitats boosts the local wildlife diversity. Both ground squirrels and tree squirrels frequent the campground, Mule Deer are tame, and Common Raccoons are attentive. Four species of hummingbirds have visited the feeders at Wallowa Lake Lodge, most often Rufous or Calliope, and dippers splash along the lake and river. Other summer bird species you might encounter are Red-naped Sapsuckers, Pileated Woodpeckers, Varied Thrushes, and Cassin's Finches. A few nature trails link the lake with the Wallowa River, and several longer trails depart into the day-use area south of the lake itself. The West Fork Wallowa River Trail heads up into Wallowa-Whitman National Forest's Eagle Cap Wilderness, dotted with alpine lakes. While the human population around Wallowa Lake shrinks greatly in the winter, it is a favored wintering spot for waterfowl and Bald Eagles.

CONTACT Wallowa Lake S.P., Oregon State Parks and Recreation, 72214 Marina Lane, Joseph, OR 97846-8192; 541-432-4185. **HOW TO GET THERE** Drive 6 miles south of Joseph on Hwy. 82. **SEASONAL ACCESS** Year-round; some areas are closed in winter. **VISITOR CENTER** The park office on the entrance road has an outdoor information kiosk.

MALHEUR NATIONAL WILDLIFE REFUGE   Princeton

Malheur has an august reputation among birders; its popularity among Northwest birders is unrivaled, and the late birding sage Roger Tory Peterson listed it as one of the country's "Dozen Birding Hotspots." The 186,000-acre refuge embraces one of the most extensive freshwater marshes in the West, an oasis surrounded by

Malheur National Wildlife Refuge with Steens Mountain in background

the dry and unforgiving high desert of the northwestern corner of the Great Basin. Malheur has more to offer than birds, but it surely has many birds to offer. Besides attracting lots of Northwest migrants and a remarkable array of nesting birds, this carefully managed refuge has a reputation for pulling in lost and out-of-range migrants.

Rarities aside, the lakes, ponds, marshes, wet meadows, isolated tree stands, and adjacent uplands promise a rich experience for wildlife observers. Because Malheur is such a large site, it takes a bit of strategy to make the best use of your time here. A few days are ideal to get a real feel for its range of possibilities, but even a one-day visit will be memorable. The Center Patrol Road leads from north to south through the heart of the refuge, and you can stop all along this road on marsh edges or at various ponds, and continue south to more upland habitats near "P" Ranch and Page Springs Campground. A short list of the refuge's more glamorous nesting birds includes American White Pelicans, Trumpeter Swans, Ferruginous Hawks, American Avocets, Sandhill Cranes, and Burrowing Owls. Brilliantly iridescent White-faced Ibises visit the refuge in wetter years, and Short-eared Owls grace the open tracts of sage at dusk. Yellow-headed Blackbirds bray from the Broad-leaved Cattail marshes on hot summer days. Many thousands of migrating waterfowl visit the uplands, where Pronghorns graze. The latter half of May is the best time to visit.

CONTACT Malheur N.W.R., HC 72 Box 245, Princeton, OR 97721; 541-493-2612. **HOW TO GET THERE** From Bend, take U.S. 20 east to Burns, then take Hwy. 205 south to the refuge. **SEASONAL ACCESS** Year-round. **VISITOR CENTER** Refuge hdqtrs. with adjoining museum is located at the southern end of Malheur Lake on Narrows-Princeton Rd.

STEENS MOUNTAIN NATIONAL RECREATION LANDS

Frenchglen

Big Indian Gorge with Steens Mountain in background

Steens Mountain—a giant fault block riven with glacier-cut gorges near the top—is the tallest peak (9,733 feet) in the Basin and Range Province and just might be the most impressive natural area in Oregon. The Steens Mountain Loop Road is the designated means to explore this singular highland. The 66-mile loop road (often blocked by snow in places until mid-July) starts near the town of Frenchglen, then joins Highway 205 about 10 miles south. Habitats along the loop include sage grasslands, strips of riparian growth, aspen groves, mountain meadows, and high-altitude lakes. Pronghorn, Bighorn Sheep, Elk, Mule Deer, and jackrabbits might be encountered, and carnivores such as Bobcats and Cougars, though much less common, are in residence as well.

The Kiger Gorge Overlook, roughly halfway along the loop, makes an exceptional viewing spot. The glacial cirque below is a reminder of how recently sheets of ice carved out this rounded valley. Large mammals may be seen foraging on these slopes, but Bighorns are more likely seen at the East Rim Overlook. At both Kiger Gorge and East Rim Overlooks, aerial predators like Golden Eagles, Prairie Falcons, and Red-tailed Hawks may meet you eye-to-eye, while White-throated Swifts zip by at racing speeds, leaving Violet-green Swallows in their jet stream. At high elevations near snow patches, you may see Gray-crowned Rosy-Finches or even a striking Black Rosy-Finch. Mid-elevation habitats might produce a Northern Goshawk, Flammulated Owl, or Pine Grosbeak. The aspens around Lily Lake host hummingbirds and songbirds in the spring and summer, before turning yellow-gold in the fall.

The arid, alkaline Alvord Desert lies just to the east in the shadow of Steens Mountain. Birders travel to this unique area in search of Black-throated Sparrows, but it is Alvord's reptiles that make this area exceptional. Look along the Fields-Denio Road or the road to Mickey Springs for Longnose Leopard Lizards, Western Whiptails, and handsome Mojave Black-collared Lizards, which stand and run erect on their hindlegs when startled.

CONTACT Steens Mountain N.R.L., Burns District Office of B.L.M., HC 74 12533, Hwy. 20 West, Hines, OR 97738; 541-573-4400. **HOW TO GET THERE** From Hwy. 205 at Frenchglen, drive past Page Springs. **SEASONAL ACCESS** Depending on snow accumulation, the loop is open from July through October. **VISITOR CENTER** Information is available at Burns B.L.M. office.

HART MOUNTAIN
NATIONAL ANTELOPE REFUGE   **Plush**

Hart Mountain is a massive fault block ridge that rises up to 8,065 feet above sea level and 3,600 feet above the surrounding valley, dropping off abruptly on the western side and more gradually on the east. The steep canyons and rugged cliffs of the western side are favored by Mule Deer and Bighorn Sheep. On the hills and low ridges of the eastern side bands of Pronghorn (also known as Antelopes) wander from spring through fall before heading for wintering grounds in Nevada. Bighorn Sheep are often seen along the road entering the 275,000-acre refuge. Pronghorn are typically seen in early morning or late afternoon from this primary road or from Blue Sky Road, which runs south from the headquarters. Pronghorn are the big draw, but other wildlife such as Pygmy Rabbits, jackrabbits, Sage Grouse, Mountain Bluebirds, and Golden Eagles are plentiful.

CONTACT Hart Mountain National Antelope Refuge, P.O. Box 111, Lakeview, OR 97630; 541-947-3315. **HOW TO GET THERE** From Lakeview, drive north on U.S. 395, and east on Hwy. 140, then north on Plush Cutoff Rd.; follow signs to the refuge. **SEASONAL ACCESS** Year-round. **VISITOR CENTER** Information is available at the refuge hdqtrs.

SUMMER LAKE WILDLIFE AREA   **Summer Lake**

Located in the southwestern corner of dry eastern Oregon, this large alkaline lake lies on the migratory flyway along the eastern slopes of the Cascades. Thousands of Snow Geese, Canada Geese, Greater

White-fronted Geese, and Tundra Swans, and small numbers of dainty Ross's Geese, pass through on their way to and from northern breeding grounds. Summer Lake's marshes and canals provide nesting for American White Pelicans, Black-crowned Night-Herons, egrets, teal, avocets, stilts, Wilson's Phalaropes, Willets, gulls, and terns. Marshes and sagebrush sustain many songbirds, from Yellow-headed Blackbirds to Sage Thrashers. The 9-mile loop road (closed from October to mid-January) is the traditional way to explore the site. Nearby Lake Abert has nesting Snowy Plovers and Sandhill Cranes; Bighorn Sheep can be found at Abert Rim.

CONTACT Summer Lake W.A., 36981 Hwy. 31, Summer Lake, OR 97640; 541-943-3152. **HOW TO GET THERE** From Bend, drive south on U.S. 97; at La Pine, drive southeast on Hwy. 31 for about 70 miles. Hdqtrs. and entrance (Headquarters Rd.) are 1 mile south of the town of Summer Lake. **SEASONAL ACCESS** Year-round. **VISITOR CENTER** Hdqtrs. on Hwy. 31.

JOHN DAY FOSSIL BEDS NATIONAL MONUMENT

John Day

Painted Hills

Flora and fauna dating from 6 to 40 million years ago are found, at least in fossil form, in this site, which encompasses 14,000 acres in three separate units—Clarno, Painted Hills, and Sheep Rock. Plant fossils of palms, bananas, and figs reveal an earlier tropical era, and saber-toothed cats are among the extensive mammal remains. Landscapes and geological features are striking, among them towering Cathedral Rock and the Painted Hills, whose richly colored slopes of volcanic ash are lit up in June by the yellow flowers of endemic John Day Chaenactis. Plantings around the visitor center attract brilliant Lazuli Buntings and Bullock's Orioles. The canyon walls of Picture Gorge, in the Sheep Rock Unit, are inhabited by Prairie Falcons, Golden Eagles, and Canyon Wrens.

CONTACT John Day Fossil Beds N.M., H.C.R. 82 Box 126, Kimberly, OR; 541-987-2333. **HOW TO GET THERE** Clarno Unit is 20 miles west of Fossil on Hwy. 218. Painted Hills Unit is 9 miles northwest of Mitchell off U.S. 26. Sheep Rock Unit is 28 miles west of John Day, on U.S. 26 near the junction of Hwy. 19. **SEASONAL ACCESS** Year-round. **VISITOR CENTER** Information is available at all units, but the main visitor center and museum are located at Sheep Rock Unit.

UMATILLA AND COLD SPRINGS NATIONAL WILDLIFE REFUGES

Umatilla

These sister refuges, crucial migration resting areas for waterfowl, lie near the Columbia River and are close enough to each other that waterfowl fly back and forth between them. The 29,370-acre Umatilla National Wildlife Refuge skirts the Columbia on both the Oregon and Washington shores; the best waterfowl viewing is often near McCormack Slough. In the same area,

McCormack Slough

Russian Olives host wintering Long-eared and Barn Owls. The reservoir at the 3,117-acre Cold Springs National Wildlife Refuge is a shorebird hotspot in late summer and early fall. During migration times, hundreds of thousands of swans, geese, and ducks appear at both of these refuges.

CONTACT Mid-Columbia River N.W.R. Complex, P.O. Box 700, Umatilla, OR 97882-0700; 541-922-3232. **HOW TO GET THERE** For Umatilla N.W.R.: From I-84 west of Hermiston, drive northeast on U.S. 730, then north on Paterson Ferry Rd. For Cold Springs N.W.R.: From I-84 east of Hermiston, take U.S. 395 to Stanfield Loop Rd. **SEASONAL ACCESS** Year-round; some areas are closed during hunting season. **VISITOR CENTERS** Refuge hdqtrs. is at 830 6th St. in Umatilla, and information kiosks are at individual refuges.

WARNER WETLANDS AREA OF CRITICAL
ENVIRONMENTAL CONCERN   Plush
More than 51,000 acres of protected wetlands lie along the western edge of Hart Mountain. Many thousands of migrating birds pass through, and nesting species are also abundant. Pelican and Crump Lakes are among the best for seeing wildlife. **CONTACT** Warner Wetlands Area, Lakeview District Office of B.L.M., P.O. Box 151, Lakeview, OR 97630; 541-947-2177.

MALHEUR NATIONAL FOREST   Burns
Idlewild Campground, located 17 miles northeast of the town of Burns in this 1½-million-acre forest, is in a beautiful setting of Ponderosa Pines mixed with brushier realms that harbors birds such as White-headed Woodpeckers, Williamson's Sapsuckers, and Pygmy Nuthatches. **CONTACT** Malheur N.F., Burns Ranger District, P.O. Box 909, John Day, OR 97845; 541-575-1731.

LAKE OWYHEE STATE PARK   Adrian
The drive along the beautiful Owyhee River toward the campground of this 730-acre park is loaded with wildlife, especially in the early morning. **CONTACT** Lake Owyhee S.P., P.O. Box 247, Adrian, OR; 541-339-2331.

WALLOWA-WHITMAN NATIONAL FOREST   Enterprise
The 358,461-acre Eagle Cap Wilderness in this 2,260,000-acre forest is heralded for its high alpine lakes and meadows, granite peaks, and glaciated valleys. **CONTACT** Wallowa-Whitman N.F., Eagle Cap Ranger District, 88401 Hwy. 82, La Grande, OR 97850; 541-426-4978.

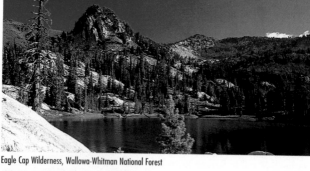

Eagle Cap Wilderness, Wallowa-Whitman National Forest

HELLS CANYON NATIONAL
RECREATION AREA   Imnaha
Not just a fantastic whitewater run, this more than 650,000-acre recreation area includes Hells Canyon Wilderness along both sides of the Snake River in Oregon and Idaho. **CONTACT** Hells Canyon N.R.A., 88401 Hwy. 82, Enterprise, OR 97828; 541-426-5546.

MCKAY CREEK NATIONAL
WILDLIFE REFUGE   Pendleton
Nearly 2,000 acres of open water, marshes, and grasslands provide critical habitat for thousands of Canada Geese and other waterfowl. **CONTACT** Mid-Columbia River N.W.R. Complex, P.O. Box 700, Umatilla, OR 97882-0700; 541-922-3232.

LADD MARSH WILDLIFE AREA   La Grande
Bobolinks, Sandhill Cranes, American Bitterns, and Black-crowned Night-Herons, plus the full gamut of other regional marsh species find a summer home here. **CONTACT** Ladd Marsh W.A., Oregon Dept. of Fish and Wildlife, 107 20th St., La Grande, OR 97850; 541-963-2138 or 541-963-4954.

The Authors

Peter Alden, principal author of this volume, is a naturalist, author, and tour guide who has lectured and led nature tours all over the world for Harvard's Friends of the Museum of Comparative Zoology, Massachusetts Audubon Society, Overseas Adventure Travel, Lindblad Travel, and many cruise lines. He has written books on North American, Latin American, and African wildlife. Alden lives in Concord, Massachusetts.

Dennis Paulson, contributing author and regional consultant for this guide, is the Director of the Slater Museum of Natural History at the University of Puget Sound, Tacoma, Washington.

Daniel Mathews wrote portions of the flora and invertebrates sections of this guide. He is a naturalist writer and photographer who has published books, articles, and poetry on the nature of the Pacific Northwest. Mathews lives in Portland, Oregon.

Bob Sundstrom, author of the parks and preserves section, leads natural history tours in North America and abroad, conducts birding workshops, and has served on the boards of numerous conservation and natural history organizations. He lives in Seattle, Washington.

Eric A. Oches co-wrote the topopgraphy and geology section of this book. He is an assistant professor in the Department of Geology and Environmental Science and Policy Program at the University of South Florida.

Amy Gregoret, co-author of the topography and geology section of the guide, is working on her Ph.D. in geology at the University of Minnesota.

Wendy Zomlefer, Ph.D. wrote the introductions to the flora sections. She is a post-doctoral associate in the botany department at the University of Florida and courtesy assistant curator of the University of Florida Herbarium.

Acknowledgments

The authors collectively thank the thousands of botanists, zoologists, and naturalists we have worked with over the years and whose books and papers provided a wealth of information for this book. The staff and members of the following organizations were most helpful: National Audubon Society, Harvard's Museum of Comparative Zoology, the Nature Conservancy, North American Butterfly Association, and American Birding Association. We also thank the staffs of the many federal and state land, game, and fish departments.

We thank all of the experts who contributed to each section of this book. Carter Gilbert of the Florida Museum of Natural History reviewed the fish species accounts, Sylvia Sharnoff wrote the lichens section, Gary Mechler reviewed the weather and night sky spreads, and Chuck Keene reviewed many species photographs. We also thank Jeff Stone of Chic Simple Design for initial editorial and design consultation.

Special thanks go to James Baird, Richard Carey, Bob Fleming, Jr., the late Richard Forster, Karsten Hartell, Michael Kleinbaum, Vernon Laux, Donna Nemeth, the late Roger Tory Peterson, and Guy Tudor.

We are grateful to Andrew Stewart for his vision of a regional field guide encompassing the vast mosaic of the Pacific Northwest's topography, habitats, and wildlife, and to the staff of Chanticleer Press for producing a book of such excellence. Editor-in-chief Amy Hughes provided fundamental conceptual guidance as well as constant encouragement and supervision. Series editor Patricia Fogarty was the project's guiding light. The success of the book is due largely to the considerable skills and expertise of project editor Lisa Leventer. Editor Miriam Harris and contributing editor Pamela Nelson thoroughly examined and refined the flora and invertebrates sections, respectively. Managing editor Edie Locke shepherded the book through the editorial process. Assistant editor Kristina Lucenko and editorial assistant and map researcher Michelle Bredeson provided boundless editorial support while they meticulously fact checked, copyedited, and proofread the book through all stages. Contributing editor Holly Thompson made many valuable contributions to the project. Publishing assistant Karin Murphy and editorial intern Tessa Kale offered much assistance and support. Dan Hugos's editorial database helped keep track of the species lists and text. Thanks also to Kerry Acker and Natalie Goldstein.

Art director Drew Stevens and designer Vincent Mejia took 1,500 images and tens of thousands of words of text and created a book that is both visually beautiful and eminently usable. The design contributions of interns Anthony Liptak and Enrique Piñas were invaluable. Howard S. Friedman created the beautiful and informative color illustrations. Ortelius Design made the detailed maps that appear throughout the book. The mammal tracks were contributed by Dot Barlowe.

Photo directors Zan Carter and Teri Myers and photo editor Christine Heslin sifted through thousands of photographs from hundreds of photographers in their search for the stunning images that contribute so much to the beauty and usefulness of this guide. They carefully chose the images that best represented each subject, and worked patiently with the authors, consultants, natural history experts, and the editorial and design teams. The team from Artemis Picture Research Group, Inc.—Linda Patterson Eger, Lois Safrani, Yvonne Silver, and Anita Dickhuth—brought considerable skills and experience to the task of researching and editing many of the species photographs. Permissions manager Alyssa Sachar facilitated the acquisition of photographs and ensured that all records and photo credits were accurate. Kate Jacobs, Leslie Fink, Jennifer McClanaghan, and intern Mee-So Caponi helped sort and traffic photographs and offered endless additional support.

Director of production Alicia Mills and production assistant Philip Pfeifer saw the book through the monumentally complicated production and printing processes. They worked closely with Dai Nippon Printing to ensure the excellent printing quality of these books.

In addition, we thank all of the photographers who gathered and submitted the gorgeous pictures that make this book a delight to view.

—Peter Alden, Dennis Paulson, Daniel Mathews, Bob Sundstrom, Eric A. Oches, Amy Gregoret, Wendy B. Zomlefer

Picture Credits

The credits are listed alphabetically by photographer. Each photograph is listed by the number of the page on which it appears, followed by a letter indicating its position on the page (the letters follow a sequence from top left to bottom right).

Kevin Adams 132a

Ronn Altig 336c, 342

Walt Anderson 96a, 100d, 101a & b, 104a, 117b, 133c, 135a, 145c, 160a, 163b & d, 250b, 251a

Ron Austing 135b, 213d, 266b, 271a, 273a, 274a, 275b, 295d, 299d, 300c, 303b, 305c, 311a, 316b, 329b, 351b

Marianne Austin-Mc-Dermon 377

Noella Ballenger 48

Frank S. Balthis 23

Robert E. Barber 164a, 357b

John Barger 11c, 34b, 35c, 393, 394b, 413a

Lance Beeny 168e, 219a

Tom Boyden 174e, 175b & c, 181c & e, 204d, 208a & b, 209b & c, 210d, 216d & e, 224c, 226c, 230b, 231b, 235, 240b

Wayne & Karen Brown/Brown & Co. Photography 178c

Gay Bumgarner 327b, 359a

Frank Burek 186b

Joyce Burek 175a, 183d, 229a, b & c, 230c & d, 231c

Francis & Donna Caldwell 20b, 28g, 40b, 42a, 46b, 141a, 403b

Francis E. Caldwell 152d

Edgar Callaert 41b

John Cancalosi 341b, 344a

Larry Carver 11b

David Cavagnaro 96e, 102c, 107d

Rick Cech 212c & d, 213c, 214a, 215b & c, 216b & c, 217b & d, 218a

Herbert Clarke 139e, 209d, 271d, 278d, 279b, 282c & d, 290c, 296d, 299a & b, 300b, 304b, 308c, 311b, 315c & d, 317d, 319b, 320c, 322c, 323a, 324a, 326d, 329c, 346b

John M. Coffman 199a, 219b

Eliot Cohen 381a

Mark Conlin 42b, 169e, 171c, 175d, 176c, 179e, 184b, 234d, 236c

Ed Cooper Photo 18a & b, 28c, 32b, 34a, 84d, 372, 379, 380, 392b, 404a & b, 407b, 410b, 411a, 418

Gerald & Buff Corsi/Focus on Nature, Inc. 84b & f, 97a & e, 100c, 102b, 107c, 111b, 112d, 113c, 123d, 140b, 155e, 164b, 165f, 170a, 176b, 179c, 181a, 185a, 236a, 270c, 305d

Daniel J. Cox/Natural Exposures, Inc. 51b, 355a & b, 362b

Bob Cranston 237c

Sharon Cummings 260c, 285a, 295a, 324c, 347a

Rob Curtis/The Early Birder 140c, 165a, 198b, 219e, 289d, 308a & d, 309a, 310d, 312b, 319a, 322a

Mike Danzenbaker 265d, 279a, 296c, 345a & b, 347b

Larry Dech 46a, 89d, 92a

E. R. Degginger/Color-Pic, Inc. 80d, 81a & c, 82b, 90b, 92e, 97c, 99f, 111a, 120a, 123c, 134e, 152c, 158a, 170b, 173a, 183e, 185d, 187a, 199d, 200c & e, 203d, 204c, 206e, 207a, 216a, 217c, 218d, 240d, 241b, 247b, 248b, 251b, 252a & c, 288d, 294c, 295c, 299c

Phil Degginger/Color-Pic, Inc. 242c

Dembinsky Photo Associates
Rod Planck 341d

Jack Dermid 273b, 335a

Alan & Linda Detrick 137d

Larry Ditto 311c

Christine M. Douglas 157a

Andrew Drake 231a

Sidney W. Dunkle 195b, 196a, b & d, 197c & d

Don Eastman 104c, 111c, 113a, 114b, 115d, e & f, 117c & d, 134b, 141e, 147a, b & c, 149d, 157b & c, 159b, 162d & e

Priscilla Alexander Eastman 134a, 136d

John Elk III 15b, 36b, 41a, 49b, 407a, 408

Ellis Natural Photography
Michael Durham 362c

Dennis Flaherty 13b, 105c, 141d

Jeff Foott 171a, 174a, 233b, 234c, 240e, 262b, 267b, 277b, 278c, 310c, 358c, 365c, 367b

Richard Forbes 336b, 346a, 352b & c

Michael H. Francis 45b, 202d, 273c & e, 288b, 314d, 315b,

327a, 349d, 354a, 356b, 357c, 362a, 363b, 365a

Dennis Frates 414a, 415b, 426a & b

Cary Given 28a, 30b, 32a, 33a, 39b, 50a, 385, 388b, 391b

Curt Given 10a, 29, 33b, 39a, 342a, 397

Chuck Gordon 259d & e, 265b, 267c & e, 268c, 270b & d, 284a, 286d, 340c

Daniel W. Gotshall 234b, 236d, 241d

Lois Theodora Grady 105e

Al Grillo 240a

Richard T. Grost 239b

Darrell Gulin 122c, 160e, 162f, 184c, 185e, 278a, 325c, 401b

Charles Gurche 12a, 22c, 27g, 35a, 374, 388a, 389, 390, 391a, 412a

Thomas Hallstein/Outsight 19b, 415a, 425

Peter Hartlove 190b, 211c

Richard Herrmann 237b

Ralph Lee Hopkins 114c, 151e

Howard Horton 227d, 238b

Joanne Huemoeller 138d

Chris Huss 84c, 229e, 230a, 232b & d, 234e, 240c

John B. Hyde/Wild Things 367a, 369b

Innerspace Visions
Saul Gonor 223b
Jeff Pantakhoff 366d
Doug Perrine 368a
Robert L. Pitman 368b

David Jensen 13a & c, 19a, 21c, 22a & b, 28h, 39a, 44, 47a & b, 402a, 403a, 423

Gregory C. Jensen 237a

Jet Propulsion Laboratory 63b & c, 65c

John G. Shedd Aquarium 226a, 228b, 232a, 233a, 238a

Bill Johnson 202e, 206a

Emily Johnson 81d & e, 143d

Wolfgang Kaehler 59a, 89a & e, 118a, 151b, c & d, 153b, 155c, 158d, 159d, 177a, 381d

Kevin T. Karlson 259b & c, 276d, 281a, 289c

Richard A. Keen 63e, 65a

G. C. Kelley 265c, 266e, 271e, 283c, 284b, 302b, 325b, 341c, 345d

Brian Kenney 204b & e, 210b, 212b, 253b, 254a & b

Kirkendall/Spring Photographers 27d & e, 61e, 378

Lee Kline 340a

Eugene N. Kozloff 168a, 170d & e, 171b & e, 179d, 180b

Thomas M. Lake 226b

Wayne Lankinen 314c

Dan Lay/Fern Ridge Wildlife Area 409

William P. Leonard 244a, b & c, 248c, 250a, 251c & d, 253a & d, 348c, 353b

Jack N. Levy 209a, 214d, 217c

David Liebman 96c, 197a, 207b, 244d

Harold Lindstrom 258c, 263d, 268b, 269d, 283d, 290a, 309c, 321c, 329d

Kathy Lindstrom 268d

Bates Littlehales 258d, 270a, 277e, 312a

Janet Loughrey 413b

Chris Luneski 24a, 410a, 412b

Stephen G. Maka 264a, 313b

Andrew J. Martinez 27c, 84e, 176e, 185c, 233c

Bruce Matheson 43b, 398, 399a, 405b

Daniel Mathews 102d, 138f, 142d, 145b, 161a, 162c, 163a

Buddy Mays/Travel Stock 395

Karen McClymonds 358a, 366a

Joe McDonald 338a,

350b, 356a, 360a

Charles W. Melton 203a, 267d

Linda J. Moore 10b, 11a, 27b, 28b, d & f, 31, 34c, 35b, 36a, 37b, 38b, 40a, 376, 382b, 383a, 384, 417, 427b

C. Allan Morgan 262c, 302c

Arthur Morris/BIRDS AS ART 259a, 264b, 274b & d, 275e, 279c, 281b, 282b, 288c, 289b, 290b, 292c, 293, 321d

The National Audubon Society Collection/ Photo Researchers, Inc.
Franz Bagyi/OKAPIA 57c
Barbour 350c
Edna Bennett 61
Biophoto Associates 25e
Howard Bluestein 57b
Bob & Elsie Boggs 297a
John Bova 6a, 62a
Scott Camazine 188a, 205b
M. Claye/Jacana 24d
Joseph T. Collins 246, 247a
Suzanne L. & Joseph T. Collins 248a
Stephen Dalton 348b
Kent & Donna Dannen 155a
E. R. Degginger 25d, 81b, 178b, 186a
Alan & Linda Detrick 45d
R. J. Erwin 218b, 219d, 352a
David R. Frazier 61a
Gary G. Gibson 174c, 177d, 181d
François Gohier 85b
Patrick W. Grace 136e
Gilbert S. Grant 202a
Ken M. Johns 305b
A. B. Joyce 224b
Joyce Photographics 24c, 27a
L & D Klein 177b
Stephen J. Krasemann 273d
Calvin Larsen 184a, 139f, 343c

Index

Converting to Metric

Limited space makes it impossible for us to give measurements expressed as metrics. Here is a simplified chart for converting inches and feet to their metric equivalents:

	MULTIPLY BY
inches to millimeters	25
inches to centimeteres	2.5
feet to meters	0.3
yards to meters	0.9
miles to kilometers	1.6
square miles to square kilometers	2.6
acres to hectares	.40
ounces to grams	28.3
pounds to kilograms	.45
Farenheit to Centigrade	subtract 32 and multiply by .55

Prepared and produced by Chanticleer Press, Inc.

Founder: Paul Steiner
Publisher: Andrew Stewart

Staff for this book:

Editor-in-Chief: Amy K. Hughes
Series Editor: Patricia Fogarty
Project Editor: Lisa Leventer
Managing Editor: Edie Locke
Editor: Miriam Harris
Contributing Editors: Pamela Nelson, Holly Thompson
Assistant Editor: Kristina Lucenko
Editorial Assistant: Michelle Bredeson
Photo Directors: Zan Carter, Teri Myers
Photo Editor: Christine Heslin
Photo Research and Editing: Artemis Picture Research Group, Inc.
Rights and Permissions Manager: Alyssa Sachar
Art Director: Drew Stevens
Designer: Vincent Mejia
Design Interns: Anthony Liptak, Enrique Piñas
Director of Production: Alicia Mills
Production Assistant: Philip Pfeifer
Publishing Assistant: Karin Murphy
Illustrations: Howard S. Friedman
Maps: Ortelius Design

Series design by Drew Stevens and Vincent Mejia

All editorial inquiries should be addressed to:

Chanticleer Press
665 Broadway, Suite 1001
New York, NY 10012

To purchase this book or other National Audubon Society Field
Guides and Pocket Guides, please contact:

Alfred A. Knopf
201 East 50th Street
New York, NY 10022
(800) 733-3000